Latour and the Passage of Law

Critical Connections

A series of edited collections forging new connections between contemporary critical theorists and a wide range of research areas, such as critical and cultural theory, gender studies, film, literature, music, philosophy and politics.

Series Editors
Ian Buchanan, University of Wollongong
James Williams, University of Dundee

Editorial Advisory Board

Nick Hewlett
Gregg Lambert
Todd May
John Mullarkey
Paul Patton
Marc Rölli
Alison Ross
Kathrin Thiele
Frédéric Worms

Titles available in the series
Badiou and Philosophy, edited by Sean Bowden and Simon Duffy
Agamben and Colonialism, edited by Marcelo Svirsky and Simone Bignall
Laruelle and Non-Philosophy, edited by John Mullarkey and Anthony Paul Smith
Virilio and Visual Culture, edited by John Armitage and Ryan Bishop
Rancière and Film, edited by Paul Bowman
Stiegler and Technics, edited by Christina Howells and Gerald Moore
Badiou and the Political Condition, edited by Marios Constantinou
Nancy and the Political, edited by Sanja Dejanovic
Butler and Ethics, edited by Moya Lloyd
Latour and the Passage of Law, edited by Kyle McGee

Forthcoming titles
Agamben and Radical Politics, edited by Daniel McLoughlin
Rancière and Literature, edited by Julian Murphet and Grace Hellyer
Nancy and Visual Culture, edited by Carrie Giunta and Adrienne Janus
Balibar and the Citizen/Subject, edited by Warren Montag and Hanan Elsayed

Visit the Critical Connections website at
www.euppublishing.com/series/crcs

Latour and the Passage of Law

Edited by Kyle McGee

EDINBURGH
University Press

© editorial matter and organisation Kyle McGee, 2015
© the chapters their several authors, 2015

Edinburgh University Press Ltd
The Tun – Holyrood Road, 12(2f) Jackson's Entry, Edinburgh EH8 8PJ

www.euppublishing.com

Typeset in 11/13 Adobe Sabon by
Servis Filmsetting Ltd, Stockport, Cheshire

A CIP record for this book is available from the British Library

ISBN 978 0 7486 9790 8 (hardback)
ISBN 978 0 7486 9792 2 (webready PDF)
ISBN 978 0 7486 9793 9 (epub)

The right of Kyle McGee to be identified as the editor of this work has been asserted in accordance with the Copyright, Designs and Patents Act 1988, and the Copyright and Related Rights Regulations 2003 (SI No. 2498).

Contents

Introduction
Kyle McGee ... 1

1. From the Conseil d'État to Gaia: Bruno Latour on Law, Surfaces and Depth ... 17
   David Saunders

2. Politics and Law as Latourian Modes of Existence ... 38
   Graham Harman

3. On Devices and Logics of Legal Sense: Toward Socio-technical Legal Analysis ... 61
   Kyle McGee

4. 'The Crown Wears Many Hats': Canadian Aboriginal Law and the Black-boxing of Empire ... 93
   Mariana Valverde and Adriel Weaver

5. Providing the Missing Link: Law after Latour's Passage ... 122
   Serge Gutwirth

6. The Life and Deaths of a Dispute: An Inquiry into Matters of Law ... 160
   Niels van Dijk

7. Plasma! Notes on Bruno Latour's Metaphysics of Law ... 197
   Laurent de Sutter

8. The Conditions of a Good Judgment: From Law to Internal Affairs Police Investigations ... 209
   Cédric Moreau de Bellaing (trans. Solène Semichon)

9. In The Name of the Law: Ventriloquism and
   Juridical Matters   235
   François Cooren

10. *Laboratory Life* and the Economics of Science in
    Law   273
    David S. Caudill

11. Bartleby, Barbarians and the Legality of Literature   304
    Faith Barter

12. The Strange Entanglement of Jurimorphs   331
    Bruno Latour

    List of Contributors   354
    Index   357

Introduction
Kyle McGee

Like the actors he studies, Bruno Latour is many things. A patient and creative anthropologist of the sciences, a skilled observer of technological practices, a boundary-pushing political and ecological thinker, even a formidable philosopher, to be sure; however, a fixture in legal studies he is not. *Latour and the Passage of Law* goes to great lengths to challenge this state of affairs, for every chapter that follows demonstrates the indispensability for legal theory of conceptual and empirical resources developed in Latour's work – including but by no means limited to his 2002 ethnography of the Conseil d'État, *La fabrique du droit* (*The Making of Law*, 2010). And although each chapter shows more than it tells, by descending from the lofty heights of conventional reflection on law (for instance the natural and social foundations of legal order, the systems, structures and apparatuses of norms or rules and the ideals of justice, equity or liberty touted in analytical and critical jurisprudences alike) to zoom in on the constructive practices that shape legal truths – much to the credit of the individual authors – a distinctive vision of law as a mode of existence nevertheless materialises across the volume.

Law enjoys prominence, even pre-eminence, in Latour's recent anthropology of the Moderns (*Enquête sur les modes d'existence*, 2012; *An Inquiry into Modes of Existence*, 2013) (hereafter AIME). As he points out, the legal institution seems somewhat immune to the 'jolts of modernism'[1] that tend to deform the institutions of, for example, religion or politics or the sciences. There is a 'fairly satisfying correspondence',[2] in other words, between the institution of the Law and the elemental, irreducible modality of truth rigorously unique to legal enunciation. The corruption of other institutions has largely to do with the prevalence of what Latour calls Double-Click [DC], a pseudo-mode charged with levelling the other modes to support the demand of unmediated, direct speech: thus religious experience is sacrificed to the purportedly rational restrictions necessary for the conveyance of information, the curvature of the political Circle is rejected as the mere crooked talk of politicians and interest groups, and even the carefully coordinated chains of reference constitutive of scientific truth are crushed under the weight of representational models of knowledge that insist on logics of resemblance sustaining a subject-object correlation. Law, nearly unique among the modes, seems quite able to resist a similar fate: no one bats an eye at the suggestion that a proposition can be held as 'true in the legal sense' or 'taken as true' and thereupon made the ground for a multitude of important consequences, and there is no implication that in doing so any error has been made. In this limited sense, then, law can be offered as a veritable archetype of the modes of existence drawn out in the first version of Latour's immense, ongoing project.

There is much more to the theorisation of modes of existence than the establishment of a specific kind of truth, of course, and there is also much more to law than the formalism of veridiction. But this is a useful starting point. Readers familiar with legal philosophy (and, again to the credit of the authors of the individual chapters, an extensive background in this field is not mandatory in order to benefit from the arguments developed in this volume) may note that Latour's account of law differs considerably from the dominant traditions. He cites H. L. A. Hart alongside Pierre Bourdieu – avatars of, respectively, analytical positivism and continental critical legal theory – but can hardly be said to adhere to either approach. Latour's account, drawing more on the under-appreciated traditions of descriptive legal semiotics and legal ethnography, is arguably the first to fall more or less completely outside the brackets of modern jurisprudence. Seeking neither the foundations of law nor the formula for justice, Latour's approach insists on tracking the hesitant composition of fragile trajectories linking together the most wildly disparate of actors in order to suture, with lace-like thread, the planes of enunciation emitted in other controversies, other practices, other scenes. As Latour notes time and again, 'the other modes *do not archive* their successive shiftings or translations',[3] so although any enunciation may produce a predecessor and a successor, a here and a now and a not-here and a not-now, a me and a not-me and a you and a not-you, and so on, none of this is *recorded* in a reliable way. The originality of law, according to Latour, consists in a counter-movement of reprisal that '*reattach[es]* what the continual movement of dispatches never stops *detaching*'.[4] Law – as a regime of truth – serves to stabilise collectives of humans and non-humans by engendering durable correlations between utterances and their authors, deeds and their doers, actions and those responsible for them. These are not pre-established correlations; they must be created anew each time. Rather than an ethereal set of methodological principles, then, legal reason is the concrete art of establishing continuity out of the radically discontinuous levels of enunciation that proliferate elsewhere, such that attributions can be made. In this way, by weaving its invisible threads, 'law brings off the miracle of proceeding as though, by particular linkages, we were held to what we say and what we do', despite that 'in fact there is neither real continuity of courses of action nor stability of subjects'.[5]

Clearly, then, despite his obvious attachment to law, Latour could never produce a self-contained, hermetically sealed Legal Theory. The account very briefly sketched above already demonstrates that legality is fully enmeshed with heterogeneous modes of existence, regimes with which law sustains uncertain and perhaps delicate relationships. Latour's legal thought thus sits uncomfortably within the prevailing architecture of legal philosophy.

Rather than rooting law in the will and positive command of the Sovereign or in the transcendent norms of Nature, Latour insists on the stepwise practice of drawing successive links between facts and principles – where both 'fact' and 'principle' must be understood as problematic, not given, terms. The principle inscribed in the judgment will emerge only gradually from the shudders and hesitations of legal reason; the legal facts become so only through an exhausting process of qualification and a cascade of transformations set in motion by the resonance among allegations, proofs, rhetorical acumen, ingenious readings of texts, a curious detachment (*libido judicandi*) and a litany of semiotic objects that the case engenders and puts into circulation.[6] One implication of this approach, which drives familiar concepts like power and legitimacy into a state of suspension or redundancy, is that the *burdens* we can ask law to bear are thrown into question. Though it is said that law is the great civiliser of nations, the guarantee of the very difference between civilisation and barbarity, the breath of life infusing cherished values like individual autonomy, the dignity of personhood, the right to property, or accountability and transparency in government and policy-making, law, by itself, is not able to sustain these weights. To demand otherwise is to commit a series of category mistakes, charging law with the requirements of, for example, technics [TEC] or fiction [FIC] (which, more than any other modes, create new virtual enunciative positions and so condition the exercise of individuality), or politics [POL] or organisation [ORG] (which, here, would alone be capable of adequately explaining the practices of governance), or attachment [ATT] (which marks the passionate, possessive interests of economic actors in their belongings, among other things), in addition to its own specific requirement of reprising the conditions of enunciation and connecting scattered acts and utterances coherently. Autonomy, personhood, property and public accountability are perhaps impossible without law, but it is a grave error to entrust law alone with their maintenance, as legal and political philosophies so frequently do. Law justifies nothing but its own assignations. It is up to other modes, other practices, other ontologies to shelter these complex, multi-hued values.

But this is not to say that, for Latour, law is the exclusive province of professionals. For just as the legal institution oversteps the passage of law (by, for example, investing the latter with the unbearable cargo of political economy, morality and so on), the uneven trajectory of transformations that Latour associates with the production of legal truth outstrips the institution that claims to house it. Although the domain of Law generally succeeds in safeguarding the irreducibility of its veridiction, legal truths proliferate in the most informal, everyday occurrences. This is so not only as regards disputes over the rightful extent of a property line or the termination of a pregnant woman's employment, but in any interaction that alters the total mix of legal relations, i.e. that renders actors responsible or, better, *answerable* for their deeds, utterances or actions. Non-lawyers are quite frequently 'doing law' or speaking legally, usually despite themselves, and indeed – on at least one view of the consequences of Latour's legal theory – non-human actors tirelessly conduct their own assignations and attributions of answerability, imposing their own claims and obligations.[7] Legal sociologists argue that law is 'embedded in' society; Latour's account, by contrast, shows that law and society are not, as the legal sociologist assumes, two separate poles or spheres or domains at all, but that the associations we register as legal themselves make societies.

How, then, can we discriminate between legal and non-legal utterances? Plainly, it is not possible to rely on the nature or essence of entities; we can talk about things customarily considered 'legal', like contracts, constitutions, judgments, patents, marriages and criminal sentences, and never come close to speaking legally, just as we may conversely talk about things that have no apparent legal significance or other connection to 'the juridical sphere', like dustbins, joys and disappointments, marshes, solar systems and films, in a 'key' that leaves no doubt that they are being drawn into a distinctively legal trajectory. That interpretive key carries no new information, but simply marks off the utterance it modifies as doing something quite other than conveying information; what is flagged is the discontinuity that must be bridged in order to allow the passage of law, which tells us only what types of connections would be capable of prolonging the trajectory without falling into error. From the vantage point of any other practice than law itself, such a trajectory can only appear illogical, discontinuous, radically heterogeneous or brutally inconsistent. Its connections, its cascades of 'and therefores', compel the one that speaks legally to adopt a strange gait that would surely earn her a diagnosis of madness in other quarters. This is why the notion of *interpretive keys* developed in AIME is so important: to make an assessment, to take an inventory, to talk the talk and walk the walk of [LAW] requires a preliminary adjustment, a pre-positioning, to orient the flow of what follows. This notion, which is central to Latour's study of modes, may suggest an affinity to transcendental philosophy inasmuch as the keys seem to supply a priori conditions for particular kinds of experience; however, this is misleading because they are comparative tools unmoored from substance and subject, part of a meta-language (or infra-language) designed to detect heterogeneous values in their contingent subsistence, and are decidedly not offered as immutable structures of cognition.[8] It would be preferable to coin a term for this alternative deployment of immanence. Latour playfully speaks of 'trans-descendence',[9] so we may suggest *descendentalism*, a term that has a suggestive alliance with the pragmatist and empiricist philosophies that captivate Latour.

As staggering in breadth and ambition as the AIME project undoubtedly is, however, not all of the authors writing for this volume have chosen to test its arguments or conceptual resources. It would, in truth, be quite difficult to confuse this volume with an exercise in 'Latour scholarship', devoted to parsing out the meaning of particular statements or to identifying the presuppositions and intellectual predecessors that have made AIME possible. As the majority of the contributions demonstrate, the versatility of actor-network theory (ANT) continues to attract incisive scholars determined to shatter the dogmatisms of modern legal epistemology and to rethink alike the complexity of law's immanent operations and its bonds to the sciences, politics, literature, the environment and the economy. If their explorations happen to shed light on Latour's grand project or other aspects of his thought as a philosopher or anthropologist, this is, in the end, merely a (welcome) by-product of their attachment to the problems they treat. By the same token, of course, this only ensures that each chapter is all the more committed to precisely the kind of descendentalist approach – part philosophy and part ethnographic or other fieldwork, but completely invested in the recovery of *pragmata* – sketched out briefly above.

However, two critical surveys introduce the volume. David Saunders's chapter, 'From the *Conseil d'État* to Gaia', artfully scans the surface of *La fabrique du droit*, ably summarising that book's arguments and drawing a series of provocative connections to Latour's subsequent enchantment with that secular figure of the earth, Gaia.[10] Saunders detects in Latour's ethnography of the French administrative law court a hint of the turn to metaphysics that would come to fruition ten years after the book on law: the *conseillors* practise a specific kind of hesitation, but perhaps Latour's point in studying it so closely is rather more general, more speculative, a pluralist's plea to remain 'open' to the variety of experience. The law, Latour argues, must be tracked at the surface, the observer must achieve a superficiality as demanding as that of the law itself – a prospect that presents a considerable challenge to the figure of the 'philosophically minded' ethnographer that narrates the book's asides. Saunders, acknowledging a sort of presentism or lack of historical concern in *La fabrique du droit*, suggests in an echo of his powerful critique of critical theory in *Anti-Lawyers* that remaining doggedly irreductionist, at the surface, as Latour advocates, presumes precisely the sort of political-legal stability that a historical investigation would have revealed to be a circumstantial and highly contingent, perhaps comparatively rare, condition.[11] The difficulty of lingering at the surface, however, turns out not to be the difficulty of bypassing history or the orthodox theories of modern law but a fully ontological difficulty: an 'epochal re-discovery of all that had been excluded – even repressed – by the Moderns' hegemonic intellectual abstractions'.

From Saunders's diagnostic reading of *La fabrique du droit*, culminating in the perverse image of a 'Gaia-Heidegger', we pass to Graham Harman's assessment of a vital, highly disputed, frequently perplexing contrast, namely that of the trajectories of political and legal enunciation. With an air of clinical detachment, Harman patiently disentangles the mesh of legal obligations and places this strange, non-referential chain into proximity with the political Circle, drawing on the dichotomy of Power Politics and Truth Politics offered in his recent study of Latour's political philosophy.[12] According to Harman, politics must precede law because it is the charge of politics to collect groups, which may in turn develop a legal order. Similarly, law relies more or less directly on the existence of political authorities – without politics, in other words, law is mere empty, unenforceable, unreliable words. Concluding with an enticing set of questions about the implications of this arrangement for a Latourian international relations theory, Harman's chapter skilfully demonstrates the promise and the peril of a comprehensive scheme of modes of existence.

Next, Kyle McGee argues for the enrichment of socio-legal studies by re-evaluating the operation of rules in legal enunciation, particularly in the 'judicial *Umwelt*'. Opposing the tendency to black-box legal rules, prevalent in doctrinal as well as critical or socio-legal research, McGee develops a new articulation of the content of law that would not, in his view, countenance the reduction of law to information. In a departure from his more exploratory book on Latour and legal theory, he focuses here on the means of formal legal speech, walking very slowly, 'intolerably' slowly, through the weeds of a US trial court's opinion in a class lawsuit concerning injuries and property damage suffered by residents of a small community allegedly resulting from a chemical company's pollution of nearby aquifers. Narrating the slow composition of a legal trajectory out of a multitude of non-legal actors and the court's methodical de-stratification of complicated levels or planes of enunciation, McGee introduces the *jurimorph* as a semiotic tool for capturing the peculiar translation that must precede entry into the trajectory and which results in a new legal figure – a value-object or, in later stages, after certain trials have been met, an obligation. The litigants propose competing sequences of value-objects, each leading to the endorsement of their respective positions; the court must submit the virtual sequences to tests, and draws out, actualises, only one pathway of obligations leading to the instauration of a principle.

Following McGee's critique of the black-boxing of legal rules comes the far more ambitious but no less earthbound critique of the 'black-boxing of empire' by Mariana Valverde and Adriel Weaver. Adroitly tracing the construction and deconstruction of the spectral *corpus mysticum* in Canadian legal discourse, the authors – one of whom, it bears noting, was among the very first legal scholars to engage with Latour's *La fabrique du droit*[13] – interrogate the weird legal agency of the Crown in aboriginal rights cases, disclosing the relentless production of novelty concealed beneath the conservative image of a continuous, eternal office and recalling the Latourian lesson about law's *soi disant* homeostatic character: 'even in this case [in which legal principles are modified], it will only be a matter of making the body of legal doctrine still more coherent, so that, in the last analysis, nothing will really have budged.'[14] These cases, Valverde and Weaver show, contract into themselves Canada's colonial/postcolonial histories and the full weight of its legal tradition's contradictory commitments. The sovereign gesture of recognition, offered by way of the 'honour of the Crown', paradoxically deprives the aboriginal nations so recognised of their very claim to existence, their nationhood: 'the Canadian state now has obligations of sovereign/royal honour toward all aboriginal peoples . . . but the naming of those obligations simultaneously performs a kind of re-coronation of the very colonial sovereign whose servants caused so much harm to aboriginal peoples over the centuries' (Valverde and Weaver this volume). Valverde and Weaver allow us to linger on this troubling sense of the uncanny, of the historical déjà vu or phantasm of repetition that takes on materiality in the bilateral movement of the Crown – ever 'ventriloquised by judges', in a phrase that conjures François Cooren's inquiry, discussed below – through the networks of public law. It is a phantasm that reappears in the discursive techniques of judges that are, in fact, elaborating and reinventing precisely the discretionary doctrinal construct ('honour of the Crown') that they claim, instead, to merely appeal to, hearkening to an eternal spring of sovereign virtue through the mists of antiquity.

Where the two preceding chapters zoom in on the techniques of legal black-boxing to recuperate surprising insights about the making of law, Serge Gutwirth's chapter constitutes a decisive philosophical intervention pitched at the level of law's ontology. In 'Providing the Missing Link', Gutwirth renders the difference between law as an institution or a body of norms (what he calls 'Law1') and law as a mode of existence or value ('law2') a crucial point of passage for any future philosophy of law.[15] Law1, Gutwirth argues, isn't really law at all, but a political and organisational phenomenon easily confused with other norms and normative systems, from the rules of sporting groups or trade associations to ethical codes. Law2 is a far narrower concept keyed to the production of novel solutions under a particular kind of *constraint* and has nothing to do with the establishment of standards to be followed. Gutwirth's argument resonates deeply with Harman's study of the fault lines dividing law and politics, but also with the more granular inquiries in McGee's and Valverde and Weaver's preceding chapters, with the succeeding chapters by van Dijk and de Sutter (see below) and, on an even more fundamental level, with the forceful thought of Isabelle Stengers and Gilles Deleuze. Gutwirth's finely tuned theorisation of law sounds a laudable alarum designed to compel legal theorists to disencumber law of the formidable demands of the *Rechtsstaat*, while holding firmly to the evasive thread of legal enunciation. For Gutwirth, statements in the key of [LAW] require, as an absolute condition, the 'anticipat[ion of] how and what a judge or court would decide', and we are all jurists engaged in the practice of law (as law2), or at the least, we 'speak legally' and not merely 'about law', insofar as we projectively reason on the basis of that anticipation. The passage of law depends on this anticipatory structure, from which Gutwirth derives the signal *operations* of law (qualification, hesitation, imputation and so on), which work in essentially the same way as they did for the Romans. Perhaps the most intriguing claims Gutwirth advances, however, are those concerning the joint articulation of Law1 and law2, which turns on a strange temporality found only in the legal mode's hall of mirrors, a temporal structure that unevenly distributes 'the general norms of yesterday, the concrete issues and uncertainties of today, and the legal bond of tomorrow'. Law alone, he concludes – even after it has been unburdened of the political, economic, moral and other duties recklessly imposed on it – remains 'the rightful and ultimate provider of stability and security', as the loops of this temporality ensure that a resolution to any controversy can indeed be fashioned, even where every other mode fails.

Niels van Dijk deepens Gutwirth's emphasis on the value of law (the latter's 'law2') by taking up the Latourian challenge of offering an alternative empirical account of what it is, precisely, to 'do' law. In 'The Life and Deaths of a Dispute', van Dijk mobilises insights gleaned from ethnographic research conducted at a law firm and courts in Belgium to formulate the legal-theoretical concept of *matters of dispute*. Tracing the gradual transformation of these matters into legal cases and finally judgments and accomplished facts, van Dijk names each step in the biography of a dispute, sharpening our understanding of the nature of legality along the way. Moving from the development of the dispute through a series of contractions, condensations and extensions to its reduction to contentious points and the judicial linearisation of its complicated folds, van Dijk invents a conceptual topology of law that he calls, suggestively, *legal pointillism*. Rather than a mere 'aestheticisation' of law, this represents a philosophical ungrounding, or re-grounding, of all existing jurisprudence and legal epistemology, stimulating a new look at fundamental concepts (thing, cause, effect, ground, point . . .) that have been locked for too long in the dusty inventories of metaphysics. Van Dijk claims an affinity not only with Leibniz, Whitehead and Deleuze, but with Harman's object-oriented philosophy as well. Finally, though his indebtedness to Latour's ethnography of the Council of State is clear on every page, van Dijk marks a number of differences with him on crucial questions, like the nature of the legal totality and the role of tautology in legal reasoning, arguing that, in the end, it would be better to speak of *assignation as a mode* rather than law.

If van Dijk ended with a subtle critique of Latour's account of law, the following chapter represents a direct confrontation with a principal tenet of Latour's metaphysics. In his contribution, Laurent de Sutter challenges Latour's commitment to empiricity, positivity and above all *the trace* by which alone an actor is grasped in actor-network theory. De Sutter embraces Latour's argument about the ontological openness or generosity of law – it is the only mode, de Sutter reminds us, capable of seizing any being whatsoever and attaching it to an utterance or an action and thereby registering its agency and, importantly, rendering it compossible with beings of quite other pedigrees.[16] As such, law is the only 'ontologically neutral' mode, but there is much more at stake than the harmonics of existential modes, namely the real composition of worlds and, indeed, of what must be defined as *the unworldly*: 'all that exists only as non-existing', 'all that is present only as absent', or again, 'all that has form only as unformed'. These missing masses that Latour occasionally acknowledges, de Sutter argues, escape from the tendrils of the networks that define the real and the knowable, but enjoy something more than a mere negative or emptily theoretical existence. For Latour, plasma is simply the 'dumping ground' where he deposits the things that do not awaken his interest, a realm of obscurity that must be set off from the world of which clear and distinct representations are possible. To undo this surprisingly Cartesian tendency in Latour, perhaps, de Sutter suggests, it would be possible to recover plasma as the genus to which Deleuze's dark precursor would belong. If there is identity, similitude, resemblance, traceability, in short the whole modern system of representation, it is only as a plasmatic excrescent. As a first step along this path, de Sutter makes a pitch for the recovery of what he calls *the beings of sensitivity*, which may affect other beings profoundly but which themselves leave no measurable trace.

Despite the force of de Sutter's argument, Cédric Moreau de Bellaing's chapter mobilises a bewildering array of traces to build a provocative account of police internal affairs investigations. Such investigations concern accusations of wrongdoing made by civilians against police officers. By deploying analytical resources drawn from Latour's work, it becomes quite possible to make such ordinary administrative procedures reveal something essential about the nature of state violence, what counts as legitimate authority, and how law fits into the modern architecture of power. What entities, Moreau de Bellaing asks, must be enlisted, and what relations must be established between them, in order to produce a 'good judgment' in these inquiries into alleged police misconduct? Having followed the police investigators in their work for several months, the author is in a position to tell us. Confronting the 'enigma' of a severe disproportionateness between the frequency of reports of illegitimate violence and the frequency of the imposition of sanctions for such misconduct, Moreau de Bellaing notes that the compiled data themselves give no hint of the qualitative details of any particular case: as Garfinkel showed long ago, statistical reports reveal, at most, the management techniques of the organisation that prepared the reports. Thus we must plunge into the disciplinary records to extract the phases of investigation and to assemble a logic of the case grounded not in numerical abstractions but in the 'torturous progression' of concrete transformations, the interplay of leads, dead ends, ulterior motives, defensive strategies and proliferating uncertainties, and the circulation of value-objects required for the generation of an acceptable conclusion warranting closure of the disciplinary file. Moreau de Bellaing's conclusion is stark and sobering: the establishment of the legitimacy or illegitimacy of police violence has nothing to do with the magnitude of force applied, as civilians would expect, but only with the successful capture, by the investigators, of the many moving pieces composing the relational situation in which any quantum of force was applied in the first place.

The next chapter, by François Cooren, also develops fascinating theoretical resources on the basis of immersive research. Cooren here applies his model of ventriloquism[17] to law and to the performances of legal speech, which allows him to detect the slight shifts in agency so characteristic of legal argumentation, and which helps reveal the complexity and polyphony of the apparently homophonic judicial utterance. From the Latourian notion of distributed action and the structure of *faire faire* – a theorem that consistently earns a central place in Latour's *oeuvre*, from some of the earliest work on the sciences and technology to the recent *Inquiry into Modes of Existence* – Cooren launches his study by problematising anew canonical givens such as the binaries of passivity/activity and autonomy/heteronomy. We must not forget that ventriloquism involves not only the ventriloquist's manipulation of the puppet but also the puppet's manipulation of the ventriloquist, insofar as the latter says things that she, quite frankly, would never say were the puppet not attached to her hand. It is this strange loop of action and passion, autonomy and heteronomy, animation and inanimation, that characterises not only the puppeteer's performance but also the lawyer's and the judge's performances, and, indeed, the structure of communication in general. What, then, does it mean to speak *in the name of the law*? Without succumbing to the snares of spontaneous hypostatisation, Cooren argues, in contrast to numerous theorists including several appearing in this volume (Valverde and Weaver, van Dijk, perhaps Gutwirth), that the law indeed possesses a sort of agency of its own. A host of legal and non-legal beings (prior judgments, witness testimony, documents of all kinds, emotions like frustration and anger, balances of power, statutes, healthcare reform policies, duplicity, etc.) are *figured* and mobilised to say certain things in the saying of the law: they are voiced by lawyers and judges, of course, but they also lend their own voices to the latter, shaping the means through which the law may pass.

Issuing a bold and, in light of current preoccupations with AIME, untimely call for the continued relevance of *Laboratory Life*, Latour's early study co-authored with Steve Woolgar and based on participant-observation at Roger Guillemin's lab at the Salk Institute, David Caudill's chapter realigns the question of Latour's value for legal theory. Rather than mapping the unstable, unpredictable movements of the legal trajectory – a term that, in preceding chapters, has taken on several perhaps inconsistent layers of meaning – Caudill proposes to reconsider the relationship between law and the sciences (and revisits some of the drama of the Science Wars) under the auspices of the economics of science, a flourishing sub-field of science studies veritably inaugurated by *Laboratory Life*'s influential discussion of cycles of credit and credibility. Deftly untangling the law-sciences-economics knot, Caudill stages the matter of *Philip Mirowski* v. *Bruno Latour (and Michel Callon)*, in which the defendants were accused of complicity with neoliberalism and charged, by proxy, with the allegedly pernicious effects of the increasing commercialisation of research on the scientific establishment. Mirowski's critique runs out of steam, Caudill shows, and runs off the rails as soon as the details of law's appropriation of scientific research and evidence are examined. But the often dismaying implications of Science Wars era disputes – now being recapitulated or replayed in miniature, in the economics wing of the science studies field and in legal studies – continue to haunt contemporary law as well as science policy, because it remains unclear to what extent judges and regulators (and legal academics) appreciate the material contributions of works like *Laboratory Life* to the improvement of our understanding of the sciences, and to what extent the co-production thesis developed by Latour, Callon and others still registers as a fanciful exercise in debunking.

If Caudill studies the entanglement of law, economics and the sciences, Faith Barter renews the conjunction of law and literature through the lens of 'their shared interest in troubling the definition of the human'. Bartleby, in Melville's story, traverses the superhuman and the subhuman, rendering him illegible and object-like to his frustrated employer, while the young girl in Coetzee's novella (who is already, as a native, deemed non-human by the law of the Empire) approaches objecthood by virtue of the indecipherable traces of imperial torture she bears. Barter examines the twin dilemmas in Melville's and Coetzee's texts while also placing them into dialogue with the infamous 1857 *Scott* v. *Sandford* opinion of the US Supreme Court. She analyses the three texts along a temporal axis, from which emerges a set of dynamic historical oscillations and intertextual patterns of world-building. Suspicious of the 'complete[] singular[ity]' of law, conceived as a mode of existence, Barter reframes the relationship of law and literature by passing each through the partial regional ontology of the other, opening up a space for the interrogation of a new hybridity: literature as law. Perhaps all modes of existence are also, simultaneously and necessarily, modes of coexistence.

Bruno Latour closes out this volume by taking hold of several threads running through the preceding chapters. In addition to responding to a few of the criticisms that have cropped up, Latour offers remarks on the specific analyses developed in several of the chapters in order to shed light on crucial elements of the *AIME* project and his view of the legal mode of existence, addressing among other things *domains, institutions, normativity, jurimorphs* and a few modal *crossings* stimulated by the work of the book's contributors. The outlines of a new concept – the *red letter of the law* – even begin to take shape as Latour moves between and among the compelling and original arguments of the individual chapters.

Latour and the Passage of Law thus exposes the law in all its complication and co-implication with the other modes, while driving ever more deeply into the specificity of law. It should be quite impossible, therefore, to overload law with commitments it is not capable of sustaining, or to confuse the tumultuous passage of law with the stable transfer of information, or to insist on the adequacy of existing legal epistemologies. Despite the breadth of the volume's interventions, however, the quarry has not been exhausted, not nearly. Instead, a cloud of new questions, ever more precise, ever more foreign to modern legal theory, arises as we pass from chapter to chapter. Perhaps, in this light, the book can be seen as setting the stage for the next great movement in the study of law, one that would overcome critique while leveraging elements of formalism and realism, ethnography and jurisprudence, ANT and philosophy in a completely unforeseeable constellation.

Notes

1. Bruno Latour (2013) *An Inquiry into Modes of Existence: An Anthropology of the Moderns*, trans. Catherine Porter. Cambridge, MA: Harvard University Press, p. 360.
2. Ibid., p. 358.
3. Ibid., p. 369 (emphasis in original).
4. Ibid.
5. Ibid., p. 370 (emphasis removed).
6. Latour (2010) provides a list of legal value-objects in *The Making of Law: An Ethnography of the* Conseil d'État, trans. Marina Brilman and Alain Pottage. Cambridge: Polity, pp. 194–5. These do not reappear as such in AIME, but are redistributed in his formulation of the passage of law, from the particular hiatus it may cross to its unique manner of extracting an alteration from being. See the table in AIME at pp. 488–9.
7. This is a point I first developed in an article (see Kyle McGee 2012) 'The fragile force of law: mediation, stratification, and law's material life', *Law, Culture and the Humanities* (June) and extended in chapter 3 of *Bruno Latour: The Normativity of Networks* (2014) New York: Routledge. It turns out that this thesis has generated some (productive) controversy, as reflected in Serge Gutwirth's reflection in this volume. Thus, in this introduction, I refrain from elaborating on a view that may be inconsistent with that of others contributing to this project.
8. See the discussion in AIME at pp. 61–4.
9. Ibid., p. 162.
10. On the secular figure of Gaia, see, most importantly, Bruno Latour (forthcoming) *Facing Gaia: Six Lectures on the Political Theology of Nature*. Cambridge: Polity.
11. David Saunders (1997) *Anti-Lawyers: Religion and the Critics of Law and State*. London: Routledge.
12. Graham Harman (2014) *Bruno Latour: Reassembling the Political*. Cambridge: Polity.

13. See Ron Levi and Mariana Valverde (2008) 'Studying law by association: Bruno Latour goes to the *Conseil d'État*', *Law and Social Inquiry*, 33 (3): 805–25.
14. AIME, p. 365.
15. Gutwirth (2013) earlier developed the foundations of this piece in an influential short article, 'Le contexte du droit ce sont ses sources formelles et les faits et moyens qui exigent son intervention', *Revue Interdisciplinaire d'Etudes Juridiques*, 70: 108–16.
16. De Sutter extends similar lines of argument elsewhere, including De Sutter (2012) 'The Kamis of Kapital', *Cardozo Law Review*, 33 (6): 2499–511, and his provocative championing of a brand of active (legal) nihilism in De Sutter (2009) *Deleuze: La pratique du droit*. Paris: Michalon.
17. See François Cooren (2010) *Action and Agency in Dialogue: Passion, Incarnation and Ventriloquism*. Philadelphia: John Benjamins.

I

From the Conseil d'État to Gaia: Bruno Latour on Law, Surfaces and Depth

David Saunders

La fabrique du droit

In *La fabrique du droit. Une ethnographie du Conseil d'État* (now translated as *The Making of Law*), Bruno Latour reported on his months of first-hand observation of how law-making proceeded in the French Conseil d'État. One of the country's three 'supreme' courts – the others being the Cours de cassation and the Conseil constitutionnel – the Conseil d'État serves as a court on matters of administrative justice. In this role, it can satisfy a claimant by annulling a prior judgment by another court or tribunal or it can reject the claim. The court also acts as a legal advisor to government on the drafting of legislative bills and decrees. More rarely and if requested by the government – as in the 'headscarf' controversy – the Conseil d'État can proffer an 'opinion'.

In selecting the Conseil d'État as his object of observation, Latour had picked a legal institution atypical of the French system. Founded by Napoleon, the court has 'the task of conjuring up, from start to finish through the mere interplay of its previous decisions and in the absence of any written text ... a *sui generis* form of law whose specific objective is to protect the citizen from the excesses of the administration' (Latour 2002/2010: 14). The court's jurisdiction, then, is not code-based but rests its decisions on the authority of its own accumulated administrative case law.

Latour's account of the Conseil d'État's manner of proceeding went much wider than a concern with this institution's atypicality. The procedural and case-based – as opposed to code-determined – dimension of the court provided passage to a broader intellectual programme whose concern was to detour around conceptual determination. The outcome was a comprehensively 'superficial' description whose focus ranged from the judges' particular habits of legal mind and their regular techniques of dealing with the cases coming before them to the architecture of the building and all the bits and pieces of equipment. This sweep – from the intellectual to the material, from the spiritual to the technical – is in keeping with the distinctive approach Latour has developed in his style of 'science studies' on the working practices of scientists and laboratories.

La fabrique was notable, though, for its satirical verve. Rather than writing a straightforward, even banal account of a court of law at work, Latour adopted a quasi-literary figure to do the describing: 'the ethnographer', an *ingénu* or innocent persona, who was loosed into the Conseil d'État equipped with an overly knowing philosophical outlook on law ... at least initially. This 'ethnographer' wasn't a Voltaire's Candide or a Montesquieu's Usbek. Latour's satire inverted these classical models by setting a persona with a hyper-developed capacity for abstraction – the 'philosophically minded' one – into the remorselessly mundane context of the court.

In one sense, though, this satirical device was just a means to the main ambition of the work: a 'thick' description of law-making in the Conseil d'État that wasn't hostage to conceptual depth. For this, a protocol was to be observed: to make 'description of the law compatible with the practice of judges'. And to this end, the report proclaimed a constraining resolution: 'to *remain on the surface of things*, stubbornly following the hesitant course of judgment' (Latour 2002/2010: 143).

In fact a triple commitment was promulgated: first, to a descriptive stance; second, to a description compatible with the experience of the practitioners; third – and perhaps least expected but most important – to a recognition of law's 'superficiality'. Law was to be observed as:

> Nothing but surface, nothing but filaments, nothing but laces; just the links that ... hold us and protect us – provided that they remain at the surface, that they engage us lightly, that we ourselves remain at the surface, hardly engaged, so as to be able to monitor and interpret them. (Latour 2002/2010: 266)

From this observation we were to reach a rather sharp conclusion: 'the difficulty of law stems from its superficiality' (Latour 2002/2010: 267).

This stance on 'surfaces' carried a powerful corollary but this was negative: law must not be encountered as a matter of 'depth'. Or, as it turned out, a matter of 'height'. For the purposes of *La fabrique*, this corollary had the force of a double proscription. It entailed rejecting 'the contradictory advice given to us, by sociologists on the one hand and epistemologists on the other, about how to grasp the hidden reality of Law'. The former reduce law to the armature of an underlying social structure, a sublimated ideology, a 'fancy dress', an 'elaborate camouflage for precisely those power relations that we should be attempting to overthrow' (Latour 2002/2010: 142–3). The epistemologists reduce law to a 'scaffolding' of overlying rules or norms – epistemic or moral – whose practical realisation the legal order exists merely to secure. To embrace either of these 'abstracting' perspectives would

> compel us to leave the winding path of practice in order to focus on another reality, one that is invisible to the [legal] actors themselves but which is supposed to explain their behaviour: either the true reality of society and social violence or the true reality of the rule and its immanent logic. (Latour 2002/2010: 142)

At issue here – as it were alongside the actual details of the Conseil d'État – was a more general question. It concerned the disposition to be adopted against a practice of 'abstraction' but towards a practice of 'irreduction'.

Latour's insistence on law's essential 'superficiality' raised a further issue. If *La fabrique* staged a demotion of 'depth' and 'height' as would-be attributes of law – attributes articulated only when law is approached in terms of either underlying explanatory social structures or overarching directive norms – Latour's account of the Conseil d'État also staged a promotion of what he would count as the right line of approach.

To specify this approach in *La fabrique*, Latour promoted 'slowness' as central to his ethnography of the Conseil d'État ... and perhaps to the legal process itself. A court judge-assessor was heard invoking a 'duty to hesitate', insisting that 'before accepting the solution of the Cassation, I believe that *we must hesitate*' (Latour 2002/2010: 32, note 41). In Latour's account, hesitating – slowing a rush to judgment – became a distinguishing feature of law's practice. Judges displayed a 'capacity that is marked by hesitation, doubt and the recognition of indisputable resistances defining what we can and cannot do'. Here Latour warned against haste on our part too: 'Again, we should not be too hasty to purify the nature of this movement [of hesitation]' (Latour 2002/2010: 151). Hesitation was a duty: 'we need to be hesitant' (Latour 2002/2010: 179). This was a call for an intellectual deceleration, one deemed prerequisite if we were to appreciate the judges' commitment 'to doubt properly, thereby avoiding any precipitously reached solution' (Latour 2002/2010: 219).

But is this as straightforward as it might seem? It's not that there are never urgent circumstances in which the law should act with all due speed. Nor is it that procedural slowness will always guarantee a judgment of high quality. But what if the issue lies less with the actual process of the law itself than with a philosophical investment in advocating 'slowness'? Is this another sort of 'slowness', one that requires its practitioners to 'hesitate' not before they reach a judicial decision – we are not all judges in courtrooms – but as the condition of a particular stance or outlook: to keep ourselves 'open' to a greater 'plurality of experience'? Is this something we'll do by endlessly deferring 'too hasty' categorial interventions ... or are such interventions by definition always 'too hasty'?

At issue here is a certain displacement. In recommending deferment, does Latour use the figure of law's 'slowness' as a proxy? Does 'the breadth of the disjointed elements which [the judges] managed to retain after having extensively and decently "hesitated"' (Latour 2002/2010: 168) then go proxy for something quite different: a desire that experience be self-disclosing?

Meanwhile, back in the Conseil d'État, the judges reached decisions, sometimes very quickly. Cases came to an end. However, this is 'superficial' too:

> The end of a case never reaches a limit that is any more grandiose than this particular kind of exhaustion [of the available channels of appeal]: 'it's reported in the *Lebon* volume', 'the issue has been decided', 'as the law now stands', 'unless the European Court of Human Rights rules to the contrary'. Nothing said in the Council of State is more juicy, or more sublime, than these sorts of expressions. (Latour 2002/2010: 238)

Appropriately, then, the judges 'take care to ensure that this ending is not clothed in the grandiose forms of Incontrovertibility'.

This was a further element of a law that's 'superficial', a law not 'overloaded' with 'impossible virtues' that included 'sovereignty, law, morals, the social link, justice, politics and even religion' (Latour 2002/2010: 267).

Instead of some such law 'overloaded' with doctrine and other abstractions, *La fabrique* invited us to look at law as a domain of deliberative work and scriptural activities having lateral ties and entanglements with other such domains. We were to see an almost endless array of precedents, modes of inscription, exegetical practices, rhetorical moves, routines of deliberation and procedures of decision and judgment. Latour described the current organisation and practices of the Conseil d'État, its judicial and other officers and their varied *cursus vitae*, and – not least – its diversity of material equipments: the 'files' and 'dossiers' that accompany a 'case' in its 'passage' through the court, the 'systemic' armchairs, even the 'hierarchical' mail-box.

For all its evident contingency, it's within this historical framework – and nothing ontologically deeper – that cases are decided without 'incontrovertible' guarantees that a present decision will determine future decisions. It's within this framework that we live our juridified Western life. If the 'ontology' of a legally ordered existence is one fashioned by the decisions that courts happen to have taken in this way, then it's not an 'ontology' at all.

Yet it's precisely the ontological specificity of law that was made a major theme of *La fabrique*. And it remains so, ten years on, in Latour's *Enquête sur les modes d'existence: Une anthropologie des Modernes*.

The *Enquête* looks beyond the law's 'mode of existence' to contemplate the modes of science, art, politics, religion, economy. There's a moment of reflection early in the *Enquête*: 'It would have been more reasonable, I recognise it, to limit the inquiry to its ethnographic dimension alone' (Latour 2012: 33). Why not stay within the disciplinary register of *La fabrique*? Because, as Latour says, he couldn't see how his subsequent inquiry into the 'modes of existence' could 'proceed without philosophy'. There's an immediate caveat. If there's a turn to philosophy, it's not to seek 'foundations'. Rather, it's in order to have a 'chance of forging the metalanguage that might allow us to do justice, in theory, to the stupefying inventions that the terrains reveal at every step'. The idea of 'terrains' revealing their 'stupefying inventions' sounds very like a promise of things to come.

The *Enquête* does not provide further empirical descriptions of judges at work. We're now on philosophical ground. The wider investigative programme of the *Enquête* is designed to tell us we're on the edge of an epochal 'crisis' – that of the world's ecology – and proceeds under the tutelary spirit of 'Gaïa'. Unlike the Conseil d'État, 'Gaïa' is not an empirically describable object of knowledge. Just what it might be I'll come to in my concluding remark.

Law among the modes

After a hard session at the Conseil d'État, Latour asked: 'But who is going to describe this pedestrian work . . .?' (Latour 2002/2010: 77). As for his readers, they 'have to absorb much more law than they would wish' (Latour 2002/2010: 127). *La fabrique* therefore entailed a pedagogical triple task: to bring us to see law in terms of 'surfaces' not depths or heights, to have us master a certain form of 'slowness' and thence to make us recognise law as a particular 'ontology', a specific 'mode of existence'.

To ease the task, for *La fabrique* Latour adopted a rather winning literary device: the persona of 'the ethnographer' serving as an in-text avatar for hard-working readers. The ethnographer started out as 'philosophically minded' but was soon puzzled by what he met within the court. Listening to the Conseil's commissioner of law, he encountered a 'form of subtlety *divorced from conceptual foundations* – even doctrinal foundations – that is characteristic of the law even though it never ceases to surprise the philosophically minded' (Latour 2002/2010: 16). Something kept eluding the ethnographer's too-deep-seeing gaze:

> 'How can this be? Is there really nothing more elevated going on in this supposedly *supreme* court, beyond these infinitely small discussions on words and drafts?', the ethnographer asks himself while adjusting his tie and straightening his posture at the foot of a grand staircase . . . 'Is there really nothing above the law?' (Latour 2002/2010: 68)

But there isn't. Through a series of such experiences, the ethnographer learned to dismiss old 'abstracting' ways of thinking that would 'compel us to leave the winding path of practice in order to focus on another reality, one that is invisible to the [legal] actors themselves but which is supposed to explain their behaviour: either the true reality of society and social violence or the true reality of the rule and its immanent logic' (Latour 2002/2010: 142). The lesson of *La fabrique* was stark: 'There is no point in studying law in depth!' (Latour 2002/2010: 265).

The *Enquête* invents a different avatar and constructs a different narrative. Latour has gone for 'the anthropologist' – now gendered female – who's naively going to learn about 'the Moderns'. Of them at first she has little idea. Progressively, as she pursues her trail through the modes of existence, she comes to see through the Moderns' 'delusions' and to decipher their 'fantasies'.

Law enjoys a star spot in the anthropologist's *Bildungsroman*. She recognises law's mode of existence as the very model for her project to 'reconstitute the system of values of "western societies"' (Latour 2012: 40). Indeed, 'better than all the others, [law] lends itself to an analysis in terms of mode of existence', such that the anthropologist finds law 'preformed for her analysis' (Latour 2012: 359, 363).

A programmatic venture in philosophy, the *Enquête* presumes acquaintance with the concrete descriptions of law-making in *La fabrique* and, perhaps, retrospectively discloses the latter's philosophical dimension. Major themes that transfer between the two books include the anti-reductionist stance, the proscription of abstraction and the advocacy of law's 'slowness'. The *Enquête*, though, spans several modes of existence, elaborating the specificity of each. As in *La fabrique*, law is shown as distinguishing itself by a specific form of veridiction, that is by its special capacity to enunciate a specifically judicial truth not beholden to any moral or religious sense of justice:

> When I require a case decided by a court also to provide me with the peace of mind that would let me, as one says, 'mourn my grief', I'm asking the impossible, because the closure particular to the judicial apparatus simply doesn't have as its purpose, as I discover in my pain, to provide a balm to my soul, but instead simply links texts with facts and texts with texts in treating opinions according to the vertiginous pathway that's designated, without being described, by the terms 'means' or 'procedure'. (Latour 2012: 66)

A line of demarcation is drawn between a truth that is legal truth and a truth that is moral or religious. Thus a court's 'decision [that is] juridically founded is not necessarily just' (Latour 2012: 361).

A similar demarcation is drawn to illustrate the particular 'force' of the law: You'll find it quite futile, in your outrage at a law of which you're ignorant, to complain about its coldness, its formalism, its findings that don't satisfy you, its 'jargon' that's inflicted on you, all its endless paperwork, its *obligations tatillonnes*, the signatures and the seals, and yet this doesn't stop you clearly sensing, the moment you encounter the judge's ermine or the advocate's black gown, that you're going to have to comply with an order of practices that will not be reducible to any other and which, despite this, will retain its own dignity and where it will also be an issue of true and false, but in a different way. (Latour 2012: 72)

The documents constituting your case dossier, the appeal to precedents and prior legislative enactments, the collective intelligence of those who work together in the legal institution ... all these are material to producing the legal verdict, the legal truth-telling. Though 'very different from the practices of scientific knowledge', law 'nonetheless possesses a similar sort of solidity, stability and seriousness ... one that requires from you a similar respect' (Latour 2012: 72).

As one piece in Latour's philosophical depiction of law's specificity this account of legal veridiction might seem clear enough. But it's as if the legal demarcation of true and false simply derived from law's present practices and procedures. Is it telling that there's nothing historical in Latour's account? Historically speaking, at times and in circumstances where no demarcation was being drawn between legal and religious modes of veridiction, European legal systems have adjudicated and enforced religious truths, to the point of pronouncing a heresy 'juridically false' and then executing the heretic according to the law. If at certain times and in certain circumstances law has come to be demarcated from religious imperatives, this has been the contingent effect of shifting political, legal and religious forces playing themselves out, sometimes in conflict, sometimes in settlement.

The *Enquête* derives law's specificity in a second manner: from its 'particular way of extending itself' (Latour 2012: 247). Law 'extends' along:

... a trail of transformations, translations, transmutations, transsubstantiations that, degree by degree, and by payment – often very costly – to line up a multitude of notaries, advocates, judges, commentators and specialised professors, bit by bit modifies the relation between, as it were, the *quantity* of facts, emotion and passion, and the *quantity* of principles and texts on which law can be made. (Latour 2012: 364)

Law's way of connecting facts and principles is its particular mode of extension, its particular 'enchainment' (*chaînage*) of links.

In the *Enquête* as in *La fabrique*, the 'extension' theme plays a crucial role in the author's advocacy of 'the principle of irreduction' (Latour 2012: 45). This principle marks the primary line of defence against pre-emptive strikes by 'abstractions' that would prematurely curtail the ever fuller 'extension' of a mode of existence. For instance, a pre-emptive reductionist turn to 'Society' – as the 'explanation' of law, despite 'law being its own explanation of itself' (Latour 2012: 359) – would entail 'the amalgamation of all the modes and all the networks whose threads one has declined to unravel and which one takes as the foundation so as to explain how all the rest holds together – religion, law, technique, even science and of course politics' (Latour 2012: 352-3).

Latour's response is to elevate 'irreduction' to a 'principle'. But with this move, is he himself closing-off the possibility that we can be 'anti-reductionist' and yet remain capable of recognising that in certain social and historical conjunctures law and legal institutions have been fully aligned with religious, political or other social institutions and functions? This more historically open form of 'irreduction' is absolutely precluded when Latour's 'principle' forecloses on the possibility – or the fact – of law sometimes being 'reduced' to or aligned with what's taken to be a 'deeper' or 'higher' level of reality, be this an underlying social structure or a set of overlying norms. To stay true to Latour's 'principle', we would refuse to see law's 'specificity' – its separate existence or *apartheid* – as a variable, as opposed to an essential condition of its existence. As for 'the principle of irreduction', does it then become the new a priori prerequisite of a hermeneutics of surfaces?

By way of clarifying what 'anti-reductionists' object to, I'll cite four instances – sociological, historical, moral, political philosophical – in which law and legal institutions are 'reduced' to some other domain of life or related to some more fundamental level of reality.

Following Niklas Luhmann (1982, 1985), Gunther Teubner has traced the specificity of law to the legal system's formal conditions of possibility. This is a work of high abstraction. It excludes interest in 'multitudes of notaries, advocates, judges, commentators and specialised professors', not to mention this personnel's more than copious *matériel*. As an 'autopoietic' or self-referential system, law differentiates itself from other social systems by forming its own limits:

> The law itself determines which presuppositions must be present before one can speak of a legally relevant event, a valid norm, and so forth ... The degree to which law becomes autonomous is determined by the extent to which it constitutes self-referential relationships, ranging from minor normative cross-referencing to the circular closure of a hypercyclically constituted law. (Teubner 1993: 33–4)

Law might draw on all manner of moral, aesthetic and even metaphysical assumptions about human beings but – as viewed in this systems-theoretic light – it deals with them only insofar as they are legally re-constructible to function in a specifically legal ordering of conduct.

At the antipodes of Luhmann's and Teubner's reductionist sociology, Alan Watson locates law's specificity in its historical conditions. His anti-sociological stance 'reduces' law to its historical existence, providing a different instance of what 'anti-reductionists' would have us resist. Taking the French *Code civil* for illustration, Watson argues from the historical evidence that law 'has to a very considerable degree a life of its own':

> The proposition is that in any country, approaches to lawmaking (whether by legislators, judges or jurists), the applicability of law to social institutions, the structure of the legal system, the formulation and scope of legal rules are all in very large measure the result of past legal history, and that the input of other even contemporary societal forces is correspondingly slight. (Watson 1988: 20)

Because historical legal systems rest on 'legal borrowing and the ancient roots of law', the extent to which law is explicable in terms of social theory – especially when theory is highly abstracted – remains limited. Watson's empirical historiography allows him to adduce supporting evidence that law has 'a life of its own' from law's very 'failures' to mirror societal forces. These forces change but, for the most part, the law 'remains, not because of any particular message, but simply because it is there' (Watson 1988: 55).

The conclusion is no less brusque: the 'dynamic causal relationship between law and society which is often thought to keep the former in close harmony with the latter simply does not exist' (Watson 1988: 133). Yet a certain room to move comes with the historian's qualifier: law 'has to a very considerable degree a life of its own', but not absolutely so.

A third instance of 'reduction' involves a hand-over of law to 'values', in the event to supreme values invoked in the name of human rights. Confronting the issue of political-legal responses to terrorism, David Dyzenhaus has proposed an 'aspirational conception of law' to ensure all executive government responses are constrained by the rule of law. The means to this end is a 'continuum of legality' (Dyzenhaus 2005: 231) that goes, as it were, all the way down (or up) into the bedrock of human values. It is, we might say, a 'hyper-legality' distinguished by an indiscriminate expansiveness:

> [I]t does not matter much from the perspective of the rule of law how the furniture is arranged: whether the legal orders are civil or common law, or have entrenched bills of rights or no written constitution at all. What places [different legal orders] on the continuum is their commitment to the constitutional project of realising the values of the rule of law. (Dyzenhaus 2005: 231)

Dyzenhaus's 'rule of law project' relies on a convergence between 'common-law constitutionalism' and the values and principles of international human rights. These 'values' and 'principles' are to accompany 'a substantive conception of the rule of law that is appropriate at all times' (Dyzenhaus 2005: 58). They include 'fundamental legal values', 'fundamental or constitutional values', 'fundamental values of legal order', 'rule-of-law principles developed by the common law' and 'fundamental constitutional values, whether writen or unwritten' (Dyzenhaus 2005: 66, 87, 98, 116, 147). The law – here common-law constitutionalism – is in effect 'reduced' by being bound into human rights doctrine. 'Anti-reductionists' will puzzle over what sort of legal persona is being created: is it still a legal persona ... or is it the occupant of a quasi sacerdotal office for the moral admonition of executive government?

The formulation 'overloaded with too many values' returns in the *Enquête*. As in *La fabrique*, it comes in the guise of a risk to warn against. The 'values' that law has been asked to bear are now itemised as morality, religion, science, politics and the State (Latour 2012: 362). The 'principle of irreduction' requires Latour to set law apart from all of these, not to retrace the shifting patterns of their conflicts and resolutions, their convergences and separations.

But what of a reduction of legal institutions to philosophical principles? I'm reluctant to apply the epithet 'reductionist' to Martin Loughlin's *Foundations of Public Law* – my fourth example – without acknowledging that Loughlin opens the issue of public law's exceptional deficiency in the English constitutional situation to historical investigation:

> The system of administrative law that emerged in continental Europe during the eighteenth and nineteenth centuries was antithetical to English ways of governing. Every facet of the emerging system ran contrary to the common law tradition. (Loughlin 2010: 440)

There's a real sense that circumstances vary. For instance, the nineteenth-century English constitutional traditionalist Dicey could dismiss the Conseil d'État as a most un-Englishly pliant instrument of despotic statism on the grounds of the court's Napoleonic origins. But Dicey 'had misunderstood the degree to which the *Conseil d'État* in France had during the latter-half of the nineteenth century established its independence as an administrative court' (Loughlin 2012: 443).

But in pursuit of his advocacy for a better ordered system of administrative law in England, Loughlin turns primarily to European canons of *droit politique* and *Staatsrecht*. Here he locates the philosophical 'foundations' too long occluded in the English legal context. To recover, restore and bring these lost foundations into use, he looks back to the 'political jurisprudence' of public law's supposed 'founding fathers': Bodin, Hobbes and Grotius, Pufendorf, Kant and Hegel.

But having recovered the philosophical foundations of public law, Loughlin finds himself confronting a still deeper depth-charge in the form of the 'network' model of modern government, formulated initially by Léon Duguit and in recent times by Edward Rubin's (2005) *Beyond Camelot: Rethinking Politics and Law for the Modern State*. The network is the new ensemble of institutions – parliamentary, administrative and judicial, elected representatives and unelected technocrats, public and private – now identified as 'government' for a vast range of 'social' requisites:

> It is the concept of the social that now seems to determine regulatory objectives and to shape the variety of techniques (some public, others private) required to ensure their realisation. Once the network metaphor is set in place, the foundational elements of public law need to be reconsidered. (Loughlin 2010: 462)

In Loughlin's stark assessment, this rise of 'the social' would 'mark the destruction of the modern edifice of public law'.

It's not hard to imagine how 'anti-reductionists' would respond to these four instances of 'reduction'. The question of how they'd respond to Latour's account of law is more difficult, despite his stance on behalf of 'the principle of irreduction' and his promotion of 'extension' as the antidote to 'abstraction'. The *Enquête* sets law and us down on philosophy's 'terrain' because its author was unable 'to proceed without philosophy'. Could this proceeding too be a form of reduction?

In the *Enquête*, the 'principle of irreduction' is invoked also in relation to the tracing of 'ontologies'. The plural matters, because these 'ontologies' are taken to respond to 'the *pluralism* of the modes and thus the *plurality* of the keys by means of which we can judge their veracity or their falsity' (Latour 2012: 29). In its turn, the pluralising of ontologies is taken to be an effective means of 're-materialising' the empirical details of each mode of existence. What's more, this 'ontologisation' is accorded the status of liberator, the very means of a *désincarcération*. That is, a 'de-incarceration' from the prison-house of abstractions. In fact, these multiple ontologies promise not only our release. They also promise our recovery of 'the simple respect of the plurality of experience' (Latour 2012: 385, 310).

We need to see what's at stake in his promotion of 'ontologies' as the antidote to imprisoning abstractions. One possibility is to set Latour's ontological promotion of ontologies as the way to resist abstractions against a historiographical account of 'abstracting'. In 'The History of Thought: A Methodological Inquiry', John Pocock proposes treating philosophical 'abstracting' as 'an activity of thinking' that's susceptible to historical description. Pocock thus envisages historicising 'the actual processes of abstraction' that produced a 'rational coherence'. This leads him to propose that in certain historical situations abstractions – or 'theoretical principles' – may well have played a very concrete role:

> It is still perfectly possible that expressions of principle were frequently put forward in the course of the action, and absorbed much of the time and energy of those engaged in bringing it to completion. At this point we shall find them spoken of as 'propaganda', 'rationalisations', 'myths' and so forth – vaguely dismissive language designed to indicate that, whatever part they played in the story, it is not worth considering. But from what standpoint is it not worth considering? (Pocock 1962: 11)

It would be cheeky but correct to answer: from Latour's ontological standpoint. This is a standpoint that rejects – even proscribes – 'abstraction' as always, everywhere and only a 'reduction' of the 'plurality of experience'. There's no equivalent act of exclusion for Pocock's 'historian' who's as interested in 'men thinking [abstractly] about politics just as in them fighting or farming or doing anything else' (Pocock 1962: 9). What matters to this historian is to describe how 'abstractions' were actually put to use ... perhaps more in fighting than in farming, but who knows what actually goes on out on the land?

Unlike the 'philosopher', the 'historian' does not deal with abstractions via 'an act of disengagement' (Pocock 1962: 6). Where law is concened, Latour's 'disengagement' from abstractions – treated as impediments to access to experience of our 'modes of existence' – is the preliminary to his crediting law with a 'particular ontological tonality' (Latour 2012: 363). By virtue of its own 'tonality of ontology', law in its irreducible 'superficiality' can then be depicted as proof against reduction to the usual categorial abstractions: society, economy, religion, politics, ideology and – as dire as any other abstraction – established values.

Latour is not alone in rejecting reductive abstractions where the study of law is concerned. But there's more than one way of doing rejection. Pierre Schlag, Paul Campos and Steven D. Smith – individually or together, as in their tri-authored *Against the Law* (1996) – have left standing as little as possible by way of philosophical justifications or ontological alibis for the practices of American law. Schlag targets the normative abstractions that legal scholars endlessly project onto law. Like any non-incremental repetition, their immense labour risks becoming comic. Though their uplifting tracts continue to be written as if they actually guided America's lawyers, if Schlag is right then actual legislators, judges and the profession at large remain utterly indifferent to the scholars' theoretic industry.

In *The Enchantment of Reason*, Schlag portrays those who elevate legal judgments into realisations of higher-order reason as would-be 'enchanters' of law. The fact, however, is that they themselves are the ones suffering enchantment:

> When one is enchanted by reason, it does not feel like enchantment at all. Instead, it feels quite reasonable. Suppose you were in thrall to the enchantment of reason, how would you know? ... You would be trying to reason your way through everything. (Schlag 1998: 1)

So a prime task is to extricate law from enchantment – and abstraction – by reason: 'Reason is unstable. Law is not benign. This is not a great combination' (Schlag 1998: 145). If extrication worked, the pursuit of reason, the posing of normative questions – 'What should the law be?' – and the performance of normative gestures like seeking 'to bring law into greater consonance with moral value' might be somewhat suspended (Schlag 1991: 802–3). This is the limit of hope. In fact Schlag shares Paul Campos's dismay at the bloated belief that ever more law will solve ever more social and personal problems, the 'hypertrophic' juridifying of American life Campos (1998) has termed 'jurismania'. In the face of the 'messianic normativity' of an American doctrinal tradition whose 'perfectionist jurisprudences' preach a 'redemption' for law, the counter has to be very modest: to decline any 'redemptive' programme for a motley American law that is 'an admixture of thinking habits, jargons, ideals, anxieties, and canonical materials ... reproduced with sufficient regularity ... to produce the appearance of an intellectual discipline' (Schlag 1996: 10, 165; 1998: 12).

Are we still tempted to look away when Pierre Schlag describes law as that 'ugly bureaucratic noise that grinds daily in the nation's courts, legislatures, and agencies'?

Closing with questions

I permit myself to close with a reference to the current European scene – the Italian situation in particular – at the time of this writing. Silvio Berlusconi's attack on Italy's judiciary has been rejected by opponents of his demagogic populist politics as unbefitting European norms. They're surely right, but there's reason to explore the matter further.

On 19 October 2013, the judges of the Milan Court of Appeal took another step in respect of Berlusconi's 1 August conviction for tax fraud. With the political establishment looking on, the court determined the duration of the ex-premier's disqualification from holding public office. Whether they decided on one, two or three years of disqualification – in the event it was two years – the Milan judges were sure, yet again, to be denounced by Berlusconi's political entourage as 'communists' and 'unelected usurpers' of legitimate democratic government. In one sense this is ridiculous.

However, we should look at Italy's postwar political history, so marked by intractable conflict between Catholic and Communist political forces. For thirty years, since the anti-Mafia 'pool' of judges emerged in the 1980s – the yet-to-be assassinated Giovanni Falcone and Paolo Borsellino were among the members – and the *Mani pulite* or Clean Hands movement in 1991, the judiciary has taken on the role of 'counter-power', filling the political vacuum occasioned by the incapacities and corruptions of the political class. Having filled the vacuum, Italian judges found themselves carrying the political can, in effect adopting quasi-sovereign powers that should have stayed with parliament.

When Berlusconi's governments enacted *leggi ad personam* favouring his personal interests he infringed a boundary he should have respected, yet he now protests at what he terms a *golpe giudiziario*, a *coup d'état* by judges. There's no question of endorsing his protest, let alone tolerating Berlusconi's demand that his sort of 'democratic' government – in the sense of sanctioned by the electors – is the pre-condition of a rule of law and of legality. This would end the rule of law, the *stato di diritto*. Yet we have to recognise that an organised section of the judiciary, the Magistratura Democratica – operating within the broader Associazione Nazionale Magistrati – has openly pursued a leftist line.

Today's terrifying fractured political-legal situation in Italy provides real-time evidence that, in a European state, law remains anything but proof against politics and ideology. This convergence is circumstantial but it raises two substantial questions. Is it in politically unsettled times that judges might 'capture' the law in accordance with an ideological – or philosophical or religious – programme? Conversely, is it then a settled political-legal situation – that of France since 1958 under the constitution of the Fifth Republic – that allows Latour to describe law in terms of Conseil d'État judges who decide cases via an 'attitude of indifference' to external determinations? Either way, the lesson is that an anti-reductionist approach to law is a matter of circumstance.

This second question returns us to the issue of law's place in the *Enquête* programme of 'metaphysics'. 'Metaphysics' is Latour's term. As an appellation for the whole project, 'experimental metaphysics' is floated, along with 'cosmopolitics' and 'practical ontology' (Latour 2010: 479). Towards the end of the *Enquête* the author reflexively asks himself:

> ... whether I've done enough in this provisional report to distinguish, one, the experience; two, the metaphysics in which it has been shrouded – in my view always inappropriately; and finally, three, a different metaphysics, mine, disposable and provisional. (Latour 2012: 478)

The turn to a 'metaphysics' – one that must be 'disposable and provisional' if it's not prematurely to close off access to experience – is immediately qualified by a confirmation of the priority of description: 'only meticulous description of the situations' of each mode of existence can furnish the 'foundation without foundation' envisaged in this metaphysics. That the description must be 'meticulous' only intensifies the imperative to extend the description, as if to avoid a too-early closure of access to the 'plurality of experience'.

And the description has to be extended, because law 'can go everywhere and make everything coherent, provided it drops almost everything':

> If we have such difficulty in focusing precisely on what constitutes law's particular autonomy, if we have to take such care in unfolding law's fine tissue without breaking it, it's perhaps because of the strength of delicate connections. If it holds everything, if it makes it possible to link all people and all acts, if for example – by providing a continuous route – it authorises the Constitution to be linked to a minor case, it's also because in all situations law only extracts a minuscule part of their essence. Its tissue resembles a net of lace. (Latour 2012: 373–4)

This characterisation of law's 'fine tissue' replays that in *La fabrique* of law as 'nothing but filaments'. It evokes philosophical notions of 'network' and 'gathering' as condition and object of Latour's account of law. But the question remains: why does Latour fit the practice of law into a metaphysics that's as slow, as extended, as web-like and as 'disposable and provisional' as it can be?

In the final chapter of *La fabrique*, a move was already under way: by opening up to the life-world of surfaces, each with its multiple determinations, we could 'reopen negotiations with the other collectivities' provided we adopt a 'more diplomatic anthropology' (Latour 2002/2010: 267). An ethnography of the Conseil d'État was already tipping into the vision of a cosmopolitics to come. The move advanced – as if in keeping with history – in Latour's preface to *Making Things Public*, a thousand-page catalogue for an art installation designed to demonstrate 'an assembly of assemblies' and an interactive politics germanically christened *Dingpolitik*, a 'parliament of things'.

To the appeal for a 'more diplomatic anthropology', the *Enquête* brings something much sharper: the threat of 'crisis' in the form of an impending global ecological breakdown. 'En attendant Gaïa' – not Godot – we're now confronted by a force, Gaïa, that can eliminate us mere 'Terriens' (Latour 2012: 483). Against the threat of 'apocalypse', though, there's the chance of a salvific access to a common world, a collective 'gathering' of all and everything. Latour calls this 'the civilisation to come'. Given the evidence of persisting jurisdictional differentiation, however, this 'elective' vision of a coming unity has not persuaded scholars committed to social and legal 'differentiation' (Teubner 2006).

And indeed there's reason to hesitate before going with Latour. It concerns his commitment 'to *remain on the surface of things*' and to address law 'superficially':

> Nothing but surface, nothing but filaments, nothing but laces; just the links that . . . hold us and protect us – provided that they remain at the surface, that they engage us lightly, that we ourselves remain at the surface, hardly engaged, so as to be able to monitor and interpret them. (Latour 2002/2010: 266)

Insisting on law's superficiality continues to play the surface/depth game, only now it's the surfaces that count. The life-world of surfaces, each with their multiple determinations. To become properly 'superficial', like the ethnographer in *La fabrique*, we must enjoy the exorcism imposed on the still 'philosophically minded' ones.

But the point is not just a better description of law-making. It's to get us to prepare ourselves to enter 'the civilisation to come'. Seen in this light, we must re-describe Latour's re-descriptions of law and review his emphasis on its hard-to-describe 'superficiality'. If 'the difficulty of law stems from its superficiality' (Latour 2002: 267), the difficulty isn't that of describing the mailboxes in the Conseil d'État as an integral part of the process of lawmaking. Nor is the difficulty – and pain – that of jettisoning old ways of explaining what law is and speculating on what it ought to be. These ways and speculations too are to be exorcised as 'horrible phantoms'. No, the difficulty has to be ontological, as Latour conceives it. Law has to be depicted as *ontologically* difficult if it's to prepare us for 'the civilisation to come'. Things might not be what they seem. In this preparatory process, does law have a decoy role as a lure – or provisional stand-in – for an anticipated 'existence'? Perhaps, for 'juridically' we do well to read 'philosophically'.

We begin to see how 'surface' plays in this new 'depth' game. If the descriptions are detailed and objective, their verisimilitude is only one element of the exercise. They might bring law and all its equipment into fuller view, but their function is to direct us to an ontological uncovering, an epochal rediscovery of all that had been excluded – even repressed – by the Moderns' hegemonic intellectual abstractions, especially in Kantian variants. The endlessly interconnected elements that make up the network-existence of law serve to display its mode of 'being in the world', at least to those who know how to look. They prepare us to accede to the 'civilisation-to-come'. We're en route to 'meet with the "others" – the ancient others – and with Gaïa – the Other that's truly other' (Latour 2012: 33).

But is this such a new game? And is it so radical? In *Making Things Public*, Latour has no hesitation in writing: 'As every reader of Heidegger knows ...' (Latour 2005: 22). Quite so. The lexicon is explicitly Heideggerian, with *Sorge* – 'worries' or 'concerns' for the world – and 'gatherings' that bring things and peoples together. Does Heidegger's *Gelassenheit* – calmness, reticence, withdrawal almost – appear in *Making Things Public* or elsewhere in Latour's writings? It captures his mode of ascribing to law's procedure a 'slowness' that isn't Pierre Schlag's 'ugly bureaucratic noise that grinds'. To the contrary, it's as if when Latour's judges 'hesitate', to the point of almost but not quite suspending action, then the decision can arrive – oh so cool – in its own time and of its own accord. As in *La fabrique*, at places in the *Enquête* it could be Heidegger speaking:

> Through a long series of detours, each more tricky [*astucieux*] and more unforeseeable than the next, we encounter atomic physics in the service of a hospital to treat cancer. Through yet another detour, wood and steel call to each other in the handle of a well-balanced hammer. (Latour 2012: 220)

Which raises the question: will the walls of the courtrooms in Latour's civilisation-to-come be emblazoned not with a crucifix but with whatever might be the effigy of an old-new deity, Gaïa-Heidegger?

Acknowledgment

My thanks to Ian Hunter for his comments on the first draft of this chapter.

References

Campos, P. (1998) *Jurismania: The Madness of American Law*. New York: Oxford University Press.

Dyzenhaus, D. (2005) *The Constitution of Law. Legality in a Time of Emergency*. Cambridge: Cambridge University Press.

Latour, B. (2002) *La fabrique du droit. Une ethnographie du Conseil d'État*. Paris: Éditions la Découverte.

Latour, B. (2005) 'From Realpolitik to Dingpolitik or How to Make Things Public', in B. Latour and P. Weibel (eds), *Making Things Public: Atmosphere of Democracy*. Cambridge, MA: MIT Press.

Latour, B. (2010) *The Making of Law. An Ethnography of the Conseil d'État*, trans. M. Brilman and A. Pottage. Cambridge: Polity Press.

Latour, B. (2012) *Enquête sur les modes d'existence: une anthropologie des Modernes*. Paris: Éditions La Découverte.

Loughlin, M. (2010) *Foundations of Public Law*. Oxford: Oxford University Press.

Luhmann, N. (1982) *The Differentiation of Society*. New York: Columbia University Press.
Luhmann, N. (1985) 'The self-reproduction of law and its limits', in G. Teubner (ed.), *Dilemmas of Law in the Welfare State*. Berlin: De Gruyter.
Pocock, J. G. A. (1962) 'The history of political thought: a methodological inquiry', in P. Laslett and W. G. Runciman (eds), *Philosophy, Politics and Society*. Oxford: Blackwell.
Rubin, E. (2005) *Beyond Camelot: Rethinking Politics and Law for the Modern State*. Princeton: Princeton University Press.
Schlag, P. (1991) 'Normativity and the politics of form', *University of Pennsylvania Law Review*, 139: 801–932.
Schlag, P. (1996) *Laying Down the Law: Mysticism, Fetishism, and the American Legal Mind*. New York: New York University Press.
Schlag, P. (1998) *The Enchantment of Reason*. Durham, NC: Duke University Press.
Schlag, P., Campos, P. and Smith, S. D. (1996) *Against the Law*. Durham, NC: Duke University Press.
Teubner, G. (1993) *Law as an Autopoietic System*. Oxford: Blackwell.
Teubner, G. (2006) 'Rights of non-humans? Electronic agents and animals as new actors in politics and law', *Journal of Law and Society*, 33 (4): 497–512.
Watson, A. (1988) *Failures of the Legal Imagination*. Philadelphia: University of Philadelphia Press.

2

Politics and Law as Latourian Modes of Existence

Graham Harman

At the time of this writing, Bruno Latour's loyal readership is still in the early stages of mastering his recent treatise, *An Inquiry into Modes of Existence* (hereafter *Modes*).[1] In this work Latour presents a system of fifteen distinct modes of existence, each with its own three-letter abbreviation and, more importantly, its own truth conditions. The scientific criterion of adequate reference to an outside world must not be applied to other modes; this would amount to a simple category mistake. The reader cannot fail to notice that politics [POL] and law [LAW] are grouped with religion [REL] as the three modes pertaining to quasi-subjects. (By way of contrast, technology [TEC], fiction [FIC] and reference [REF] are the modes pertaining to quasi-objects.)[2] In what follows, I will focus on Latour's distinction between politics and law, leaving religion and the other twelve modes for my forthcoming book on Latour's later philosophy.[3]

One of the features that politics, law and religion share in common for Latour is their negative trait of being ungovernable by reference to objective facts in the outside world. It should already be clear to everyone that politics is not primarily an effort to ascertain objective truth. Most political controversies cannot be calmly and decisively settled by incontestable evidence, since most political 'evidence' can and will be contested ad infinitum until finally implemented by force. Nor can law be viewed primarily as an attempt to establish the true external facts of a given case. Many so-called facts in law are simply 'taken as true', and even the winning plaintiff can feel empty in victory, as if his or her truth-claim was not sufficiently appreciated by a favourable legal decision that aims at a different sort of resolution. Missed deadlines, botched paperwork, inadequate signatures and other apparent legal trivialities can derail an entire case. The same holds all the more for religion, whose claims surely cannot be verified by rigorous empirical inquiry. While for rationalists this is enough to disqualify religion altogether, for Latour it is merely a spur to determine what *other* sort of truth religion possesses, impenetrable to scientific research. Politics and law, our twofold subject in this chapter, are similar to religion insofar as they provide another standard of truth than the scientific kind. Yet they are markedly different from one another in what we might call *topological* terms: for Latour, politics is a *circle* and law is a *chain*.

The political circle

In his September 2008 Frankfurt acceptance speech for the Siegfried Unseld Prize, Latour recalls that 'beginning in Easter 1987, I started in earnest the first project about comparing regimes of enunciation (what I now call *An Inquiry into Modes of Existence*), even though I have not published a line about it ever since – until today that is.'[4] While this statement is mostly true, Latour seems to have momentarily forgotten several earlier publications on the modes project, including one that is perfectly suited to our topic: his 2003 article 'What if we *talked* politics a little?'[5] Nowhere else does Latour discuss the political circle in such detail. The final sentence of Latour's abstract to the article gets straight to the point: 'The "political circle" is reconstituted and thus also the reasons why a "transparent" or "rational" political speech act destroys the very conditions of group formation.'[6] What is most typical of politics in our time (other than politics of radical Left aspirations) is that intellectuals join almost unanimously in viewing it with contempt:

> Political expression is always *disappointing*; that is where we must start ... truisms, clichés, handshakes, half-truths, half-lies, windy words, repetitions mostly, *ad nauseam*. That is the ordinary, banal, daily, limp, tautological character of this form of discourse that shocks the brilliant, the upright, the fast, the organized, the lively, the informed, the great, the decided. When one says that someone or something is 'political,' one signals above all this fundamental disappointment...[7]

What the supposedly clear-headed thinkers prefer instead is *straight talk*, without all of the hedging, bluffing, flattering, and haggling that characterises the standard politician:

> For a start, we could say that [straight talk] consists of information, transparency, exactitude, rectitude and *faithful* representation. That is the dream of honest thinking, of non-deformation, of immediacy, of the absence of any mediator, what I like to refer to as *double-click* communication . . . It is in relation to this demand, this utopia, this myth, that political expression always has to admit to being skew, underhand, sly, compromising, unfaithful, manipulating, changing.[8]

Yet Latour has little regard for attempts to judge politics by the measure of the straight line: 'saying that political discourse is "twisted" has a very different meaning, depending on whether one has chosen the curve or the straight line as the ideal for all utterances.'[9] But readers familiar with Latour will recall that even his conception of *science* does not resemble a straight line, let alone his view of *politics*.[10] As Latour puts it in the same 2003 article:

> If politicians are to be hated for their lies, what can be said about scientists? Demanding that scientists tell the truth *directly*, with no laboratory, no instruments, no equipment, no processing of data, no writing of articles, no conferences or debates, at once, extemporaneously, naked, for all to see, without stammering [or] babbling, would be senseless. If the demand for transparent and direct truth makes understanding of the political curve impossible, remember that it would make the establishment of 'referential chains' by scientists even more impracticable.[11]

Science and politics are both incompatible with straight lines, though science involves 'referential chains' and politics deals with 'circles' which shall be described shortly. In any case, politics must not be expected to provide direct referential truth: 'One could just as well complain about the poor quality of a modem that was incapable of percolating coffee ordered on the internet.'[12] For:

> Political discourse appears to be untruthful only in contrast with other forms of truth. In and for itself it discriminates truth from falsehood with stupefying precision. It is not indifferent to truth, as it is so unjustly accused of being; it simply differs from all the other regimes in its judgment of truth.[13]

The truth condition of politics is simply that it must *succeed* in creating a group. Namely:

[Politics] aims to *allow to exist* that which would not exist without it: the public as a temporarily defined totality. Either some means has been provided to trace a group into existence, and the talk has been truthful; or no group has been traced, and it is in vain that people have talked.[14]

This implies that politics has a far wider scope than that of public rallies, parliaments, sovereign edicts and acts of war, a point Latour makes himself with blunt humour:

For *any aggregate*, a process of redefinition is needed, one that requires curved talk to trace, or temporarily retrace, its outline. There is no group without (re)grouping, no regrouping without mobilizing talk. A family, even an individual, a firm, a laboratory, a workshop, a planet, an organization, an institution: none have less need for this regime than a state or nation, a rotary club, a jazz band or a gang of hooligans. For each aggregate to be shaped and reshaped, a particular, appropriate dose of politics is needed.[15]

We now brush up against the circular structure of politics. For when we compose an aggregate, this means 'transforming the *several into one*, initially through a process of representation . . .'[16] That is to say, we cannot think of the aggregate as a group with fixed opinions or demands that the representative or sovereign would then be bound to reflect faithfully. If this were the case, then the representative would simply be a transparent intermediary repeating what the aggregate had already told it. But this is impossible. For one thing, an aggregate is too diverse for *all* of its opinions and demands to be faithfully represented; certain idiosyncratic or minority wishes are bound to be deleted from the end result. And for another, the representative or sovereign faces a different world from that of the aggregate, confronting other forces that sometimes need to be dealt with in ad hoc or improvisational fashion without direct instruction from the aggregate. What good would a senator or defence attorney be if they simply ventriloquised what we had already told them ourselves? What good would a diplomat be who stuck to the initial script from home and made no opportunistic surgical cuts into an emerging conversation in the foreign capital? In short, when the many become one, a certain degree of *betrayal* is needed.

Yet the same holds in the opposite case of the 'retransformation of the *one into several*, [which] is often called the wielding of power but [which] I more bluntly call obedience.'[17] Here too, the ruled cannot simply obey the ruling power transparently, without translation or interpretation; even the most imperious command contains a certain degree of vagueness as to the means for carrying it out. Once the political decision is made, always in partial betrayal of its constituency, that constituency in turn must partially betray the abstract and formalistic command it receives, by implementing and negotiating it with a view to concrete local conditions. When the general orders: 'Take that hill!', the lower officers still have many fateful decisions to make. This results in the creation of new conditions, which results in turn in the aggregation of all the new conditions into a new sovereign decision, which once more feeds back into commands that must be translated in order to be obeyed. Only in this way can the circle make a sufficient degree of healthy contact with the world outside itself. In other words, 'politics is tautological, not only in the ... sense of signifying a stream of platitudes, but also because it does always say the same thing *again and again*, without any hesitation at being boring. It *has to be* repetitive.'[18] Latour summarises his discussion as follows:

> She who talks in the name of all *must* necessarily *betray* those she represents, otherwise she will fail to obtain the transformation of the multitude into a unit; in turn, those who obey *must* necessarily transform the order received, otherwise they will simply keep repeating it without implementing it. In other words, either there is a double betrayal and the loop is looped, or there is fidelity, exact transfer of information, straight talk and the circle will never be closed. Truthful political talk – in the sense of double-click information – is as impossible to achieve as perpetual movement or the squaring of the circle. Hence, by an extraordinary paradox, autonomy would be impossible without this double betrayal – which goes some way to explaining the horror that the sudden appearance of politics never fails to arouse in reasonable people.[19]

Let this suffice as a description of the political Circle, which gives us Latour's topology of politics as a mode, and which plays such a prominent role in all of his recent discussions of politics. Yet along with this topological structure of politics, Latour also ascribes a *chronological* aspect to politics that ought to be mentioned here, even if it receives less development in his work than the theme of the Circle. In his 2007 exchange with Gerard de Vries, Latour describes five different stages in the political life of any issue,[20] making use of a metaphor from astronomy: 'In the same way as stars in astronomy are only stages in a series of transformations that astronomers have learned to map, issues offer up many different aspects depending on where they are in their life histories.'[21]

- *Political-1*: 'new associations between humans and nonhumans'.[22] Something from outside begins to perturb the *polis* that never perturbed it before, though it still remains vague just what that thing is.
- *Political-2*: the perturbation is now sufficiently distinct that the focus shifts to how the political sphere should reshape itself in reaction to the new issue, as in '[Walter] Lippmann and [John] Dewey's beautiful argument that the public is always a *problem*.'[23]
- *Political-3*: the state now feels the need to take some sort of stand on the new issue, a moment that is obviously 'much closer to the hard core of political theory, from Machiavelli to [Carl] Schmitt'.[24]
- *Political-4*: the deliberative stage, 'when fully conscious citizens, endowed with the ability to speak, to calculate, to compromise and to discuss together, meet in order to "solve problems" that have been raised by science and technology.'[25]
- *Political-5*: the issue has now 'become part of the daily routine of administration and management'.[26] For instance, 'the silent working of the sewage systems in Paris has stopped being political, as have vaccinations against smallpox or tuberculosis. It is now in the hands of vast and silent bureaucracies that rarely make the headlines.'[27] But Michel Foucault does often treat such things in political terms, as do certain feminist thinkers and science studies scholars.

To my knowledge, Latour does not discuss any other mode of existence in terms of its chronological life: a gradual coming-into-focus followed by a slow fade into the background infrastructure of the *polis*. We now turn from politics to law.

The legal chain

We now turn to Latour's book *The Making of Law*, published in 2009 in English, seven years after its appearance in French under a somewhat different title.²⁸ In the Preface to the English edition, Latour gives us a glimpse of his wider *Modes* project:

> I have to confess that, until I had carried out this field work, I was not too convinced that my overall project had any chance of succeeding. Having tried to compare scientific felicity conditions to, for instance, those of religion or politics, I knew it was feasible, but there was always the nagging feeling that it was a lost cause, so powerfully had the ideology of science squashed those other contrasts beyond recognition. Whatever I tried to do, religious and political enunciations seemed always to lament and repent for not being scientific enough. The immense advantage of law ... is that they never have any doubt (a) that their way of arguing is entirely specific; (b) that there is a clear distinction, inside this way of arguing, between what is true and what is false ... and (c) that this difference between true and false is totally different from what might be taken to be scientifically true or false.²⁹

And furthermore, 'only law has maintained, throughout the modernist parenthesis, a sturdy confidence in the validity of its own felicity conditions quite independently of what has happened to science ...'³⁰ The key legal word, for Latour, is 'the [French] word "moyen," for which the translators and I had a lot of trouble trying to find an equivalent. It is uttered ten times a minute by lawyers and judges, and yet this key term has no definition in law dictionaries.'³¹ The point of his book, Latour tells us, is to 'study in detail what is meant by this strange ambiguous and ubiquitous word "moyen," that has been translated by the words "argument," "reason," "ground" or *"mean."*'³²

In fact, the word *moyen* and its English equivalents are not actually discussed in the book as often as Latour's mission statement might suggest. Nonetheless, we realise while reading that we are learning all about 'means' and their role in the fabric of the law. Latour shows us how it works in cases that range from the amusing to the mortally perilous. A sunflower farmer sues the nearest town for not killing the pigeons that later devoured his crop of seeds; a lonely widower files suit following the death of his only son on a municipal ski slope under hazardous conditions; the illustrator for a gardening magazine succeeds in her quest to receive a coveted press card; a convicted Iraqi drug dealer, married to a French woman and the father of French children, fights deportation to Baghdad where he claims certain death awaits. Needless to say, the personal emotions of the claimants in these cases do not themselves appear at the Council of State:

> We can sometimes still recognize the smothered echo of the original complaint ... rage, indignation, scandal, something which belongs to the psychological, anthropological and sociological subject matter and which has given rise to sadness and anger somewhere in France. However, it concerns an anger and a sadness which are not only expressed by violence and tears, screams and blows, but which – through a rather mysterious mutation – decide to transform into fraud and grievance: in short, in more or less well argued writing which is addressed to an administrative tribunal. There is quite a distance between groaning, growling or protest and the writing of a claim.[33]

Alongside this *objectivity* of the law, we find an almost comical *materiality*: 'Every case, at least in our countries of written law, is physically enveloped in a carton folder held together with elastic bands. Even though it is not attributed any place in legal theories, it is by moving through this palace while following this little animal that we are going to become acquainted with all the various functions of the Palais-Royal.'[34] Another feature of the law is its *heteronomy*, since there are times when one cannot remain trapped within the letter of the law without keeping extra-legal circumstances in view:

> For the past six months, both lawyers and counselors, for once united, have been trying hard to find some way of escaping the jaws of the argument directed against the President of the Republic and his decree by an obscure stockholder of the Epsilon corporation, who has obtained twelve shares worth 35 francs each, and whose only objective is to stir things up and remind the State that there is a law against revolving doors ... The choice of one solution rather than another, and hence one way of linking the texts of the Penal Code to the case at hand, *depends* on the spirit of the time, on the image we have of the administration, on the shrewdness of lawyers, on the stubbornness of the claimant and on the multi-formed pressure of the press.[35]

The fact that the Council rules *against* the President of the Republic and in favour of the minor stockholder may seem to teach the opposite lesson: that of the immovability of the law in response to circumstantial and political pressures. Nonetheless, the Council's ruling is made entirely under pressure from the 'spirit of the time'. After all:

> The praetorian construction proposed by the Jacobins in the Council ... would have allowed the members of the Council to find an ad hoc way of saving at least this particular appointment in the interests of the State, the bank in question being in a state of collapse and therefore very much in need of an unimpeachable director. A few years ago, perhaps even a few months ago, that is precisely what would have happened.[36]

However, recent public enthusiasm for transparency in government finally shifts the deliberations of the Council against the President. On another occasion, the solemn principle of 'legal stability' really amounts to nothing more than two Council members agreeing colloquially that 'it would be a mess' if they allowed contracts to be disputed indefinitely.[37] On yet another occasion, Bruno Latour himself (observing quietly from the fringes of discussion) is asked only half-jokingly to weigh in on a case:

> *Luchon (turning towards the author)*: What does the philosopher say?
> BL: The philosopher is not sufficiently prepared to opine.[38]

The means of establishing truth in the law are not what we might expect, if we have just arrived in court from the laboratories of natural science. When a Council member says 'this is undisputed', Latour comments as follows: 'This expression [in law] does not mean that it is true [in the scientific sense of the term], but that the opposing party has not disputed it and that therefore the part of the file which, according to the file, has not been contested by the opposing party can be counted as fact.'[39] Another aspect of legal truth is that it must *hesitate* rather than sleekly apply rules to obtain automatic and efficient results:

> It is impossible ... to define the expression 'to say the law' if we eliminate from it the hesitations, the winding path, the meanders of reflexivity: the reason why we represent justice as blind, and holding scales in her hands, is precisely because she hesitates, and proceeds feeling her way forward ... Justice only writes law through winding paths. In other words, if she had refused to make mistakes, if she had

applied a rule, if she had summed pieces of information, we could not identify her as being either just or indeed legal. *For her to speak justly, she must have hesitated.*[40]

In the same passage Latour calls hesitation the *je ne sais quoi* of the law, a 'reserve of degrees of freedom in the definition of our capacity of judgment, an aptitude to *unbind* which permits us only to *bind again* without attaching ourselves in any durable manner either to ... external events ... or to the strict application of rules and texts.'[41] In an especially Latourian passage, we read that 'the power of Law, like that of a chain, is exactly as strong as its weakest link and we can only detect this link by following the chain link after link, without omitting a single one.'[42] Yet we recall that Latour also described *science* as having the structure of a chain. In what respect, then, does law differ from science? This is the subject of the brilliant Chapter 5 of *The Making of Law*, probably the most detailed comparison/contrast that Latour ever draws between two of his modes of existence.

Chapter 5 begins by telling us, among other things, that 'readers [will] learn to their surprise that objectivity and detachment defines law rather than science.'[43] We might normally think of science as if it were a cold, remote, logical enterprise undertaken by the likes of Mr Spock, yet 'however surprising it may seem, scientific articles are much more passionate than administrative law texts. That is because they push a claim as far as possible, by throwing everything into the pot ...'[44] Unlike judges, scientists work 'by means of a chaos of hesitant observations and in a flourishing of partial (in both senses) texts which are published as quickly as possible, to generate claims that are fiercely defended, and which at the same time judge that claims previously published by themselves or by their colleagues are invalid, obscure, false, unfounded or quite simply banal and uninteresting ...'[45] For this reason 'it is impossible ... to base ourselves on the prevailing idea that the sciences are pure, objective, disinterested, distant, cold and self-assured.'[46] For in the laboratory, 'the act of writing [is] always an intensely passionate moment, and the rewriting of articles prior to publication [involves] heated discussion about what [can] or [cannot] be said, about how far one [can] go without going too far, or about what [has] to be concealed for tactical or political reasons.'[47] By contrast, counsellors of the law 'are as a rule indifferent to their file, and this indifference is punctuated by pulled faces, sighs, lapses of memory, a whole *hexis* of disinterest which contrasts very sharply with the obligations that laboratory researchers should be deeply, bodily, and passionately engaged in their observations about a matter of fact.[48] Scientists, in a word, are entirely *sincere* about their subject matter. And while counsellors of the law are not entirely lacking in passionate interests, 'every effort is made to ensure that they are not attached to the file, to the bodies of opinion-givers or to solutions adopted . . . because they are held apart by the matter at hand, the object itself, by a distance that progressively becomes almost infinite.'[49]

More generally, Latour provides a meticulous chart showing no fewer than seventeen ways in which science and the law are *opposites*.[50] Nonetheless, he calls these differences 'superficial' since both are rooted in a deeper distinction between 'chains of reference' and 'chains of obligation'.[51] Whereas science gives us information, Latour tells us that 'wanting to transport knowledge via the routes of law would be like trying to fax a pizza . . . it is simply not the right medium. Law, like religion, like politics, deceives those who want to transport information.'[52] But what is at the heart of the difference between science's chains of reference and law's chains of obligation? Some of the difference can be seen in the different professional dramas involved in the two cases. A scientific claim 'is characterized by uncertainty and risk [as] the authors release [their work] into the mass of existing publications. The truth value of [their] statement will be attributed retroactively, from the treatment that the claim or petition receives at the hands of other authors, supporters as well as detractors.'[53] Admittedly, law also needs to trace references sometimes: as when hunting for an appropriately paid parking slip in a legal file, or when consulting maps or photographs in the course of reaching a decision. Yet for the most part, law links immanent means with other immanent means, not instruments with an outside reality in the manner of science. 'Would a judge agree to entrust his judgment to an electronic microscope which requires 100 or so adjustments, each of which completely transforms the initial sample? A judge would exclaim indignantly that he needed a "more direct" contact with reality.'[54] To give a more concrete example, Latour relates the case of one Mrs Eyraud, 'the illustrator of a gardening magazine, who had been refused a highly coveted press card on the grounds that she did not deal with current affairs . . .'[55] In negating her initial rejection by the journalists' professional syndicate, the Council of State does not proceed as scientists would and try to establish what it 'really' means to be a journalist:

> The question is not whether an illustrator of current affairs is really, truly, fundamentally or referentially a journalist, but whether, as against the professional body of journalists, she is able to establish that quality 'within the meaning of article L 761-2 of the Labour Law Code.' There is simply no relation between this and a definition of essence, nature, truth, or exactitude.[56]

This helps explain Latour's constant sense that the law is a *superficial* mode of existence:

> If [law] holds everything, if it makes it possible to link all people and acts ... it is also because it extracts only a tiny part of their essence from all situations. Its fabric resembles that of a delicately knitted lace ... Unlike science, it never embarks on the impossible trial of constructing, in powerful calculation centres, the scale models that resemble the world and make it visible at a glance.[57]

Latour continues:

> What is a notary's act in relation to the dwelling in which we live? How can this fragile sheet of paper be compared to the thickness of walls and memories? No resemblance, no mimicry, no reference, no plan ... The link is tiny yet total; the grip is infinitely small yet capable of linking up with all the rest.[58]

And finally, 'the ethnographer feels despondent: will he ever be *superficial enough* to grasp the strength of the law?'[59] This harmless failure to plunge into the depths is paralleled by the fact that law, unlike science, aims at something different from referential truth. As Latour puts it, 'when Roman lawyers intoned the celebrated adage *res judicata pro veritate habetur* [the matter which has been adjudicated shall be taken for the truth], they were declaring that what had been decided should be taken *as* the truth, which means, precisely, that it should in no way be confused *with* the truth.'[60] It also helps clarify the difference that 'whereas in science everything is done to ensure that the impact of new information upon a body of established knowledge is as devastating as possible',[61] in law the goal is continuity and minor modification.

The book ends with Latour drawing contrasts between law and still other modes of existence: technology (which becomes increasingly more efficient while law remains as slow as ever), fiction (which does not bind or oblige us in the way that law does), metamorphosis and organisation.[62] The closing words of the final chapter herald an important lesson of *Modes* a decade later – law is the only mode that retains traces of itself. As Latour puts it, giving law a bona fide metaphysical significance: 'Without [law], we wouldn't be human; without it, *we would have lost the trace of what we had said*. Statements would float around without ever being able to find their enunciators. Nothing would bind the space-time entity in a continuum. We would be unable to find the trace of our actions.'[63] Latour even makes a passing critique of Niklas Luhmann, who wants to see law, politics and the like as *systems* rather than modes. Never a great admirer of Luhmann, Latour complains as follows: 'We can see why jurists like to believe themselves safe in a sub-system *à la* Luhmann, just as scientists take great pleasure in fortifying the walls of their scholarly autonomy... They all see themselves as King Midas and believe that everything they touch becomes scientific or legal.'[64] Latour's complaint seems to be that Luhmann allows too easily for homogeneous zones of society where only the dominant regional mode has an impact (law in courts, religion in churches, politics in parliaments...) rather than an interweaving of different modes in different locations. As Latour puts it:

> Law plunges into everything without having its own domain. We have witnessed this amply: the Council of State is not made 'of law' but consists of walls, corridors, frescoes, files, a body of members, texts, careers, publications, controversies. If there is law in it, if it is capable of saying the law, it is surely not because it belongs to a system distinct from the rest of the social world, but because it stirs it in its entirety *in a certain mode*.[65]

If Luhmann tends to locate each of his 'social systems' in a distinct professional place, Latour conceives of his modes as separate radio frequencies all occupying the same air space.

Even more important for our purposes are three passages in the book where Latour confronts law with politics directly, comparing and contrasting them as modes. We have already mentioned the first, which groups them together with religion, in a negative sense: 'Law, like religion, like politics, deceives those who want to transport information.'[66] Yet even if they are all negatively similar in not transporting information, they are nonetheless not alike. The other has to do with law's existence as a creature of the surface, described by Latour with what might sound like a backhanded compliment: 'There is no point studying law in depth! The relationship between appearances and reality, which is so important in science, politics, religion, and even art, is meaningless here: appearances are everything, the content is nothing.'[67] And finally there is the following important passage, directed against those philosophers of law who think that law itself has any force:

> If public life had only law to defend itself from violence, it would have sunk into nothingness long ago. For law to be a force, to have teeth, the entire circle of representation and obedience constantly has to be covered; this is statesmen's job. If there is one thing law does not know how to replace, it is the gradual composition of sovereignty that is achieved by politics ... Confusing the autonomy of politics with the heteronomy necessary to law is more than a crime, it is a major political mistake. Law alone can never create totalities that have not already been spawned and maintained by the never-ending circle of sovereignty. Here again, one chooses the wrong medium if one thinks that the vehicle of law transports authority; on the contrary, authority has to be pre-established for the real work to begin.[68]

To summarise, law and politics belong together in the negative sense that neither transmits information. Yet they differ insofar as: (1) law is entirely a superficial matter of appearances; (2) politics has a circular structure while law is a chain of translated obligations; and (3) law relies on the authority already pre-established by politics. On this note, we can turn to Latour's recent major work *An Inquiry into Modes of Existence*.

Politics [POL] and law [LAW] as modes of existence

As mentioned previously, Latour groups politics [POL] and law [LAW] with religion [REL] as the triad of modes of existence said to pertain to 'quasi-subjects'.[69] Elsewhere in the system of modes, we find technology [TEC], fiction [FIC] and reference [REF] as the triad pertaining to quasi-objects; repetition [REP], metamorphosis [MET] and habit [HAB] are the modes said to ignore altogether the differentiation between quasi-subject and quasi-object; attachment [ATT], organisation [ORG] and morality [MOR] are supposed to link quasi-subject with quasi-object; and finally, network [NET] and preposition [PRE] have an overarching status of governing the other modes, with double click [DC] unconvincingly added to complete this final trio, although Latour generally treats double click more like a lamentable category mistake than a mode of existence in the proper sense.

We leave a full discussion of these modes for another occasion, for now simply recalling that politics and law are relatively close neighbours in the system outlined in *Modes of Existence*. Politics [POL] is highlighted in Chapter 12 of the book, but also discussed in Chapters 5, 13, 14, 15 and 16. Meanwhile, law is the central topic of Chapter 13, and remains confined to that chapter except for a quick opening appearance in Chapter 1. This does not necessarily indicate that politics has a greater importance for Latour than law, but simply means that politics is so easily confused with other modes that those confusions must be disentangled locally as they arise. One of Latour's greatest concerns in *Modes* (as elsewhere) is that 'the Moderns are those who have kidnapped Science to solve a problem of closure in public debates.'[70] Whereas genuine politics involves uncertainty about the elements and issues with which it must deal, there is a style of Truth Politics (on the Left and Right alike) which holds that the political truth is *already known*, and would already be implemented too, if not for certain empirical obstacles (greedy class interests for the Left, the dangerous stupidity of the unphilosophical masses for the Right).[71] In other words, Truth Politics holds that in a perfect world, politics could simply engage in 'straight talk' about the truth, which is precisely the opposite claim of Latour's political Circle.[72] As he asks, rhetorically enough: 'Who speaks better, who is more sensitive to the requirements of [the mode of politics]? The one who learns to speak "crooked" in an angry crowd, looking for what it wants, or the one who claims to speak straight, perhaps, but leaves the crowd to its disorderly agitation?'[73] Or a few pages later: 'The only rigor that matters to us is learning to speak in the right tonality, to speak well – shorthand for "speaking well in the agora to someone about something that concerns him."'[74] In fact, Latour sees most of the history of political philosophy as stuck on the notion of politics as straight talk: '[it] began with Socrates and has never stopped, through Hobbes and Rousseau, Marx and Hayek, to Habermas. "If only we could finally *replace* the crookedness of the political with the path of right reason or science – law, history, economics, psychology, physics, biology, it hardly matters!"[75]

Latour is so worried about the confusion of politics with other modes that he even suspects that politics is being *lost*, perhaps in the same way that religion was almost lost.[76] Under the modern monopoly of truth granted to science (reference [REF]), everyone has come to assume that politics contains no truth at all. 'The case is closed: to go into politics, to take courses in political communication, to participate in an electoral campaign would be to *suspend* all requirements of truth.'[77] But politics does have its own form of truth, as we have seen: the truth of successfully creating or mobilising a public, a *phantom public* (in Walter Lippmann's phrase) that does not pre-exist its political mobilisation in the name of this or that issue.[78] In fact, 'political beings are always accused of lying, whereas they begin *truly* to lie, to lie *politically*, only if they "go off on a tangent' . . . by beginning to proffer straight talk, that is, wanting [to] be "faithfully" represented or "faithfully" obeyed.'[79]

Yet politics must also remain in contact with the surprises or resistance of an outside reality that it has not yet mastered: 'How could [someone] claim to be speaking well about something to someone if her speech were not also engaging the reality of what is said?'[80] When we begin to see politics as nothing but a self-contained power struggle with no ulterior reality principle, we begin 'to overestimate unreason, and to brandish lies, skills, power struggles, violence, no longer as defects but as qualities . . . Such is the temptation of Machiavellianism . . .'[81] Here Latour is asking us to think two things at once. Much of modern political theory polarises between the Truth Politics that aims to ground politics on some sort of *knowledge* of human beings (from Marx on the Left to Strauss on the Right), and the Power Politics that abandons all hope of a trans-political knowledge and views politics in terms of struggle rather than truth (from Foucault on the Left to Hobbes and Schmitt on the Right). Latour is consciously trying to steer us between both extremes. For if (like Hobbes) Latour is allergic to any appeal to transcendent standards beyond the political sphere, he is equally suspicious of a self-contained circle that cannot be moved by the appeal of the newly discovered entities and ethical scruples to which the scientists and moralists of the world draw our attention.[82] It is true that Latour's natural sympathies (as all of his early work attests) lie more on the side of power politics. In one passage he even scolds the ominous Carl Schmitt for *limiting* the state of exception (in which grim existential struggle with the enemy replaces reasoned political discussion) to specific moments of political emergency. For Latour, the state of exception is *always* underway and is found in all places. However, the point of this claim is not to argue for omnipresent ontological dictatorship, but to *eliminate* the exceptional character of those situations that seem to entail the need for Schmitt's dictator or 'exceptional man', the one who comes to save us from real or imagined national peril. For Latour, the state of exception is no longer an 'event' but a constant feature of the political, even at the micro-scale of family dinners and clubhouse electoral politics.

> Schmitt's error lay in his belief that it is only on high, among the powerful and on rare occasions, that the political mode has to look for exceptions. Look at the [political] Circle: it is *exceptional at all points*, above and below, on the right on the left, since it *never goes straight* and, in addition, it must always *start over*, especially if it is to spread.[83]

At the same time, this proposed global Schmittian immanence is countered by Latour's words on behalf of a reality principle, against the Machiavellian temptation. There is also the surprising conclusion of *Modes*, where it is said that morality [MOR] is a mode governing all the others. As he puts it there: 'Everything in the world *evaluates,* from von Uexküll's tick to Pope Benedict XVI – and even Magritte's pipe ... On this point Nietzsche is right, the word "value" has no antonym – and especially not the word "fact."'[84]

We now turn to the discussion of law in Chapter 13 of *Modes*. Latour tells us at the outset that law 'offers special difficulties ... owing to its strange mix of strength and weakness, its scarcely autonomous autonomy, and the fact that it has been charged with too many values.'[85] But in another sense, there are fewer difficulties with law than with any of the other modes: 'Unlike the other modes, law does not strike the ethnologist as an insoluble brainteaser, for it promises a fairly satisfying correspondence between a domain, an institution, and a contrast whose specificity, technicity, and centrality seem to have been recognized by everyone.'[86] And furthermore, 'it has its own mode of veridiction, certainly different from that of Science, but universally acknowledged as capable of distinguishing truth from falsity *in its own way.*'[87]

Politics and Law as Modes of Existence 55

Whereas the other modes have suffered greatly from the modernism of double click, with its demand for unmediated access and explicit statements, law has somehow resisted double click and retained its ancient prestige:

> Whether we are running into a legal problem, spotting a justice's black robe, reading the fine print of a contract, signing a document before a notary... each of us is well aware that there is something quite particular going on, something frightfully technical, which will establish the difference between truth and falsity in a way that is at once obscure and respectable. Without even being surprised at this, we may say that a statement is true or false 'in the legal sense,' which means both 'in a narrow and restricted sense' and 'with a completely original interpretive key that one has to learn to recognize.'[88]

Yet our accustomed distance from law gives rise to disadvantage as well: 'Whereas technology, fiction, reference, religion, and politics have penetrated everywhere (thereby multiplying the risks of cascading category mistakes), law suffers from the advantage of having been kept too respectfully at a distance.'[89] And finally, the law remains filled with disappointments:

> We feel the weakness [of law] every time we despair at seeing that the 'legally justified' decision is not necessarily just, opportune, true, useful, effective; every time the court condemns an accused party but the aggrieved party has still not been able to achieve 'closure'; every time indemnities have been awarded but doubts still remain about the exact responsibilities of the respective parties. With the law, we always go from surprise to surprise: we are surprised by its power, surprised by its impotence.[90]

Law does share with politics the characteristic of often being viewed cynically by the public. The fact that the law is flexible leads to 'the symmetrical temptation to take [law] not just as superficial and formal but as a mere cover, as a rather clumsy disguise for inequalities.'[91] Latour also sees in law the interesting peculiarity of not existing only in the present tense:

> All the other modes identified up to now [before law] have this distinctive feature: they pass, they move forward, they launch into the search for their means of subsistence. Each one does it differently, to be sure,

but they have in common the fact that they never *go back* to the conditions under which they started. Even the political Circle [POL], while it always has to start over, disappears . . . as soon as it is interrupted, without leaving any traces behind but the slight crease of habit . . . [The other modes] leave wakes behind, of course . . . but they do not *go back to preserve* the traces of their movements . . . If law [LAW] is so original . . . it is because law alone ensures this *reattachment* of frames of reference.[92]

Amid Latour's metaphysical preference for instability in the world, law provides the semblance of a stable anchor: 'While in fact there is neither real continuity of courses of action nor stability of subjects, law brings off the miracle of proceeding as though, by particular linkages, *we were held to what we say and what we do*. What you have done, signed, said, promised, given, *engages* you.'[93] Or more beautifully, '[Law] paves with continuities a world of which it has become the author despite a cascade of shiftings.'[94]

Conclusion

We have seen that politics and law are placed side by side with religion as three modes of existence that obviously cannot function according to scientific canons of truth-seeking. Politics must avoid self-righteous Truth Politics just as it must avoid cynical Power Politics, since the political sphere can detect truths currently lying outside it while never being able to claim direct access to those truths. Politics is at best a *lover* of truth, just as the philosopher is a *lover* of wisdom, not an incarnate sage. Latour recommends the same double avoidance for law, which must steer between

> the two main schools of thought, jusnaturalism and positivism which, as we know, provide polar-opposite definitions of the foundations of Law. Each in its own way – despite the great divides that seem to oppose them – simply repeats firmly that Law is 'always already present.' Either, like the jusnaturalists, we take as a base the existence of a law that *precedes* all positive law or, on the contrary, we decide, like the positivists, to recognize as law only that which has *already* been defined by a legally constituted authority. In neither case can one go beyond law and establish it on some heterogeneous foundation.[95]

The same holds for religion, where Latour accepts neither a foolproof reference to an objective God existing outside the mind, nor a purely ceremonial sense of religion that merely serves as a golden casing for secular social purposes.

That said, politics and law quickly diverge despite their presence in the same trio of modes of existence. Politics has a circular structure of representation and obedience, which lasts for only as long as a given political culture is maintained, and which is completely autonomous in the way it is grounded on no prior state of nature or anything else. But law has the structure of a chain of obligations, one that preserves the traces of our commitments even as we ceaselessly shift across the years through a range of new passions, interests and moods. It is heteronomous, despite the views of the jusnaturalists and the positivists, since it considers consequences and complications in a way that does not leave it the prisoner of formalistic principle but that may earn the accusation of inconsistency. Finally, Latour is clear in his view that law is grounded in politics rather than the reverse. Authority does not emanate from the law; law presupposes the authority that is established by politics. At least one interesting question arises from this ordering: is Latour committed to a Schmittian view of international relations? That is to say, if law emerges only on the interior of some political authority on which it depends, then there seems to be no way to harness state actors in any sort of legal arrangement. But if this were the case, Latour would be forced to adopt a classical realist position on international relations, which views the Hobbesian state of nature as preserved on the international level even as it is tamed in the heart of each individual nation by the police. The danger of such a commitment is that Latour would lose his otherwise careful sense for the middle ground between Truth and Power. Would the international scene become a theatre of untrammelled Power Politics if law is subordinated to politics? Or is it the role of some other mode (perhaps morality [MOR]?) to tame the *bellum omnium contra omnes* between states?

Notes

1. Bruno Latour (2013) *An Inquiry into Modes of Existence: An Anthropology of the Moderns*, trans. C. Porter. Cambridge, MA: Harvard University Press.

2. Latour, *An Inquiry into Modes of Existence*, pp. 488–9.
3. Graham Harman (forthcoming 2015) *Prince of Modes: Bruno Latour's Later Philosophy*. Melbourne: re.press. For a systematic treatment of Latour's politics, see Graham Harman (2014) *Bruno Latour: Reassembling the Political*. London: Pluto.
4. Bruno Latour (2010) 'Coming out as a philosopher', *Social Studies of Science*, 40 (4): 599–608. The passage cited is from p. 603.
5. Bruno Latour (2003) 'What if we *talked* politics a little?', *Contemporary Political Theory*, 2: 143–64.
6. Latour, 'What if we *talked* politics a little?', p. 143.
7. Latour, 'What if we *talked* politics a little?', p. 145.
8. Latour, 'What if we *talked* politics a little?', pp. 145–6.
9. Latour, 'What if we *talked* politics a little?', p. 146.
10. Bruno Latour (1987) *Science in Action: How to Follow Scientists and Engineers Through Society*. Cambridge, MA: Harvard University Press.
11. Latour, 'What if we *talked* politics a little?', p. 147.
12. Latour, 'What if we *talked* politics a little?', p. 147.
13. Latour, 'What if we *talked* politics a little?', p. 147.
14. Latour, 'What if we *talked* politics a little?', p. 148.
15. Latour, 'What if we *talked* politics a little?', p. 149.
16. Latour, 'What if we *talked* politics a little?', p. 149.
17. Latour, 'What if we *talked* politics a little?', p. 149.
18. Latour, 'What if we *talked* politics a little?', p. 150.
19. Latour, 'What if we *talked* politics a little?', p. 151.
20. Bruno Latour (2007) 'Turning around politics. A note on Gerard de Vries' paper', *Social Studies of Science*, 37 (5): 811–20.
21. Latour, 'Turning around politics', p. 815.
22. Latour, 'Turning around politics', p. 816.
23. Latour, 'Turning around politics', p. 816.
24. Latour, 'Turning around politics', p. 816.
25. Latour, 'Turning around politics', p. 817.
26. Latour, 'Turning around politics', p. 817.
27. Latour, 'Turning around politics', p. 817.
28. Bruno Latour (2010) *The Making of Law: An Ethnography of the Conseil d'État*, trans. M. Brilman and A. Pottage. Cambridge: Polity Press. In what follows, all page references to this book are to the Wiley e-book edition.
29. Latour, *The Making of Law*, p. 10 (e-book).
30. Latour, *The Making of Law*, p. 10 (e-book).
31. Latour, *The Making of Law*, p. 10 (e-book).

32. Latour, *The Making of Law*, p. 19 (e-book).
33. Latour, *The Making of Law*, pp. 86–7 (e-book).
34. Latour, *The Making of Law*, p. 86 (e-book).
35. Latour, *The Making of Law*, pp. 168, 170 (e-book).
36. Latour, *The Making of Law*, p. 170 (e-book).
37. Latour, *The Making of Law*, p. 183 (e-book).
38. Latour, *The Making of Law*, p. 185 (e-book).
39. Latour, *The Making of Law*, p. 140 (e-book).
40. Latour, *The Making of Law*, p. 157 (e-book).
41. Latour, *The Making of Law*, p. 157 (e-book).
42. Latour, *The Making of Law*, p. 101 (e-book).
43. Latour, *The Making of Law*, p. 211 (e-book).
44. Latour, *The Making of Law*, p. 216 (e-book).
45. Latour, *The Making of Law*, p. 216 (e-book).
46. Latour, *The Making of Law*, p. 218 (e-book).
47. Latour, *The Making of Law*, pp. 222–3 (e-book).
48. Latour, *The Making of Law*, p. 223 (e-book).
49. Latour, *The Making of Law*, p. 223 (e-book).
50. Latour, *The Making of Law*, p. 243 (e-book).
51. Latour, *The Making of Law*, p. 232 (e-book).
52. Latour, *The Making of Law*, p. 277 (e-book).
53. Latour, *The Making of Law*, p. 236 (e-book).
54. Latour, *The Making of Law*, p. 236 (e-book).
55. Latour, *The Making of Law*, p. 239 (e-book).
56. Latour, *The Making of Law*, p. 239 (e-book).
57. Latour, *The Making of Law*, p. 274 (e-book).
58. Latour, *The Making of Law*, p. 274 (e-book).
59. Latour, *The Making of Law*, p. 274 (e-book).
60. Latour, *The Making of Law*, p. 247 (e-book).
61. Latour, *The Making of Law*, p. 241 (e-book).
62. Latour, *The Making of Law*, pp. 282–4 (e-book).
63. Latour, *The Making of Law*, p. 287 (e-book).
64. Latour, *The Making of Law*, p. 272 (e-book).
65. Latour, *The Making of Law*, pp. 272–4 (e-book).
66. Latour, *The Making of Law*, p. 277 (e-book).
67. Latour, *The Making of Law*, p. 274 (e-book).
68. Latour, *The Making of Law*, p. 279 (e-book).
69. Latour, *An Inquiry into Modes of Existence*, pp. 488–9.
70. Latour, *An Inquiry into Modes of Existence*, p. 129. Latour ascribes these words to the fictional hero of his book, a female ethnographer who starts off as an actor-network theorist before tiring of the

monotony of Latour's former theory and heading off in search of the modes of existence.
71. See Graham Harman (2014) *Bruno Latour: Reassembling the Political* (London: Pluto Press.
72. Latour, *An Inquiry into Modes of Existence*, p. 123.
73. Latour, *An Inquiry into Modes of Existence*, p. 135.
74. Latour, *An Inquiry into Modes of Existence*, p. 139.
75. Latour, *An Inquiry into Modes of Existence*, p. 333.
76. Latour, *An Inquiry into Modes of Existence*, p. 327.
77. Latour, *An Inquiry into Modes of Existence*, p. 331.
78. Latour, *An Inquiry into Modes of Existence*, p. 355.
79. Latour, *An Inquiry into Modes of Existence*, p. 344.
80. Latour, *An Inquiry into Modes of Existence*, p. 140.
81. Latour, *An Inquiry into Modes of Existence*, p. 336.
82. See Bruno Latour, *Politics of Nature: How to Bring the Sciences into Democracy*, trans. C. Porter. Cambridge, MA: Harvard University Press.
83. Latour, *An Inquiry into Modes of Existence*, pp. 347–8.
84. Latour, *An Inquiry into Modes of Existence*, p. 453.
85. Latour, *An Inquiry into Modes of Existence*, p. 357.
86. Latour, *An Inquiry into Modes of Existence*, p. 358.
87. Latour, *An Inquiry into Modes of Existence*, pp. 358–9.
88. Latour, *An Inquiry into Modes of Existence*, p. 360.
89. Latour, *An Inquiry into Modes of Existence*, p. 360.
90. Latour, *An Inquiry into Modes of Existence*, p. 361.
91. Latour, *An Inquiry into Modes of Existence*, p. 362.
92. Latour, *An Inquiry into Modes of Existence*, pp. 368–9.
93. Latour, *An Inquiry into Modes of Existence*, p. 370.
94. Latour, *An Inquiry into Modes of Existence*, p. 371.
95. Latour, *The Making of Law*, p. 268 (e-book).

3

On Devices and Logics of Legal Sense: Toward Socio-technical Legal Analysis
Kyle McGee

The problem with black-boxing rules

The production of legal statements is a peripheral concern among socio-legal scholars, philosophers, anthropologists, critical theorists and others engaging law from what, according to a conventional doctrinal perspective organised around the artifact of the legal rule, is itself a peripheral vantage point. Perhaps this is as it should be. This chapter suggests otherwise.

Perhaps, by moving beyond the matrix in which legal statements are assembled in order to access such complex but relatively common phenomena as variances in legal effect and enforcement, or the work of legal rules and modes of reasoning in the construction of social attributes (such as class, race, gender) or other broad *topoi* of the socio-legal, scholarship disserves its very object of study. Perhaps it even neutralises the force of its own argumentation: having eclipsed the entire scenography in which the legal artifact under scrutiny came to be, is it not plausible that diagnoses, recommendations and critiques will serve in the last analysis only to entrench a problematic mode of legal production? By starting from (what is understood as) a refined, stable legal rule or set of rules and proceeding to an examination of its empirical interpretation or its appearance in patterns of legal activity, by making it pass, unaltered, through diverse social channels, does the analyst not render the rule more opaque, even as she sheds light on its failures and achievements? In doing so, socio-legal studies makes itself parasitic on doctrinal analysis: quite different, to be sure, but committed all the same to the integrity of the law's black boxes and performatively complicit in the macro-structuring of a particular normative world – often strikingly similar to the one purportedly critiqued.[1]

This failure of legal studies is basic and spread widely beyond the field, in virtually every domain for which rules, standards, principles and other normative artifacts are endowed with quasi-spiritual powers to regulate, restrict, govern, dominate or rule quite effortlessly. It is a metaphysical failure. Thought and speech, things and practices alike are delocalised so that their normative effects become untraceable and emanate, somewhat mysteriously, from no particular site or act of enunciation. Unbound from such terrestrial constraints, disembedded legal particles move swiftly through the normative void. There is, therefore, tremendous value in modes of thought that slow down to peer into these sorts of artifacts and the material, conceptual and semantic constructs that enable law. The laboratory construction of administrative legal references[2] and the transactions and procedures through which competing techno-politico-economic visions come to populate regulatory frameworks,[3] for example, are analytically invisible events if deceleration is not made into a virtue. Those turning to analytical tools, like actor-network theory, that are capable of decelerating, of re-encumbering the legal, disclose the field's rather desperate need for new sensors capable of registering the ordinary in all its unremarked complication.

In this chapter, I want to step on the brakes even more firmly than have those that have so admirably begun the socio-technical legal revolution.[4] I want to narrow the scope of inquiry to an almost unbearable degree and ask the reader to examine a single, most ordinary American legal case in a most ordinary procedural posture at the trial court level. Yes, one decision on one motion. The near-universal practice in legal scholarship is, of course, to ignore or, where this is not possible, to pass over lower court decisions as quickly as possible, in order to reach the more rarefied articulations of the appellate court. There are distinct advantages to refusing this particular temptation, however. To track the slow composition of a unique trajectory of legal truth; to register the specific processes and techniques deployed to fuse a continuous pathway out of scattered elements of uncertain relevance and to thus achieve an order that is witnessably legal; to map the decisive yet easily overlooked transformations of volatile value-objects into disciplined obligations or the multiple transfers of agency implicated in the fabrication of a legal statement: none of these 'earthbound' jurisprudential phenomena are accessible without a dogged insistence on a kind of casuistry that places a premium on the actions occurring in courts of first instance. The conceptual point of this casuistic method is that, when we bypass the radically uncertain, tenuous, hesitant production of judgments, we carelessly afford a set of pricey values – neutrality, objectivity, certainty, integrity, *sécurité juridique*, even the rule of law – to wonky artifacts that perhaps do not deserve them or, more interestingly, that have in fact acquired alternative versions of some of these values in ways quite different than we had imagined.

Content and its discontents

The discussion that follows, then, is about the *content* of law. This content is peculiar. When philosophers or sociologists of science speak of the content of a science, they often mean the theorems and axioms that are said to underlie the particular physical observations recorded in laboratories, among other sites: the 'internal' or the 'endogenous' or the 'immanent' stuff of scientific knowledge and practice, as distinguished from its external, exogenous, transcendent, contextual conditions. The nature of that boundary was the subject of much dispute among science warriors, as is well known. In law, the same quandaries cannot resurface, at least not in the same ways: no one, not even Niklas Luhmann, thinks that legal utterances bear no relationship to the problems that prompted their utterance. While philosophers of science fiercely rejected what they saw as the relativism and nihilism implicit in the claim that scientific knowledge is inexorably and, according to some, causally tethered to the institutional and general social conditions that prompted its formulation, I doubt very much whether any academic lawyer would react similarly to the claim that legal statements bear birthmarks binding them to their own social conditions. Indeed, such traces would seem to be distinguishing marks of good legal speech.

So what is legal content? We know that it is not something distinct from 'context', an arcane 'thought process' or the inaccessible mental undulations of professional legal reasoners, but neither is it the objective semantic value of a legal proposition. This would reduce the content of law to mere information [LAW-DC]. We want not to eliminate or obfuscate the actions and actors to which such a semantic value is necessarily attached, as this reduction requires, but instead to give them their full due.

Risking a degree of obscurity, we can say that the content of law is not only irremediably bound up with its conditions of enunciation, but is fully identical with those conditions. And some of those conditions are packaged in *legal devices* that we can unwrap and explore. Provisionally, we can define legal devices as assemblages of mostly non-legal beings deployed for a legal purpose, namely to give consistency and objectivity, as well as direction, to a specific legal trajectory. The device *formats*, translates the diverse strata bound up in a disputed matter into legal discourse, but while this entails certain technical reductions, it entails no ontological reduction of agency. Technically, the various entities and agents at stake are semiotically re-figured – jurimorphised. This, we will see, amplifies their agency rather than (or in addition to) diminishing it.

Legal content – or what I will also call *sense* – thus exists only by way of the mediation of jurimorphs (i.e. value-objects and devices). A value-object materialises when it impacts the course of enunciation. If it does, it shifts semiotic registers to become an *obligation*. This transition from value-object to obligation is what would be described semiotically as a modal transformation from *wanting-to-do* to *not-being-able-to-not-do*.[5] The difference is that the demands of value-objects can sometimes be quieted without impacting the pathway of means: a wanting-to-do (value-object) can fail to attain the modality of not-being-able-to-not-do (obligation), thus found to be without any justificatory relevance, failing to signify within the judicial *Umwelt* and safely discounted from the legal trajectory.

In the formal legal discourse of the judiciary, value-objects are the principal media of legal expression. (There are others too – gestures and bodily *hexis*, for instance.) Thus they enact and construct what I have elsewhere called the law's *administrative force*, that is its reflexive, self-policing articulation within the institution of official organs such as courts.[6] The composition of this force depends upon the mediative activity of the 'constraints' of legal practice so valorised by Serge Gutwirth (indeed, to the exclusion of all other media and thus all other forces of law).[7] But Gutwirth fails to register the normativity of these very constraints. Value-objects, understood as constraining, interlocutory, administrative legal actors, serve then as invisible barriers that at once guide the legal trajectory as it unfolds and actively define its contours, as we will see in detail below. Although the problematic of expression is not pre-eminent in this chapter, it is important for an understanding of my argument as a whole to appreciate that media ecologies other than those of discursive value-objects and the interlocutory practices of counsellors and judges can and do generate other kinds of jurimorphs, and thus produce other logics of legal force than the administrative – for example, the 'delegated' or technologically 'ballasted' force of law or the imagistic/cinematic 'affect checkpoint'. For those other forces of law, the semiotics of value-objects no longer suffices to trace the enunciation of law within the particular institutional arrangements sustained by those other media. Instead, new analytical tools must be developed with respect to each mode of expression. Even the lowly speed-bump or the film image are legal actors if they are caught in trajectories that produce legal effects, which constitute a particular subspecies of normative effects in general.

Transitioning back from expression to content, it is clear that the content of law retains a number of important connections to the contentious matters of concern that have been translated, jurimorphised and packed into discursive legal devices. Just like the expressive media of legal force, the devices of legal content are profoundly, constitutively entangled in material-semiotic networks of controversy and dispute – i.e. matters of concern. Matters of concern are things, issues or problems that simultaneously gather and divide populations of actors – their local, differentiated and involuntarily convoked 'publics'.[8] Of particular importance is the multiplicity of enunciative strata organising any matter of concern, shaping and populating what Latour calls a public space. This space is, of course, an agonistic, political space in which contradictory voices merge or fail to merge, but it is much more. First, there are not only two positions bound up in a disagreement (for/against), but *at least* four.[9] And this minimal fourfold presumes that the disagreement implicates only two enclaves, when typically many more are interested – exponentially increasing the quantity of accounts. Second, all manner of technical knowledge (scientific, technological, economic, etc.) may be in play, meaning that competing and mutually supportive 'expert' enunciative positions must be considered. These will fold the agencies of certain non-humans, for which they claim to speak, into themselves, but always imperfectly, so even more complication may develop when 'things strike back'. Third, relatedly, no matter concerns *only* expert knowledges; lay positions cannot be ignored. Everyone affected in their daily lives by the issue – residents, farmers, schoolchildren impacted by the oil refinery management's decision to dispose of waste in the local river – will have a distinctive position in the mesh of concerns, defined by their *attachment* [ATT] to, for example, a lifestyle, a legal right, a tract of land, a well, an income stream, a building, an object, a planet.[10]

The space of the issue simultaneously gathering and dividing these diverse actors is thus complex and multidimensional: it is stratified. In other words, every implicated actor is busy (mis)representing other actors – shifting-out from its deictic *ego-hic-nunc* to encompass and speak for, characterise, modify other actors and strategically shifting-in again to its own register[11] – resulting in a panoply of scattered and asymmetric enunciative planes. Each strives to define the totality of the situation, as 'Irreductions' so powerfully demonstrated. But the hierarchy or scale of these layers or planes or strata (I will use the terms interchangeably) is not pre-given; it is to be determined by those involved.[12] If that is so, then everything turns on how the issue is articulated, and we cannot presume uniformity across planes – indeed, the issue is defined by the variability of its articulation.

The transformation of a contentious issue into a *legal case* is monumental, in terms of the arrangement of these many layers. In a sense that merits serious reflection but which lies beyond this chapter's compass, the crossing of that invisible boundary is an entry into a room the disputants are already inside. This signals the paradoxical tautology of law's totality, according to which, when one utters a promise, for instance, or declares 'this is mine, that is yours', the whole of the law passes through her mouth. That is to say, legal statements appeal implicitly (or otherwise) to the archive of legal statements – from the lowliest petty appropriation to the loftiest provision of the constitution, charter or international treaty – with which they claim solidarity and kinship. And not only this, for the appeal is simultaneously to the archive as totality, rendering the latter a proper condition of legal enunciation, which, of course, can only be recognised as such retrospectively and never *in the act*, as it were. But let us suspend this line of inquiry before going further astray, however gripping the enigma of the totality may be: back to the matter of concern and the legal case.

The issue enters a professionalised, ritualised representational space, providing conditions in which entirely new actors come into play, and in which existing actors can be figured as jurimorphs

– that is value-objects and, potentially, obligations. While it is true that '[t]he public focus on litigation obscures the sources of power and hegemony of law',[13] which materialises instead in diverse expressive substances like technological artifacts, from speed-bumps to drones, or in films and other images regulating affect,[14] litigation remains a key site for the production of the sense or truths of law among those claiming to be modern. Where matters of concern *do* wind up in litigation, the interesting thing is not merely the 'institutional displacement' or diversionary effect of removing the locus of dispute from the ordinary run of things, avoiding self-help or physical violence on the spot in favour of formalised proceedings in distant hallowed halls,[15] or the related effect of de-politicisation and expropriation of conflicts;[16] instead, it is that within this formalised space, the issue will be subjected to a fascinating technique designed 'to ensure the continuous passage' from one enunciative plane to another, generating 'continuity through astounding discontinuities'.[17] The threads knotted together in the stratified issue will be untangled and reassembled in a distinctive way to arrive at the unmistakably legal truth of the matter. The complex issue will be contorted, simplified and brought into alignment with rules. This transformation of the issue allows the rules to 'apply' – but as we will see, such application also entails a transformation of the rules themselves.

Rules and devices: *Gates* v. *Rohm & Haas Co.*

The issue does not automatically 'speak legally', but must be made to do so through certain techniques of representation. A new mediator is required to bridge the hiatus separating what, in legal discourse, would be called 'fact' and 'law'. This goes unacknowledged in legal practice: the facts are 'just there' and 'must be dealt with'. Academic commentators reproduce this same blindness by uncritically dividing fact and law in order to focus only on the 'properly legal' aspects of judicial speech. However, anthropologically, we can see that this divide arises only through the traumatic re-articulation of the matter of concern. The congeries of attachments, as well as scientific, technological, economic, governmental and other knowledges, and alternative cosmologies defining the issue are first flattened and forced into a 'fact' box, to be kept separate from the 'law' box. Certain enunciative positions are emphasised and elaborated or exaggerated, others ignored, played down or silenced altogether. What seemed inconsequential or peripheral to the engaged publics now seems central, *material* to the dispute: in changing the means, the ends also change. Moreover, adversarial procedures reduce the multiplicity of perspectives from four, or 16, or 256, to merely two opposed sides. But new strata quickly accrete within and between the fact/law division, as we will see, and neither box is able to contain them. The complexion or general balance of the inconsistent, knotty threads composing the issue is radically changed by the time a court or other adjudicator receives it.

This re-articulation or juridical translation of the issue conditions what counts as a legal argument or what may have justificatory relevance[18] in the case. In adversarial litigation, that translation is the work not of judges but of advocates. As spokespersons for divided publics, advocates select only certain elements of the issue (e.g. the plaintiff's injury or the defendant's bad acts; for the defence, the plaintiff's carelessness or the defendant's good faith) to thread into narratives that, in their estimation, queue up a set of favourable rules. The other elements of the issue may be forgotten or later thrown back at an advocate by her opponent. As for rules, the narrative seems more or less squarely to fit their shape, and it is up to the opponent to push them out of alignment. The two sides quickly blossom into four as there is no agreement between the advocates regarding what each is arguing, in terms of either 'fact' or 'law'. If the *moyen* or means nominated by Latour as the vehicle for the transmission and passage of law in its interlocutory dimension can be understood as the *basis of the claim* (including both elements that will have been factual and elements that will have been doctrinal), then the fractured, inconsistent assemblage made up of the advocates' competing translations of the matter of concern and competing accounts of what the rules mean is, in my view, the aperture or window through which such means must *of necessity* be apprehended – certainly by the court (no grounds ever appear in abstraction from a concrete dispute) but also by scholars. It is a mistake to see the *moyen* as an abstract legal rule. It is a hybrid actor (fact/law, or better, transformed issue/transformed rule) that may be encountered only through what I call a legal device.[19] Legal devices are just those assemblages that materialise legal materiality, whose particular mediation of the issues that they translate allows a trail of legal means enjoying justificatory relevance to appear through a particular

– hesitant – sort of evaluation. The device constitutes a specifically legal internal referent. Practitioners have no analogous concept; there are facts and there are rules, there is a plaintiff's side and a defendant's side, and all these things are different. The legal device allows us to register their pragmatic entanglement, which practitioners of course appreciate, but without conceptualising.[20]

It is a truism that doctrinal constructs are not self-executing, self-applying creatures, but must be manipulated, balanced, coordinated not unlike a piece of laboratory equipment. Their contours, sometimes appearing very rigid, nevertheless undergo transformation in every case. This is ultimately a lesson imparted by pragmatic semiotics: the doctrinal category, figure or rule does not exist except as a function of its application which varies every time. Performance precedes (and conditions) competence. Certain legal analyses demonstrate this more clearly than others: a conventional negligence analysis, for example, makes no secret of the doctrine's dependence on 'social context' or of the contingency of when a duty of care exists and what constitutes a breach; similarly, any test involving a standard of 'objective reasonableness' clearly turns on the court's perception of what is customary or generally expected by participants, or of what 'everyone knows' or 'should know',[21] as the lawyers present it and as the court imagines it. These are what some would call 'standards' – doctrinal tests or rubrics claiming flexibility, inclusiveness and similar qualities as opposed to 'rules', which claim to exhibit certainty, rigidity, etc. But the conventional rule/standard dichotomy is a poor description of how legal veridiction works. It forgets that there is only performance (and in forgetting, generates dead-end analyses of an arrested dialectic), even though that is the sole positive point made in the deconstruction of the dichotomy. (It's true that legal arguments repeat stereotyped forms advocating 'rule-like' and 'standard-like' performances – in the same sense that scientists use the same instruments to do many things or that novelists use the same narrative structures to tell different stories – but that is a sign only of the importance of different kinds of standardisation to different practices, not of the meaninglessness or vacuity of legal reasoning.) Once we appreciate that, there is no compelling reason to think of rules and standards as separate or opposed forms: every doctrinal directive or test brings along its 'context of application'. If you think rules oppose standards, you are thinking about purified competences determined *ex post applicatio*.

I will discuss a recent class certification analysis in an American federal court because it is a multi-part inquiry bearing some of those points out, and because the kind of public issue I initially thought of – toxic spillage – often leads to group litigation and must pass through this formidable doctrinal obstacle to proceed to trial, and because I wanted to know what exactly happened in that transition from *res publica* to legally certified (or uncertified) class.[22]

Although the modern American class action dates to 1938 when the Federal Rules introduced it, and the phenomenon of aggregate litigation more generally appears at least as early as the thirteenth century, the contours of the litigation class are unsettled, indeed constantly changing and subject to vigorous contention. The modern class action responds to the imbalance of power created by the coexistence of unaffiliated consumers and well-capitalised industrial outfits carrying on mass production of goods, as the more ancient form responded to asymmetries favouring wealthy elites and manorial proprietors against peasants, villeins and other poor and middling groups.[23] The very notion of a unified 'class' of unaffiliated persons similarly injured by a single entity's conduct is highly suggestive of John Dewey's notion of a 'public' of unaffiliated persons drawn together solely by virtue of the indirect consequences of unrelated transactions.[24] It is the way in which modern law has resolved one of the eponymous 'problems' of the Deweyan public. The financial stakes riding on class action technicalities are extremely high; each year, settlements and verdicts in class cases amount to tens of billions of dollars in losses for corporations.

The Federal Rules state that a class must satisfy four initial criteria – numerosity (making joinder of all members impracticable), commonality (questions of fact or law are common to the class), typicality (the class representative's claims or defences are typical of those of other members) and adequacy (the class representative will fairly and adequately protect other members' interests) – and at least one of a second set of criteria. The two most frequently invoked parts of the second set are the 'cohesiveness' of the class unit[25] and the 'predominance' of common questions of law or fact over any questions affecting only individual members.[26] These analyses are similar.

Rule 23 is a script directed to the federal judiciary, a creature of organisation [ORG], but requires the intervention of other actors to become a legal rule. Through attorneys, the script is transformed into a bundle of value-objects that demand to be taken into account. And as the script unfolds, it mixes with the other value-objects.[27] Each attorney explains what the script requires in the case at hand and how she has met its requirements or how her opponent has failed to – in other words, each becomes a channel through which value-objects may protest, asserting their modal qualification we described as *wanting-to-do*. Rule 23 guides their arguments and focuses their disagreements, itself – in their hands – translating the dispute into its own narrow semantic universe. But what constitutes numerosity, commonality, typicality, adequacy, cohesiveness or predominance is thrown into question; no general principle can supply an answer in the particular case. The class device fuses these inconsistent accounts, resulting in a motley disorder that the court must rearrange, charting a trajectory that must create continuity out of discontinuity, flatness out of rugged terrain. In federal class cases, the class device is created in the certification papers and is subjected to ordeals, is 'tried', in the court's written opinion granting or denying certification.

In the 1990s and 2000s, several residents of a small community in McCullom Lake, Illinois developed brain cancers. Chemical companies with facilities about a mile from the community had, since the 1960s, disposed of wastewater in unlined waste pits and on-site lagoons. These series of events are distinct; no conclusive environmental studies or epidemiological research had linked them, no economic frame could enable a transaction capable of making the series converge. One unique quality of law is that it is well-suited to forging connections between actions and harms despite insurmountable disagreement between those summoned by a common divisive issue. The residents, through self-appointed spokespersons including individuals living in McCullom Lake and the *Northwest Herald*, the local newspaper, centred the issue squarely on the existence of a cancer cluster, which would imply a singular cause for all tumours; the companies and other individuals living in McCullom Lake disputed the existence of a cluster.

Gates v. *Rohm & Haas Co.* concerned whether the companies could be held liable not for actually causing any cancers but for medical monitoring costs for the cancer-free residents and the diminution in value of the allegedly affected real estate. The case was not about the existence of cancer clusters but a seemingly more limited version of that issue: the tumour-producing agency of vinyl chloride found in McCullom Lake and its traceability to the chemical facilities. Donna and Glenn Gates, two residents, through their attorney, Aaron Freiwald, sought to speak legally on behalf of their entire community. Before the liability problem could be raised, the Gateses had to show that they could represent the community as a single unified group.

The class device in *Gates* was, like virtually any other, loaded with incompatible things drawn from the complex matter of concern it translated: more than 1,000 people with different physiological traits and water and air consumption habits, different loyalties (e.g. employees/retirees of the defendant companies versus non-employees), different understandings of their risks and different levels of concern about potential exposure; hundreds of homes with different histories, designs and layouts and different distances from the facilities; domestic and multinational chemical companies; wastewater disposal techniques and conflicting accounts of what was known when and precautions taken; vinyl chloride; air pollution modelling techniques and isopleth maps; toxicology reports and risk assessments; hydro-geologic models of groundwater flows; genetic predispositions and mutations; more than thirty rare brain and pituitary tumours (seen once in every 100,000–300,000 people) concentrated in a single residential village of about 1,000; neuropathological evidence for and against the link between brain cancers and exposure to toxins; international, federal and state environmental standards; property values and real estate appraisals; health costs; MRIs and CAT scans; remediation technologies; moral failings and plausible denials; limited judicial resources; statements interpreting each of these things. It is a hotchpotch of value-objects that want to be heard: [LAW-ORG] considerations, such as Rule 23 and other cases interpreting it, as well as elements of the divisive issue giving rise to the case such as, among others, referential pathways [REF], moral scruples [MOR] and a multitude of passionate interests in land, water, buildings, atmosphere, money, health, etc. [ATT], all mobilised to sustain two irreconcilable positions. In the certification papers submitted by the parties, all of these value-objects clamour and demand to be taken seriously, to become norms or obligations, but their relative weight and proper connection is not at all apparent. Although the class device is a modified and in some ways simplified translation of the stratified issue, it too contains multitudes – disjointed enunciative planes piled atop one another, elements of a matter of concern locked into homogeneous aggregates that must be reintegrated, connected horizontally to form a chain, to construct a specific trajectory of relevant legal grounds.

It is worth noting parenthetically that class certification is – or was – a relatively minor procedural inquiry, largely bracketing the merits of the claims and defences. Increasingly, however, federal courts, including the Supreme Court, have aggressively advanced the merits inquiry (usually reserved for summary judgment or trial) to earlier points in the litigation, which is, according to plaintiffs, a boon for corporate defendants that can more easily escape liability on an underdeveloped record and, according to defendants, a welcome due-process safeguard against unmeritorious class actions.[28] Class certification now requires a 'rigorous analysis' that 'overlaps' with the merits inquiry, although what that means is often unclear.[29]

The Gateses, the class proponents, freely leverage the moral failures and environmental consequences of the defendants' actions and capitalise on the plight and risk of the residents. But the companies dispute whether the evidence is so clear: there are uncertainties about the plaintiffs' ability to prove that the residents have suffered any harm, let alone any uniform harm, whatever the truth of their allegations about the moral value or environmental consequences of their conduct. The inconsistencies and complications built into the device are so onerous as to render class treatment unmanageable; whatever efficiencies or benefits the parties and the court might have otherwise enjoyed by unifying the group of interested claimants would not come to fruition because every claimant has a materially different claim, if any at all. Their written legal argument demonstrates how such burdensome complexities proliferate, while rendering moral and environmental considerations irrelevant to the legal problem. There is no common proof that all residents were exposed to the carcinogenic chemical in excessive quantities, only statistical computations about what a fictional 'average' resident would have been exposed to, given certain assumptions that may or may not be supported by data.

The Gateses, by contrast, emphasise the commonalities: the defendants acted no differently toward the group as a whole (carelessly dumping contaminated wastewater), and now, since some residents developed brain cancers, everyone must undergo regular screening. The statistical evidence is not based on the chemical exposure of an unrelated or hypothetical cohort but on what the actual residents themselves would have experienced.

For both, legal argument consists in soliciting and enlisting heterogeneous actors as support for the advocate's own position, for the application of the rule she desires. Each acts as though the 'rule' about the adequacy of proof in this case is not preordained and must take shape only through the circulation of value-objects. Through successive rounds of argument (without judicial involvement), the parties carve out a series of possible pathways, possible means of aligning the bulk of enunciative strata. That multiplicity of alternative routes to coherence defines the boundaries of the class device and the freedom of movement of the agencies it hosts.

The device, so conceived, looks similar to a technological project. Like Aramis, for instance, the class device is freighted with inconsistent visions, incompatible designs, unworkable functions. Aramis failed – not for lack of interest or ingenuity or capability on the part of engineers, politicians, capitalists, regulators, or non-human assemblies, but thanks largely to the proliferation of many 'nominal' or inflexible, perfect Aramises.[30] In a sense every technological project encompasses many possible worlds, and that is also true of legal devices. Unlike Aramis, legal devices do not (necessarily) require the solicitation of the RATP or of motors, doors and non-material couplings, but they do require the recruitment of value-objects, the jurimorphised issue-elements and archival statements of law. Opposing counsel work to interrupt these recruitment processes, acting as spokespersons for the ignored aspects of the issue and of the legal statements invoked by the other party, converting enemies and obstacles into allies. In both the legal and the technological cases, such *negotiation* is indispensable.

The decisive difference between legal and technological practices, it may be thought, is that technological projects are not typically reviewed, critiqued and adjudicated by an authority able to redesign the project, trimming away parts that do not fit. This brings us to the judicial opinion, that many-voiced chorus.[31] The opinion is, as I've written elsewhere, a record of the movements of value-objects and the court's hesitation over them. The most profitable way to understand the place of the court in the enunciation of law is not as a transcendent, distant authority but as an actor that must, like the non-legal materialities assembled in the issue or archival utterances of law, be solicited and enrolled by the parties. The judicial opinion 'says the law' and, in doing so, carves out one narrow pathway of legal materialities from the contested, inconsistent assemblage manufactured by opposing advocates that we have been calling a legal device. If the legal device somehow encompasses many possible worlds, the trajectory of legal reasoning is the progressive actualisation of only one. The doctrinal or analytical framework is a script the court implements; the art of judging lies not in following a script but in this technique of destratification, of tracing the *topoi*, the pleats and creases defining the topography of the matter to figure out where the parties disagree (only, of course, by adding a new enunciative stratum of its own – simplification is simultaneously complication because the whole is always smaller than the parts, circulating inside them) and collecting and weaving an indeterminate set of value-objects into a somewhat more stable *chain of obligations*, culminating in the enunciation of a legal principle crowning that still-wavering trajectory. That trajectory owes its shape to the conflicting value-objects rapidly passing through the device, which the judge does not control, but which, through a sort of *techne* of self-government, she can perhaps slow down. We can even affirm that the judge's peculiar forms of agency themselves owe something fundamental to legal devices, as material-discursive assemblages, because it is their complications that are translated in every legal statement.[32] The judge, perhaps striving to maximise her legitimacy,[33] takes as many clamouring value-objects into account as possible, amplifying her own value (and credibility) not through unassailable deductive logic but through maximum extension and appropriation of many (individually weak) allies.

In his written opinion, the district court judge, Judge Gene Pratter, takes the class device over from the feuding parties to submit it to a disciplined interpretation, further stripping away irrelevancies and rearranging the remaining components in a new sequence. Straight away, Judge Pratter notes that in the certification papers, the parties ended up agreeing that only one pollutant and one particular means of contamination (the chemical was present in a shallow aquifer and volatised into the air) might form the basis of a viable class, so limits his discussion to that proposal. Thus certain value-objects – the directional flow of groundwater in the deeper bedrock aquifer and evidence and arguments about it, for example – are 'no longer germane to class certification[.]'[34] The many remaining considerations the court tests in the order prescribed by the Rule 23 script. The numerical order is less telling than the amount of attention the court lavishes on a particular consideration; those that occupy it for more textual space and for which it constructs more elaborate arguments are more important. In every instance, the court tries to bridge a miniscule hiatus separating one value-object from another, discarding as irrelevant those that turn out, on inspection, to be incapable of connection.

In *Gates*, the first such difficulty was argued extensively by the parties: since the class would include all residents not yet diagnosed with brain cancer, and seeks no personal injury damages, it is conceivable that some class members would have viable personal injury claims for injuries *other than* brain cancers barred as a result of the class certification.[35] Thus the chemical companies appropriated the interests of the potential class members to support their bid opposing class certification. The court overcomes this hiatus not by denying it exists but by seizing two additional elements to form a coherent chain: that several residents have already initiated separate legal claims against the companies regarding their present injuries (thus freeing them from being bound by the result of the class case) and that the alleged contamination has been well publicised, making it unlikely that residents with injuries other than brain cancers would be unaware of their ability to sue.[36] These value-objects (other residents' lawsuits, media coverage) thus find a place in the trajectory, becoming obligations, modalised, from the perspective of the trajectory itself, as not-being-able-to-not-do. A second such difficulty soon crops up: vinyl chloride (whose carcinogenic properties are well documented and which is regulated, however lightly, by environmental standards[37]) may not be 'hazardous' to particular individuals, whose physical dimensions (height, weight, breathing rate, medical history, physiology, presence or absence of particular enzymes) will alter the precise level of risk they bear. Given such differences, the companies argue, class treatment is inappropriate. These value-objections are quieted not by taking new value-objects into account and transforming them into obligations, but by a slight displacement of the problem and a minor legal fiction: 'At some point, a given chemical must be considered 'hazardous' to all humans, for purposes of exposure claims – even if it does not actually cause harm in everyone exposed to it because of physiological differences.'[38] In this way the court can safely discount the relevance of the physiological differences value-object, which does not become an obligation.

But the last hiatus is the most challenging. The Gateses relied on statistical risk assessments that computed the average level of chemical exposure of the residents. The average exposure rate was computed using monitoring well data to simulate the average annual concentration of vinyl chloride in the air between 1940 and 2006. Isopleth maps showing the distribution of vinyl chloride in different years and different locations within the community visualised the reality of the residents' risks. The Gateses' experts also calculated the risk of developing brain cancer as a result of the average exposure level. The companies, rather than directly undermining the evidence, deflated its legal value by arguing the class could not be certified unless a common set of figures could prove the *actual* exposure levels of individual residents; averaging by its nature overestimates the exposure level for some and underestimates it for others.[39]

The parties disagreed about whether the averages would suffice under a 'rigorous analysis', each excising statements and fragments of statements made by other judges in other circumstances to support their interpretation of what a 'rigorous analysis' in this case is. Judge Pratter struggles to link the averages to the actual residents. The hiatus becomes a problem of mismatched scale: how do the residents themselves fit into the calculation? And how closely must they fit, for the law's purposes? Judge Pratter does not seem to know *in abstracto*. To find out, he looks to the explanation offered by the person that performed the calculations, the Gateses' air dispersion expert. His own testimony protests against forging such a connection: he conceded in deposition that the actual, not average, exposure level ultimately matters for individual claimants. Seeing that this evidence undermines rather than supports the class, making the hiatus seem unbridgeable, Judge Pratter attacks the expert's methodology (his report uses 'advantageous' data), further confirming that this particular evidence does not belong in the legal trajectory in quite the way the Gateses suggested. Judge Pratter finds this key evidence for the class fails to signify: it 'says nothing about a common minimal level of exposure'.[40] In doing so he blends a statistical, calculative mode of reasoning into the work of legal reasoning; the average/actual distinction becomes a legal operation. The court proceeds for pages to turn value-object after value-object into an obstacle to class certification: the amount of time spent outside versus inside, the amount of years in residence and the amount of time spent away from the community at work, school or on extended leave will differ for each individual resident and potentially affect the actual level of exposure suffered. Even the isopleth maps are turned against the Gateses, signifying now their failure to provide actual metrics. A cascade of materials quickly overtakes them. These are each transformations in the content of law – even though none of these techniques can be found in handbooks on procedure or legal reasoning.[41]

Unlike the lawyers' assertive arguments, the court's reasoning is tinged with anguish and marked by hesitation – a difference in tone attributable perhaps to what Latour calls the *libido judicandi* – as for example when it recognises the 'puzzling, frustrating and, above all, certainly tragic' set of brain cancers suffered by community residents, yet feels compelled, by attachment to the practice of legal veridiction and the 'immutable legal requirements' of the Rule 23 script, to deny certification.[42] Worth noting also is the lapse of time between the briefing period and the issuance of the court's opinion: initial briefing was complete by July 2007 (with supplemental briefing extending into January 2009), but the opinion was issued on 5 March 2010. This hesitancy indexes the court's trepidation in uttering a legal principle that must 'do justice' in the case itself while also cohering, somehow, with archival utterances: there is an element of the Jamesian *salto mortale* (or the Holmesian 'leap in the dark') in every link of the chain of obligations, which, whatever their agency, cannot arrange themselves.[43] Phrases like 'immutable legal requirements' – uttered precisely when those requirements are being determined, when the *operative* rule is being pieced together – attest not to the solidity of law but to its fragility, its entanglement with demanding value-objects of uncertain justificatory relevance that must be inspected with a juridimeter. Fragility, contingency, perplexity – but not arbitrariness, since the *libido judicandi* is itself the materialisation of juridical sensitivity to the subtle demands of the principle to be instaured.[44]

The trajectory of the court's reasoning achieves its consistency and objectivity, its 'technical rationality' in Greimas's curiously Weberian language,[45] only by passing through jurimorphs. We see very specific casuistic techniques (seizing free value-objects, fictionalisation, rescaling) deployed to destratify the legal device and create a peculiar sense. We see value-objects, whose agency consists not only in moulding the trajectory but also certain specific effects (smoothing it, slightly reorienting it, bending it to the breaking point) animate the whole drama. But note what Judge Pratter did *not* do, namely skip ahead to the unbridgeable hiatus. His text tells a longer and more nuanced (analytical) story, putting a host of value-objects into circulation to register their mutual reaction. His analysis endows the decision to deny certification with a sort of *narrative causality*. This causality, like others, names only the silencing and appropriation of the agency of the value-objects that have defined the trajectory. But in law as in literature the causal sequence is not totally committed to the hands of the writer. In literature the logic of the story regularly exceeds the storyteller. The teller is subject to the demands of the elements of the story, which link up in sometimes surprising ways. In this, legal analysis is like storytelling. The thread of causality the judge narrates is traceable to the legal device (here, in three instances of impassable controversy), and this is why the judicial narration cannot be understood apart from the advocates' briefs that set up the device. And, relatedly, we cannot fail to notice that the opinion makes the judgment a *collaborative* one: Judge Pratter is careful to focus only on controversial matters but makes strictly no decisions without the guidance of the parties, finally stating that the class device is doomed because the parties themselves, through the proxy of their experts, agree that averages aren't enough to prove actual residents' exposure levels.[46] If we see the court as a particular actor contending with diverse obligations that are not 'legal' in any textbook sense, rather than as a scion of a reified, automatic (indeed, autopoietic) Law, we understand immediately that broad-based ideological criticisms of its reasoning are misplaced. As we'll see, however, that does not mean it is beyond reproach.

But the legal principle carefully excised from the trial court's 'rigorous analysis' is not yet stable; the Gateses challenged the trial court's decision not to certify the class. Judge Scirica, writing for the appellate panel, explained that the trial court correctly analysed the case and rejected the Gateses' argument that Judge Pratter had improperly considered 'merits' questions instead of the merely procedural 'certification' questions.[47] Judge Scirica's discussion is learned, professorial and confident, and stands in contrast to Judge Pratter's more laboured, hesitant text. But it is Judge Pratter's text that more openly informs the anthropologically oriented reader about the terrestrial production of legal truth, and while most lawyers familiar with *Gates* think only of the appellate court's decision (which bears the same name), we have opted for the lower court's analysis for precisely that reason. Judge Pratter's text exhibits superior 'eloquence', as Latour's *Dingpolitik* essay reimagines the term.[48] What is significant – anthropologically – in

Judge Scirica's opinion is its precise and masterful execution in securing Judge Pratter's legal principle not to the mix of value-objects constituting the case itself (which Judge Pratter succeeded in doing) but to the rest of the legal archive, with which it claims solidarity and compatibility: Judge Scirica's achievement is to have refined and fastened that principle to a line of descent, including the Supreme Court's (in)famous opinion in *Wal-Mart* forcefully restating the need for a 'rigorous' certification analysis overlapping with the merits and the Third Circuit's similar statement in *Hydrogen Peroxide*, as well as securing horizontal commensurability with other appellate courts throughout the nation.

Freedom bound

The theory of legal materiality that Judge Pratter enacted – which, as noted, was inherited from the contentious composition of the class device – demands a durable connection between act and harm. Judge Pratter refused to certify the class, pinning this decision on the insufficiently common character of the evidence that the defendants' wastewater disposal had introduced to the residents' elevated risks of brain cancer. It is tempting to say that the legal principle is that 'hypothetical average calculations of exposure to hazardous chemicals do not suffice to render the act/harm connection durable' or that 'average calculations do not demonstrate that actual class members' injuries can be proven with common evidence' or similar variations, but try as we might to capture it with some precision and make it look like a definite, stable, resilient rule, it will slip through our hands. There obviously may be cases where average calculations *do* suffice to render the connection durable or to demonstrate commonality – even in *Gates* itself, if, for example, the various spatial and temporal differences concerning residents' exposure to the air were found to be insignificant, such that the statistical models were more firmly fused to the judicial construal of the bodies of the residents. If we succumbed to the temptation of postulating the principle in propositional form, as doctrinalists and those relying on their accounts do, we would take a misleading short cut. The point is that the real rule – the operative rule, that is the *principle* crowning the legal trajectory – does not pre-exist the case and depends on a network of value-objects that are modified (remodalised as not-being-able-to-not-do) and strung together in a scripted, yet ad hoc manner. Judge Pratter's analysis is a written narrative and so, of course, the objectification achieved by virtue of committing it to paper renders it more durable and capable of acting in specific ways in later, unrelated interactions. But every *visa* or later citation to *Gates* will appropriate its principle for ends foreign to the veridictory procedure in which it was enunciated: advocates will deploy *Gates* to restratify the legal space as they dispute its meaning, and judges will fit it into an entirely new, unrelated analytical series, silencing Judge Pratter by representing his judgment – a kind of 'immanent', infra-legal overflowing. The principle took shape out of the device, that assemblage of vociferous value-objects, which Judge Pratter simplified and rationalised to fabricate a continuous pathway of relevancies, and the principle remains bound to it. The lesson to lawyers: doctrinal transformations depend not on vague social, cultural or ideological shifts but on particular legal devices, which are constantly evolving and building non-legal elements into themselves.

The *Gates* 'rule' is not a self-subsisting snapshot, a freeze-frame, but part of a moving image – something practitioners know well (as they must analogise to *Gates* so it becomes relevant or irrelevant for their own legal devices), but theorists seem to forget. In this it is not dissimilar from a scientific fact that is easily mistaken for a substantial being but is merely part of a complicated chain of references. Sense is not localised anywhere in particular within the judicial utterance; it runs along the chain of obligations resulting from the hesitations of judgment and is coterminous or coextensive with it. To state the principle we could only repeat the entire *Gates* opinion, recitation of the date included, which of course would nevertheless remain inadequate to the original scenography of utterance. Regarding science and law, we reverse Rousseau's formula: facts and principles are born in chains (of reference, of obligation), and everywhere the epistemologists set them free (to go forth and multiply in the world, without intervention).

Translation *redux*

Each step in the translation from matter of concern to legal principle more or less violently reduced the thing translated: the issue and the publics articulating it began as a disjointed multiplicity of enunciative planes scattered in all directions, but were embedded in a standardised legal framework that dramatically flattened them and eliminated their dispersal by regrouping them (composition of the 'facts'); these were bound up with competing articulations of the legal grounds that would permit or prohibit the cause of action by the advocates, through tendentious narratives that re-produced a multiplicity of levels, better organised but just as disconnected and uneven as before (composition of the device bridging the fact/law hiatus); and the hesitant destratification of the device components by way of the court's modifications of the value-objects put in play by the parties, resulting in the production of a new legal principle responding to the case and claiming to cohere with archival legal utterances (a complementary practice of *restratification*, forcing the accretion of a new archival layer). Other courts sometimes say that *Gates* 'means' that class certification should be denied where the class proponents are unable to connect the alleged wrongful act to the alleged injury suffered with more particular proof than statistical averages, and while that is a new transformation of the principle that in fact goes no further than *Gates* itself (that is it is one part of a longer chain or trajectory that is detachable only on condition that it takes on new meanings in a new trajectory), it has a bearing on the Rule 23 script, the doctrinal requirements for a toxic exposure claim, and any other construct to which advocates and judges in later cases decide to analogise it. The meaning of those doctrines is not what it was prior to *Gates*. The successive transformations of the issue experienced in Lake McCullom led to the principle altering the meaning of procedural scripts and technical legal doctrines invoked in the unforeseen circumstances of later cases.

We thus conclude our discussion of the case at the very point that other legal theories, including the spontaneous theories of the law review and the law school classroom, arrive to take inventory. By the time the court has uttered its holding and explained its reasoning, it is too late: we have missed the practice of law, overlooked the slow composition of a unique trajectory through the transformation of value-objects into obligations, and fumbled our handling of the legal principle, which we promptly mistake for an ordinary rule. By spinning out studies of the meaning, source, derivation and coherence of legal rules abstracted from any trajectory, treating law as mere information [LAW-DC], legal theory serves then only to reproduce the natural and naturally objective, irrefutable, 'immutable' qualities of a reified Law. Ultimately, it buys into the victor's narrative of history, for which legal truth is obvious and automatic rather than fragile and constantly renegotiated.

If there is room for (valuable) criticism, it may come from those affected by the judgment or others 'speaking legally' in subsequent cases. The latter criticisms may look like positive or negative modalisations, in the language of *Science in Action*: they either accept the principle and cite it as authority for a new argument, rendering it more opaque and increasing its stability, or on the contrary trace the principle back to its conditions of enunciation to reveal its dependence on value-objects that fail to protest in the new case. Or they ferret out inconsistencies in the court's reasoning.[49] The former criticisms – those voiced by the participants – tell us what happened to the articulation of the issue after *Gates*.

According to the *Northwest Herald*, surprisingly, the Gateses viewed the failed class lawsuit as a success: 'The Gateses said the awareness the lawsuit raised, and the settlement with another defendant [Modine Manufacturing] that led to two early detections of brain tumors, made it a success.'[50] The Modine settlement provided a $1.4 million fund for medical monitoring, and two of the 100 residents that sought monitoring exhibited tumours. Absent the Modine settlement, in other words, the *Gates* decision would have resulted in a failure to detect at least two tumours.[51] Rohm & Haas Co., for its part, said that it is 'gratified by the results and the due process followed all the way along' and 'believe[s] this is the correct outcome in this case',[52] and continues to deny any responsibility for the tumours that have already developed or the risks faced by other residents: whatever is acting to produce tumours in the community, it is not vinyl chloride traceable to its facilities.

Following the sequence of legal translations, including the appellate court's affirmation, the community president had the air tested (by the Aires Consulting Group, with funds provided by Rohm & Haas) and no abnormal levels of vinyl chloride were detected.[53] Would-be representatives of the community announced that the black cloud had been lifted: this independent study was in accord with prior studies done by local agencies and the US Centers for Disease Control and Prevention, which concluded that no unusual cancer cluster existed in the area (as compared to county and state statistics). The new testing was promptly criticised by other representatives and the idea that the cloud was lifted denounced as an 'illusion'.[54] Disgruntled residents and investigative media invoked a series of allies – a 1977 order from the state pollution control board shuttering the waste pit and an attorney general lawsuit brought in the 1970s on behalf of area residents;

the local department of health's failure to investigate the pollution as a cause of the unusual group of brain tumours 'based on their personal perceptions about the direction the wind blows',[55] exposed in a 2007 media report; and faults in all the studies claiming to show the non-existence of a cancer cluster – to rekindle the controversy. Certain residents have launched a social media campaign to bring awareness of the cancer cluster, providing running updates on health and legal news – trying, in a small way, to make their problem everyone's problem, in Sandra Harding's memorable phrase. Other residents, by contrast, persist in claiming that the matter is finished, this painful chapter of the community's history definitively completed. After the passage of law in *Gates*, then, we see that the issue lives on, transformed: suppressed enunciative strata reappear, old perplexities are reborn and though the legal truth has been 'instituted', new legal events continue to surface. Thirty-three residents allegedly suffering brain and pituitary tumours as a result of the chemical companies' conduct continue to litigate their individual claims; new tumours continue to develop; different actors – residents, media, corporations, government agencies – continue to claim to speak for the community as a whole. Formatting is never total; excessive, unpredictable overflow results because the jurimorphised agencies were never really disentangled from the issue. And the issue does not disappear with the enunciation of the legal principle; it begins again.

Notes

1. Callon and Latour (1981).
2. Lezaun (2012).
3. Cloatre and Wright (2012).
4. Socio-technical legal analysis is different things for different writers; in Annelise Riles's minimalist statement, it means 'tak[ing] the agency of [legal] technological form seriously', refusing to reduce legal technicalities to pretexts for political, cultural, historical, economic or other preferences (2005: 1029). Other major works in the genre might include Riles (2011), Pottage and Sherman (2010), Twining (2009) and Valverde (2003). Latour's (2010) ethnographical account of law qualifies as socio-technical analysis as well.
5. I prefer the cumbersome 'not-being-able-to-not-do' to the more prosaic 'having-to-do' because the latter implies a peremptory structure that is lacking in this particular transformation.

6. See McGee (2013: chapter 3), especially on the failings of H. L. A. Hart's theory of legal normativity.
7. Gutwirth, this volume. I will respond to Gutwirth's valuable arguments in another paper, but it suffices here to mention that his theorisation suffers from a professional parochialism that denies the experiential dimension of the value of law, rendering law incapable of bearing real ontological or, indeed, anthropological interest, and further undermines itself by situating the judge, institutional actor par excellence, at the heart of the purportedly non-institutional account of law as a mode of existence.
8. The great bulk of such matters never generate litigation or stimulate administrative intervention, of course; instead, they are resolved locally, provisionally, tentatively, informally, in interactive practices of 'law uncoupled from legal institutions' (Silbey and Ewick 1998: 22). But they remain legal events despite the typical absence of the state – a point I cannot develop here.
9. Recall the Valladolid controversy (Latour 2004b). To wit, each 'side' mobilises its self-interpretation and its interpretation of the other.
10. On attachments and issues, see Marres (2007).
11. On shifting, see Latour (2013: 246–9) and Akrich and Latour (1992: 260).
12. That is why recent debates in science studies over the role and authority of expertise, addressing the 'right' of experts to unilaterally resolve technical matters, have been crucial to the field of political theory (for example, Callon (1999), Callon et al. (2009), Collins and Evans (2009) and McGee (2013: section 2.3).
13. Silbey (2005: 331); see also Silbey and Cavicchi (2005). On the materialisation of legal normativity, see McGee (2013: chapter 3).
14. On expression and legal force, see McGee (2013: chapter 3).
15. Diversionary techniques of dispute resolution have been examined in several non-Western collectives; Roberts (2013) is a good overview. Silbey and Ewick (1998) also address the reification of law achieved through the removal of courts and other legal organs from everyday life among Americans. Of course, we should remember that the Icelandic Althing was a place apart, drawing a public once per year.
16. This is common to Marxists/postmarxists – see Balbus (1977), Christodoulidis (1997) and other forms of anti-liberalism such as that of Carl Schmitt (2007).
17. Latour (2013: 361).
18. On justificatory relevance, see Weinrib (1995).

19. Incidentally, American federal courts seem to agree: the Supreme Court not long ago stated that the 'grounds' of a party's entitlement to relief are something distinct from 'a formulaic recitation of the [purely legal] elements of a cause of action'. *Bell Atlantic Corp.* v. *Twombly*, 550 US 544, 555 (2007).
20. As a legal translation of the matter of concern, the legal device retains its *thingly* character, remaining, in Yan Thomas's words, 'a common object that *opposes* and *unites* two protagonists within a single relation' (quoted in Latour 2005: 23). It is precisely this opaque thingliness that is overlooked in the common sense of practitioner and doctrinalist alike.
21. On the construct of common knowledge in judicial reasoning, see Valverde (2003).
22. And because it allows a subtextual dialogue with Michel Callon's economic sociology, which uses similar examples frequently (e.g. Callon 1998).
23. For an influential history of the modern class action, see Yeazell (1987). Medieval group litigation, according to Yeazell, grows out of a communal or collectivistic sensibility and thus differs in character from the modern class action, which bands members together based on shared individual interests.
24. Dewey (1988: 15–16). Indeed, one of the modern class action's innovations seems to be to have eliminated the need for a pre-existing relationship among class members.
25. Federal Rule of Civil Procedure (FRCP) 23(b)(2).
26. FRCP 23(b)(3).
27. I differ from Latour on the question of what constitutes a value-object: for me, anything that enters into the process of creating a trajectory of legal reason is (or may be) a value-object, but Latour seems to limit them to considerations bearing on the constraints of legal speech generally, without regard to specific cases. Because I find it impossible to separate 'fact' and 'law' prospectively, Latour's more limited range seems unrealistic and even to play into the simplistic epistemologies academic doctrinal lawyers peddle.
28. The key recent Supreme Court opinion is *Wal-Mart Stores, Inc.* v. *Dukes*, 131 S. Ct. 2541 (2011), although purists will argue that the 'rigorous analysis' point runs back to an opinion issued thirty years prior, *General Telephone Co.* v. *Falcon*, 457 US 147 (1982). In the Third Circuit, the Circuit to which the trial court in *Gates* must answer, the key opinion is *In re Hydrogen Peroxide Antitrust Litigation*, 552 F.3d 305 (3d Cir. 2008).

29. For a critical assessment of recent transformations in class action doctrine, see Spencer (2013).
30. Latour (1996).
31. Leubsdorf (2001) usefully examines the polyphony and heterogeneity of the judicial opinion.
32. This highlights the connection of legal to economic devices, which remain, nevertheless, very different. On market devices as economic assemblages, see Muniesa et al. (2007).
33. See Bellaing, this volume, analogising to the police investigation scenography.
34. 265 FRD at 211 n. 5.
35. Ibid. at 217.
36. Ibid. at 218.
37. See, for example, National Resources Defense Council (NRDC) (2010). Federal environmental regulations take account of vinyl chloride's potential impact on the liver, but not other organ systems, which reduces the cancer potency quantification of the chemical, which lightens the burden on industry in terms of production and remediation costs.
38. 265 FRD at 220 n. 21.
39. Ibid. at 223.
40. Ibid.
41. Propositionalist accounts fail here because the operative agencies (isopleth maps, statistical reasoning techniques, residents' lifestyle habits, etc.) are engaged in the construction/performance of something like a 'relevance rule' rather than being subjected to a pre-existing one taking a propositional form. There is a small, undervalued (non-propositionalist) literature combining legal semiotics and ethnomethodology that is probably an exception to the claim made in the body, for example, Dupret (2011).
42. 265 FRD at 231.
43. There is no better account of the precise communicative channels through which non-human agents activate apparently autonomous humans than Cooren (2010).
44. The similarity of this point to the first-wave critical legal theorists' point about legal indeterminacy is palpable, but it should be noted that indeterminacy, for CLS, implies that legal reasoning is camouflaged *political* reasoning, whereas this *salto mortale* remains immanent to the legal trajectory. If there is a politics within law, it is in the movements of the value-objects. This alternative represents a path not taken in contemporary post-CLS theorising, which has

moved decisively away from the production of legal statements and toward metaphysical reflection on themes such as biopolitics and resistance to neoliberalism. In a sense the fusion of legal studies and STS that draws us to examine in detail the praxis of legal enunciation (*clinical* legal studies?) can claim inheritance from first-wave CLS more readily than contemporary critical legal theorists – though this is no complaint against the latter, who are doing rigorous and groundbreaking work in what can be described as simply a different register.

45. Greimas (1987: 176).
46. This suggests that, viewed according to their use and regardless of what the official discourse may claim, some, perhaps many, legal norms in fact represent mere bargaining chips that parties and courts may deploy rather than determinative statements. This would render modern American law commensurate with what earlier legal anthropologists called acephalous societies like the Arusha of Northern Tanzania (see Roberts 2013: 99–102). It is entirely possible that American acephaly is a product of deregulatory initiatives and the deployment of market devices as enforcers of law, but that is a different matter.
47. *Gates v. Rohm & Haas Co.*, 655 F.3d 255, 265 (3d Cir. 2011).
48. Latour (2005: 17–22).
49. For example, why were the statistical averages of exposure levels insufficient evidence of common proof, while the (unquantified) unlikelihood of injured but non-cancerous residents not knowing of their right to sue was found sufficient to overcome objections to the Gateses' adequacy as class representatives? Both depend on similar probabilities, and only the one that failed (average exposure levels) was actually quantified. The answer may be that the hiatus in the two instances posed different challenges, but a closer look at them is not possible here. The same question arises in connection with the court's supposition that '[a]t some point, a given chemical must be considered "hazardous" to all humans, for purposes of exposure claims – even if it does not actually cause harm in everyone exposed to it because of physiological differences.' The court bridged the difference between hypothetical and actual harm for that inquiry but not the predominance inquiry.
50. *Northwest Herald* (2012).
51. The remaining residents opted not to pursue monitoring, suggesting that regardless of the way the *Gates* decision turned out, it would have had no impact on them. This recalcitrance, if that is what it is,

evokes David Engel's (1984) classic study of the community's moral disapproval of personal injury litigation in rural Illinois.
52. *Northwest Herald* (2012).
53. *Northwest Herald* (2011a).
54. *Northwest Herald* (2011b).
55. *Northwest Herald* (2011a).

References

Akrich, Madeleine and Latour, Bruno (1992) 'A summary of a convenient vocabulary for the semiotics of human and nonhuman assemblies', in Wiebe E. Bijker and John Law (eds), *Shaping Technology/Building Society: Studies in Sociotechnical Change*. Cambridge, MA: MIT Press, pp. 259–64.

Balbus, Isaac (1977) *The Dialectics of Legal Repression: Black Rebels Before the American Criminal Courts*. New Brunswick, NJ: Transaction Books.

Callon, Michel (1998) 'An essay on framing and overflowing: economic externalities revisited by sociology', *Laws of the Markets*. Oxford: Blackwell, pp. 244–69.

Callon, Michel (1999) 'The role of lay people in the production and dissemination of scientific knowledge', *Science Technology Society*, 4: 81–94.

Callon, Michel and Latour, Bruno (1981) 'Unscrewing the big Leviathan: or how actors macrostructure reality, and how sociologists help them to do so', in Karin Knorr-Cetina and Aaron Cicourel (eds), *Advances in Social Theory and Methodology: Toward an Integration of Micro- and Macro-Sociologies*. London: Routledge, pp. 277–303.

Callon, Michel, Lascoumes, Pierre and Barthe, Yannick (2009) *Acting in an Uncertain World: An Essay in Technical Democracy*, trans. Graham Burchell. Cambridge, MA: MIT Press.

Christodoulidis, Emilios (1998) *Law and Reflexive Politics*. Dordrecht: Kluwer.

Cloatre, Emilie and Wright, Nick (2012) 'A socio-legal analysis of an actor-world: the case of carbon trading and the clean development mechanism', *Journal of Law and Society* 39: 76–92.

Collins, Harry and Evans, Robert (2009) *Rethinking Expertise*. Chicago: University of Chicago Press.

Cooren, François (2010) *Action and Agency in Dialogue: Passion, Incarnation and Ventriloquism*. Philadelphia: John Benjamins.

Cover, Robert M. (1983) 'Nomos and narrative', *Harvard Law Review*, 97: 4–68.

Dewey, John (1988) *The Public and Its Problems*. Athens: Ohio University Press.

Dupret, Baudouin (2011) *Adjudication in Action: An Ethnomethodology of Law, Morality, and Justice*, trans. Pascale Ghazaleh. Burlington: Ashgate.

Engel, David (1984) 'The oven-bird's song: insiders, outsiders, and personal injuries in an American community', *Law and Society Review*, 18: 551–82.

Greimas, A. J. (1987) *On Meaning: Selected Writings in Semiotic Theory*, trans. Paul Perron and Frank H. Collins. Minneapolis: University of Minnesota Press.

Latour, Bruno (1996) *Aramis, or the Love of Technology*, trans. Catherine Porter. Cambridge, MA: Harvard University Press.

Latour, Bruno (2004a) 'Why has critique run out of steam? From matters of fact to matters of concern', *Critical Inquiry*, 30: 225–48.

Latour, Bruno (2004b) 'Whose cosmos, which cosmopolitics? Comments on the peace terms of Ulrich Beck', *Common Knowledge*, 10: 450–62.

Latour, Bruno (2005) 'From *Realpolitik* to *Dingpolitik*, or how to make things public', in Bruno Latour and Peter Weibel (eds), *Making Things Public: Atmospheres of Democracy*. Cambridge, MA: MIT Press, pp. 14–43.

Latour, Bruno (2010) *The Making of Law: An Ethnography of the Conseil d'État*, trans. Marina Brilman and Alain Pottage. Cambridge: Polity.

Latour, Bruno (2013) *An Inquiry into Modes of Existence: An Anthropology of the Moderns*, trans. Catherine Porter. Cambridge, MA: Harvard University Press.

Leubsdorf, John (2001) 'The structure of judicial opinions', *Minnesota Law Review*, 86: 447–96.

Lezaun, Javier (2012) 'The pragmatic sanction of materials: notes for an ethnography of legal substances', *Journal of Law and Society*, 39: 20–38.

MacCormick, Neil (2005) *Rhetoric and the Rule of Law: A Theory of Legal Reasoning*. Oxford: Oxford University Press.

McGee, Kyle (2013) *Bruno Latour: The Normativity of Networks*. New York: Routledge.

Marres, Noortje (2007) 'The issues deserve more credit: pragmatist contributions to the study of public involvement in controversy', *Social Studies of Science*, 37: 759–80.

Muniesa, Fabian, Millo, Yuval and Callon, Michel (2007) 'An introduction to market devices', *Market Devices*. Oxford: Blackwell, pp. 1–12.

Natural Resources Defense Council (2010) 'Vinyl chloride'. Online at <http://www.nrdc.org/health/files/vinylChloride.pdf>.

Northwest Herald (2011a) 'Counley: McCullom Lake Air Clean Of Contaminants', 23 September. Online at <http://www.nwherald.com/2011/09/22/counley-mccullom-lake-air-clean-of-contaminants/atlr5n6/>.

Northwest Herald (2011b) 'While tests call McCullom Lake air and water safe, not all are reassured', 18 December. Online at <http://www.nwherald.com/2011/11/17/while-tests-call-mccullom-lake-air-and-water-safe-not-all-are-reassured/ak1cor1/>.

Northwest Herald (2012) '"If we save one life, we succeeded"', 26 February. Online at <http://www.nwherald.com/2012/02/15/if-we-save-one-life-we-succeeded/adbboal/>.

Pottage, Alain and Sherman, Brad (2010) *Figures of Invention: A History of Modern Patent Law*. Oxford: Oxford University Press.

Riles, Annelise (2005) 'A new agenda for the cultural study of law: taking on the technicalities', *Buffalo Law Review*, 53: 973–1033.

Riles, Annelise (2011) *Collateral Knowledge: Legal Reasoning in the Global Financial Markets*. Chicago: University of Chicago Press.

Roberts, Simon (2013) *Order and Dispute: An Introduction to Legal Anthropology*, 2nd edn. New Orleans: Quid Pro.

Schmitt, Carl (2007) 'The age of neutralizations and depoliticizations', in George Schwab (ed.), *The Concept of the Political*, trans. Matthias Konzett and John P. McCormick. Chicago: University of Chicago Press, pp. 80–96.

Silbey, Susan S. (2005) 'After legal consciousness', *Annual Review of Law and Social Science*, 1: 323–68.

Silbey, Susan S. and Cavicchi, Ayn (2005) 'The common place of law: transforming matters of concern into the objects of everyday life', in Bruno Latour and Peter Weibel (eds), *Making Things Public: Atmospheres of Democracy*. Cambridge, MA: MIT Press, pp. 556–65.

Silbey, Susan S. and Ewick, Patricia (1998) *The Common Place of Law: Stories from Everyday Life*. Chicago: University of Chicago Press.

Spencer, A. Benjamin (2013) 'Class actions, heightened commonality, and declining access to justice', *Boston University Law Review*, 93: 441–91.

Twining, William (2009) *General Jurisprudence: Understanding Law from a Global Perspective*. New York: Cambridge University Press.

Valverde, Mariana (2003) *Law's Dream of a Common Knowledge*. Princeton: Princeton University Press.

Weinrib, Ernest (1995) *The Idea of Private Law*. Cambridge, MA: Harvard University Press.

Yeazell, Stephen (1987) *From Medieval Group Litigation to the Modern Class Action*. New Haven, CT: Yale University Press.

Cases

Bell Atlantic Corp. v. Twombly, 550 US 544 (2007).
Gates v. Rohm and Haas Co., 265 FRD 208 (ED Pa. 2010).
Gates v. Rohm and Haas Co., 655 F.3d 255 (3d Cir. 2011).
General Telephone Co. v. Falcon, 457 US 147 (1982).
In re Hydrogen Peroxide Antitrust Litigation, 552 F.3d 305 (3d Cir. 2008).
Wal-Mart Stores, Inc. v. Dukes, 131 S. Ct. 2541 (2011).

4

'The Crown Wears Many Hats': Canadian Aboriginal Law and the Black-boxing of Empire
Mariana Valverde and Adriel Weaver

Introduction

Latour's *The Making of Law* encouraged us to think about 'law' as a set of overlapping networks in perpetual motion, networks in which such lowly entities such as paper clips, wooden mailboxes and file folders play important roles (Latour 2010; Levi and Valverde 2008). Latour's approach and choice of object of study are in keeping with much of today's legal anthropology, in part because today's legal anthropologists are more likely to be doing fieldwork in the backrooms of constitutional courts and even central banks than to be investigating the norms and 'customs' of Pacific Islanders (e.g. Riles 2011).

Our contribution to this volume is at one level a study that echoes Latour's and Riles' work on the anthropology of legal modernity (Mundy and Pottage 2004; Latour 2010). But since we will here highlight an innovative re-assembling of certain legal actors that reek of pre-modernity – those associated with the British/imperial/Canadian 'Crown' – it might be more accurate to say that our study shows how the modern v. pre-modern binary deconstructs itself in a legal assemblage elaborated mainly by means of current-day Canadian judicial decisions regarding aboriginal rights, an assemblage that makes strikingly novel use of very ancient notions about monarchs and their material and spiritual accoutrements.

'The Crown' – an ontologically hybrid term if there ever was one (Latour 1987) – is one of the most frequently used terms of Canadian law. It is found, with performative effects, in lofty documents, such as treaties between states or between the Canadian government and aboriginal nations. But it is also mechanically reproduced thousands of times a day in criminal proceedings, which are always styled *Regina* or *Rex* – abbreviated 'R.' – v. *Smith* or *R. v. Jones*. The genderless 'R.' is thus an interesting actor. It is first of all a tiny printed letter serving as a label telling the reader that a criminal prosecution is at work, a letter whose effective legal meaning is exactly the same as that of the US phrase 'The people of the state of X'. And yet, because the letter abolishes distinctions between actual monarchs, making it seem that the (male) sovereign who prosecuted someone in 1948 is the same as the (female) sovereign that is prosecuting Canadians and English people today, the 'R.' creates a supernatural and political 'body mystical', today's successor to the king's second body (Kantorowicz 1975), by literally erasing the historical markers dividing reigns.

This leap from an apparently trivial rhetorical convention (using 'R.' instead of either *Rex* or *Regina*) to the loftiest realms of theology and political theory is typical of the logic of the Canadian 'Crown': in the complex assemblage that is 'the Crown', ordinary historical temporality and everyday legal processes are not so much abolished as subsumed or *aufgehoben* into the mystical, almost timeless temporality of that curious medieval political actor, the king's second body.

While evoking the special powers of monarchs, the term 'Crown' has also been quietly appropriated by a good number of commoners. A public prosecutor (in English Canada) will answer the cocktail-party question, 'What do you do?' by saying, 'I'm a Crown'. This speech act is unique to Canada – no commoner Australian answers a routine question about occupation by claiming to be 'a' Crown – but unless there are foreigners present who marvel at this way of describing one's workaday existence, and thus draw attention to the black-boxing exercise that produced the crown-as-prosecutor, Canadians express no amazement at the fact that an ordinary person with a law degree can claim not just to represent but to *be* nothing less than the jewelled object worn, thousands of miles away in another jurisdiction, by Queen Elizabeth on solemn occasions. In another deployment of the royal crown, Canadian coins and bills usually feature Queen Elizabeth's crowned head, as is the case in Britain; but since the prosecutorial 'agencement' of the ultimate symbol of royal power has long been black-boxed in Canadian society, nobody feels it is peculiar that a prosecutor should daily use images of the very Crown that they claim to 'be' for such non-official purposes as buying a coffee.

A century ago, the great English legal historian F. W. Maitland, who as a moderniser was upset to see that English as well as colonial/imperial law persisted in granting 'the Crown' a great deal of agency and continued to multiply its personifications and thus its powers as colonial and postcolonial jurisdictions multiplied, declared: 'As a matter of fact we know that the crown [not capitalised] does nothing but lie in the Tower of London to be gazed at by sight-seers' ([1908] 1961: 418).

A. V. Dicey, another great moderniser, similarly complained that 'no-one, indeed, but a child fancies that the King sits crowned on his throne at Westminster and in his own person administers justice' (1902: 10). It is only because English law lacks even a word for 'droit administratif', Dicey explains (ibid.: 323) that it is still necessary to talk about the Crown and its powers. The English refusal to admit that there is a British state creates confusion, Dicey argued, since the true powers and jurisdictions of 'the Crown' (that is, the British state) are 'concealed under the fictitious ascription to the sovereign of political omnipotence' (ibid.: 11).

The English modernisers who a century ago cast aspersions on English law's fondness for using 'the Crown' (and also 'the crown', i.e. the object that lies in the Tower of London) as a confusing label for all manner of personifications of 'the state', while still retaining the old meaning of 'Crown' as 'the sovereign', would be shocked to learn that in a country whose legal system is arguably a great deal more modern than that of Britain, namely Canada, the older English Crown networks have not only persisted but multiplied and given rise to novel assemblages. Against the expectations of modernisers, and against the grain of liberal human rights logics, a new legal network has been created in which the very mysticism and quasi-divine temporality that have characterised the (English) Crown since the sixteenth century (Kantorowicz 1957; Engster 2001) has acted as a key resource for aboriginal nations seeking to assert their rights in novel ways.

We will tell the story of the contemporary effects of the mystical body politic that is the Crown in two parts. First, we will unpack the curious notion, invented almost from scratch by the Supreme Court of Canada, that if aboriginal peoples now have greater rights, especially in respect to natural resource development, than they did a century ago, this is not because of either international conventions or domestic laws, but rather because 'the Crown', being essentially by nature honourable, is obligated, by its own internal virtue, to accommodate aboriginal interests. The story of the 'honour of the Crown' will be followed by a reflection on a curious phrase that has been repeatedly deployed to subtly undermine aboriginal claims: 'The Crown wears many hats.' The practical meaning of the rather incongruous image is as follows: the government of Canada may well have a historic responsibility to guard the interests of aboriginal people in the face of rapacious white settlers, but the same government also has to protect non-aboriginal persons' private property rights and has to promote capitalist economic development. Typically, judicial decisions first acknowledge special governmental responsibilities towards aboriginal communities (often by invoking 'the honour of the Crown'), but then undermine the promise of justice by stating, as a fact, that 'The Crown wears many hats,' i.e. has responsibilities towards groups other than aboriginal nations. The 'many hats' trope thus acts to undermine, in a highly indeterminate manner, the beneficent effects attributed to the (hatless?) honourable colonial/postcolonial Crown.

The odd, even ridiculous image of a bunch of hats perched on top of a royal crown is currently being repeated from text to text, without having thus far evoked any comment in the vast relevant legal literature.[1] The commentators' silence corroborates our argument that the multiple and clashing personalities and functions of the Crown, or rather 'the Crown', have been so successfully black-boxed that both the Crown and its accoutrements have become invisible to the very judges who perform the feat of superimposing the trite image of multiple hats/duties on sovereignty's head covering.

Unfortunately for aboriginal people, the mixed metaphor is not a purely textual or symbolic entity. It wields a great and purposively indeterminate power to undermine the very benefits conferred on aboriginal peoples by the doctrine of the Crown's honour, as will be shown below.

The honour of the Crown

Civics textbooks notwithstanding, classifying a particular country as a constitutional monarchy is not very informative. The formal classification sheds no light on the specific powers, symbolic as well as practical, that flow from or accrue to the monarchical apparatus and to whatever other assemblages have in that particular nation-state claimed to speak on behalf of 'the Crown'. Just to give one example: in Spain, a country that (unlike Canada) has since the 1870s experienced two republics and two dictatorships, but (like Canada) is currently headed by a monarch, there is a sharp distinction between the monarchy and his 'Casa Real' (royal household) on the one hand, and 'the state' on the other. A public prosecutor would no more think of invoking 'Rex' to prosecute than he/she would think of referring to him- or herself as 'una Corona'. By contrast, in Canada, the federal government often appears, especially in litigation contexts, as 'The Queen in Right of Canada'. And when playing the role of respondent in a criminal appeal, the state appears not as 'the People' or as 'the Department of Public Prosecutions' but rather as 'Her Majesty the Queen'.

Federalism complicates an ontology of sovereignty that was already, in the purely domestic English context, rather fuzzy. Canadian provincial governments too are often referred to as 'the Crown' and/or as 'the Queen in Right of Ontario', or 'the Queen in Right of British Columbia', etc. Complicating matters, the usage is not consistent: governments also appear in court as 'The Attorney General of Canada' or 'the Attorney General of Ontario', with lawyers consulted by the authors about usage dismissing the inquiry as an unimportant technicality (Riles 2005; Valverde 2009).

This semiotic fluidity could lead to the conclusion that the term 'the Crown' is a decorative anachronism of no real legal consequence. In some contexts that is true. However, in the context of aboriginal rights claims, the Crown has been recently revived and reinvented, by aboriginal legal writers as well as by courts (Borrows 2010; Henderson 2009), and the network studied here – that linking 'the honour of the Crown' doctrine to the notion that 'the Crown wears many hats'– forms an important part of this 'invention of tradition' (Hobsbawm and Ranger 1975).

The honour of the Crown is not mentioned in the Canadian constitution. It is not found in Acts of either the old imperial or the current Canadian Parliament, and it makes only the most fleeting of appearances in the common law. This latter point is important: whereas laws and norms about frankly modern Canadian legal inventions (official bilingualism, multiculturalism) are based strictly on statutes and on the written 1982 Constitution, aboriginal law in general and this doctrine in particular conspicuously lack black-letter support. In the absence of contemporary statutes, creative readings of the common law have been used by judges and by legal scholars attempting to find legal footholds for aboriginal rights claims. Aboriginal title, for example, was for many years viewed as justified by old English law concerning certain feudal forms of land tenure (see McNeill 1989, a text often cited by the Canadian Supreme Court); this anachronistic but useful recycling of pre-capitalist land law is not unique, since other pre-modern bits of law have also been creatively repurposed.

One case that has been cited as a precedent for current views on the honour of the Crown is Lord Coke's decision in a 1613 dispute with the Sherlock Holmesian name of 'The Case of the Churchwardens of St. Saviour's Southwark'. Here, Coke said that if a royal grant of interests in land can be read two different ways, and one would render the grant void, then the other meaning should be chosen, for the King should not be imputed with the intent of making a void grant (10 Co. Rep. 66b, 77 ER 1025). This is a pragmatic and limited judgment on a purely private matter: but the act of citing it (alongside another, even less obviously relevant case, Roger Earl of Rutland's Case (1608), 8 Co. Rep. 55a, 77 ER 555) creates an atmosphere of antiquity and continuity that, like so much incense, acts to conceal the novelty and the very specific political-historical purpose of the doctrine. The current deployment of ancient doctrines and cases with names such as 'the Churchwardens of St. Saviour's Southwark' works, like incense, to infuse proceedings with an air of mysticism. And switching to the mystical temporality of 'the Crown' is useful to aboriginal interests precisely because the logic of ordinary, everyday blackletter law rarely works in favour of aboriginal peoples. One of the many Canadian fans of the honour of the Crown doctrine, Saskatchewan Treaty Commissioner David Arnot, tellingly states that by 'resurrecting' (his words) the ancient doctrine by which the Crown must be assumed to always already harbour nothing but honourable intentions, the Canadian Supreme Court is appealing to 'a standard of fair dealing that stands *above and outside* the black-letter law' (Arnot 1996: 341, emphasis added).

When the honour of the Crown was first resurrected by the Supreme Court, it was largely bound up with the concept of fiduciary duty, a doctrine which recognises that when the Crown (i.e. the state) undertakes discretionary control in relation to a specific aboriginal interest, it assumes equitable obligations enforceable in the courts. A fiduciary is always under an obligation to act honourably, and so the honour of the Crown was initially seen as merely an aspect of its fiduciary obligations. In *R. v. Sparrow* – the first modern constitutional aboriginal rights case in which the honour of the Crown was invoked – the Supreme Court held that 'the honour of the Crown is at stake in dealings with aboriginal peoples. The special trust relationship and the responsibility of the government vis-à-vis aboriginals must be the first consideration in determining whether the legislation or action in question can be justified [notwithstanding that it infringes aboriginal rights]' ([1990] 1 SCR 1075 at para. 73). Subsequently, in *R. v. Van der Peet*, Lamer CJ suggested that the duty to act honourably was grounded in the government's fiduciary duty: 'The Crown has a fiduciary obligation to aboriginal peoples *with the result* that in dealings between the government and aboriginals the honour of the Crown is at stake' ([1996] 2 SCR 507 at para. 24, emphasis added).

It was not until its 2002 decision in *Wewaykum Indian Band* that the Court began to separate honourable duties from legal fiduciary obligations: the 'need to uphold the "honour of the Crown"' is only 'somewhat associated with the ethical standards required of a fiduciary in the context of the Crown and Aboriginal peoples', Justice Binnie stated, for the court. And in *Haida Nation v. British Columbia (Minister of Forests)*, [2004] Chief Justice McLachlin, writing for the Court, effectively reversed the formulation set out by Chief Justice Lamer. The honour of the Crown is now understood to be the *source* of legal fiduciary obligations: 'The honour of the Crown gives rise to different duties in different circumstances. Where the Crown has assumed discretionary control over specific Aboriginal interests, *the honour of the Crown gives rise to a fiduciary duty*' (at para. 18, emphasis added).

By resituating the Crown's honour over and above – and prior to – its fiduciary obligations, the Court is able to transcend the limitations of black-letter law. It might seem that by resurrecting the feudal idea of the Crown as essentially honourable Canadian judges were grasping at legal straws, but there were good reasons to try to find ways to address historical injustice, over and above fiduciary law. First, despite its progressive effects – and notwithstanding the Supreme Court's repeated assertions to the contrary– the doctrine of fiduciary duty, based on the trust-like relationship between aboriginal peoples and the Crown, carries more than a whiff of older colonial notions of 'Indians' as childlike and primitive 'wards of the Crown'. Moreover, as a practical matter, fiduciary duty is firmly bounded both temporally and jurisdictionally. In regard to temporality, since breach of fiduciary duty is a claim in equity, it is subject to the equitable defence of laches – which requires that a claimant act diligently in prosecuting his or her claim, even though for much of Canadian history aboriginal nations were materially and legally prevented from pursuing their rights in court. In addition, claims for breach of fiduciary duty can also be subject to statutes of limitations. Jurisdictionally, the government's assumption of control over aboriginal interests must be legally established before any trust-like obligation will be recognised, and since 'Indians, and lands reserved for the Indians' fall within the powers assigned exclusively to the federal government by the Constitution Act 1867, fiduciary duty attaches only the federal and not the provincial Crown. As we shall see, once it is unmoored from the law of fiduciary duty, the honour of the Crown exceeds both the temporal and jurisdictional bounds of black-letter law. The network that produces the honourable Crown, in other words, is one that lives and has effects in the material world of aboriginal communities, but one that simultaneously escapes, to some extent, ordinary, worldly temporal and spatial limits.

Mystical temporality and jurisdictional expansion

Importantly, it is never clear in the legal sources whether the Merlin-like entity that allows judges to leap above and outside of 'black-letter' law while still speaking law is the Crown itself or only its honour: the phrase 'the honour of the Crown' is used as if it were a single word. But however vague its ontology might be, the temporality of the Crown's inherent honour is not in doubt: it is the quasi-sacred temporality of the king's second body. As a recent article by Lior Barshack puts it, immanent sovereignty is a here-and-now entity embodied in a particular group or person and engaged in governing social relations: but transcendent sovereignty, which unites generations dead and unborn with the current generation in a single 'communal' (not merely collective) body, is 'outside the social' (Barshack 2009: 554). And the transcendent sovereignty of the communal *ecclesia* or Crown exists not in clock time but in 'a mythical time' (ibid.: 559).

It is the sacred temporality of the 'sacred communal body' (ibid.: 556), functioning as an actor in its own right, that enables judges to greatly extend the reach and the scope of the idea that governments owe fiduciary and quasi-fiduciary duties to aboriginal peoples. The mystical temporality of the Crown's honour has been used to supersede and trump the temporal limitations that constitute ordinary law. In the most recent relevant case, concerning the Métis Federation of Manitoba's complaint about the half-hearted performance of an 1870 solemn Canadian government promise of 1.4 million acres of land, the Supreme Court innovatively decided that the Métis claim, despite being more than 100 years late, was not barred by statutes of limitations (*Manitoba Metis Federation Inc. v. Canada (Attorney General)*, 2013 SCC 14). While an action for breach of fiduciary duty – had it been made out – would have been statute-barred, a claim for a declaration that the Crown had not acted honourably in carrying out its solemn promise to the Métis was not so constrained. Reasoning from the uncontroversial premise that statutes of limitations cannot prevent the courts from issuing declarations on the constitutionality of legislation, the majority held that '[b]y extension, limitations acts cannot prevent the courts from issuing a declaration on the constitutionality of the Crown's conduct' (para. 135) – and in particular on whether that conduct was in accordance with the constitutional principle of the honour of the Crown. How the honour of the Crown became a 'constitutional principle' rather than a mere guide to statutory and treaty interpretation will be addressed below, but here we need only note that the majority concluded that the courts, as guardians of the constitution, 'cannot be barred by *mere statutes* from issuing a declaration on a fundamental constitutional matter' (para. 140, emphasis added). The majority further concluded (against what the lower courts had found) that the Métis action was also not barred by the equitable doctrine of laches, which requires that claims in equity – such as breach of fiduciary duty – be prosecuted without delay.

The legal work performed by the supra-statutory and thus supernatural temporalisation of the Crown's honour did not escape the eagle eyes of the two judges who dissented in the Manitoba Métis case. They complained that: 'This Court has never recognized a general exception from [temporal] limitations legislation for constitutionally derived claims' (para. 254). The dissenters also expressed a worry that if courts are seen to hitch a ride on the magic carpet of the Crown's honour in order to open up centuries-old deals and disputes that normal law cannot address, this will retroactively open up history through reparations claims made by groups well beyond the traditional 'Indians' to whom fiduciary duties are owed. If groups are allowed to dig up evidence of old injustices, in the expectation that the usual legal barriers to reparations claims will be lowered or shaken, the two dissenters warn that 'this has the potential to open the court system to a whole host of historical social policy claims' (para. 265). As Walter Benjamin put it in a different but apposite context, 'even the dead shall not be safe' (Benjamin 1967: 255) from being pursued by justice seekers.

Before the Métis Federation case was decided in 2013, the key judgment on the honour of the Crown was the previously mentioned case of *Haida Nation* v. *British Columbia (Minister of Forests)* [2004]. The Haida Nation went to court to prevent the provincial government from giving out generous logging licences to forestry companies working in the old-growth Pacific coast forests on unceded Haida territory. Because of the policies concerning colonial settlement and aboriginal title in British Columbia, the Haida were never sought out for treaties. They therefore did not have any agreement with the federal government that might engage the Crown's fiduciary obligations. Although the Haida had maintained their claim to Haida Gwaii (the 'Queen Charlotte Islands') for over 100 years, they had not yet established aboriginal title in the courts. As a result, the aboriginal interest in question was insufficiently specific to give rise to fiduciary duty let alone to ground a claim for breach. The Supreme Court recognised that the Haida claim to title to Haida Gwaii was strong, but also that it was complex and would take 'many years' to prove (para. 7). Without a land cession treaty (which would have recognised the pre-existing aboriginal interest in land) and without established aboriginal title, the Haida Nation's claims had little foothold in law – at least up until 2004. But in the precedent-setting decision in *Haida*, the Supreme Court acknowledged that while fiduciary duty did not exist, the 'honour of the Crown' doctrine demands that where the Crown has knowledge of a credible but unproven aboriginal right or title claim, it has a corresponding duty to consult and if necessary to accommodate aboriginal interests (Newman 2009; Morellato 2008). 'The government's duty to consult with Aboriginal peoples and accommodate their interests is *grounded in the honour of the Crown*. The honour of the Crown is always at stake in its dealings with Aboriginal people . . .' (*Haida* para. 16).

Canada's Aboriginal peoples were here when Europeans came, and were never conquered. Many bands [tribes] reconciled their claims with the sovereignty of the Crown through negotiated treaties. Others, notably in British Columbia, have yet to do so ... The honour of the Crown requires that these rights be determined ... This in turn, requires the Crown, acting honourably, to participate in processes of negotiation. (Para. 25)

Thus the honour of the Crown functions to impose duties on government even in the absence of – or prior to the establishment of – the kind of specific aboriginal interest that would be sufficient to give rise to a fiduciary obligation.

Further, and hugely important from the point of view of forestry and mining, key issues in those parts of Canada with significant aboriginal populations, the Supreme Court held that the duty to consult and accommodate, which flows from the honour of the Crown, lies not only on the federal but also provincial governments/Crowns – bodies to which the fiduciary obligations of aboriginal law do not attach. This was a marked departure from the long-standing view that as Canada became independent, it was the federal government, exclusively, that inherited the imperial Crown's treaty and other obligations to 'Indians'. For over a century, provincial governments had refused to deal with aboriginal claims, whether based on treaties, other documents or the common law, referring all of these to the federal government. In 2004, however, the Court disposed in three brief paragraphs of the argument advanced by the Province of British Columbia that any duty to consult or accommodate rests solely with the federal government (paras 57–8). Thus provincial governments, which sometimes appear in court as 'the Queen in Right of British Columbia' etc., now also have a legal responsibility to consult and to accommodate aboriginal interests. Since provinces, in Canadian law, have exclusive jurisdiction over natural resources, the jurisdictional expansion of the honour of the Crown doctrine to include the provinces was a hugely important win for aboriginal communities attempting to both regulate natural resource development and share in its benefits.

To the two expansionary moves performed in *Haida Nation*, the Court very recently added a third, one which underscores both the mystical temporality and the jurisdictional fluidity of the honour of the Crown. As we have discussed, the Haida could not rely on the doctrine of fiduciary duty because their interest – although unquestionably aboriginal – had not yet been legally recognised. In the 2013 *Manitoba Métis Federation* case, the Métis were equally unable to rely on the doctrine of fiduciary duty, but for effectively the opposite reason: their interest was abundantly well-established in law – indeed, enshrined in the Manitoba Act, which forms part of the Canadian constitution – but was insufficiently 'aboriginal'.

The Métis nation emerged over many generations in the prairies from marriages between the largely French-speaking Hudson's Bay Company personnel and aboriginal women from the late 1600s onward. Since they did not exist before contact, the Métis obviously have no 'pre-contact' ancient hunting and gathering practices, those practices being what is primarily protected as 'aboriginal rights'. The Métis therefore could not deploy the symbolic and legal resources of original occupation, tradition and time immemorial that are the usual currency of aboriginal rights litigation. But aboriginal people, in official Canadian discourse, do include First Nations, Inuit (formerly 'Eskimo') and Métis, and for the majority of the Supreme Court this classification trumped the Métis' inability to claim original occupation and thousand-year-old, pre-contact custom.

In *Manitoba Métis* the lower courts and the numerous government lawyers involved at all levels of appeal had worked hard to emphasise the modernity and private property habits of the Métis, a move that by denying their aboriginality helped to defeat their claim that fiduciary obligations were engaged and had been breached. As the Attorney General of Canada's brief put it, 'in 1870 the Métis already had a history of private land-holding which included buying and selling land' (factum of the Attorney General of Canada, para. 128), and being good Lockean individuals, should not be granted the benefit of either fiduciary obligations or of those duties of honour the Crown imposes on itself when thinking about its vulnerable primitive subjects. The Attorney General of Manitoba similarly stated that 'the Métis at Red River [now Winnipeg] did not live a communal lifestyle. They owned land on an individual basis' (factum of the Attorney General of Manitoba, para. 6). But the Supreme Court, while not directly challenging the sharp distinction between modern, private-property owning Métis and 'primitive', perpetually collective 'Indians' – indeed, while agreeing that the evidence failed to establish pre-existing communal aboriginal title held by the Métis – nevertheless concluded that a promise of land embodied in the 1870 federal law that founded the province of Manitoba qualified for the honourable treatment. Again, we see the honour of the Crown being put to work where black-letter law falls short.

Thus the mystical temporality that has long attached to 'the Crown' as the transcendent dimension of monarchical sovereignty is no mere medieval anachronism: it can become an important legal resource that enables judges to reach legally innovative results when black-letter law has come to be seen as either inadequate in its content or overly limited in its jurisdictional and temporal reach.

The honour of the Crown in the interpretation of treaties and constitutional provisions

From its modern inception in the 1960s until around 2000, the honour of the Crown was essentially a principle used to interpret treaties. As mentioned earlier, in the 1613 Churchwardens case, Coke had stated that when interpreting ambiguous language contained in a royal grant in interest in land, the text should not be read in such a way as to negate the grant. This rather slim precedent was invoked to support the argument that in interpreting the meaning of treaties signed long ago, any ambiguity as to the intentions of the parties should be resolved in favour of the aboriginal peoples involved – not because of contemporary rights doctrines but rather because the Crown's honour is 'at stake', and the Crown's honour demands a generous interpretation.

The earliest example of this use of the doctrine is the dissenting judgment of Supreme Court Justice Cartwright in *R. v. George*, [1966] SCR 267, which arose when an aboriginal man shot two ducks on lands that had been reserved to the Chippewa (Ojibway) pursuant to treaty as hunting grounds. The birds were shot out of season, contrary to the Migratory Birds Convention Act. Holding that the Act should not be permitted to extinguish rights guaranteed by treaty, Justice Cartwright noted:

> In St Saviour's Southwark (Churchwardens) [(1613), 10 Co. Rep. 366 at 66b and 67b, 77 ER 1025 at 1027] case, Lord Coke said: 'If two constructions may be made of the King's grant, then the rule is, when it may receive two constructions, and by force of one construction the grant may according to the rule of law be adjudged good, and by

another it shall by law be adjudged bad; then for the King's honour, and for the benefit of the subject, such construction shall be made that the King's charter shall take effect, for it was not the King's intent to make a void grant, and therewith agrees Sir J. Moleyn's case in the sixth part of my reports.'

And since then courts have often used the notion of the Crown's inherent honour to read statutes in a more generous spirit than the letter of the law or historians' research into the circumstances of various statutes might suggest.

We now turn to the key case in regard to the honour doctrine's role in treaty interpretation – a decision arising out of an Indian man's supposedly illegal sale of 463 pounds of eels caught out of season and without a government licence: *R. v. Marshall*, [1999] 3 SCR 456. Donald Marshall's eels acquired a deep historical significance as soon as he was charged because the fishing took place in an area famous for the major battles between the English and the French during the 1760s Seven Years' Wars that, as every schoolchild knows, were the most important moment in the formation of the white Canadian nation-state. On top of that rather heavy weight of history, Donald Marshall too was no ordinary person; he was the hero of a very long story of wrongful prosecution and wrongful conviction that had begun when as a 17-year-old he was charged with murder by police officers who turned out – as discovered by the subsequent major government inquiry into the conviction – to be incompetent and racist.

Therefore, when the case appeared in the Ottawa courtroom, it was not a little tale of eels and regulations: it was a truly monumental assemblage of several key events in Canadian history and several equally significant processes in Canadian criminal justice. The 1990 Royal Commission into Marshall's criminal conviction is not mentioned in the later eels case, but it undoubtedly played a role, if only unconsciously, as the Supreme Court deliberated on the specific matter at hand, namely the proper meaning of a 1760 treaty between the Mi'kmaq and the English Crown.

In 1760, the English had just defeated the French army at Louisbourg and expelled the French-speaking population of Nova Scotia (the Acadians), many to Louisiana. After that victory but before the 1763 Treaty of Paris, the English military powers signed a treaty with the Mi'kmaq, a populous and well-organised nation that had long allied with the French Crown. The specific issue before the Court was the relatively minor question of what the treaty 'really' said about how fish caught by the Mi'kmaq were to be sold and to whom. But the treaty was only incidentally about fish; it was really about securing British sovereignty in the northern part of North America, just as the thirteen colonies were getting restless, by establishing and regulating bonds between aboriginal nations, including those formerly allied with the French, and the new English colonial authorities. In his erudite judgment, Justice Binnie, speaking for the court, provides a very lengthy account of the military and political context in 1760–1, and uses this to reach the conclusion that if the treaty had been merely a commercial document regulating fishing it would have to be interpreted very narrowly, thus upholding Marshall's illegal fishing conviction; but since it was a political document of some importance in the formation of Canada, a 'narrow' interpretation was not adequate. The eels thus disappeared into the background, or rather became an emblem of a key, founding moment in the history of white Canada: the replacement of the French Crown of Nouvelle France by the British Crown.

Avoiding any consideration of the nature of the French Crown, by consistently using the term 'Crown' to mean only the imperial government, Justice Binnie concluded that the honour of 'the' Crown – its current honour – requires the court to read the treaty non-technically – that is, 'above and outside black-letter law' (to reiterate the words of Saskatchewan's David Arnot). A technical legalistic interpretation is

> not consistent with the honour and integrity of the Crown ... This was no commercial contract. The trade arrangement must be interpreted in a manner which gives meaning and substance to the promises made by the Crown. In my view, with respect, the interpretation adopted by the courts below left the Mi'kmaq with an empty shell of a treaty promise. (Para. 52)

(The 'empty shell' phrase is a reference to the St Saviour churchwardens case, of course.) Binnie thus concludes that whatever the words of the treaty might say, 'certain assumptions are therefore made about the Crown's approach to treaty making', an approach which has to be assumed to be 'honourable'. The Crown's inherent honour requires courts to be 'flexible' in 'treaty interpretation' (para. 14).

For most of the very long, impeccably learned judgment, Binnie emphasises the positive outcomes that result when the Crown is assumed to be honourable. This distracts attention from the sociopolitical fact that if beneficial effects arise out of a quasi-chivalric self-imposed duty that sovereigns take on precisely because they are all-powerful, the long-term effects are perhaps not wholly beneficial to the subjects involved.

But interpreting the words of written treaties is only one purpose or function of the 'honour' doctrine. Courts, especially the Supreme Court, have invoked the Crown's inherent honour when interpreting the very terse words of section 35 of the 1982 Constitution: 'The existing aboriginal rights ... are hereby recognized and affirmed.' The Supreme Court, in dealing with the indeterminacy created by the gnomic sentence that constitutes the whole of the aboriginal rights content of the Constitution, has stated that 'the purpose' of section 35 is 'reconciliation' – a very capacious term used to perform all manner of political manoeuvres, but which in the cases being discussed here usually means the reconciliation of Canadian (Crown) sovereignty with some collective rights for aboriginal peoples, rights which are sometimes substantive (fishing out of season for food purposes) and sometimes merely procedural.

There is a vast literature on 'reconciliation' and its conflicting Canadian meanings which cannot be canvassed here. For present purposes, all that needs to be said is that the version of 'reconciliation' pioneered in South Africa has had but small purchase in official Canada.[2] In the cases under consideration here, 'reconciliation', purged of its potential to challenge colonial violence, is, as it were, itself reconciled with the Crown's inherent virtue. 'It is a corollary of s. 35 that the Crown act honourably in defining the rights it guarantees' (*Haida Nation*, para. 20). Section 35 is thus described not as a human-rights style clause empowering the previously oppressed, but rather as a statement whose logical corollary, apparently, is that the Crown must act decently not because of international human rights norms but because of its internal, self-imposed honour.

A final point in the discussion of the honour of the Crown doctrine is that, curiously, a phrase that highlights the most visible symbol of sovereignty (the actual crown) acts precisely to blackbox sovereignty. It should be noted that whenever, in the legal materials before them, appeal court judges see statements that challenge Canada's sovereignty, they do not directly confront or challenge them. The only time the Supreme Court has had to directly address the question of sovereignty is in the 'Reference' on whether Quebec could legally move to separate from Canada. And it is interesting that this 'Quebec Secession Reference' – which decided that Quebec could take steps toward separation only if a substantial majority of the population supported this in a referendum with a 'clear' question – makes only the briefest cameo appearances in aboriginal law cases. Aboriginal legal materials do sometimes challenge sovereignty, usually in offhand remarks that are not integral to the argument: but such implicit claims are consistently ignored by judges, with the same manoeuvres that they use to ignore implicit sovereignty claims embedded in such Canadian linguistic conventions as calling the legislature of the province of Quebec 'the national assembly', as is done routinely in both law and in media accounts of Quebec politics.

A good example of how sovereignty is and is not contested at the same time is the text produced by the Assembly of First Nations for the Manitoba Métis Federation case, which, in its very first paragraph, states that the fundamental goal of current Canadian aboriginal law is the reconciliation of the pre-existence of aboriginal societies with the '*de facto* sovereignty of the Crown' (para. 1). By adding 'de facto', the organisation leaves a door open for a future challenge, but the 'de facto' does not do any work at all in the document at hand, and if the Court took any notice of it, the record is silent.

If Canada's sovereignty is now largely black-boxed, this was not always so. The Prime Minister who was responsible for the 1870 creation of the province of Manitoba and who made the promise of 1.4 million acres of land to the Métis, John A. Macdonald, did not black-box sovereignty, at least not in private correspondence. Writing to his beleaguered local representative, who had been scared off and prevented from entering Winnipeg by an imposing group of armed Métis, he warned his officials that if he declared sovereignty prematurely and was once more unable to actually take possession, the locals, who were majority Métis, had the legal right to set up whatever government they wanted: 'In such a case, no matter how the anarchy is produced, it is quite open by the law of nations for the inhabitants to form a government *ex necessitate* ... and such a government has certain sovereign rights by *ius gentium* ...' (letter from Macdonald to would-be lieutenant governor Macdougall, quoted in Bumsted 1966: 92).

The Métis materials (including briefs from the Métis organisations of Alberta and Ontario) in the Manitoba Métis case do not cite Macdonald's interesting letter, but they consistently use the word 'nation', as discussed in detail below. This is not anachronistic: the Métis called themselves a nation in 1870 (Morton 1957). But whether the Métis were then or are now a nation was not directly addressed by the court. Put in its larger political context, then, all the talk about the Crown's honour requiring governments to negotiate and requiring lower courts to interpret treaties and constitutional provisions generously and flexibly has the effect of distracting attention from the fundamental issues of jurisdiction and sovereignty.

We thus see how in the line of cases discussed here, the current Supreme Court, despite being fully aware of all manner of challenges to sovereignty, from uprisings by Mohawks in Eastern Canada, to Quebec separatism, to the reminders, such as the phrase 'de facto sovereignty', scattered throughout the materials, repeatedly invokes the image of the eternally honourable Crown to somewhat extend aboriginal rights – while simultaneously performing the amazing political feat of black-boxing sovereignty itself. The judicial action performed here is similar to what a magician does to distract the crowd's attention from the real trick, but the difference is that the magician fully intends to deceive the audience, whereas in the case of Canadian judges, there is no deception: the refurbishing and polishing and retrofitting of the Crown being achieved in these cases is there in the texts for all to see.

Another example of the black-boxing of sovereignty is found in a grandiose phrase in the Métis Federation judgement about a 'rift in the national fabric'. Discussing this will also illuminate one problematic effect of using the honour of the Crown as a tool of justice, namely that its inherent indeterminacy then makes any remedy the court might order equally indeterminate.

Like other sacred entities, the honour of the Crown is, if not infinite, indeterminate, in terms of time, space and scope: therefore, it does not generate any specific remedies, as ordinary, black-letter law does. Courts – or the Supreme Court, to be specific: lower courts would not take such legal leaps – can ride on the spatio-temporally powerful magic carpet that is the Crown's honour to tell the government that it is obligated to treat aboriginal groups, all aboriginal groups and not just 'Indians', differently (again, mainly procedurally, since the 'duty to consult' does not necessarily result in greater material resources for the aboriginal people in question than they would have obtained by non-legal means). And addressing the question of why the government of the day – today's 'Crown' – should be obligated to do things not contained in any treaty and not arising from the law of fiduciary duty, the answer given is that the Crown of today, judges feel, has to make an effort to repair 'the ongoing rift in the national fabric' (*Manitoba Métis*, para. 140) that the history of aboriginal–white relations has created.

The phrase 'ongoing rift in the national fabric' here is telling. In regard to temporality, the word 'ongoing' moves the case into a supra-legal as well as supra-historical register. From the black-letter law perspective, if there was a rift or a historic injustice, that rift is firmly located in the past – specifically, the years after 1870, when the federal government surveyed the land in question and proceeded to distribute the interest in the land to young Métis who may or may not, depending on who one believes, have been fairly treated. But from the sacred perspective of claims to a justice that is beyond written law (Derrida 1992), any shady activity by governments long past can suddenly flash up in today's present, as Walter Benjamin famously put it (Benjamin 1967): the fabric of today's nation-state can thus be said to be still torn.

But while addressing the usually suppressed issue of justice claims beyond law, the Supreme Court's phrase simultaneously denies the 'victims' of historic injustice the crucial status of 'nation'. In their written submissions to the Court, Métis groups (not just the Manitoba Métis Federation but the other Métis associations presenting intervener briefs) used the word 'nation' to refer to their own status as a distinct nation within a larger state. By 'nation' they mean either the Métis nation of Canada or the Métis nation of Ontario, Alberta, etc. In its decision, the Supreme Court quietly ignores these indirect claims of nationhood, and indeed contradicts them, insofar as the only 'national fabric' they acknowledge is the pan-Canadian one. The Manitoba Métis Federation was granted standing by the Supreme Court, with this legal victory being tantamount to recognising a collective interest that is more than the sum of the individual interests of the descendants of the original beneficiaries of the land grant, but while the federation is found to have standing (unlike in the lower courts) because 'the appellants advance a collective claim' (para. 44), the appellants are said to represent the Métis 'people' – not nation.

This dual move – going against the grain of black-letter law by recognising collectivities other than traditional, official 'Indian' bands or nations, while then subtly undermining the most important claim made by the Métis since the 1860s, that is their self-perception as a nation – is reiterated in slightly different ways in every judicial statement about the 'honour of the Crown'. The common denominator of all of the moves described in this chapter is that the current Canadian state now has obligations of sovereign/royal honour toward all aboriginal peoples, even the non-original Métis, that go beyond the texts of black-letter law, but the naming of those obligations simultaneously performs a kind of re-coronation of the very colonial sovereign whose servants caused so much harm to aboriginal peoples over the centuries.

A final point in regard to the onto-temporal dynamics of the entity named in the doctrine is that the doctrine is rarely actually named as such. As a matter of legal fact, it is the *doctrine* that obliges the government to take some measures to fix the tear in the national fabric. But when the words 'the doctrine of' are deleted by judges, and the words 'the honour of the Crown' are treated as both the grammatical subject and the motor force of law, a miraculous act, for which the word 'performative' is inadequate, is achieved.

Through judicial activity, then, the Crown's honour (ventriloquised by judges, of course) is said to be in the process of achieving the world-historical task of reconciling the sovereignty of the Canadian state with the acknowledgment of aboriginal rights. In keeping with previous case law, the Manitoba Métis decision states that 'the *ultimate purpose of the honour of the Crown* is the reconciliation of pre-existing Aboriginal societies with the assertion of Crown sovereignty' (para. 66, emphasis added; note the quote does not say 'the ultimate purpose of the doctrine of the honour of the Crown').

And if the reader cannot be sure which Crown is being talked about in this passage (the Ottawa government in 1870; the British Crown that gave the Hudson's Bay Company its charter in the seventeenth century; the current federal government, etc.), it is even more difficult to discern how 'it' could have a purpose. Clearly, it is *the doctrine* that has a purpose (as articulated by judges). But deleting the words 'the doctrine of' has the useful effect of bringing the spectre of transcendent sovereignty into the room and treating it as a powerful legal and political actor: 'The honour of the Crown thus recognizes the impact of the "superimposition of European laws and customs" . . .' (*Manitoba Metis*, para. 67). Similarly, we read in the earlier Haida case: 'The honour of the Crown also infuses the processes of treaty making and treaty interpretation . . .' (para. 19). And, also in *Haida*: "The honour of the Crown may require *it* to consult with and reasonably accommodate aboriginal interests pending the resolution of the [land] claim' (*Haida Nation*, para. 27, emphasis added). In this quote, the honour of the Crown is, as in the previous quotes, turned into an independent actor that appears not only in the courtroom but also on the political stage. But over and above the legal fetishism inherent in the deletion of the words 'the doctrine of', the word 'it' is a switch point through which the duties apparently incurred (without their knowledge) by long-dead imperial government officials are quietly imposed onto current government officials.

The government of the day is clearly in the present and it is composed of identifiable individuals, but 'the Crown' is both past and present and even future, and is both transcendent and immanent simultaneously. Governments are elected and fall, just as individual monarchs are born and die, but 'the Crown' remains self-identical and has no temporal limits, or at least none that judges have discerned. Its sacred temporality furthers the judges' ability to claim that it is always by definition honourable – despite the fact that 'the Crown', in the person of the Governor General, the military envoys signing treaties, the Ministry of Indian Affairs, etc., has certainly been known to sign documents that do not always reflect honourable intentions. But while particular actions by particular servants of the Crown can be acknowledged to be devious and/or illegal (cf. the 1984 *Guerin* decision), treaties and constitutions and laws, being signed by the Crown, can never be acknowledged to contain injustice. In order to preserve the doctrine of sovereign self-identity and eternal honour against all evidence, judges can only read statutes and constitutional texts creatively and/or against the grain.

The fact that the Canadian Crown has even more multiple personalities than the imperial Crown (due to federalism) is important here. One might think that in a federal country with a history of multiple European Crowns, courts would be a little more careful to distinguish one personification of the Crown from another, distinguishing Queen Victoria's emissaries from the later Ottawa government, the federal government in turn from 'the Queen in Right of Ontario', and so on. But the court, in these cases, speaks about the Crown in general (not any particular person or institution defined in space and time). Using the ambiguous word 'it' in phrases about how the honour of the Crown requires 'it' to do X or Y, the legal fiction of a unified and historically continuous monarchy whose essence in no way depends on the actions of officials or even particular monarchs is perpetuated (Kantorowicz 1957). Inventively, the sacred and timeless 'Crown' is given new life by the very same moves that also place aboriginal peoples in a much better bargaining position than they were in colonial times.

The elision of the words 'the doctrine of' thus allows judges to write as if, contrary to the frustrated complaints of Dicey and other modernisers, the Crown's honour were a free-standing actor – rather than a textual creation of recent Canadian Supreme Court judges. But the indeterminate, fluid, a-temporal logic of 'the Crown' in general has a defect, namely that it cannot produce particular remedies. In the Manitoba Métis Federation case the final result was 'declaratory relief' – that is a judicial statement that the federal government is obligated to negotiate but is not ordered to give back any land or provide any specific monetary or other compensation. This is in keeping with current jurisprudence and current governmental practice; consultations have proliferated but without the Crown ever giving up its ultimate grasp not only of jurisdiction but also of territory: even judicial decisions that demonstrate considerable sensitivity to the oral history have not resulted in declarations of aboriginal title (*Tsilhqot'in Nation* v. *British Columbia*, 2007 BCSC 1700).

The flowery language of the Crown's honour, therefore, has done a great deal to generate judicial texts that make current Canadian Supreme Court justices sound wonderfully post-racist, even post-colonial, but the same language has in practice done nothing but give a slight push to government–aboriginal negotiations. While the circumstances of First Nations, Métis and Inuit communities vary widely, there are many that experience desperate poverty and dysfunction. That it is not easy for those aboriginal nations, few of whose members go to law school or otherwise gain the tools necessary to meaningfully negotiate, to significantly change their situation by means of negotiations is not a matter within the purview of the courts.

The Crown wears many hats

A different black-boxing of sovereignty is achieved through a phrase used by Justice Ian Binnie in a 2002 decision: 'The Crown ... wears many hats' (*Wewaykum Indian Band* v. *Canada* [2002] 4 SCR 245 para. 96). This sounds innocuous, even meaningless. But when judges utter this curious sentence they are consistently speaking not about the Crown's duties toward aboriginal peoples but about the exact opposite: the fact that the same Crown that has honourable obligations towards a particular group, aboriginals, also has other legal and political responsibilities, such as promoting capitalist development. Thus: 'The appellant Crown argued that because the Crown wears many hats and represents many interests ...' it did not agree to the aboriginal people's demands (*Samson Indian Nation and Band* v. *Canada* [1998] 2 CNLR 199). And: '... the Crown is no ordinary trustee. The Crown wears many hats, and acts not only in the interest of Indians, but also...' (*Buffalo* v. *Canada* [1995] 3 CNLR 10). And more recently, 'Canada [here, the government's lawyer] says that the Crown wears "many hats" and is responsible to the whole of the Canadian population...' (*Ross River Dene Council* v. *Canada (Attorney General)* [2010] 1 CNLR 345).

Government lawyers have thus found it very useful to counter claims about trust-like obligations and honourable duties not by directly denying such special duties towards aboriginal peoples but rather by emphasising that the government is after all not 'an ordinary trustee' with a single duty, but rather an internally torn trustee who is perpetually distracted from its duties by having to also tend to all the other subjects of Her Majesty the Queen in Right of Canada, including corporations engaged in natural resource extraction and descendants of white settlers.

In the Manitoba Métis Federation materials, the phrase is wielded by the Attorney General of Canada's lawyers, in keeping with the cases just quoted. These lawyers argue that the 1870 law that founded the province of Manitoba and promised the children of the Métis 1.4 million acres of land was not meant to turn the Métis into a territory-bound collective aboriginal nation that would stay in place forever; the 1.4 million acres was a small part of the whole province, and in any case, having individual title (as distinct from Indian collective, unalienable title), the Métis were expected to either farm the land individually or, more likely, sell it to whites. 'It was not Parliament's intention to anchor the Métis to the ground in Manitoba, but to facilitate the orderly settlement of Rupert's land [the Hudson's Bay Company territory] ... and the construction of the transcontinental railway' (para. 106).

In other words, according the Crown's representatives, the Métis of 1870 had to be given a bone, but the bone chosen was fully alienable, and so not really aboriginal anyway, and the government that passed the bill into law was not primarily interested in the historic rights of the Métis but interested precisely in dispersing them so that they would not impede capitalist exploitation. All of these claims are certainly true, and accepted by the Court. But where the Attorney General of Canada (in the Métis case) then veers off in a direction that the majority of the Supreme Court rejected in that case is precisely when they quote their just-retired colleague Justice Binnie: 'The Crown wears many hats' (factum of the Attorney General of Canada, para. 123). The 'many hats' metaphor has the effect of directly undermining the obligations, which are specific to aboriginal peoples, contained in the 'honour of the Crown' phrase; it undermines the potentially beneficial effects of the honour of the Crown doctrine. However, the contradiction between one phrase and the other is subtly lessened in this legal document by the fact that the Attorney General of Canada does not speak in its own voice as the government but rather attributes the 'many hats' doctrine to none other than Justice Binnie, the author of the *Marshall* and other key judgments, i.e. the well-known pioneer of inventive readings of law furthering aboriginal interests.

That the undermining of the obligations imposed by the Crown's honour is done through a homey metaphor rather than serious law is by no means an accident. The trite metaphor creates a great swamp of discretion and indeterminacy that is very useful both to government representatives and to judges fearful of ordering specific remedies. The deadness of the metaphor prevents readers from asking themselves the uncomfortable questions: how many hats does the Crown/government actually wear? How do Crown representatives know when or how to pay attention to one duty rather than another? How many hats can possibly fit on a Crown – and does even a single hat not undermine the majesty and sovereignty of the venerable object?

Mining companies, forestry firms, individuals owning farming or residential property and municipalities are among the many candidates for 'hat' treatment, since they all have interests, legally protected interests, that are in direct conflict with the historic claims of aboriginal people. As seen in the first part of this chapter, the doctrine of the Crown's inherent honour has not been seen as necessitating any particular action by today's governments other than engaging in some form of negotiation and accommodation as seen above. And as just shown, this already fuzzy and easily evaded obligation has been further undermined, in a more direct manner, by an offhand, quite extra-legal metaphor drawing attention to the government's multiple responsibilities. ('Extra-legal' in the sense that we are not aware of any constitutional or legal texts authorising the use of the hats metaphor as a legal doctrine.)

Conclusion

In a recent work, Daniel Engster has argued that contrary to most (liberal) academic opinion, early state theorists in the sixteenth and seventeenth centuries did not so much replace the old medieval idea of divine right of kings by a secular idea as infuse the modern state with the old sacredness that had long attached to the person of the monarch. This move took place not just in Jean Bodin's France, he argues, but even in England, and not just in Hobbes' writings (Engster 2001).

Engster's argument sheds light on some of the peculiarities of current Canadian judicial discourse on 'the honour of the Crown', particularly the key role played in the judicial games analysed here by the sacred temporality of 'the Crown'. However, going beyond the rather static image of the state and of sovereignty found in political theory texts, including Engster's book, we have shown here that the sacred qualities and temporalities of the transcendent Crown can be creatively deployed by courts to push state officials to take responsibility for problems that lie more in the realm of justice and of politics than in the realm of black-letter law – with the brilliance of the judicial knowledge move lying in the fact that the very act of acknowledging past injustices, instead of furthering claims to new-old counter-sovereignties, only confirms the claim that the Crown that is the direct descendant of the British imperial Crown is not only legitimate but is positively virtuous and imposes duties on itself that go beyond those created by ordinary law.

'Canada is a young nation with ancient roots.' So says the Supreme Court of Canada in the opening words of its judgment in *Manitoba Metis Federation*. Although never explicitly identified, the ancient roots the Court has in mind appear to be the aboriginal nations whose presence long pre-dated the assertion of Crown sovereignty. Yet, as this chapter describes, other ancient roots continue to bear considerable fruit. As noted aboriginal legal scholar John Borrows observes in relation to a different area of aboriginal law, 'simply conjuring sovereignty is enough to change an ancient people's relationship with their land'; at the same time, the 'words that unlock sovereignty's power' are themselves 'of ancient origin. Practitioners of [sovereignty's] craft can summon a tradition that reaches deep into the past' (Borrows 1999: 558). Sovereignty, Borrows points out, is conjured through the 'cant of conquest', the chant of 'historic rites' (ibid.: 561) that continue to echo in contemporary jurisprudence. 'Sovereignty's incantation is like magic. Its mantra is "Aboriginal title is a burden on the Crown's underlying title"' (ibid.: 562).

The honour of the Crown – the honourable Crown – is conjured in much the same way. Despite the Supreme Court's insistence in *Haida Nation* that the honour of the Crown is 'not a mere incantation' (para. 16), it is the incantatory repetition of the phrase 'honour of the Crown' that makes it seem as if the doctrine which is in fact being elaborated there is merely being appealed to – though the lack of citations to standard common law sources or legal treatises suggests otherwise. Incantations and shaman-like moves by which eternal or at least temporally indeterminate entities magically set aside normal law's temporal limits are precisely what make this doctrine work. Indeed, the very claim that the doctrine is *not* an incantation is itself a symptom of judicial unease, just as the claim that 'I am not a racist' is often a sign that one is protesting too much.

One Victorian commentator whose reading of the 'Crown' was extremely influential was Walter Bagehot (Bagehot 1867). Bagehot's best-seller *The English Constitution* is the elaboration of a single, simple distinction: that between the 'efficient' and the 'dignified' parts of the constitution. The efficient parts, including the Cabinet and the bureaucracy, do pretty much all the governing, but Bagehot notes that this has not rendered the monarchy superfluous. 'The Queen is only at the head of the dignified part of the Constitution,' he says (2001: 9), but those dignified elements that 'excite and preserve the reverence of the population' (ibid.: 4) are very important, in all countries but especially in Britain – because 'of all nations in the world the English are perhaps the least a nation of pure philosophers' (ibid.: 42). The country would fall apart if the state apparatus (not Bagehot's word, obviously) were to rid itself of mystic elements. And among these elements, the monarchy is the most important one. In a statement that he meant to apply to the monarchy but we apply to the doctrine of the honour of the Crown, Bagehot concluded that 'its mystery is its life' (ibid.: 50). Indeed.

Notes

1. While there has been commentary on the work done by this metaphor, the metaphor itself has gone unremarked (see, for example, Luk 2013).
2. For example, on 11 June 2008 Prime Minister Stephen Harper stood in the House of Commons and apologised on behalf of the government for the treatment of aboriginal children in Indian Residential Schools. He said nothing, however, about the larger context of colonialism and violence that made such assimilationist and abusive practices possible.

References

Arnot, David (1996) 'The honour of the Crown', *Saskatchewan Law Review*, 60: 339.

Bagehot, Walter (1867 [rpt. 2001]) *The English Constitution*. Cambridge: Cambridge University Press.

Barshack, Lior (2009) 'Time and the constitution', *I-Con*, 7 (4): 553–76.

Benjamin, Walter (1967 [1940]) 'Theses on the philosophy of history', in *Illuminations: Essays and Reflections*, trans. Harry Zohn. New York: Schocken, pp. 253–64.

Borrows, John (1999) 'Sovereignty's alchemy: an analysis of *Delgamuukw v. British Columbia*', *Osgoode Hall Law Journal*, 37: 537.

Borrows, John (2010) *Canada's Indigenous Constitution*. Toronto: University of Toronto Press.

Bumsted, J. M. (1966) *The Red River Rebellion*. Winnipeg: Watson & Dwyer.

Derrida, Jacques (1992) 'Force of law: the "mystical foundation of authority"', in Drucilla Cornell and Michael Rosenfeld (eds), *Deconstruction and the Possibility of Justice*. New York: Routledge.

Dicey, Albert Venn (1902) *Introduction to the Study of the Law of the Constitution*, 6th edn. London: Macmillan.

Engster, David (2001) *Divine Sovereignty: The Origins of Modern State Power*. Princeton: Princeton University Press.

Henderson, James [Sake'j] (2009) 'Dialogical governance: a mechanism for constitutional governance', *Saskatchewan Law Review*, 72: 29.

Hobsbawm, Eric and Ranger, Terence (1975) *The Invention of Tradition*. Cambridge: Cambridge University Press.

Kantorowicz, Ernst (1975) *The King's Two Bodies: A Study in Mediaeval Political Theology*. Princeton: Princeton University Press.

Latour, Bruno (1987) *We Have Never Been Modern*. Cambridge, MA: Harvard University Press.

Latour, Bruno (2010) *The Making of Law: An Ethnography of the Conseil d'État*. Cambridge: Polity Press.

Luk, Senwung (2013) 'Not so many hats: the Crown's fiduciary obligations to Aboriginal communities since *Guerin*', *Saskatchewan Law Review*, 76: 1.

Levi, Ron and Valverde, Mariana (2008) 'Studying law by association: Bruno Latour goes to the Conseil d'État', *Law and Social Inquiry*, 33 (3): 805–25.

McNeill, Kent (1989) *The Common Law of Aboriginal Title*. Oxford: Oxford University Press.

Maitland, Frederic William [1908] (1961) *The Constitutional History of England*. Cambridge: Cambridge University Press.

Morellato, Maria (2008) *The Crown's Constitutional Duty to Consult and Accommodate Aboriginal and Treaty Rights*. West Vancouver, BC: National Centre for First Nations Governance.

Morton, W. L. (1957) *Manitoba: A History*. Toronto: University of Toronto Press.

Mundy, Martha and Pottage, Alain (2004) *Law, Anthropology and the Constitution of the Social: Making Persons and Things*, Cambridge Studies in Law and Society. Cambridge: Cambridge University Press.

Newman, Dwight G. (2009) *The Duty to Consult: New Relationships with Aboriginal Peoples*. Saskatoon, SK: Purich Press.

Riles, Annelise (2005) 'A new agenda for the cultural study of law: taking on technicalities', *Buffalo Law Review*, 54: 973–1033.

Riles, Annelise (2011) *Collateral Knowledge: Legal Reasoning in the Global Financial Markets*, Chicago Series in Law and Society. Chicago: University of Chicago Press.

Valverde, Mariana (2009) 'Jurisdiction and scale: legal "technicalities" as resources for theory', *Social and Legal Studies*, 18 (2): 139–57.

Woolford, Andrew (2006) *Between Justice and Certainty: Treaty Making in British Columbia*. Vancouver: University of British Columbia.

5

Providing the Missing Link: Law after Latour's Passage
Serge Gutwirth

[On] ne peut parler juridiquement sans être juge.
(Bruno Latour 2002: 273)

Ce qui m'intéresse ce n'est pas la loi ni les lois (l'une est une notion vide, les autres, des notions complaisantes), ni même le droit ou les droits, c'est la jurisprudence. C'est la jurisprudence qui est vraiment créatrice de droit : il faudrait qu'elle ne reste pas confiée au juges. Ce n'est pas le Code civil que les écrivains devraient lire, mais plutôt les recueils de jurisprudence.
(Gilles Deleuze 1990: 229–30)

Every time a person interprets some event in terms of legal concepts or terminology – whether to applaud or to criticize, whether to appropriate or to resist – legality is produced.
(Patricia Ewick and Susan Silbey 1998: 45)

Introduction

There are two ways to speak of the law, which, both for jurists and laypersons, coexist like an optical illusion. Either you see the naked young woman, or you see Freud's profile, and the passage from one view to the other is difficult to grasp or control. You're caught 'in' the one or 'in' the other. Similarly, law is evoked in two modes referring to two distinct significations. On the one hand law is referred to as an intertwined whole of statutes, rules and regulations, and thus, in one word, as norms (or 'normativity'), while, on the other hand, it can as well be understood as decision-making or as a practice that produces solutions. Thus: norms or solutions, that's the question.

While it is not clear how we have been mixing up and shifting from the one register to the other, we surely have. In fact – and maybe this is clearer in continental legal systems – we have long been confusing the 'sources of law' with 'law' as such. It is not Latour's least merit that his passage through law and legal studies has made it possible to spot and lift this confusion, and to start exploring and learning how to speak well of law. A reboot, as we might say today.

In this chapter, I want to show that this incessant switching between two ways to evoke or invoke the law is blurring our understanding of what the law does, what it produces, what it makes possible and how it is articulated to what is not law, to other practices or modes of existence. As a result, this chapter focuses upon the *role* of law much more than upon the *rule* of law, a shift of interest and sense which is induced not only by Bruno Latour's research on the law, but also by his startling project to anthropologically rethink, almost from scratch, what 'we', the moderns, actually have been, now that we have come to understand that we never have been modern. Latour already showed that the same sort of double invocation is not only at work when we speak about law, but he convincingly argued that it is also noticeable when we speak, for example, about science or religion (very clear in Latour 2013). As the Native Americans are supposed to have said about the white cowboys conquering their territories: 'Ils ont la langue fourchue' (Latour 2012). The moderns never (seem able to) say what they do.

In the first two sections of this chapter I intend to describe and distinguish the two voices in which we evoke the law, and to put the contrasts in the spotlight. In the third section I consider a number of consequences of the distinction as regards, firstly, the relation between law as an institution and law as a value (in the sense Latour gives to these words). Secondly, I try to explore what this means for the understanding of law in a democratic constitutional state, arguing that well describing the role of law might be more useful and needed than to continue to affirm its rule. Thirdly, I reconsider the notion of the 'force of law' in the light of the former. And fourth, finally and pursuing the same perspective, I address the question of the embodiment of law into technology.

I Law1:
setting and enforcing norms; law as normativity

I.1 'What is law?'

In response to this question, very often, not to say always, law is declared to be a whole of rules and norms – commandments, injunctions, permissions, prohibitions . . . – which are imposed and sanctioned by a society, typically a state, but indeed supra-, inter-, infra-national law do exist as well. From that perspective law is constituted of binding norms, directives, decrees and/or rules. That is, certainly in continental European legal systems, what introductory courses to law and legal manuals propose as a description or 'definition' of the law to their students and readers. Such rules can be deemed to exist in any sort of society or collective, a position that fuels the assumption of many researchers in comparative law that, although in very different forms and expressions, law exists everywhere, be it in its western, state-bound and written form, or in a different, often more informal, traditional, religious, oral and communal expression. But it is 'law' all the same.

I.2 'Formal' and 'material' sources of law

Next to this the same handbooks systematically enumerate the different 'formal sources' of the law, which are: legislation (or statute law), case law, legal doctrine (the authoritative writings of jurists), custom, general principles of law and, according to some, contracts. These 'formal sources' have a double character: on the one hand they point to the body of obligatory references that allow the emergence or making of law, while on the other hand they also indicate the tangible places where the current operational law formally expresses itself, can be 'found' and is read. Interestingly, this double sense of the notion of 'formal source' is paradoxical *ab initio* because in the first sense the sources aren't yet law, but rather condition law's emergence – the sources, here, are the mandatory tools and materials that will make the production of law possible – while in the second sense, the sources are deemed to already express the law and hence to contain it, to be it. The notion of 'formal sources' thus embodies a short circuit between two fundamentally different temporalities, i.e. those of a law that still has to become, and those of a law that is already there.

According to the legal handbooks, the 'formal sources of law' are indeed not levitating in a void, but emanate from what the manuals call the 'material sources of law'. The latter refer to all the factors and contexts that influence and substantiate the former. Culture, history, economics, agriculture, transportation, science, technology, industry, morals, religion and last but not least politics provide the 'contents' that will be translated into the formal sources and will be re-expressed through them. A statute making euthanasia for terminal patients possible under certain conditions can be considered as the expression of a decision by a competent representative political body, which in turn reflects a very complex compromise involving religious and ethical convictions, scientific knowledge, medical practice, cultural perceptions and technical conceptions of life and death, economic reasoning, etc. An exploration of the ecology of the 'material sources' linked to a particular Act of Parliament or to a ruling of a court, might indeed provide explanations about the alterations of the matter at stake in its trajectory from the 'societal' issue to its translation into a formal source, and then again to its processing by a judge when she decides a pertinent case.

The transformations of contents in the movement from the 'material sources' to the 'formal sources' – mainly legislation – and, if applicable, further to the rulings of judges and courts, are the object of interest of meta-juridical disciplines, as law-and-economics, legal sociology or philosophy of law. Are the statutes and judicial decisions correctly and fully translating the collective endeavours expressed through the formal sources? Are they meeting their stated goals? Do they produce perverse effects? Undoubtedly, these are interesting questions, but they do not alter the fact that judges deciding cases must restrain the scope of their hermeneutics to the hierarchically organised 'formal sources'. In fact, judges and courts have to suspend reliance upon the material sources, not to mention their own moral, political, cultural and economic views. This is why I have argued elsewhere that the context of law is constituted by its formal sources and not by its material sources (Gutwirth 2013).

I.3 Definitions and formal sources of law: strange loops

Three aspects particularly catch our attention in the preceding descriptions.

First, it appears that the institutionalised definitions of law are very vague and not really distinctive from morals, religious requirements, customs, largely accepted social conventions, political programmes and the explicit or implicit regulations and codes of, for example, sporting, ethnic, professional and/or cultural communities and associations, which also constitute rules and norms that effectively carry a certain degree of coercion and sanction. In fact, the proposed definitions barely contribute to extricate law's singularity.

Second, such accounts of law also encompass each of the enumerated sources of law on its own. Legislation and statute law are indeed 'norms', and so are customs and 'general principles of law', but the same is true not only for the whole of pre-existing case law from which regularities and trends and, thus, norms will be extracted, but also for the systematisations and prescriptions of the legal scholars, which also are – emblematically for the point made here – called 'doctrine' and 'authorities'. From this perspective, evocation of the law turns into the evocation of its sources.

Third, it remains surprising to see both jurists and profanes spontaneously associate law with legislative norms, while those are, be it on the inter-, supra-, infra- or just the national level, the result of negotiations and agreements between the members of representative bodies, between diplomats, between representative organisations and so on. Legislative processes are thus political processes, and statutes, treaties, collective compacts, regulations, decrees, etc. are a political and organisational outcome par excellence. And yet, still we are inclined to define law with reference to legislation and what the latter does: setting norms and objectives to meet, and organising things in conformity with these . . .

I.4 Legislation

Legislation is thus at least two things: on the one hand, it is the final result of a political decision-making process by a legislative body, and on the other, certainly in continental European law, it is also the most important and predominating source of law. That is to say that not only is it the concluding and conclusive expression of a choice of policy, but it is also an obligatory and constraining reference point for the judge, the legal practice and the legal enunciation (see below). This accounts for a very interesting articulation of politics and law, wherein the laying down and fixture of a decision in a legislative form is instantaneously relayed by its coming into existence as a legal source, which in turn (indeed, only if applicable) will be picked up by the legal practice.

That legislative acts exist in at least two different ways is, as a matter of fact, strongly expressed by the existence and role of the Legislation Section of the Belgian Council of State which must advise on legislative and statutory matters: this Section especially analyses and comments upon bills and proposed legislation from a legal perspective, with a view to anticipating how judges and judicial bodies will take hold of them, how they will legally interpret their terms and conditions. This Section, which also exists in the Dutch and French Councils of State, has precisely been called into being in order to worry about the consequences of the entanglement of the political or legislative regime and the legal one.

1.5 Axiomatic law

In the vast majority of cases the image of law is abstract and normative, or 'axiomatic'.[1] Cayla is clear when he notes 'une appréhension quasi unanime de l'univers juridique sous l'angle de la *norme*' (Cayla 1993: 3, original italics). Law, then, is conceived as a hierarchical whole of pre-existing binding rules, with legislation or statutes as their strongest expression, but nonetheless also including many sorts of other rules. All in all, this means that such a notion of law – Law1 – refers to what the (continental) lawyers understand as the legal sources.[2] In fact, the sources of law do include more norms than one might expect: in addition to the acts of legislative assemblies there are indeed subsidiary legislation and executive acts, but also 'general principles', rules distilled from precedents (especially where *stare decisis* applies), the systematisations detected and proposed by legal doctrine, rules in sports, customs . . . which turn out to be normative as well.

It is to this whole of norms that a person must turn if she is called to practise law, and such obligatory and hierarchically ordered reference to the pre-existing sources – where the qualifications and ensuing hermeneutics stem from – is indeed peculiar, because it implies that jurists work with means that are per se older than the facts[3] and thus that, for example, judges, who *must* decide, must do it with tools that may originate from another century (as is often the case in criminal law). This indeed explains not only the redundant litany that the law is always 'too late' and overtaken by the pace of developments in science and technology, in economy, (geo)politics, morals, etc., but also why this critique is so poorly aimed and totally misses the point.

I.6 Why is a constitution legal, after all?

As a totality of norms, Law1 is often, if not always, assumed to embody, convey or carry a worldview, a perspective on humans and their collectives, a project of society for its subjects. Even more, in a *Rechtsstaat*, Law1 seems to be the instance that is ultimately in charge of protecting and carrying such a Big Project on its shoulders, and of imposing and perpetuating it. In this sense, no doubt, the American Constitution is 'the supreme law of the land', the European Convention on Human Rights is a supreme law for the Member States of the Council of Europe as are the WTO treaties and through these the so-called 'laws' of the market for the world. Today, Law1 and especially constitutional law in this tonality (often as a remnant of colonialism) generally convey the ideal of a fair and just society, namely the liberal constitutional and representative democracy, of which the roots can be historically retraced in the simultaneous development – the *Gleichursprunklichkeit* – of democracy and the rule of law in the ancient Athenian *polis*.[4]

Law1 is thus intimately interwoven with government and governance, economy, power balances, geopolitics, ethics, religion, history – it carries, expresses and imposes the content and values of the material sources – but nonetheless, it remains persistently characterised as 'law'. The latter implies that Law1 must at least possess a 'legal dominant' but, remarkably, there are very little convincing arguments explaining where this 'legal colour' exactly comes from, or to clarify what then characterises Law1 as law. More bluntly: what is it that makes the American Constitution the supreme 'law' of the land, since it is the ultimate result of a long historical, political, religious and economic struggle for independence and it embodies the proclamation of the end of a colonial, arbitrary and absolutist reign and states (a compromise about) the high-level principles of the new organisation of the US? This is indeed not meant to diminish the role of the Constitution and the named principles, but only to raise the question of their 'legal' nature as such. Why would a document organising checks and balances between state powers, a division of powers between states and the federation, and recognising a number of human rights already be 'legal'? In Latourian terms, aren't we rather meeting a very high-level script [ORG] issued by a revolutionary collective [POL:ORG] that has the ambition to organise nothing less than the institutional and administrative governance of the USA and its people? Where is the distinctive legal 'touch'? Where is [LAW]⁵ here ?

If, more generally, *norms* are the core of law and thus not its 'source', how then to distinguish law from governance, regulation or (state) organisation? What I wrote about the Constitution can be extended to all legislation: a statute or a governmental decree/decision indeed organises things until a new one will be enacted, altering, superseding or replacing the former. Aren't statutes and decrees typical organising deeds? Don't they provide for multiple, sometimes overlapping, sometimes even conflicting frames that are meant to steer our actions and decisions? Aren't they influential role distributing scripts (that we are supposed, even obliged and assumed to know), which are again interconnected with another flurry of non-legislative scripts like interpersonal arrangements, labour rules, common projects and so on? In Latourian terms again: legislative processes [POL] produce pieces of legislation assumed to steer our conduct [POL:ORG]. And again: where then is [LAW]?

II law2:
fabricating links where they are missing, law as an experience

II.1 *'Who practises law?'*

When it comes to answering this question, the responses given take a completely different turn in comparison with the 'What is law?' entry. Now, they will invariably consist of an enumeration of legal professionals: judges, advocates, attorneys, public prosecutors, paralegals, the jurists in the legal services of enterprises and administrations, bailiffs, registrars and so forth, not the political representatives that populate the representative assemblies nor the members of bodies with legislative powers, but all those who are involved in the production not of rules but of decisions, among which the judges and the members of courts are the most emblematic examples.

From this perspective, hence, something becomes legal when grasped, seized, caught or subsumed by the singular regime of the legal enunciation, or, in other words, by the distinctive hermeneutics that characterises the legal approach. That does not necessarily mean that someone has studied law or is a legal professional, no, it is the mere 'entering' into the regime of the law that makes the difference: you become a legal practitioner, or literally, a jurist, because you (have to) abide by the constraints of the legal regime.

II.2 Anticipating what judges would do

Hence, a thing becomes legal when it is seized in a singular way, which is unmistakably framed or modelled by the constraints of a judge seizing that precise thing. Put differently, a thing becomes legal when it is processed or thought from a position that anticipates how a judge could or should do it. Justice Oliver Wendell Holmes Jr famously wrote as much in 1897 in the *Harvard Law Review*: 'The prophecies of what the judges will do in fact, and nothing more pretentious, are what I mean by the law' (Holmes 1897).

Hence – and this is no longer 'Holmesian'[6] – a person turns into a jurist when she is constrained to think as a judge: it is not a legal degree that makes the legal practitioner, but the mere fact that one thinks legally, i.e. as a judge. A person with a claim will, with the support of a lawyer or not, anticipate how the judge might cope with her claim, and will try to find the strongest way to make her case considering the constraints – the whole of *obligations* and *exigencies* – that 'hold' the judge, and thus the legal practitioner (cf. Stengers 1996, 1997 and 2014; see also Gutwirth et al. 2008).[7] This is the precise sense of the three mottos I have used to launch this chapter: the distinctiveness of law lies in the singular mode in which it seizes cases. In other words: everyone can practise law, everyone (who is called to do so) can become a legal practitioner, and that is, when she is moving or moved forward by the legal regime of enunciation with its many particular constraints and value objects, which have been so well described by Latour (2002) and that we will summarise later. But eventually this way of 'moving forward' and 'making the law' always – and it can't be said enough – amounts to anticipating how and what a judge or court would decide.[8] Once this happens, to switch to the Latourian idiom, the [LAW] preposition has been set, 'legality is produced' and the law starts to pass.

Clearly, *what* the judge will decide is never completely predictable, the only thing that is certain is *that* she will decide, which is precisely what we call 'legal certainty': the certainty that a judge will bring closure and stability, even if no one else does it, wants to do it or succeeds in doing it. This omnipresent possibility of law might explain why law paradoxically is both 'autochtonous' ('already there') and anticipatory ('not yet stated by a judge') (cf. Latour 2002). In other words: before the intervention of the judge one can anticipate how she will decide this case, and that will often be in the line of what the rules extracted from the sources of law – legislation, executive orders, former decisions, customs, etc. . . . – allow one to expect, but it is never a straightforward and purely deductive 'application'. In that sense, all cases are 'hard' and routine is the main enemy. However, the fact that the instauration, statement or the 'putting down' of the legal bond by a judge or court is *always an open possibility* generates a sense that, although anticipated, the law is always already there.

Henceforth, a thing starts to exist legally when it is comprehended in a way that anticipates how a judge could possibly seize and decide it under the given circumstances and claims. As Latour (2004) rightly observes: nothing that refers to the legal *institution* (cf. below) – a *codex*, togas or robes, official charges, authentic documents, court houses, registrars, lawyers and judges . . . – must already be present for the law come to life or into existence.[9] No, law's singularity is tied to its 'regime of enunciation' that we – Westerners – spontaneously recognise as such, much like we instantaneously recognise a sense or feeling of 'if' or 'but', 'blue' or 'cold': it is prepositional (Latour, especially 2004 and 2012, also McGee 2014: 124, both with references to the work of William James). It is, put differently (and in the sense that Isabelle Stengers gives to these concepts), constituted by the 'constraints' of the legal 'practice' (Stengers 1996 and 1997). Law is a particular 'mode of existence';[10] it is another world: it gives a legal existence to the things it seizes (Hermitte 1998). A car, a chair, words or a human become legal beings when, for one reason or another, they are 'seized' by the juridical forms and processed by the 'moulds' and ways of legal hermeneutics, or, to use an expression of Kyle McGee, when they get 'jurimorphed' (McGee 2015) by *whoever* – a legal specialist or professional or a lay person – is brought to do it. Or, in the words of Cayla, 'le signe auquel on reconnaît immanquablement le juriste reside avant tout dans sa façon de discourir sur le monde en assurant sa *traduction* [...] dans la grille conceptuelle des categories juridiques' (Cayla 1993: 4).

Every issue – the property of a good, the harm caused by speech, the treatment of a mentally ill person, the love of an animal, a foul play in soccer, the use of public transportation, human rights[11] ... – can remain untouched by law and hence stay non-legal forever, but when the need develops (e.g. when harm is not processed satisfactorily without a legal intervention), our civilisation provides for the legal mode, and that has been the case since the Roman age (Schiavone 2008; Latour 2002 and 2012). At a certain point, earlier or later depending on those concerned, but always knowing that eventually there is no other way to obtain a stabilised bond,[12] the protagonists might start being embraced by (or will embrace) the clef of the law, and start to think and act in anticipation of how a judge would cope with their issue and which hermeneutical and material steps should or should not be set in order to have the anticipated judge doing what comes the closest possible to their interests. Lawyers or advocates do indeed play a very important role here, since they will try to pre-structure and prepare the claims, means and files in order to build a *dispositif* and to set the scene in anticipation of the hermeneutical trajectories they wish the judge to take (and indeed the other parties will do the same[13]). But the 'entry' into the legal mode – its 'launching' ('l'envoi', Latour 2004) – definitely precedes their intervention: the mobilisation of lawyers by parties is already a consequence of this 'entry'; it is a next step in a possible trajectory. Indeed, a judge might be convinced by and confirm the qualificatory pretensions of one of the parties, implicitly disqualifying the other pretensions, but she might well also impose her own qualification (Cayla 1993: 12).

II.3 Topical law

Law2, then, provides for decisions/solutions under the form of judgments, where no other way or mode succeeded in making and respectively finding them. This is the pragmatism of the Roman *casus* rather than the Athenian political philosophy:[14] law as a practice, which again and again, case by case, is reactivated to produce, state or 'draw' the *vinculum iuris*. From this perspective, law2 is 'topical':[15] it produces solutions to cases through its regime of enunciation, its proper *conditions de félicité* and more concretely its '10 value objects', as they have been extracted and described by Bruno Latour in particular in the fourth chapter of *La fabrique du droit* (Latour 2002; see, further, McGee 2014, 2015; Audren and Moreau de Bellaing 2013; Van Dijk 2011). The legal approach then is characterised as well by distinctive operations, such as the testing of 'legal means', 'qualification' (below), 'distinguishing', 'subsumption', 'imputation'[16] and, finally, 'assignation'. Other aspects of law's singularity are also manifest, such as the 'detachment' of jurists coping with facts, their singular obligation to *hesitate*, to de-bind and re-bind, to reassemble and disassemble, to redo the hermeneutical loop again and again, until the issue is ripe for a decision, and thus for the law to be 'solemnly' stated or put down, for a *dictum*, a ver*dict*.

Typical for law2 is that the facts of a case will be read and interpreted in view of their *qualification* (Cayla 1993; Rigaux 1997; Latour 2002), an operation that is constrained by the tools the jurist has available for use. Jurists must seize (or 'subsumate' in Frenglish) the facts at stake with 'containers' or 'forms' they must derive from sources of law which are well known, at least so far as their enumeration goes:[17] the applicable legislation, the pre-existing case law, possibly with its different tendencies, the systematisations of the matter at hand by the legal doctrine (very often, the first step taken by professional jurists in continental legal practice), and more occasionally customary rules, the general principles of the law and 'equity'. Contrary to scientists, jurists do not want to learn from the facts, and neither do they want to produce knowledge about or put those to the test, no, the person called to practise law will first operate an intensive and repeated to and fro between the facts (generally the files in which they have been stated or archived, 'frozen', often in mandatory forms) and the named 'formal sources of law' (also texts, of statutes and of cases, and books) from which the optimal or best-fitting qualification for this case must be extracted (Latour 2004; Gutwirth 2010; Cayla 1993). Indeed, such a *demarche* cannot ever be confused with ordinary speech or 'straight talk', or be done routinely, since all cases, all sets of facts, are an appeal to the creativity (not in an artistic sense, but literally: the constraint to produce and thus 'create' a legal bond where it is disturbingly lacking) of the judges and their interpretive tools and techniques. As a consequence, the 'optimal fit' is never a given that should be found, unveiled or discovered, but it has to be fabricated or constructed through the process of hesitation, pondering and tinkering (so well described by the ethnography undertaken by Latour and later, in commercial courts, by Van Dijk 2013).

II.4 *The sources of law and the law, again: law2 as proof of the pudding*

Strikingly, among the sources of the law, only the case law meets the generally accepted representation of law wherein law is derived, extracted or produced from 'the sources of the law'. The judicial bodies are effectively obliged to produce law by mobilising all the pertinent sources of law, there where it had not been posited yet formerly by another judicial instance. And eventually *only* a judicial instance will be able to say or speak the law, to *assign* the legal bond and to make it exist in the void where it wasn't explicitly stated yet. It is the judgment – in French the double signification of 'arrêt' is emblematic here: it refers both to a decision and a 'stopping' (cf. McGee 2012[18]) – that creates and decrees the stabilising bond, the attachment that will once and for all (*ne bis in idem*) be taken as the legal truth (*res iudicata pro veritate habetur*), even if that decision is not the one you expected as a party to the dispute, even if a majority disagrees from a moral or economic perspective, even if scientific knowledge points in another direction.

It is thus only from the perspective of law2 that an unequivocal and consistent understanding of the relation between the 'sources of the law' and the law itself, which 'springs' from them, can be built. Consequently, only legal practice – the coping with things in anticipation of what a judge can do or does – extracts or derives law from its sources. On the contrary, from the perspective of Law1, as we said, this crucial relation between the sources of law and the law itself appears to be blurred and ambiguous.

In other words, the widespread, if not generally accepted, doctrine of the sources of law can only be underpinned and evidenced through the taking into account of law2, since it is only through the seizure of things by the particular hermeneutics of the law that the model is at work. Only then do we see law being fabricated from the sources of law. Legislators are not bound by these hermeneutics when they make laws, they are driven by other motives and objectives, and will in fact 'only' give law2 new meat to process.

If, as it is generally agreed upon, the Romans did already possess law such as we know it today, it is indeed not because of the contents of its rules and decisions, as is clear from the position of slaves and women in ancient Rome, but because today we still judge and produce legal bonds in the same way, through the same regime, through the same *operations*: those of law2. To say it with a jest of Latour's: 'Cicéron prendrait place au Conseil d'Etat ou à la Cour de Luxembourg sans avoir d'autre effort à faire que d'apprendre le français!'[19] Consequently, there can indeed be 'law' (law2, as a matter of fact) in other institutional designs than that of the democratic constitutional state, with its specific articulation of the principles of the sovereignty of the people through representative democracy, the respect for human rights and of the rule of law (limiting the power of government).[20] That is the case for such non-democratic regimes as those of Hitler, Stalin, Ceauşescu and Pinochet, that could not afford to bluntly do without law and had to maintain at least (very meticulously!) the appearance of a judiciary in order to permit the production of stabilising bonds, the assignation of responsibilities both in civil and criminal matters, the positing of the attachments of things or words to people, and the settling of disputes that would otherwise never end, except in violence and force.

II.5 Law2:
a factory of stabilising bonds, of assignations

In *La fabrique du droit* (2002) and chapter 13 of the *Enquête sur les modes d'existence* (2013) Latour has convincingly grasped law in its singularity, i.e. in what distinguishes it from everything else. After all, even if law (just like politics, religion, organisation or science) is intimately intermingled with everything else, something must also distinguish it from all the rest; otherwise law would not exist as such, but would have vanished into its contexts. Something must bring out the distinctive 'colour' of law. And it is indeed only through law2 that we can understand and describe what law does *exclusively*, that is what law alone does.

Law, then, is a practice that provides decisions and installs 'truces' (Rigaux 1997), that weaves stabilising bonds, that assigns responsibilities, acts, words and objects to legal subjects (or legal *personae*), that produces the proverbial 'legal certainty' and so forth. During its passage[21] law thus 'attaches', 'states', 'connects' or 'links', by the production of a 'passage',[22] what for one reason or another has fallen apart or become disturbingly uncertain, and was not resolved under the sign of any other mode. To use the words of Latour: '[...] l'ensemble des fonctions permettant de relier, retracer, tenir ensemble, rattacher, suturer, recoudre ce qui par la nature même de l'énonciation ne cesse de se distinguer, fait partie de cet attachement, que notre tradition occidentale a célébré sous le nom de Droit' (Latour 2004: 34–5). Law, in that sense, provides the links that are missing and missed: it is the mode that attaches where no connection can be made, or where other connections break, are contested, or are unsuccessful. Law, in that sense, is the *residual connection*, the ever-present possibility of connection, be it 'only' a legal one: a connection for the sake of the stability it brings. It is, literally, the last recourse to obtain certainty about a problematic relation. From this point of view the legal bond only starts to exist in a hard and permanent form *after* the decision stating it in the last instance. From then on it will be 'frozen' as a *res iudicata*. Nevertheless, the law 'passes' every time such a decision is anticipated (and hence might influence the course of things) without reaching the stage of the judicial decision.

If the legal bond is residual, does that mean that it can be arbitrary as long as it is stated? No, on the contrary. If the legal solution is formal, abstract, detached and superficial, it is therefore not arbitrary, precisely because it is fabricated through fine-tuned procedures, a very demanding hermeneutics and many, indeed a maximum of, hesitations. It is not arbitrary, in other words, precisely because it is legal. Could it be said, then, that the content or non-legal consequences of the decision will be arbitrary? No, because the content conveyed is itself the result of an issue-triggered conjunction of the (not yet legal) formal sources of the law with a set of calibrated legal operations, the outcome of which is neither arbitrary nor predictable, but constrained in a precise sense.

This shines an explicative light on two other features of law$_2$. First, on law's superficiality, as Latour has so subtly described it (Latour 2002): law can bind and connect everything, only because its operations barely touch the essence of the deeds, persons, situations and words it attaches. Such *superficiality* is part of the *grandeur* of the law. In more radical terms, this implies that law$_2$ has no proper content: it links, stabilises and assigns, but it does not produce justice, morals or knowledge. When judges practise law, they do, and must, care about the legal operations that the issue, claims and legal means require them to carry out. The second feature follows from the first and is the *detachment* so characteristic of legal practitioners. When triggered, a jurist is obliged to remain distant and to keep external mobilisations at bay, a feature that actually mirrors the crucial operation of qualification. The facts must be 'seized' by the optimally fitting pre-existing concepts derived from the formal sources, as a result of which the legal practitioner will 'leap' from the factual aspects into the 'real' legal work and its hermeneutics. Such a detachment should not be denounced or crushed as being the proof of a generalised and selfish alienation of the legal caste but calls for respect: such detachment is an obligation of the legal practice that contributes to its capacity to generate stabilising bonds everywhere they are required (cf. Gutwirth et al. 2008).

Putting the focus upon law as a regime of enunciation with its own practice of veridiction; recognising the constraints of jurists and what induces their hesitations; taking seriously the register of their creativity in order to grasp what is a success or a failure and to 'speak before' the legal practitioners[23] – all of these elements together contribute to the determination of what makes law irreducibly law, to what only law does, to what only law can do. For many of us, jurists and proponents of the democratic constitutional *Rechtsstaat*, such an approach is certainly an exercise in humility, but it is ultimately a necessary and rewarding exercise – because what the law effectively does is as quintessential for what we are as are such other modes as politics, science, habit and technology. It may appear small, but it is huge: law can always bring certainty and closure. It attaches what otherwise might dissolve, explode, get lost or disintegrate. It ties together what stubbornly resists all other kinds of less formal and less abstract connection.

To put law2 in the spotlight, therefore, is also an antidote against the strong tendency to overcharge and overburden law with a long series of expectations for which it is neither shaped nor equipped to meet, such as to carry civilisation, democracy and human rights, to decide what is true and false in history or in sciences, to protect health and morals, to foster reconciliation after a crime or to provide 'good' punishments, to organise the economy, to replace religion with a secular alternative, etc. (cf. Latour 2012: 363). This tendency to overburden law is in fact a category error, a mixing up of registers:

> En droit, croire que le jugement console, fait le deuil, c'est typiquement une erreur de catégorie. Car le droit ne fait pas le deuil, il ne transporte

pas quelque chose qui s'appelle de la thérapeutique, ou du salut. [...] C'est comme téléphoner à quelqu'un qui doit vous livrer une pizza, et dire: 'Faxez-la moi.' Erreur de catégorie typique. Il n'a pas compris que le mode de transport qui fait la commande n'est pas le mode de transport de la livraison. Eh bien, demander au droit de transporter vos peines, la fin du deuil, c'est la même chose. (Latour 2008: no page numbers; see also Latour 2012: 66)

III Exploring the consequences of the distinction between Law1 and law2

III.1 Values and institutions

At first sight Law1 and law2 do not seem to have much in common. This impression is certainly further fed by the often delicate and thorny relationship between on the one hand the legal practitioners, positivists or 'internalists', and on the other the meta-jurists or 'externalists'. Indeed, legal philosophers and sociologists of law are often sharply critical of the constricting and 'alienated' approaches of legal practitioners, while the latter often indifferently shrug away 'meta-juridical' analyses that they experience as alien or denigrating. From this perspective a political or philosophical approach to the law as a whole of norms (Law1) would be radically different from, and even antagonistic to, the legal practice that provides decisions and solutions (cf. de Sutter 2009b, building on the work of Schiavone 2008[24]). However, such oppositional representation misses the point that *both* the internalist and the externalist perspective mix up the two ways of evoking law, Law1 and law2. Both meta-lawyers and positivists, legal scientists and practitioners, lawyers and laypeople, smoothly and unconsciously switch from one register to the other without faltering. From Freud's profile to the naked women, from Law1 to law2, and back, and forth, you've switched without thinking.

Latour opens a path that might help us to better understand the articulation between Law1 and law2, namely by insisting upon the distinction between 'institutions' and 'values' (Latour 2004, 2012). On the one hand, Latour endeavours to single out a (not yet limited) series of singular experiences that 'we', the Moderns (Westerners, 'whites', ...) know well and recognise easily. It is these *experiences* that make us what we are; we would not be able – as a matter of life and death – to relinquish them in a diplomatic encounter or negotiation with non-modern others. He calls these experiences *values*, a notion that covers our distinctive experience of, for example, science, technology, religion, politics, economy, art, religion, morals and law. From this perspective, legal judgments and truths obviously differ from scientific judgments and truths and we know that they are respectively produced according to two different modes (regimes or practices) and that they are singular and irreducible to each other. In the *Enquête*, Latour links each of these values to a singular mode of existence, which he notates, as we already picked up, with three capital letters between brackets ([LAW], [REF], [REL] . . .) in order to focus precisely on their singularity, on their contrasts, on their irreducibility.

On the other hand, these values never stand alone or move on their own; water and gas need infrastructure – not itself made of water or gas! – to be conveyed, to circulate in a network and to be brought where needed. In the same vein, the values identified (and the singular modes through which they can exist) need to be *institutionalised* not only in order to be sheltered and to subsist, but also to circulate and move in landscapes where they might be triggered. The institutions of Science, Religion and Law are, however, intermingled and entangled ('à la façon des marbres veinés de San Marco dans lesquels aucune figure n'est clairement reconnaissable' (Latour 2004: 35)). They all are hybrid. Thus the legal institution is indeed a mixture of politics, religion, organisation, technique and so on.[25]

For McGee, concerning law, the difference between values and institutions amounts to a distinction between law in an 'ordinary sense' and law as a singular mode or regime 'with its own singular *key* (in something approaching the musical sense of the term)' (McGee 2012: fn. 3, original italics). From this perspective, the instituted form law takes is related to the way it is generally or trivially given sense to, while the value encompasses what the law does when it is practised within its specific constraints, or enunciated within its peculiar regime. Generally, the institution of a mode of existence can be said to be closely linked to the account that a collectivity makes of it.

In other words, law as an institution is interwoven, linked up and entangled with all other institutions and it hosts law as a singular mode of existence. The legal institution then is the whole of the arrangements that make the circulation and triggering of the legal regime possible (on all these points see also De Vries and

Van Dijk 2013). The same is indeed valid for the other institutions and the values they host. But institutions, as well as the relations between institutions, are highly variable, which means that the way they host, shield and represent a singular and sustained mode of existence is often problematic and always complex. Latour even suggests that the many tensions between the Church as an institution and religion as a mode of existence, as an experience, are emblematic of the generic complexity of the articulation between institutions and values in the West (Latour 2012).

The former distinction between institutions and values shines a light upon the distinction between Law1 and law2. It is clear that law2 is the 'value' at stake: the always existing possibility of the making of a stabilising bond, of the assignation of responsibility, or of an attachment where it is missed ... [LAW] is the guarantee of continuity and connection, against disintegration and endless uncertainty. Law1, then, it seems to me, is the legal institution, especially since all the formal sources are also part of different institutions but simultaneously find themselves associated in a unique way as formal sources, as unavoidable references for the anticipation or production of legal bonds by law2. A parliamentary statute in that sense weaves together different institutions: politics (since it expresses collective decisions), organisation (since it provides high-level scripts), law (since it is a legal source), and might touch and alter religious or scientific institutions, and so forth.

The interplay between values and their institution, transposed upon the relations between law2 and Law1, shines a light on different aspects of law. First, it explains the complex conjunction between the age old and rather stable regime of enunciation of law2 (or [LAW]) that subsisted and persisted since the Romans, and the always changing (sometimes even volatile) normativity and rules of Law1 which are dependent on a lot of heterogeneous factors and their common history. Political, economic and ethical institutions change, as do technologies and sciences, and hence Law1 as well, while law2 remains at work in the same continuous way. We thus obviously succeeded in staying Greek and staying Roman at the same time. Second, it shows how an important discrepancy can develop between what law2 really does, and the expectancies, objectives and responsibilities brought by Law1. And third, it invites us, now from a renewed perspective, to reflect upon the role (rather than the rule) of 'law' in the democratic constitutional state – the democratic *Rechtsstaat* or *état de droit*

Providing the Missing Link

– hence a role that is deemed to be quintessential and characteristic of modernity.

III.2 The role of law: towards a more realistic description of the trias politica?

The last point raises the question whether the law (Law1, law as an institution) weighs more upon the characterisation of the democratic constitutional state than the other institutions, in particular politics, economics and religion. Inversely, and more interestingly, one may wonder how to understand the role of law (as law2) in the design of the democratic constitutional state, beyond the broad and underdetermined institutional representation wherein the law is supposed to warrant, protect and carry the whole edifice.[26] Such an inquiry might lead to a more modest but no less crucial framing of the law's role in the *Rechtstaat*, and particularly with regards to the *mise en œuvre* of the *trias politica* or, concretely, the role of the *judiciary* (rather than the rule of Law1) in the architecture of 'checks and balances'.

Even if legislation and executive orders are important formal sources of the law, their specific articulation to the judiciary necessarily implies that at least a bit of uncertainty remains: if triggered, how will the judiciary interpret them? There always remains some interpretative leeway. Next to this, the facts and claims submitted will give rise to new legally pertinent issues that the rulings of the judges will have to accommodate or adjust to the formal sources. Judicial decisions, although formally constrained by law's regime of enunciation, are after all still to be fabricated and taken, and thus created. Hence, what the judiciary will decide can only be anticipated with more or less certainty, but never absolutely. Retrospectively, it will become clear if the rulings of the judges followed a probable/plausible/foreseeable path, or if they turned out to have embraced a new and merely possible path, or to have been creative in other ways. The judge is not the *bouche de la loi*, neither can there be a *gouvernement des juges*. If the judges and courts stick to their obligations and constraints when they put down a stabilising legal bond in a case, it can only be wrong to hold that their decision is either the mere predictable extension of a rule or an arbitrary expression of the judges' personal preferences.

In fact, this provides for a very subtle framing of the role of the judiciary in the *trias politica*. The force of legislation then appears to be co-produced by case law and to depend on how the judges will interpret, concretise and give consequences to the piece of legislation at stake among the other pertinent sources of the law in the light of the particular setting of facts. As I have already suggested, application is never straightforward: there is always a moment of hesitation, each case being triggered by other facts, other requirements and thus other hermeneutical possibilities. That is indeed why artificially intelligent systems that aim at replacing judges are doomed to fail, or even worse, they bear the danger of turning law into something else wherein the proper legal moment (qualification, interpretation, hesitation, imputation . . .) has disappeared in favour of routine, automatism and levelling down (Gutwirth 2010).

III.3 The force of law: a subtle articulation of Law1 and law2

The preceding paragraphs account for a surprising 'loop' whereby the authority of *legislation* is co-produced by the way the judiciary will receive and interpret it as one, perhaps *the* major, source of law. The force and reach of general legislation are thus ultimately dependent on the case law that will substantiate it, but only on a case-by-case basis. The temporal gap is interesting: the actual force of legislation depends on its future interpretation by a judicial body. Again, the anticipation of what the judiciary will do is crucial, because it excludes any representation of the force of Law1 as a direct and straightforward steering power; there always remains latitude for creation.

Indeed, we ourselves – private and public persons – have to prospectively and anticipatorily weigh our choices and act as if we are judges, and more concretely when, for one reason or another, the need for legal stability pops up as an issue. Such a stance is actually as pertinent for the police officer making a decision about the organisation of the control of a demonstration or a visit of officials as for the neighbours getting still more involved in a quarrel over the shadows and roots of trees crossing the disputed limits of their gardens. Once the legal regime of enunciation is set in motion, one finds oneself at the point of articulation of Law1 and law2, i.e. between the pre-existing normative sources of law and the law that will be drawn from them, between the general norms of yesterday, the concrete issues and uncertainties of today, and the legal bond of tomorrow. In other words, one is at the precise spot where the judges intervene when mobilised to decide.[27]

If the 'force of law' is used as a concept to explain why we obey the norms and rules that emanate from the formal sources of the law (thus from Law1 and primarily from legislation), such force is a child of what is not yet there, namely law2 (cf. above, concerning 'autochtony' and anticipation). Such a state of things considerably complexifies the question of our relationship to legislation and other norms, and makes concepts such as compliance and transgression sound like impudent simplifications because they rule out the anticipative stance and the possibilities it conveys. How to act according to the law in a conflict with your neighbour before the judge states how the law will materialise in this case? How can you comply with a piece of legislation if the final decision about your compliance still has to be taken by a judge? How to bring the anticipatory dimension of compliance and transgression into our understanding of compliance with Law1, without already knowing law2?

Does this mean that our compliance with the rules of Law1 is the result of a sort of permanent individual legal practice that installs a fictive judge (a movement of [FIC]?) in our heads, trying to anticipate for every step we take what real judges would do if confronted with what we have done? Certainly not, because this would be a paralysing and unbearable burden. Just as it would be unbearable for us go through the whole range of 'folds' that have been designed in order to propel a car forward every time we push our feet on the gas pedal [TEC], or redo the same experiment every time we want to evoke gravitation in an article on physics [REF]. No, in most of our doings we conveniently – and luckily – omit the prepositions, render them implicit and 'black-boxed'. The different modes, in other words, are 'veiled' but not forgotten, as has been admirably described by Latour (cf. Latour 2012: 266 *et seq.*). We just do as we did before, but we know that a 'return to the manual' can be triggered by a difference, a problem, an obstacle, a swerve or, why not, a *clinamen*.[28]

This mode of omission, which Latour calls habit [HAB], covers 99 per cent of our existence (Latour 2012: chapter 10). Without this habit, we would go mad, confronted by endless and numerous recalls of the prepositions, the on/offs of the modes of existence. Thanks to this mode, you just know what to do next, without thinking and searching the right key; [HAB] warrants a sense of continuity spanning over multiple discontinuities. Pursuant to this, when we abide by the norms of Law1, e.g. by the scripts provided by legislation [ORG:POL], in 99 per cent of the cases, we do it in the [HAB] mode and it is only in case of a hitch that [LAW] might get launched and that we'll start to anticipate how a judge might evaluate our choices, and indeed possibly adapt our behaviour.

Rather than a consequence of the 'force of law', our compliance with norms shows our obedience to scripts [ORG], generally in the mode of habit [HAB]. We spontaneously drive on the right side without the need to remember the traffic regulations [ORG:POL], but if we cross the Channel, our habit will be disturbed, the veil will be lifted and, because we know that the English judge will not take seriously our excuse that we drive on the right hand in Belgium [LAW], we'll conform to a new script, which will (quickly or slowly, depending on our aptitudes) turn into a new habit (Latour 2012: 269). When abiding by rules, the anticipation of what a judge will decide is the final benchmark. This is quintessential since it precisely warrants the choice and liberty one enjoys, even if the legislative formulation is already unambiguous and precise; such is the tangible role of the judiciary in a system of checks and balances. Who hasn't wondered about how to interpret a legislative norm, whether to comply with it or to circumvent its consequences? Which engineer hasn't wondered if her invention is patentable or, more worryingly, whether her patent will ultimately be endorsed by a judge if contested? And is the partner of a consenting masochist infringing criminal law when giving the latter pleasure through the administration of pains by what looks like 'assault and battery'? Such questions engage law2, trigger it and set it in motion, but a definitive answer in that precise case will only be provided if a judge produces a verdict, the *arrêt*. For sure, law2 or [LAW] is an abstract and lively mode of existence. Even when the judge cuts short and closes the issue at stake, by replacing the many stippled bonds by a steady bold one (*res iudicata*, the closure), the abstraction remains primal.

III.4 A material life of law? The embodiment of law in technology

In his writings on Latour's presentation of law, Kyle McGee devotes a lot of attention to what he calls the 'modes of expression of law'. According to him, the force of law passes through a wide variety of media, 'into objects, techno-scientific constructs, artifacts of all varieties' that each impact upon the quality of the named force itself, turning it into a plural force or different forces of law (McGee 2014: 127, 2012). There is indeed a lot of literature exploring the embodiment of law in technology, especially in the field of information technology where 'privacy by design' and 'legal protection by design' receive full interest (among others Hildebrandt 2011), but I focus only on McGee's contribution, because he explicitly builds further upon Latour's work, which is the object of the present book and chapter.

As a great reader of Latour, McGee is well aware of the distinction between law as an institution and law as a practical regime of enunciation, between Law1 and law2, and that the latter may not be reduced to the utterance or decision itself, but on the contrary that '[t]he whole process of enunciation composes the beating heart, systole-diastole, of legality' (McGee 2012: 6). In other words, *'the enunciation of the judgement does not complete the enunciation of the law'* (McGee 2014: 148, original italics); law2 is more than the pronouncement of judgments. When McGee writes that 'law's passage extends beyond the verbal exchanges of counsellors, lawyers, judges and administrators' (with reference to *La fabrique du droit*) in order to focus upon its role in collective life, it at first sight meets the idea that the legal key or preposition can always be triggered, by whomever whenever about whatever, in order to give direction to the articulation of our behaviour to organisational, political and administrative norms. Then law as a regime of enunciation is indeed much broader than the interlocutory process that takes place in courts.

Though I fully join him on these points, I am not sure we interpret these statements in the same way, since I tend to stick to my understanding of law2 as an abstract mode, while McGee argues that law passes, among others, into objects and technologies and hence it materialises. McGee unambiguously takes a further step by arguing that 'dire le droit' also occurs through material objects and technological artefacts (McGee 2014: 127). For him, the 'force of law' also passes through all kinds of mediators whereby law 'juridifies' other modes of existence, such as [TEC]. Fences, pedestrian barriers, painted lines on the street, traffic lights, speed bumps, anti-parking bollards, weaponised city benches or disciplinary architecture ('spikes' to discourage beggars and homeless people to sit or sleep), surveillance cameras, electronic eyes for the operations of doors or the detection of burglars and other technological beings then develop (through a succession of 'folds'[29]) into place holders or 'lieu-tenants' of law. They 'materialize legal statements [...] make us act in specific ways [...] and so exercise a certain kind of normativity' (McGee 2014: 165). 'The pedestrian barrier, for instance, is performing the law by enfolding a space-time that is entirely distinct from the law's own' (McGee 2014: 167). Technicity prolongs law: 'This is a *delegative* legality' (McGee 2014: 169).

I would indeed agree if McGee was evoking Law1 and the formal *sources* of law or, in other words, if he was speaking of law as an institution. As I argued at the beginning of this chapter, the formal sources of law are all normative, but at the same time they are an obligatory referential component of the making of law2. Stated more radically, however, these sources are not singularly or definitively legal, not even legal per se. They are at best very weakly or possibly legally prepositioned if that preposition indicates, as we argued based on Latour's study, a specific way of hermeneutically coping with issues through a trajectory steered by legal operations and value objects: legislation is certainly dominantly coloured by [POL:ORG], customs are literally [HAB:ORG], doctrine is [REF:LAW] and pre-existing case law is difficult to coin but probably mainly [ORG:LAW] when it comes to the rules/scripts derived from legal decisions and [LAW:ORG] (or [LAW:REP] or [ORG:REP]) regarding legal bonds they have already put down in prior cases.

Undoubtedly, technical artefacts can embody rules or norms, and the examples are self-explanatory. A fence translates a rule into barbed wire, 'you shall not trespass' in the one sense, and 'you're "at home"' in the other. The beeping of your car or its refusal to ignite impose the norm that you have to wear a seatbelt. The *Amsterdammeke* makes parking impossible where the rule prohibits it. The list of illustrations could be extended ad infinitum: rules and regulations can indeed be materialised in technical artifacts. That should not be surprising, because it is precisely what technology [TEC] is about: about delegation – folding in – a succession of tasks into a durable and discrete device (not necessarily a material device, such as the techniques of plastering walls, serving in tennis or legal reasoning).

So, are we talking law here? Yes, certainly if we evoke Law1, the sources of law and the set of rules they spawn. But as we have shown already, Law1 and the 'normativity' it conveys through the formal sources of law (which are political, organisational, scientific, ethical, cultural, etc.) are far from marked by the singularity of law2, which is that it binds, assigns, holds together, retraces and stabilises, when triggered to do that.[30] But the argument doesn't hold water if it is meant to also (or only) apply to law as a regime of enunciation. As regards law2, the technical materialisation of the norms and the normativity which are its 'sources' do rather seem to have 'repulsive' or 'repellent' consequences. If the interpretations of norms, the possibilities that they leave open and the liberty we have not to abide by them are limited by hard devices that impose a particular kind of conduct, the legal momentum, the triggering of law2, is 'pushed further' or even rendered superfluous. The room for the uncertainty that may trigger the legal mode is then narrowed down: no bond or connection can even be missed, because there *is* a connection, but it is simply not legal (e.g. an [ORG:TEC]-connection). As such, for example, there will be no discussion about the justifying or excusing elements a legal practitioner would consider for a medical doctor receiving a parking ticket while urgently intervening if, due to a concrete pole, she just couldn't have done it (and the patient might have suffered more).

From this perspective a 'speed bump' is not per se a legal device. It is organisational because it imposes the script that you shall not drive more than 30 km/h in an urban agglomeration [ORG]. It is political as well since it is the choice or 'emanation' of a collective not to have people driving too fast where children are playing [POL]. It is technical, for it incorporates or 'folds in' a number actions to obtain a result, into a steady device [ORG:TEC], namely forcing people to drive slower. It is scientific [REF] because the material it is made of is experimentally known to be resistant to a billion bumps by cars and other vehicles of a certain weight. But it is *not* legal as it stands. Of course, *it can become legal* [LAW] if, for example, it has been defectively built and the public authorities start considering launching a liability action against the private builder, or if an ambulance breaks its chassis while speeding to the hospital with a mother giving birth, and both the owner of the ambulance and the mother start thinking about taking legal action against the administration for their damages.

In other words, in the examples given by McGee, the embodiment of law in technology actually should be read as the embodiment of norms, rules and regulation in technology. As a consequence, the evoked technological devices are in fact the 'lieu-tenants' of political, economic and moral governance. Designing public benches so that the homeless cannot use them to sleep or rest has nothing to do with the law, but everything to do with the (moral, organisational, political) idea that sleeping on benches should be impeached for one reason or another. Such devices rather postpone or remove the setting of the [LAW]-preposition, the coming into motion of the particular regime of enunciation that characterises the law. In that sense they are anti-law. Inscribing rules and norms into technology is an act of governance, even if it is 'well-meant', e.g. to support individual rights such as in the case of 'data protection by design'. Such acts can be both public (speed bumps) and private (fencing, spiking), but remain acts of power in the finest Foucauldian sense: they are *conduites des conduites*, they steer the conduct of others (Foucault 1984: 313–14). Nothing legal – in the sense of law2 – under the sun.[31]

IV Conclusion: the residual connection

If we want to understand what singularises law, we cannot be satisfied with an evocation of a body of more or less binding rules. On the contrary, such norms do actually express a mix of many sorts of concerns, stakes and hopes, and therefore simply do not permit us to isolate what properly distinguishes law. After Latour's passage, this appears still more clearly: approached as a practice or regime of enunciation, law – law2 – cannot be singled out by a focus upon normativity and rules. It is the opposite: the legal practice must carefully and steadily avoid falling into the trap of a normative stance. How things *should* be from a political, moral, cultural or economic perspective is not law2's concern. It does something else.

Such statements should not come as a surprise, since the tenet of the sources of law has confirmed this for ages, although we regularly overlook it, as clear as the message is: the material sources of law are not the same as its formal sources, and the formal sources of law differ from the law itself. By associating law and normativity, we confuse non-legal sources and law, legislation (*loi*) and law (*droit*). Indeed, in a first step, the material sources of law, with their moral, political, economic, cultural and other contents, are translated and transformed into formal sources of law, which may happen through legislation and executive measures, but also through precedent analysis, deduction, legal science and custom. In a second step, the formal sources may be taken as obligatory reference points by legal practitioners and judges in order to respectively anticipate or state the legal bonds in a case. So, indeed, a legal practitioner will consider a person of nineteen years as a minor if a statute sets twenty-one years of age as a threshold. And yes, she will recognise the possibility or consequences of a same-sex marriage if the conditions are met as foreseen by the legislation. But if the legislation changes, their decisions will be different *inasmuch* as they will have different consequences for those concerned. Generically speaking, however, the jurists will have done the same work and proceeded consistently with the same constraints of the same practice. If we want to single out what is immanent to law, the point is precisely what remains unchanged, i.e. *how* the judges and jurists cope with the things they seize.

In other words, law's singularity is to be located in law$_2$ and is not determined by *what* legal practitioners convey as non-legal contents and consequences but by *how* legal practitioners work, how they reason and decide, how they seize the things of the world they are triggered to comprehend. When one practises law, one is not and should not be primarily concerned with content, but rather with the opposite, with the legal operations and value objects of law, with taking and holding distance and building the detachment that makes legal coping with things so characteristic of legal activity. Indeed, the result in terms of content and interest will drive lawyers through the switches of the possible anticipations of the future decision of the judge, but in principle it is the most appropriate *legal trajectory* that will prevail.

Additionally, it is precisely because of the fact that legal practice takes no or, better, is not supposed to take a political, moral, cultural or economic position, that it may touch or seize absolutely every thinkable thing, and that we can accept it as the rightful and ultimate provider of stability and security, where these are missing and missed. If judges and jurists really had to cope with all the non-legal consequences of their decisions and anticipations, they obviously would have to be categorically distrusted, since nobody can be expected to master everything and nobody speaks a definite and unique truth. That is also why no one would agree to see the judges supersede politics, morals, economics, science and whatever else. They practise law and that is what we expect them to do.

The contrasts between Law1 and law2 turn out to be strong. If Law1 bears the whole edifice of the democratic constitutional state (its rules and principles) on its shoulders, law2's role appears very modest, but is nonetheless vital, since it must produce stabilising decisions and solutions, everywhere and whenever those are missing and missed, where no other stabilising solution has emerged. In the vast web of diverse connections that make our collectivities, the legal bond is the residual form of connection. With too much temerity, I would suggest that it is actually *the connection for the connection*: the imputation of the one connection into the whole of connections. The peculiar constraints of the legal practice (in a Stengersian sense) and its regime of enunciation (so well described by Latour) are a mirror of this role. Being the residual connection, the legal bond must just hold and stabilise, and hence, should be the result of a process with as much detachment from the passions and interests at stake as possible, with a superficiality that makes it as disengaged as possible. No wonder that the legal mode of existence is *utterly abstract*.

Does this mean that there is no articulation between Law1 and law2, between the institution and the regime of enunciation, between normativity and the making of stabilising bonds, the construction of legal security? Is the residual connection completely un-tuned, arbitrary and alienated from politics, morals, economy, etc., or in other words from the material sources of the law? Certainly not, indeed, but the two-step *dispositif*, from material to formal sources and then to the legal decision, combined with the operations of law, that further produce distance and 'objectivity' (Latour 2002: chapter 5), together amount to a complex and subtle articulation between extra-legal norms and rules, cases, legal practice and case law, wherein contents are conveyed, transformed, formalised and, yes, why not, 'jurimorphed'. When judges make decisions that displease, content-wise, the representatives of the legislative and executive powers are free to intervene using the tools at their disposal to try to steer the judges to make decisions with different consequences. Although in principle not a straightforward relation, since the impact of changes in the formal sources must still be linked to the peculiar facts of a case and interpreted by legal practitioners, this may have immediate effects. Slow adjustments are possible as well, and can be the result, on the one hand, of the influence of legal doctrine or science upon the legal practitioners, or, on the other, of judicial creativity, spawned by new issues or new hermeneutical openings. Moreover, as we saw, the legislation sections of the State Councils in Belgium, the Netherlands and France are particularly interesting interfaces between legislation as a formal source of law and legal practice, since they try to anticipate the way legal practitioners will receive legislative or executive measures in order to make possible an assessment of consequences in terms of content. Constitutional courts are also a fascinating meeting point of law with politics, economy, culture, organisation and so on, since they legally settle issues, sometimes quite loaded issues, that question the basic organisation of states from political, economic, moral, religious and other perspectives.

Many years ago, when I was writing my PhD, Latour's passage obliged me to reconsider what I was doing as a scientist. His work helped me to recognise myself in the scientific practice (even as a legal scientist!), beyond the then very trendy critique of the scientific institution. With his work on the law, he actually realised a similar thing: by unburdening the shoulders of the law of many non-legal callings, he made it possible for me to reconcile myself with a practice too often denigrated and reduced to alienated hair-splitting by critique. It is not a reduction or minimisation of the law's importance to shift the focus from the rule (of Law1) to the role of law2, because producing stabilising bonds and security [LAW] is as singular and characteristic of what we are as constructing robust and reliable knowledge [REF] or constituting the collective [POL]. Quite the contrary, in fact: when the responsibilities entrusted to practitioners conform to the possibilities of their constraints, the joy of practising emerges.

Acknowledgments

The author would like to thank Bruno Latour and Kyle McGee and all the other participants in the Law workshop of the AIME project that took place at Sciences Po on 28 April 2014, and especially for their disagreements. Many thanks also to Isabelle Stengers for the superb hours of thinking together and to Vinciane Despret for her disarmingly sharp insights.

Notes

1. For the use of the concepts 'axiomatic' and 'topical' see De Sutter (2009a) (with the references to the original work of Gilles Deleuze).
2. Interestingly called the 'capital of law' by Kyle McGee (2012).
3. That is indeed well expressed by the principle of non-retroactivity of the law.
4. Foqué (2011).
5. In the original French version of the *Enquête sur les modes d'existence* (Latour 2012), the legal mode of existence is notated [DRO] from *droit*, but I will use its English equivalent [LAW] to promote readability.
6. For Holmes, law is a profession or a 'business' rather than a practice or a regime of enunciation.
7. Cf. also the semiotic notion of 'conditions of felicity' applied to the legal enunciation and more particularly the list of ten 'value objects' that Latour extracts from his ethnographic observations at the French Conseil d'État (Latour 2002: chapter 4, pp. 139–206, with an overview table at p. 203): these value objects are the cornerstones of the step-by-step progression, 'traceable movement', propulsion or 'passage' of the law in the interlocutional interaction within the Conseil d'État.
8. I think it is worth noting that this is a description of law that avoids the tautology (cf. Latour 2012: 359)
9. This is clear in the example quoted in the former footnote: 'You don't have the right to steal my marbles!' invokes or announces the particular legal 'tune', 'twitch' or 'clef' in which the situation might, if this is pursued, be taken forth (Latour 2004: 38).
10. About these concepts see Latour (2002, 2004, 2012), Stengers (1996, 1997, 2004) and Stengers and Latour (2009). For a summary in English see Gutwirth et al. (2008) and in French see Gutwirth (2010).
11. This example might surprise because it is commonplace to conceive human rights as being a fortiori legal. But human rights, fundamental rights or natural rights are much more than legal, and in the first place their signification is political and organisational. They were conceptually built up by liberal political philosophers, mobilised by the Western revolutionary movements of the seventeenth and eighteenth centuries, written in the constitutions that expressed both the rupture with the former arbitrary and absolutist forms of government and the installation of a new – liberal – organisation or economy

of power relations and, finally, exported worldwide as political mantras through processes of decolonisation and universalisation steered by Occidental power and politics: human rights as shields against the power of the state, as higher principles to be respected and enforced even by the states. For sure, as being a crucial aspect of Western and other constitutions, human rights *are* a supreme source of national law and can even – except for States as such China and the USA – be consecrated in individual cases by international or supranational courts, turning them into a legal thing. But again, it is only when human rights are thought of in anticipation or as an element of a judicial process, and ensnared in the regime of enunciation of the law, that they become legal. What the Luxemburg Court would do with my claim that the NSA has been blatantly violating my rights to privacy and data protection for more than ten years is in this sense a question that will yield 'legality'.

12. The alternative is violence, but violence brings the opposite of stability and 'legal certainty': it destabilises even more.
13. On the crucial work done by the lawyers see the beautiful pages in McGee (2014).
14. 'En simplifiant quelque peu, mais sans trop nous éloigner de la vérité, nous pouvons dire en effet que, si nous devons au Grecs la naissance du "politique", nous devons au Romains celle du "juridique"' (Schiavone 2008: 9).
15. Cf. note 3.
16. 'Imputation' is important, because the lawyer still needs to consider the whole of the law: she needs to link the decision to the wholeness of the law: 'When a lawyer considers a case, what he hesitates about is the way that he will make this case stick to the wholeness of law – and the only way to build such a relationship between a case and the wholeness of law is to branch the individuals at stake with the case to a legal reality such as, for instance, accountability or guiltiness. To declare somebody legally accountable for something is not to impute to him a moral quality: it is to impute to him a quality which requires the wholeness of law to be applicable to him – and not only the local provision that he may have infringed. This is why the choice of a type of legal imputation is, for a lawyer, a matter of hesitation: to branch somebody on the wholeness of law cannot be realised at will [*sic*]. If the lawyer has not well hesitated, the legal imputation through which he made the case stick to the wholeness of law can be declared legally void: hesitation is a very delicate matter. Since it is not only a local provision which is at stake with a given case,

but the wholeness of law, to hesitate is for a lawyer a trial through which he will have to show his ability to manipulate this wholeness, so that the imputation he realises can be declared compatible with it' (Gutwirth et al. 2008: 200).
17. They are much less well-known, however, from the point of view of their subtle interplay and entanglements, beyond the simplistic ideal of a straightforward hierarchy: see, for example, Rigaux (1997) and Ost and van de Kerchove (2002).
18. Kyle McGee, however, refers to this feature of the judgment with another rationale: to him the decision brings an end to the process of judicial interlocution, but in his view the law still passes: *'the enunciation of the judgement does not complete the enunciation of the law'* (McGee 2012: 9, original italics). Cf. below.
19. See Latour (2012: 366). The contemporary value of Roman Law has been strikingly described in the work of the late Yan Thomas. See, for example, Thomas (1980, 1998); see also Schiavone (2008) and De Sutter (2009b).
20. The literature on that subject is enormous. See, however, De Hert and Gutwirth (2006), in particular the first part of the chapter, and Foqué (2011).
21. 'Passage' in the sense of a movement, a trajectory.
22. 'Passage' in the sense of a link, connection, bond or even a 'bridge' or a 'chain.'
23. That is why Latour writes the following: 'Bien parler sur l'agora avec les praticiens, c'est espérer qu'ils hocheront la tête avec approbation quand on leur proposera de leur pratique une version, peut-être totalement différente, mais au moins adéquate à leur expérience et si possible partageable' (Latour 2013: 2645).
24. 'Un jour [De Sutter writes] les juristes ont commencé à accepter que le droit pouvait tirer sa grandeur d'autre chose que lui même. L'intervention progressive de la philosophie dans la pensée du droit est à l'origine de la grande bifurcation doctrinale moderne, bifurcation dont nous portons encore les conséquences. Cette bifurcation peut-être formulée en peu de mots : ou bien les normes (droit), ou bien les concepts (philosophie). Qu'il puisse exister une pensée propre au droit, une dimension spéculative propre au droit, est que la doctrine de ces derniers siècles s'est escrimée à rendre impossible. Il est difficile de l'en blâmer: la mainmise de la philosophie sur le droit avait à la fin du XIXe siècle, entraîné une confusion complète de l'une et de l'autre. Parce que le langage de la justice était devenu celui du droit, la spécificité de celui-ci se trouvait anéantie par la

force de conviction de celle là. Qui aurait pu prétendre que le droit ne possède aucun rapport avec la justice, qu'elle soit naturelle ou divine? Dans *Ius*, Schiavone fait remonter le moment d'émergence de la tentation philosophique du droit à Cicéron. Cette tentation, pourtant, ne c'est pas imposée sans résistances. Les grands juristes romains connaissaient mieux que quiconque la spécificité de la pensée du droit. Il savaient aussi ce que celle-ci avait à perdre à tout céder à celle-là: elle avait à perdre jusqu'à sa plus élémentaire pertinence. Rien n'a moins de sens que le droit, une fois la détermination de ce sens réservé à la philosophie – ou bien, de nos jours, à la sociologie (Bourdieu), l'économie (Posner), la psychanalyse (Legendre)' (De Sutter 2009b: 794). For De Sutter legal theory and philosophy, just as politics, ethics, economy, science and technology, represent a threat for the autonomy and singularity of the law. The law can do without external legitimation, it is its own legitimation. In the words of Latour : 'Le droit ne remplace rien d'autre' (Latour 2002: 292).

25. This metaphor very nicely expresses the point made: 'Imaginez un jeu de Lego qui au lieu de la seule accroche par les quatre plots traditionnels en aurait plusieurs. Imaginez ensuite que chaque attache rende plus facile ou plus difficile les autres attaches. Admettez maintenant que certains blocs de ce jeu de Lego un peu particulier s'attachent par la connexion DRO et d'autres par la connexion POL. Les blocs eux mêmes sont de formes multiples [. . .]. Maintenant lâchez des gamins dans ce jeu. Ils vont produire des formes – des institutions – dont des segments plus ou moins longs seront dits DRO parce que l'attache est de type DRO alors même qu'un bloc donné peut être repris, selon un autre segment, par l'attache POL. Dans l'ensemble bigarré produit, on pourra dire, selon l'intensité des liens, "là c'est plutôt quand même en gros du droit," "là c'est plutôt quand même du politique." Ce sera toujours faux bien sûr puisque le blocs sont divers, hétérogènes etc. de couleurs variés, et pourtant ce ne sera jamais tout à fait faux car la "dominante," pour parler musique, sera bien donnée par un type particulier d'attachement ou d'ébranlement ou de contamination' (Latour 2004: 39–40).

26. Which it does not in any case: 'Ne faisons pas porter au droit – énonciation et institution – des formes de regroupement et de composition qu'ils son sûrs de ne pas pouvoir porter. Impossible par exemple de résister au totalitarisme en s'appuyant *seulement* sur la fragile barrière du droit (sous Vichy, le Conseil d'État encaisse sans sourciller les lois sur les juifs faisant pourtant le même "excellent travail" avant et après' (Latour 2004: 39).

27. The difference between the judges and the (private and public) persons doing law in anticipation is indeed that the former act from a position that is detached as much as possible from the case, while the parties are passionately committed and interested (Latour 2002).
28. 'Suivre un cours d'action parce que l'on a compris dans quelle éthologie on se trouvait, ce n'est pas du tout la même chose que ne plus suivre aucune indication sur ce qu'il convient de faire la prochaine fois. Harold Garfinkel, l'un des rares analystes de l'habitude, a proposé cette admirable définition d'un cours d'action: "for another first next time" ("pour une autre prochaine première fois"). Voilà une belle condition de félicité: on fera la prochaine fois comme la précédente, oui, mais ce sera aussi la première fois. Tout est pareil, lisse et bien connu, mais la différence veille, prêt à "reprendre en manuel." Paradoxalement, il n'y a pas d'inertie dans l'habitude – sauf quand elle bascule dans son contraire, l'automatisme ou la routine. Mais là, aucun doute, l'habitude sera perdue' (Latour 2010: 271).
29. 'Folds' are the main characteristic of the [TEC] mode; see Latour (2012: chapter 8) and Gutwirth (2010: chapter 4) for more references.
30. Self-evidently, but nevertheless interestingly, here is that the rules embodied by technological devices do not even have to be legal at all – it works for any kind of rule, even a rule that no one would consider legal, even from a very loose perspective: that is, for example, the case for a thermostat which implements your personal 'rule' that your living room should not be heated up to more than 19 degrees Celsius.
31. One may wonder if law2 could be embodied in technology, which would imply that the legal practice would be 'folded into' technological devices. That, in turn, would mean that devices be built that would anticipate decisions of judges in a case and carry out all the operations of the law taking into account the different value objects of the law's regime of enunciation. I am extremely sceptical about this endeavour (cf. Gutwirth 2010).

References

Audren, Frédéric and Moreau de Bellaing, Cédric (2013) 'Bruno Latour's legal anthropology', in Reza Benakar and Max Travers (ed.), *Law and Social Theory*, 2nd edn. Oxford: Hart, pp. 181–94.

Cayla, Olivier (1993) 'La qualification ou la vérité du droit', *Droits*, 18: 3–18.

De Hert, Paul and Gutwirth, Serge (2006) 'Privacy, data protection and law enforcement. Opacity of the individual and transparency of power', in Erik Claes, Anthony Duff and Serge Gutwirth (eds), *Privacy and the Criminal Law*. Antwerp and Oxford: Intersentia, pp. 61–104.

De Sutter, Laurent (2009a) *Deleuze. La pratique du droit*. Paris: Michalon, collection Le bien commun.

De Sutter, Laurent (2009b) 'Nous sommes tous des juristes romains', *Droit et Société*, 73: 793–5.

De Vries, Katja and Van Dijk, Niels (2013) 'A bump in the road. Ruling out law from technology', in Mireille Hildebrandt and Jeanne Gaakeer, Jeanne (eds), *Human Law and Computer Law: Comparative Perspectives*. Dordrecht: Springer, pp. 89–121.

Deleuze, Gilles (1990) *Pourparlers 1972–1990*. Paris: Minuit.

Ewick, Patricia and Silbey, Susan (1998) *The Common Place of Law. Stories from Everyday Life*. Chicago and London: University of Chicago Press.

Foqué, René (2011) *De democratische rechtsstaat: een onrustig bezit?* Utrecht: Forum Essayreeks.

Foucault, Michel (1984) 'Deux essais sur le sujet et le pouvoir', in Hubert H. Dreyfus and Paul Rabinow, *Michel Foucault. Un parcours philosophique*. Paris: Gallimard, pp. 297–321.

Gutwirth, Serge (2010) 'Composer avec du droit, des sciences et le mode technique: une exploration', in Daniel Le Métayer (ed.), *Les technologies de l'information au service des droits: opportunités, défis, limites*. Bruxelles: Bruylant, pp. 24–42. Online at <http://works.bepress.com/serge_gutwirth/14/>.

Gutwirth, Serge (2013) 'Le contexte du droit ce sont ses sources formelles et les faits et moyens qui exigent son intervention', *Revue Interdisciplinaire d'Etudes Juridiques – Droit en contexte*, 70: 108–16.

Gutwirth, Serge, De Hert, Paul and De Sutter, Laurent (2008) 'The trouble with technology regulation from a legal perspective. Why Lessig's "optimal mix" will not work', in Roger Brownsword and Karen Yeung (eds), *Regulating Technologies*. Oxford: Hart, pp. 193–218. Online at <http://works.bepress.com/serge_gutwirth/1/>.

Hermitte, Marie-Angèle (1998) 'Le droit est un autre monde', *Enquête: anthropologie, sociologie, histoire, sociologie*, 7: 17–38.

Hildebrandt, Mireille (2011) 'Legal protection by design. Objections and refutations', *Legisprudence*, 5 (2): 223–48.

Holmes, Oliver Wendell, Jr [1897] *The Path of the Law*. New Orleans, LA: Quid Pro Books; (2011) reprint from *Harvard Law Review*, vol. 10, p. 457.

Latour, Bruno (2002) *La fabrique du droit. Une ethnographie du Conseil d'état*. Paris: La Découverte.

Latour, Bruno (2004) 'Note brève sur l'écologie du droit saisie comme énonciation', in Frédéric Audren and Laurent De Sutter, *Pratiques cosmopolitiques du droit, Cosmopolitiques. Cahiers théoriques pour l'écologie politique*, No. 8. Paris: L'Aube, pp. 34–40.

Latour, Bruno (2008) 'Entretien avec Bruno Latour', by A. Fossier and E. Gardella, *Tracés. Revue de Sciences humaines*, No. 10, *Genres et Catégories*, February 2006. Online version posted on 11 February 2008 at <http://traces.revues.org/index158.html> (last accessed 29 May 2014), no page numbering.

Latour, Bruno (2012) *Enquête sur les modes d'existence. Une anthropologie des Modernes*. Paris: La Découverte.

Latour, Bruno (2013) *Facing Gaia. Six Lectures on the Political Theology of Nature* (March). Online at < http://www.bruno-latour.fr/node/486>.

McGee, Kyle (2012) 'The fragile force of law: mediation, stratification and law's material life', *Law, Culture and the Humanities*, 1–24.

McGee, Kyle (2014) *Bruno Latour: The Normativity of Networks*. Abingdon: Routledge.

McGee, Kyle (2015) 'On devices and logics of legal sense: towards sociotechnical legal analysis' (this volume).

Ost, François and van de Kerchove, Michel (2002) *De la pyramide au réseau? Pour une théorie dialectique du droit*. Brussels: FUSL.

Rigaux, François (1997) *La loi des juges*. Paris: Odile Jacob.

Schiavone, Aldo (2008) *Ius. L'invention du droit en Occident*. Paris: Belin.

Stengers, Isabelle (1996) *Cosmopolitiques. Tome 1. La guerre des sciences*. Paris: La Découverte/Les empêcheurs de penser en rond.

Stengers, Isabelle (1997) *Cosmopolitiques. Tome 7. Pour en finir avec la tolérance*. Paris: La Découverte/Les empêcheurs de penser en rond.

Stengers, Isabelle (2004) 'Une pratique cosmopolitique du droit est-elle possible?' (entretien avec Laurent De Sutter), in Frédéric Audren and Laurent De Sutter, *Pratiques cosmopolitiques du droit, Cosmopolitiques. Cahiers théoriques pour l'écologie politique*, No. 8. Paris: L'Aube, pp. 14–33.

Stengers, Isabelle and Latour, Bruno (2009) 'Le sphinx de l'œuvre', in Etienne Souriau, *Les différents modes d'existence* suivi *De l'œuvre à faire*. Paris: PUF, pp. 1–75.

Thomas, Yann (1980) 'Res, chose et patrimoine', *Archives de philosophie du droit*, 25: 413–26.

Thomas, Yann (1998) 'Le sujet de droit, la personne et la nature', *Le débat*, No. 100: 85–107.
Van Dijk, Niels (2011) 'Approaching law through conflicts', *Law and Method*, 1: 44–63.
Van Dijk, Niels (2013) *Grounds of the Immaterial. A Transversal Approach of Legal Philosophy in Intellectual Rights*. PhD thesis, VUB, Brussels.

6

The Life and Deaths of a Dispute: An Inquiry into Matters of Law
Niels van Dijk

1 Introduction

Latour has recently put forward the diplomatic proposal to embrace the value of law in our common non-modern world, and to see whether alternative accounts can be provided based on an empirical turn to the details of legal practices. These accounts will need to differ from the overly dismissive ones given by critical social theorists and from the overly purified or glorified ones provided by legal theorists and defensive legal practitioners. For the purposes of this chapter we will take up the proposal to provide such an account. This account can then be used within the diplomatic negotiations about the nature of law, both as a check and an addition to the accounts provided by more traditional legal theorists, but also to the alternative account provided by Latour himself.

In this context Latour's own account of law extracted from his ethnographical study at the French Council of State will first be discussed. Through his empirical investigations he addresses the philosophical question about the essence of law. He proposes to extract from this institutional practice what he calls the 'regime of enunciation' of law. Law has a specific way of tying a whole range of heterogeneous phenomena together in a way that allows lawyers to speak legally. Latour calls this the 'passage of law' which is characterised by several semiotic elements: a *clef de lecture*, the transfer of value objects and the acts of re-attachment. Taken together these constitute the legal trajectory of enunciation.

The conclusions that Latour draws about the nature of law, especially those related to the role of facts and legal totalities, will be compared with an alternative account of the value of law. This account will be based on empirical studies at a law firm and courts of first instance according to an approach that traces all the proceedings of the *matters of dispute*. Instead of starting a study of law at the end of the legal line in an instance of judgment in last appeal, such a conflict-based approach visualises all the things that make such a legal decision possible in the first place, by closely following everything that happens between the moment a particular conflict is first brought into contact with lawyers and the moment it is decided by the judges. This focus on the whole life of the legal dispute makes visible the whole antagonistic process in which lawyers render a dispute legally decidable that normally remains invisible in legal theory. The observation of these processes of law in action allows us to gradually and in piecemeal fashion construct an outline of the legal plane. These insights can, in turn, also be mobilised against existing legal theories and hold a promise for new ways of thinking about the nature of law.

2 Law as a regime of enunciation

In his book *The Making of Law* Latour addresses the philosophical question about the essence of law through an ethnographic study of law in action at the French Conseil d'État, the highest court in France in administrative matters. He states that:

> Although there is no clear description for what I'm doing, the closest is that of an empirical (not an empiricist) philosopher. This book tries, through the device of ethnography, to capture a philosophical question [...] that would be inaccessible philosophically [...]: *the essence of law*. Knowing an essence does not lie in a definition but in a practice, a situated, material practice that ties a whole range of heterogeneous phenomena in a specific *way*. And it is on the search for this specific way that this book is entirely focused. (Latour 2010: 10)

This empirical approach makes it possible to avoid philosophies that postulate a transcendence of the Law that would be incarnated in various legal institutional practices. Instead, Latour proposes to turn to the various details of these practices in order to extract from them what he calls the 'regime of enunciation' of law. This exercise of empirical philosophy is part of his larger philosophical project to provide an account of the modes of existence of our common world that has never been modern (Latour 2013).

Each of these modes has its own conditions of felicity according to which the success or failure of the actions and enunciations of its actors have to be understood. Law has a specific way of tying a whole range of heterogeneous phenomena together in a way that allows law to pass and lawyers to speak legally (*dire le droit*). Latour calls this the 'passage of law'.

This proposal to understand law as a 'regime of enunciation' takes its inspiration from semiotics.[1] Several semiotic elements can be detected in the way Latour characterises law: a specific *clef de lecture* or interpretive key as a particular evocative mode of send-off into the register of legal intelligibility, the transfer of different value objects that provide an orientation and specificity to the legal passage, and the acts of assignation that reconnect a statement to its enunciator by tying a local case to law as a totality. When aligned together these constitute the legal trajectory of enunciation.[2]

(i) When the essence of law consists in its passage, we are led to ask where this movement leads and when it is successfully finished in order to arrive at an accurate characterisation. To answer such questions Latour introduces the notion of 'value-objects' borrowed from semiotics. These value-objects give direction to the legal passage and their successful transfer indicates the end of the legal trajectory. They can be seen as attractors towards and through which the passage of law takes place and which animate the work of the lawyers. Throughout his studies of the activities at the Council of State Latour extracted ten different value objects (Latour 2010: 194–5):

1. the authority of the lawyer at stake;
2. the procedural progress of the claim;
3. the logistic organisation of cases;
4. the interestingness of the cases;
5. the authoritative weight of texts;
6. the control of the quality of the legal work;
7. the hesitations that provide a room for manoeuvre before producing linkages;
8. the legal means (*moyen*) that allow for the performance of certain actions;
9. the internal coherence of law;
10. the external limits of law.[3]

Interestingly, when compared to other modes of existence, the ways in which these value-objects are described does not always seem to make them primarily belong to the legal mode of existence. The logistic administration of cases (value-object 3), for instance, rather belongs to the mode of existence of *organisation*. In a certain sense the same seems to apply to the limits of law as an efficient enterprise that can effectively process cases and dispense the law in them (value-object 10). Furthermore, the control of the quality of the legal work through reflexive verification (value-object 6) seems to be a subcategory of *morality*'s mode of verification of 'the overall quality of all the links' between means and ends (Latour 2013: 460). Similarly, the hesitations that provide room for manoeuvre before producing new linkages (value-object 7) also seem to be a subcategory of morality's hesitation about the relation between means and ends more generally (Hache and Latour 2010).[4] Moreover, the interestingness of the cases (value-object 4) seems to belong to the mode of *attachment* with its related concept of *interessement*. In fact, this argument could even be applied to the very semiotic notion of 'value-object' here deployed to characterise the very passage of law, by indicating what makes actors move and tick and functioning as an attractor for their actions. This notion itself seems to belong more generally to the mode of attachment as a 'being of passionate interest' that attaches people by a common drive.[5] Where many of these value objects do thus not by themselves seem sufficiently legal, this characterisation should probably be rather sought in the specific way they are aligned in the legal trajectory of assignation of acts and actors.

(ii) The most important aspect of law in the light of its contribution to the construction of a common world is that it constitutes such a regime of *assignation*.[6] In daily life people continuously engage in all kinds of actions and utter all kinds of statements with regard to others. In the passage of things these acts and actors, these enunciators, enunciations and enunciatees, immediately and constantly become dispersed in all directions. Now, what is unique about law is the manner in which it preserves all these disengagements by keeping track of the traces that these actions have left behind and how, on this basis, it continuously reconnects people to their acts and enunciators to their enunciations. Without law these would have remained free-floating and unattributable.

People would not have been held to what they say and do and would not have been assigned to their acts and goods. In this sense law thus gives consistency to the processes of subject formation.

Law is singular in the way that it makes enunciations assignable. It is able to do so through its specific arsenal of legal operations like qualification, imputation, authentication, linking, following signatures and through its meticulous set of stabilising procedures. These operations reconnect a statement to its enunciator by tying a local case to the law as a whole. This notion of *legal totality* constitutes an important aspect of law. Latour even states that:

> It seems that there is law when it is possible to mobilize a certain form of totality with regard to an individual case, irrespective of how tiny it may be – and this is precisely why we call some reasoning 'legal'. (Latour 2010: 256–7)

Law is thus a particular way of mobilising a totality within the individual. Specific legal operations like qualification make the case pass through a series of appropriate forms that allow for the mobilisation of a legal totality and make it possible to *move away from the facts* of the case.[7] The importance of this point becomes further apparent from the ways in which both legal practitioners and legal theorists always evoke legal totalities in a circular fashion in definitions of what law is. These *tautologies* are not so much considered an embarrassment, but rather a necessary quality of law reflecting its original mode of self-explanation.

Latour's empirical approach to legal practice has the great advantage of providing an alternative account of law that demarcates it from other practices and makes us adjust our expectations of it. Our expectations should in this sense neither be too low in reducing law to something else, nor should they be too high in making law the guardian of some grand values that it cannot protect. Without understanding the proper constraints that legal practitioners face in their activities, law runs the risk of becoming mobilised too easily by other practices to be enlisted as an instrument in their service. Such instrumentality would only fuel the theoretical cynics who would all too happily jump in and reduce law to something external like economic markets (law and economics), governmental regulation (public administration), social constructions (sociology of law), cultural values (legal anthropology), political interest, class struggle or unconscious desires (critical legal studies). As a response to such accusations in the public debate, the jurist is often tempted to defensively present his or her practice by resorting to the general vocabulary of big terms (often learnt in law school) about the role of law in society as a guardian of morality, justice, the state, sovereignty, politics or public order. In this context Latour refers to La Fontaine's fable about the ass carrying relics and calls for law to be unburdened from these impossibly heavy loads, so that it may carry only itself and transport only its own values.

Latour's proposal drives a wedge between the value of law as a mode of existence and the accounts of law that have generally been provided by lawyers. This gap opens up a space for new alternative accounts of law that restitute its value, but in a way that differentiates law from the institutions that have come to betray it and from the (theoretical) domain in which it has become enclosed. Stated in this way, it thus becomes very important to take care that the nature of the legal value is sufficiently extracted from the relevant legal practices, so that the account of this value is not too greatly infected by the extravagancies of the particular institution in which it is studied. We can take up his challenge to enter the diplomatic negotiations about the value and nature of law by providing alternative accounts that restitute this value.[8] Hereafter, we will attempt to provide the brief outlines of such an account based on two empirical studies at a law firm and courts of first instance.[9] This account can then be mobilised both as a check on and an addition to the accounts provided by more traditional legal theorists, and also to the alternative account provided by Latour himself.

3 The life of the legal dispute

The studies at the law firm and the court are based on an empirical conflict-based approach partly born out of lingering dissatisfaction with both the distant abstract treatment and theoretical fixations of legal theory and the social and critical studies of law that aim to calculate its economic and societal effects or unmask its hidden presumptions. Their explanations often get before, after, above or below the legal objects of investigation in order to explain them, but they never get to the middle of things – *in medias res* – where they are still vital events in the process of happening. It could thus be asked in what way these theories have managed to *approach* legal matters at all. In order to obtain a closer understanding of law as an event, what is needed is a transversal turn to the median ground of legal practices that moves 'across' and traces the proceedings of the legal disputes at the heart of these practices.[10]

A conflict-based approach visualises all the things that make a legal decision possible in the first place by closely following all that happens between the first encounter of a particular conflict with lawyers at the law firm up until its judgment in court. This focus on the whole life of the legal dispute makes visible the antagonistic processes in which a dispute is rendered legally decidable through constructive actions of proof, disproof, qualification, disqualification, authorisation and unauthorisation, which normally remain invisible in legal theory. In this way we gradually obtain an outline of the proceedings of the dispute and the two little deaths that constitute the rhythm of its legal life. This will allow us to gradually and in piecemeal fashion construct a sketch of the legal plane. The orienting question for the investigations is here not so much 'What is Law?' – the classic question addressed by legal theory – but the question 'How does something become legal?' This shifts the focus from being to becoming, from legal objects (*Rechtsobjekt*) to things as antagonistic events. Here the fabric of the lawsuit grows from the middle, along tentative lines of proposition, towards its edges. Only on the basis of these lines of movement does it become possible to assign coordinates to the so-called 'fixed points' of legal objectivity and legal subjectivity of legal theory. In fact, it will enable us to see how the thing at stake is primarily a matter of dispute that can gradually become transformed into a legal object through the operations of legal practice.

This chapter presents an account of law extracted from the results of such a conflict-based approach. (See Figure 6.1 for a diagram of the movements we will study in this chapter.) Textual limitations will necessarily force us to abstract, which will make us lose some of the fire proper to the conflict dynamics that is nevertheless crucial to this undertaking. Some practical flesh on these conceptual bones of this account is provided elsewhere.[11] In order to get the contours of the type of issue at stake in these legal practices better into sight, a few contrasts with scientific practice and epistemology will also be drawn. These relate to the concepts of cause, effect, facts, evidence and the explication of conditions of success.

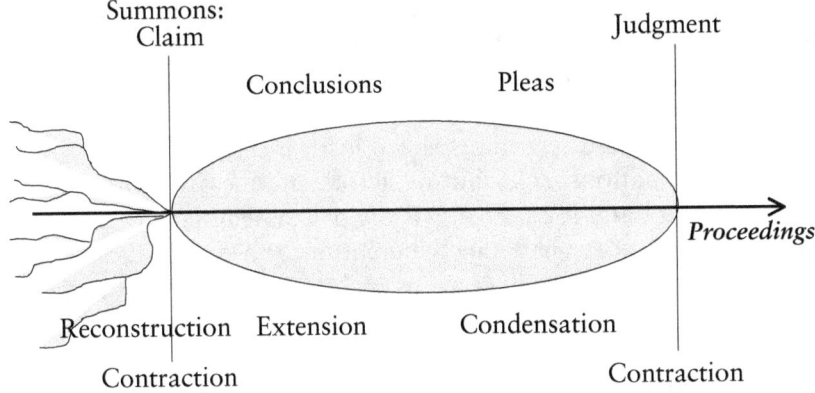

Figure 6.1 Diagram of the life of the legal dispute.

At first, the lawyers have to retrace and reassemble the dispute from the institutional network of memories and documents throughout which it has become dispersed, and contract it into the points of dispute that will determine its aboutness.

When we normally come into contact with court cases when reading about them in the newspaper, we often get the impression of issues with a precise and determinate topical value. We are often provided with a clear and concise summary on what the conflict is about. The journalist might have taken his cues from the summons or judgment documents. The main claims of the conflict are here carefully listed and seem to precisely indicate to the reader what the conflict is about. We must realise, however, that this degree of conciseness already situates us in a certain phase in the life of the conflict in which this topic of the conflict has attained a certain degree of stabilisation. This view is, however, neither exemplary for the nature of the conflict dynamics, nor for the way in which the conflict was first brought into connection with legal practice. A closer investigation of such first encounters provides us with a very different view of things. When lawyers first come into contact with the conflict it is not at all necessarily clear what the conflict is even about. The conflict has a very scattered mode of being that is never simply given. Lawyers first and foremost encounter it in its chaotic extensions, diffused over different times, spaces and people. The determination of the very aboutness is the first challenge for the lawyers for which they will have to engage in a process of *reconstruction* of the conflict through close interaction with those who have been involved in it. This process will require a careful retracing of all the fleeting memories and lost documents that have become distributed over a dispersed institutional network of long gone past situations, role-shifting actors and messy informational archives and databases. This process of reassemblage of the conflict becomes most visible in the creation of a case file. A digital and cardboard *folder* will come to enclose together the documents gathered in the course of reconstruction and all the ones that will be gathered later over the course of proceedings. These documents hereby become defined as belonging to the conflict. The file will itself become divided through several subfolders with titles like 'Agreement', 'Bills', 'Meetings', 'Correspondence', 'Pieces' and 'Lawsuits' that will further organise the body of the conflict.

When sufficient dispersed traces have been reassembled, they can be *contracted* into a few central singular points that will constitute the centres from which the conflict will unfold. These contractions provide a certain orientation and belonging to the conflict and delimit the series of possible paths along which it might further proceed.[12] This concept of the 'points of dispute' is very important. They characterise the singular *legal pointillism* at the core of the lawyer's operations of dealing with conflicts and rendering them decidable. We will return to this later.

> *The conflict is translated to the conceptual vocabulary of a certain legal regime through the typical legal act of qualification, which assigns the matter of dispute a belonging and orientation.*

This contraction of the many heterogeneous elements of the dispute finds its most intense form in the claims proposed in the summons, which is an official document that calls for a defendant to appear in court. This document provides a first formal introduction to several elements that will play a central role in the legal proceedings of the dispute.[13] It introduces the primary parties to the conflict and prepares for the inscription of the central claims. These claims provide us with the *matter of dispute*.[14] This is the central thing competed for that has gathered together all of the protagonists and the proceedings and transformations of which will have to be followed. This thing cannot at all be seen as an external physical object (*Rechtsobjekt*) for a legal subject as postulated in classical legal theories. It is not necessarily even something material or objective, but first of all consists in the way that it matters to the parties on whom it has exerted its gathering force.[15] In line with its ancient primordial meaning as *res*, a thing is before anything else the affair at stake that opposes and reunites two protagonists within the same relation, a *res iuris*. This matter of controversy finds itself posited in this common interiority: *res in controversia posita*.

When this *res* is subsequently put in legal form (*mise-en-form*) by being translated according to the conceptual vocabulary of a specific legal regime, it can become a *causa* for initiating legal action. This act of translation is known as *qualification* and is very characteristic of law. The thing is hereby introduced into the legal arena and transformed into a matter of legal dispute. From there on it can be further articulated by the specific tools and procedures of law (*lis*).[16] By assigning something a belonging in a certain legal regime, a qualification provides a first orientation to the dispute. The claim is the most contracted and simplified state of the conflict that brings together and implicates many heterogeneous elements in one single formula. Taking inspiration from Leibniz, we could call this contraction of the infinitely detailed and extensive developments of the dispute, in the claim a first little 'death' of the dispute.[17]

The short statement of the elements of the dispute in the claim could be deceiving to the extent that it might portray the activity of lawyers as a simple exercise in syllogistic logic in which the concrete complex case is subsumed as a species of a general stable legal form. This is not at all the case. Stabilities and simplicities are always local and temporary and quickly become fluid and complexified, drawn in by the chaotic dynamic movements of the dispute. This dynamic is characterised by the antagonistic dance of the opponents united in a common relation around the matter of dispute.[18] The only constant here is disputation itself. Each qualification proposed by one party is bound to be met by a disqualification from the opposed party. Actually, each qualification can itself be seen as a disqualification of other legal categories either explicitly proposed or which would have been possible to propose.[19]

> *From here on, things complexify rapidly. The dispute becomes mediated by a host of things, procedures,*

> *techniques and architectures that enable the organisation and circulation of the file in law firms and courts, and that enable the jurists to speak legally about the dispute (*ius dictum*).*
>
> *The lawsuit readily extends throughout the 'conclusion' documents, in which the matter of dispute becomes mutually affixed to or cut from pieces of evidence and conditions that will come to authorise its procession.*

After the first contraction and envelopment in the claims in the summons document, the dispute is fully sent off into its antagonistic dynamics. It will now enter a phase of rapid extension and development. In civil law cases this happens through the writing and exchange of 'conclusion' documents, which is the legal form in which the protagonists are obliged to organise their further proceedings.[20] Claims can here be checked with counterclaims, qualifications with explicit disqualifications. These are in turn often followed by counter-qualifications that can transpose the cause at stake according to a different legal regime and thus open up whole new directions in which the dispute will simultaneously come to be unfolded. According to each qualification, alternative directions are taken and alternating things become relevant.

In order to understand these extensions, one has to understand the connections that will be made to the dispute after its initial qualifications. We could introduce the term *affixation* to characterise this act of establishing connections between the dispute and all kinds of documents. To affix means not only to secure to something, attach, join one thing to another, but also to impute, attribute, ascribe, assign, and to annex or place at the end. This triple meaning nicely demonstrates the threefold nature of the connection itself (fastening attachments), its indexical location with regard to the documented body text of the dispute (annexes like sources and inventory of pieces) and what happens when these connections manage to hold (assignation).[21] We will have to fine-tune this point, however, since attachments to different kinds of documents will lead the lawyers in very different directions and will lead the matter of dispute onto different trajectories of becoming. When the matter of dispute becomes stitched to or cut from *pieces of evidence* it can gradually be turned into a *matter of fact*. When it is aligned or disconnected from raised *conditions of proceeding* it can be gradually transformed into a *legal object*.

The search for certain documents called 'pieces of evidence' will guide the lawyers onto wild goose chases, making them jump into their cars in order to ransack the sites of friends and foes, conduct implicative teleconferences with informants, or conduct thorough detective investigations on the Internet. The reassemblage of the whole network of dispersed elements from many different places will have to be intensified. All traces must be followed, all relevant leads investigated. The collection of these pieces of evidence and their attachment to the dispute constitutes a continuous task for the lawyers. These documents are gathered in an 'Inventory of Pieces', a subfolder of the case file, where they are ordered according to categories and numbers. This inventory will mediate the connection between the inscribed quotes or bracketed document titles in the text of the conclusion and the documents in the 'Pieces' folders. Through these textual operations the lawyers establish legal reference to the facts that will prove their claim. When all this work has been performed the focus in the dispute can gradually be shifted from the actions of processual actors like lawyers (and registrars and judges) to the acts of the protagonists who have been drawn into the antagonistic dance of the dispute.

The majority of these affixed pieces of evidence are documents that inscribe a variety of topics: from contacts to contracts, meetings to beatings and actions to reactions. Through these attachments the matter of dispute is made to proceed in and out of a variety of different sites, settings and situations, where it is brought in contact with a plethora of introduced actors, figures and things, and where it can be staged in ways that allow the parties involved to assume certain (op)positions with regard to it. Through the procedures of legal evidence these protagonistic elements are turned into the factual grounds for the matter of dispute, on which its procession is progressively brought to stand as a legal matter of fact, a *res facta*. The lawyers of the opponent will in turn try to *cut* as many of those established evidentiary stitches as they can and do some attaching of their own. Afterwards, severed links will be mended by new attachments and old links will be reinforced. The weft of links that makes up the lawsuit gradually unfolds through these constant adversarial processes of stitching, cutting and reinforcing of pieces of evidence.

> *Here the epistemic notion of the fact as a discussion-closer really shows its legal roots.*[22] *When we speak about what*

> the case is in fact, we have to become familiar with this very specific legal concept of proof. Just like with the notions of cause and effect, we have to forget all references to science when we want to understand the legal particularity of notions like 'matter of fact' and 'proof'. Lawyers are bound to constraints for providing valid proof that would be very unfamiliar to scientists.[23] Concepts like 'burden of proof', 'evidential value', 'evidential force' and 'inner conviction' are very characteristic for the legal mode of proof. Furthermore, a glance at the means of proof allowed in general civil proceedings shows them to be utterly foreign to science: documents, witnesses, experts, presumptions, oaths, confessions and invoices. Marking the contrast between scientific and legal proof even more is the fact that conclusions or factual confirmations by (scientific) experts have the smallest 'evidential value' of all means of proof. Article 962 of the Code of Procedural Law even determines that the judge is not obliged to follow such conclusions if they conflict with his convictions. On the other hand, certified documents which are signed by both parties provide full proof of what they inscribe (agreements). Such a document has 'evidential force' which, according to article 1319 of the Civil Code, the judge is obliged to follow even if it would be against his 'conviction'. Is this not most curious from the viewpoint of science or philosophy of knowledge? In court the so-called 'subjective' convictions of a judge are valued higher than the 'objective' statements of fact by the expert! And documents with signatures cannot even be evaluated by the judge, but force him to align. The practices of law and science in this sense both have their own divergent ways of producing facts.[24] The conditions according to which lawyers and judges either have to or cannot do certain things, characterise the legal mode of proceeding.

Whereas the hunt for evidentiary documents leads the lawyers into their cars, onto the Internet or to their phones, the search for other kinds of documents that will constitute the legal 'source material' for the dispute will lead them to their bookcases crammed with codices, periodicals of jurisprudence and books and journals of doctrine.[25] At stake here is the extraction and establishment of the *conditions* and requirements that the matter of dispute will have to satisfy in order to legally proceed. Instead of an endeavour to let the factual evidence speak for one's claims, the lawyer's work is here oriented towards letting the law and its authorities successfully speak for these propositions.[26] Through attaching the proposition to parts of text from jurisprudence, doctrine or statute law, the matter of dispute is made to pass through a variety of different legal settings. It will come to traverse some of the legal paths that have once become successfully constructed in past disputes in order to transport their requirements to the present conflict when the lawyers manage to establish sufficient 'resonances' between them;[27] it will be guided through the preparatory considerations and legal reference checks of the legislative processes leading up to the laws invoked in the dispute; or it will come to pass along the systematic pre-articulations of the webs of authorisation for the conditions that govern the proceedings of these kinds of dispute lines proposed in the interpretative writings of legal scholars.[28] In this way certain carefully proportioned alliances of legal sources become aligned with the matters of the claim in order to authorise its successful proceeding.

Once again the lawyers of the opponent will try to *cut* as many of those alignments and appended weights as they can and will themselves perform some aligning and balancing. In this way they try to unauthorise the claims of their adversary, isolate and invalidate their conditions and make the force of law exert itself in favour of their own propositions. Sometimes the mobilisation of a single new source can displace or even reverse a whole network of authorisations. Certain proposed stringent conditions can, for instance, suddenly find themselves less firmly supported, where the authority of the law is redirected and aligned with other proposed conditions that are less exigent.

These processes of (un)authorisation can also relate to conditions of proof. Apart from disputing the attachment of certain *pieces* of evidence attached to the dispute (the cut of disproof), it is also possible to dispute the evidentiary *obligations* that govern the conflict and the *scope* of proof (the cut of unauthorisation), by trying to prescribe what one is required to prove at all and to what extent. The conditions that govern the scope of evidence required in order to prove one's legal propositions are thus themselves part of the legal dispute. This also shows that, although facts and law become differentiated by two directions of attachment, they constantly lead to each other and modify each other, thus opening new directions and orientations for the unfolding of the dispute.

> *The fact that the work of making explicit the conditions of felicity is such an important, integral part of the practical proceedings is definitely a curiosity of legal practice. In scientific practice, for instance, these debates arise most clearly in those situations in which scientists are engaged in controversies and conflict. According to Kuhn such conflicts arise most in periods of crisis and revolutionary science, i.e. periods in which the 'normal' practice of scientific activity has broken down (Kuhn 1996). In law these kinds of situations are at the heart of its ongoing activity because law is a practice that deals with problems, conflicts and breakdowns.*

> **After this phase of extension, the dispute becomes gradually condensed through the pleas in court. These provide the judges certain piloting directions for passing through the assembled corpus of the case.**

In the plea the order of things is tied together differently, as compared to the conclusions. In the conclusions the complex movements of the dispute were developed at great length and detail. When the lawyer's work has been thorough, these conclusions will often have become 'corpulent' documents. In the plea this will have to be presented in such a way that the problem, the main points of conflict and the solutions will become clear and evident to the judges. There is a condensation of the dispute at work here. Years of preparations are contracted into the lines of speech of the oral pleas in ways that have to be convincing. We could say that a plea has a threefold structure of satisfaction: *satis-facere, satis-placere, satis-plicare*. A lawyer has to do enough (*satis*) work of unfolding and explicating the case, in a way that sufficiently complies with the conditions and convincingly pleases the judges, in order for them to align with the qualification proposed.

In order to please the judges, the lawyers will have to speak satisfactorily. This is not an easy achievement and there can be many obstacles. In court the flow of a plea can become interrupted by the adverse party or the judges, making the lawyer 'lose her point'. It is actually a part of the lawyer's work to try to punctuate the flow of words of one's opponent by interruptions and reversals. All these factors complicate speech and can make it stutter and stumble. Sufficient preparatory work thus needs to be done for stabilising the plea. The lawyers employ several techniques for this, like mnemonic devices to 'find things back' and optic devices to 'make things visible'. First, oral speech is supported by a number of paper items that serve to index, trace and retrieve the threads of argumentation. When the lawyer loses the aim of her story she can fall back on a paper sheet (sometimes called a 'trial brief') with the main 'bullet points' to retrieve the ammunition for her plea. Second, oral speech is substituted by 'speaking' images that serve to visualise the matters of dispute. Sometimes these images tell the story of change more satisfactorily than the lawyers can. The question here is not merely about how to do things with words, it is rather about how things enable the lawyers to speak legally and how they allow them to say things without words.

We have seen that lawyers have to be good detectives. The narratives that they have constructed must be grounded by gathering many pieces of evidence. These attachments must have been made to resist the cutting operations of the adverse party. The corpus of the case can become quite complicated through all these stitched attachments, cuts, reattachments and reinforcements, especially when it concerns detailed technical issues. Being a good detective and conclusively writing an authoritative and elaborate body of text at the law firm is one thing, but it offers no necessary guarantees for further proceeding in court. The judges have to be satisfactorily guided through the accumulated specificities and technicalities of the dispute.[29] The lawyer is always faced with the risk of losing the judges along the way. In court the lawyer has to be a good pilot and ensure that the boat that sails the stream of events safely arrives at its proposed destination with all its members still on board. It is to these judges that we will now turn.

> *Eventually the dispute will find a second differential contraction in the operatives of judgment according to a linear focus along the strong points that will come to constitute its grounds.*

To convince or to be convinced, that is the question by which much of the legal play oscillates.[30] The requirements of the advocates to convince and the requirements of the judge to be convinced diverge, however. Whereas advocates often get to work on a case for extensive periods of time, the judges cannot indulge in such 'luxury' since the time they have for dealing with each case is limited by their workload. When advocates have proceeded too rashly in extensive constructions of their case through their conclusions and pieces, it is up to the judge to slow things down.

Judgment will have to again contract the dispute. In order to perform such a contraction the judge has to select points of the dispute that will permit him or her to do so. These points are of two kinds. On the one hand, they could reflect a gap enveloped or concealed in some other extension of the dispute. These are 'weak points' that cannot bear the weight of a legal argument or might even destabilise and implode the whole legal proposition (the gap as a black hole). The judge deploys several rhetorical techniques to make the advocate get 'to the point'. On the other hand the point at stake could also be a 'strong point' that includes an intensity that could support legal arguments and thus serve as a sufficient basis for judging the case.[31] This happens when the lawyers have, as one judge states, 'put the right stepping stones for legal argument in the right place'. This is what enables the judge to go back to his office and do his job as a 'technician' in the art of judgment. The advocate has to select and align the intensive points of the dispute and highlight them as a solid path to arrive at judgment and not digress and drown in irrelevant specificities and technicalities that have accumulated in the dispute.

Once this is done well, the whole exercise of reaching an opinion boils down to the judge having to assume a point of view on the dispute, or rather an alignment of points of view, cleared from within the dispute dynamics. This happens when reasoning strikes a line that selects and connects points of intensity from the dispute dynamics and incorporates these into the connecting trajectory of a 'linear focus' from which the cases of the advocates can be arranged into an opinion (the act of judgment).[32] Once this linear focus is assumed, the selected points can be projected as the reasons that sufficiently ground the judgment (the act of reasoning). These grounds are thus unfolded and raised from within the interiority of the dispute. Such a line of reasoning is like a strike of lightning that bifurcates downwards in a tentative series of points of embranchment until one of them arrives at the ground and the charge reinforces itself as the running line of those bifurcations that constituted this passage.

This highlights the importance of two terms in the composition of judgment: that of the 'point' and that of the 'ground'. The act of judgment can be described as the pointillist art of selective contractions of intensive points of dispute in a series of operative sentences (linear focus).[33] In this sense the unit of decision-making is not so much the dispute itself, but rather the 'point of dispute'. Through this *legal pointillism* with regard to disputes (points of dispute, weak points, strong points, requisite procession points, bullet points, points of view, appointments) jurists continuously endeavour to contract zones in the extensive dispute dynamics into discrete points.[34] We have seen how lawyers performed this contraction through the reconstruction of the conflict and its legal qualification in the claims. Judgment can achieve such a contraction through its own modus operandi that consists of aligning a succession of operators, operations and operatives. First the judgment becomes organised according to a series of *operators* (e.g. scroll number, repertory number, etc.) that both link the judgment document to the case file or actually turn it into a file, and install it within the order of administration as the grasping point for further acts of organisation. The dispute subsequently becomes further compacted through a series of *operations* preceding judgment, which transform the dynamics of the proceedings of the dispute into vectors of consideration, admission and conviction that will impinge on the minds of the judges during the processes of deliberation.[35] Many of these operations will have to pass certain 'requisite procession points' that condition the felicity of the act of judgment itself (e.g. the contents that the verdict has to inscribe for not being declared null or void itself).[36] Finally, the dispute becomes contracted by a series of *operatives* that enact the judgment through a series of performative acts that carry a preceding cause or *causa* into its legal effects. The latter are enlisted in 'the operative part' of judgment that inscribes the 'dictum', the thing said legally. The court enacts this judgment through pronouncing a range of utterances, each of which performs a specific operation. The nature of these performative operations is indicated by the verb by which the utterance is initiated like 'declares', 'sentences', 'orders', 'grants', 'denies', 'prohibits', etc.[37]

> *This 'carrying out' or 'carrying into effect' is the etymological meaning of the verb 'to perform'. The act of judicial qualification according to a legal form brings about legal*

> *effects. There is a very specific notion of cause at stake here. The word 'effect' should not be misunderstood by giving an interpretation befitting a scientistic context in which it can objectively be reduced to, and thus explained by, a physical cause. Instead of having the notion of cause hijacked by physicalists and reduced to material or efficient causes,[38] we should pay attention to a mode of cause that belongs to legal practices. Can these legal effects be explained by referring back to a cause? Yes, certainly, but they refer to a very specific cause that is quite at home in a legal context.[39] We could even speak of a very specific kind of formal cause that is characteristic for law and is closely related to the notion of performativeness. It is per forma that a matter of dispute is carried into its legal effects. Cause and form are thus closely related in their own way within legal practice. The forms here point both to the forms of action within a practice, or what Austin calls 'conventional procedure',[40] of affixing the documentation and filling out the constitutive forms, rather than some explanation by some form, idea or intention in the mind of the parties or the judge, or some isolated ideal template for things that would constitute the scene.[41]*

After the contraction in the advocate's claims in the summons, the dispute finds its second most intense contraction in these operatives of judgment, selectively bringing together many of its heterogeneous elements in these few singular formulas. These two 'little deaths' of the dispute formally compose the rhythmical interval of the life of the conflict as a matter of legal dispute.

The life of the matter of dispute and the little deaths of the dispute in the operatives of judgment (and the claim in the summons) that formally enclose its legal life have to be distinguished from the *grounds* of judgment of the dispute.[42] Grounds do sometimes rise to the surface of things; they make their ingression in a dispute from a below within. The vertically raised grounds (|) are different from the horizontal extensions of the dispute (-) and the diagonal acts of grounding (/) and judgment with its striking linear focus (\ ). A ground only makes its ingression in the dynamics of a dispute when it is raised within the practice of that dispute through an act of grounding.[43] This focus on grounding as an act or operation is important. Heidegger pointed out that 'in all grounding and getting to the bottom we already walk on the path to a ground' (Heidegger 1997: 3).[44] This 'path to a ground' highlights not so much the ground, the grounded or the grounder, but the *act of grounding* which has the character of being underway, of proceeding, of seeking to arrive. These acts of grounding are indeed closely related to a judgment in which the ground will bring something (the matter of judgment) to a stand (*zum-stehen brengen*) as an object (*Gegenstand*) when it will have provided a sufficient (*vollstandig*) account of it.[45]

In a legal dispute this fixation of a position is quite an achievement. In the legal geometries of disputes no such position is ever pre-given, but has to be painstakingly established as a post-given beyond dispute in the dynamics of the legal fabric.[46] They have to be extracted from the extensions of the conflictual dynamics that constantly threaten to destabilise and engulf them. This work of extraction requires prudential acts of stitching pieces of evidence and legal documents to the matter of dispute in a way that establishes a foothold on its incessant proceeding and ground a position in relation to it. Through the grounding judgment (*arrêt*) the proceeding matter of dispute is brought to a (temporary) halt (*arrêter*), transformed into a matter of fact and the *legal object* of the relevant legal regime.

4 Modern facts, legal totalities and application

The results of the conflict-based approach presented in this chapter have led to an outline of the lives and deaths of disputes at the heart of legal practices. It has put into focus the whole process by which a matter of dispute proceeds, from the moment it becomes reconstructed and contracted in a claim, to the moment it arrives at judgment where it becomes contracted in its operatives. In this sense it makes visible all the steps that precede judgment and make it possible in the first place. A focus on the proceeding of the matter of dispute also shows all the processes in which the proceeding of the matter of dispute is gradually grounded and transformed into a matter of fact and a legal object, and how, as a cause of action, it undergoes a series of *performations* by which it is gradually carried into its legal effects.[47] Such an approach that is crucially related to the event of the dispute, casts jurisprudence into the role of the legal philosophy that deals with singularities.[48] In this sense legal practices constitute a paradigmatic site for the study of things, causes and object-formation as matters of dispute that gather protagonists in a dance of antagonism,[49] but also for the study of speech act theory in articulating what is involved in processes of performance and what allows the flows of illocutionary force.

With this account we can return to the discussion about the nature of law and enter into the diplomatic negotiations on how to restitute the value of law and which elements are important for this. First, the account can be mobilised as a check on the existing accounts of this value provided by legal theories and thus holds a promise for new ways of thinking about the nature of law.[50] For this exercise to succeed, however, it is necessary for this value to be sufficiently extracted from the different forms in which it has become institutionally rendered. In order to check the robustness of this extraction, we can start by drawing out some comparisons and contrasts with Latour's account of law. Latour has chosen the Council of State as the site for studying law in its pure form in the speech acts of the councillors. When we situate these events within the broader biography of the life of a legal dispute, we here find ourselves at the end of the legal line at the judgment in last appeal. At this point in time a lot has already happened to the matter of dispute, many events have befallen its destiny. The matter of dispute will have undergone several trials and tribulations through which it has become greatly 'canvassed', as Llewellyn so elegantly expressed it, through the pointillist 'screen' of legal practice.[51] At this stage it will in fact be in its third life-time, not yet a cat but coming quite close.

In order to understand these previous processes, we will need to envisage all that makes legal judgment possible in the first place by closely following everything that happens between the moment a particular conflict is first brought into contact with lawyers and the moment it is decided by the judges. This focus on the whole life of the legal dispute also makes visible the whole antagonistic process in which lawyers render a dispute legally decidable through their constructive actions of proof, disproof, qualification, disqualification, authorisation and unauthorisation that normally remain invisible in legal theory.[52] The observation of these processes of law in action allows us to gradually and in piecemeal fashion construct an outline of the legal plane of grounding. Several elements and concepts can be identified as important for an account of law:

- *matter of dispute* (thing, antagonism)
- *qualification* (claim, translation, legal concept)
- *performation* (cause of action, legal effect)
- *proceedings* (process and procedure)
- *evidence* (facts, conviction)
- *conditions* (authorisation, legal sources)
- *ap-plication* (affixation, extensive development, mutual folding)
- *grounding* (reasoning, bringing-to-a-halt, fixing position)
- *pointillism* (contraction, points of dispute, appointment)
- *judgment (ius dicem)* (linear focus, operativity).[53]

With this account we can open the negotiations. From this outline, some comments can be made about the role of facts and legal totalities in the characterisation of law. We could say that when the bibliographical narrative of a legal dispute has sufficiently proceeded, at a certain moment in time it might become possible for legal practice to get rid of the facts in order to pass to the composition of a legal totality. This is indeed what we could observe at the highest courts of appeal, which are procedurally required (this is a requisite procession point) to abstain from judging the facts of a certain dispute since these have been dealt with sufficiently by courts of first and second instance. Instead, they are charged with the task to only deal with the legal questions that this dispute may give rise to, which will pose to them the challenge of constructing legal coherences. These are requirements specific to a court of last appeal that has to perform a *cassation*, which, in line with its etymological meaning, makes some thing void, emptying it of its factual content. But is our empirical account of law to depend on such rules of procedure that prescribe in advance where pure law is to be found? Or do we need to engage head-first the intense chaos that announces itself in each dispute, in order to study the processes by which purifications might be achieved in practice by all kinds of laborious operations, independent of the pre-scription of the site of action?

In order to understand law we will have to look at the whole dispute trajectory, from its 'first instance' when it enters the offices of the law firm until its 'last appeal' at the court of cassation. When one thus turns to the work of lawyers at the law firm or of judges in lower courts, we get a quite different view on things. These previous proceedings of the matter of dispute are instead characterised not so much by getting rid of the facts, but rather by fully engaging with them according to the typical mode of legal evidence. To the contrary, there seems to be very little elaboration and attachment of the dispute to legal totalities here.[54] In order to reach a *ius-dicim* in a dispute, a 'speaking legally' about some thing, it is not necessary to mobilise the whole of the law. We cannot say that there is law only when there is a construction of legal totalities. The construction and connection of a legal totality is rather a by-product of the extension of disputes, especially when they have come as far as the Council of State. It is a gradually accumulated quality dependent upon and proportional to the extent of proceeding of the matter of dispute. What characterises these processes of proceeding themselves is rather a concern for attaching the two fabrics of evidence and conditions well to each other in terms of the concrete dispute at stake. We can single out this operation by reinvigorating the concept of *ap-plication*:

> Etymologically 'to apply' means to 'attach to' or to 'fold to' in order to bring something in contact with something else. Advocates bring heterogeneous elements together when they connect an extralegal thing to law in order to initiate its proceeding as a matter of legal dispute. During the legal process two different fabrics – the factual patchwork and the legal weft – have to be constantly folded to each other in such a way that they join together and something can proceed. 'Application' does not have the hierarchical or vertical connotation of 'subsumption' in which a factual matter is transformed by being syllogistically placed under a form that itself remains unaltered. Instead the term application keeps open the possibilities for the mutual change of both case and rule that might result from a connection between the two. What the case is and what a rule requires is never something given. In a lawsuit both have to be constantly worked out by being connected to each other in a way that is legally tailored to the matter in dispute.[55]

In the previous section we have seen how a twofold authorisation is operative in the practices of attaching documents to the dispute in a way that grounds the matter of dispute both in law and in facts. These affixations gradually transform the matter of dispute into a matter of fact and into a matter of law or legal object of a certain legal regime.[56] We saw how these factual authorisations were mediated by a series of special evidentiary procedures by which the facts come to decide someone's claim and by which the practitioner becomes empowered to speak in the name of what happened. We here arrive at a notion of the fact – the *res facta* – that is more properly legal and that has itself even influenced the concept of 'the modern fact'. It has indeed been argued that this modernist notion, with all its epistemological assumptions and its status as discussion-closer, historically originated in the legal practices of courts with its developing standards of eyewitnessing and testimony. This moved the figures of the witness (and the juror) into the position of the 'judge of the facts'. Afterwards this notion migrated to other practices like the sciences or empiricist philosophy in order to constitute a much broader modern culture of fact.[57] In its primordial sense this *res facta* or matter of fact was not yet 'that which is proven', but referred to the issue of proving an act itself. As such, it was closely tied up with the legal necessity of reaching reasonable closure in a relatively short period of time and to the adversarial characteristics of the trial in which all kinds of procedures for testing the credibility of witness evidence were developed (like cross-examination, the crime of perjury for false testimony, subpoena for appearing).

In this sense it is curious to see that Latour draws the conclusion that 'contrary to religion, technology, fiction, and politics, law has suffered much less from the ravages from the modernist invention of matters of fact. In a way, law has never been modern, always insisting on its original type of truth condition and its completely specific key' (Latour 2008: 9), considering that law itself contributed to this invention of the matter of fact through the procedures and figures set in its own specific key of legal evidence.

Lastly, in the project of restituting the value of law, one hypothesis remains to be explored. It relates to the installation of law as a mode of existence that inhabits the ecology of common (non-modern) values and to some conclusions drawn with regard to its tautological nature. Latour observes how law is singular in the intensity of care for itself: law constantly engages with itself, checks its own quality and continuously explicates the proper conditions for itself. He further observes how law is always encountered in its entirety and that this mobilisation of legal totalities is crucial for the essence of law and accounts for its tautological nature. We need to proceed carefully here and explore whether there is a different possible starting point of analysis that would break out of this circle, or rather never be set in motion in the first place, and thus save us from all this agonising head spinning. The exploration of this possibility requires a care for naming. As the great Confucian philosopher Xunzi remarked, if the goal is to achieve a sustainable harmony in our collective existence, we better start by using the proper names. This lesson both pertains to the more generic logic of the exercise of naming the modes of existence and to the value in our case specifically.

So what about calling this value 'law'? One problem with this starting point is that this coinage seems what sets the whole tautological circle in motion in the first place. It will then be 'law' which cares for itself and stretches its reflexive muscles. There is, however, another possible designation strategy, which Latour deploys in the case of the mode of existence that deals with knowledge and information. Latour did not choose to name this mode 'science' but called it 'reference'.[58] The term 'reference', however, applies more specifically to the success of the epistemic act, to the conditions of felicity so to say (when the words in a scientific article have managed to successfully refer to the 'thing' that was at stake through the established chains of links that manage to hold, thus securing access to remote entities). When we would take the same approach in our case, we would not call our value 'law' but *assignation*.[59] 'Okay okay,' one might object at this point. 'You are merely playing language games. Why is all this play with words so important?' The answer to this is that when our value is assignation instead of law, we might have suddenly lost the dimension of tautology and self-reference that was claimed to be essential for it (since this 'self' and this 'it' have changed meaning). In turn, this would allow us to understand 'law' as the name for one kind of attachment, next to attachments called 'facts', performed to a proceeding matter of dispute in order to make it assignable. The success of these attachments will be determined by whether an enunciation will be tied back to 'its' enunciator, the act back to 'its' actor.[60] This designation might thus change the theoretical stakes and tasks in accounting for this modal value and could give legal philosophy itself a whole new assignment . . .

Notes

1. Especially the work of Greimas – see for instance Greimas (1976). Latour, however, uses a notion of enunciation that is broader than is current in semiotics, since it extends to action. Latour defines an

enunciation as 'the whole of the acts of mediation whose presence is necessary for the meaning' (Latour 1999a).
2. This discussion will here necessarily be brief. The notion of a *clef de lecture* as a particular evocative mode of send-off into the register of legal intelligibility will not be further treated. For a more extensive discussion and some points of critique of the semiotic aspects of the legal regime of enunciation, see De Vries and Van Dijk (2013).
3. In his later writings Latour reiterates certain of these value objects in order to characterise the nature of the legal mode of existence while passing over others. Above all he reinstates the crucial singularity of the notion of 'means' in establishing a continuity of passage by establishing stable connections between the heterogeneity of elements implied in a case and the notion of 'hesitations' that determines the quality of judgment and sets law apart from organisational management. He also mentions the importance of 'procedures' for re-attaching acts to their actors, the circulation of 'dossiers' constituting the material manifestation of legal passage and 'coherence' for stabilising legal totalities (Latour 2013).
4. Perhaps these two points bear relation to the translation of the French term *moyen* as 'means' for the eighth value-object. Whereas this translation has the advantage of indicating both a middle and a 'means of transportation' (of legal force), it has the disadvantage of causing confusion with other modes due the way the term 'means' is used in discussion on technology and morality. For this purpose it might be better to translate the term as 'ground' or 'reason' in the sense that will become clear later in this section. Grounds are the true legal affordances, they provide the 'cause of action', the thing that makes specific legal actions possible and, in concordance with its etymology, lets it proceed onward.
5. In Latour's previous writings he even called law the regime of enunciation of Attachment (Latour 2004: 37).
6. In fact the way law is characterised in the pivot table of the modes of existence in terms of its hiatus, trajectory, conditions of felicity, entities and alteration is practically exclusively in the terms of this notion of assignation (Latour 2013: 488–9).
7. 'Facts are things that one tries to get rid of as quickly as possible, in order to move on to other things, namely the particular point of law that is of interest, and to which the judges will be entirely devoted from that point on' (Latour 2010: 215).
8. Latour stipulates several criteria that these alternative accounts have to fulfil. They have to distinguish between: (1) the value at stake; (2)

the theories offered to account for this value; and (3) an alternative account of the value (Latour 2013: 480).

9. More concretely, these were all cases of intellectual rights like copyright, patent and trademark law before two Belgian courts of first instance.
10. As such this approach has certain affinities with the practice turn in contemporary theory (Schatzki et al. 2001), the concept of an ecology of practices (Stengers 2005) and the tracing of circulating objects (Latour 1999b). For a more detailed account of this conflict-based approach, see Van Dijk (2011).
11. Van Dijk (2013). Here, more justice is done to the 'matters of law' mentioned in the subtitle to this chapter by a more thorough focus on the materialities of legal proceedings. These include the things that make one speak legally and the (monadic) regimes of legal visibility.
12. We can take inspiration here from Gilles Deleuze's thinking on the 'being of the problematic'. He states that 'problems must be considered not as "givens" (data) but as ideal "objecticities" possessing their own sufficiency and implying acts of constitution and investment in their respective symbolic fields.' Their 'solution necessarily follows from the complete conditions under which the problem is determined as a problem, from the means and the terms which are employed in order to pose it' (Deleuze 2004: 198), which in our case relate to legal conditions, means and terms. We can furthermore compare the contracted points of dispute to what Deleuze calls 'centers of envelopment' or 'centers of implication'. He states: 'Every contraction is a presumption, a claim – that is to say, it gives rise to an expectation or a right in regard to that which it contracts, and comes undone once its object escapes' (ibid.: 100).
13. The Dutch word here is *geding* which is commonly translated as 'proceedings'. The word *geding* is a noun relating to a conflict or dispute. The word has the grammatical form of the perfect simple of the verb *dingen* which means 'to compete'. The word *ding* as a root noun, however, means 'thing'. The word *geding* thus could be said to have the composite meaning of the competition for a thing. In a legal context *geding* refers both to 'the thing competed for' and 'the process of competing'. In the first case we will speak of the 'matter of dispute', in the second case we will use the translation 'proceedings'. In Heideggerian parlance the term *geding* could even be translated as the 'thinging'.
14. The term *matter of dispute* is a translation for the Dutch term *voorwerp van geschil*.

15. Heidegger famously stated that the ancient term 'thing' or 'Ding' means 'a gathering for the trial of a matter [*Angelegenheit*] under discussion, a contested case [*Streitfalles*]' (Heidegger 2004: 167). In ancient Germany people gathered at sites in the natural landscape with special features in order to administer the law and to settle disputes. These 'thing sites' – the *Thingstätten* – later developed into natural shelters, half-open structures, multi-purpose buildings and finally into the kinds of courthouses of our times (Dölemeyer 2005).
16. On the crucial role of the triad *res–lis–causa* in ancient Roman law, see Thomas (1978, 1980).
17. Leibniz describes death as 'envelopment and shrinking' which he opposes to generation as 'development and growth' (Leibniz 1714: §73).
18. We could think here also of Foucault's appropriation of the concept of 'agonism' as a contest which gathers and locks the two opponents in a dance of contest in which they reciprocally incite each other and act upon the other's actions, and invent new moves and strategies as a function of the actions of the other (Foucault 1982).
19. Cayla (1993).
20. The term 'conclusion' is a literal translation of the Dutch term *conclusie*. In British law the conclusion of the applicant is called the 'statement of claim' and the conclusion of the defendant is called a 'reply in defence'. In this chapter we will use the terms 'conclusion' or sometimes 'conclusion of claim' and 'conclusion of reply'.
21. It must be added, however, that the term 'affix' is here not used in its technical legal sense as a means of appropriation of something through its attachment to reality.
22. In fact, all kinds of legal features were involved in the historical development of the epistemological conception of the modern fact itself (Poovey 1998; Shapiro 2003).
23. For an extensive discussion of this difference see Murphy (2003). He, for instance, states that:

> The existence of the law of evidence is one of a number of factors which distinguish a judicial trial from other forms of inquiry into past events. All these factors go some way in explaining (though not necessarily justifying) the idiosyncratic treatment of evidence by advocates. But by far the most significant is the fact that trials are conducted by a judge using exclusionary legal rules of evidence, the effect of which is to keep from the fact-finders much material which is plainly relevant and which any rational

investigator would wish to take into account in his or her reconstruction of the facts. (Murphy 2003: 2)

24. These two modes of proceeding, however, collide in the case of expert evidence in court. Law has different models of validity of expertise and proper legal techniques and procedures that enable the jurists to dispute expert reports. The role of the scientific or technological expert within these legal forums is often hybrid. Jasanoff has stated in this context that the 'borderline between value decisions that should be the prerogative of judges and factual matters that are properly reserved for experts is itself a construct, negotiated anew from expert to expert and from case to case' (Jasanoff 1997: 48).
25. For a description of the relation between law and its sources, see Gutwirth (2015).
26. This is the etymological sense of *con-dicere*, a speaking together, in this case together with the legal sources.
27. See van Dijk (2013) for this typical jurisprudential operation of establishing *resonances* between different disputes (as opposed to the presumption of case similarity in the databases of case-law).
28. This concept of articulated 'lay-out' is in fact a more literally translated rendering of the German term for interpretation, namely *Auslegung*.
29. There might be a difference here between Continental and Anglo-Saxon legal systems on this point. In Anglo-Saxon legal systems the judge is less passive than in Continental legal systems, but has a more active role with regard to truth finding and finding out the facts. This, however, is a theoretical distinction. In practice Belgian judges do not have to just passively listen to the pleas of the advocates but can also actively intervene and pose questions. This competence has even been inscribed in article 756 of the Belgian Procedural Code.
30. The etymology of *con-vincere* is 'to conquer with', indicating that the advocate has to succeed in deploying the judge along the lines of dispute resolution proposed.
31. The role of good advocacy can here be cast as a certain art of stagecraft in constructing and lighting the way to arrive at judgment. We could say that in the conclusions the advocate is required to assume the role of the stage builder who has to construct a script and set of the dispute, whereas in the plea s/he becomes a lighting technician who has to light the way in this 'civilised theatre'. In the plea the advocate has to first *en*lighten the scene to the judge by 'situating the case'. Within this situation s/he has to direct the judge's focus

by *high*lighting the 'topics that are decisive for the judgment'. These *topoi* or places are the zones that indicate 'the important points' in the dispute, the strong intensive points of the advocate's case. Simultaneously the advocate will necessarily shade the *topoi* or zones which are 'irrelevant' in this respect.

32. In this sense it resonates with the old sense of the term 'appointment' which implied the 'coming to a point about some matter and therefore to settle it'. The term 'linear focus' is inspired by Deleuze who extracts it from Leibniz's *Monadology* as the 'power of arranging cases' referring 'to point of view as *jurisprudence* or the *art of judgment*' (Deleuze 1993: 19–21, my italics). This art of judgment of extensive cases is connected to the two conditions for monads in creating a clear point of view: 'selection' and 'closure' (Deleuze 1993: 90–1, 131–7). It is also important to add that a point of view in Leibniz 'does not mean a dependence in respect to a pre-given or defined subject or mind; to the contrary, a subject will be what comes to the point of view, or rather what remains in the point of view' (Deleuze 1993: 19). With Whitehead we could call such a point of view a *locus standi* for such a subject or mind and which is always tied to an 'event here'. 'It is that in nature from which the mind perceives. The complete foothold of the mind in nature' (Whitehead 2004: 107). In our case this event is the dispute which allows certain loci to be assumed as points of view.

33. These sketches of judgment as a selective contraction or, as we could say, a folding differently of the body of the case provide us with an alternative more detailed approach to judgment than the rather sweeping conceptualisation of the judgment as a macroscopic cut (Derrida 1992).

34. This term is not meant as an aestheticisation of the legal process but rather to unite all the characteristic actions mentioned and juxtaposed here under a singular mode of operation. In this sense it can be compared with artistic pointillism due to its technical character in which the punctual contraction manages to perform an abstraction of things. In the case of law this abstraction can often render this matter of dispute unrecognisable even to its primary protagonists but is essential for rendering it decidable.

35. We have already become acquainted with the peculiarities of the legal concept of evidence. This concept is closely linked to the other curious legal concept of 'inner conviction'. What transmits to certain pieces a certain value of evidence that works upon the inner convictions of the mind of the judge? Different legal regimes of procedural

forces and values circumscribe the room for the movements of conviction for the court and also install the mind of the judge itself within a regime of (in)visibility as a kind of mobile secret chamber of deliberation, as a movable *camera obscura*. This also shows that these are much more legal concepts than psychological ones. This 'mind of the judge' is not so much a black box of behaviourist psychology in which the processes of deliberation going on inside would be methodologically circumvented by the researcher, but rather a legal black box that is inscribed in the pre-scripts of procedural law and which circumscribe the mind of the judge within a regime of invisibility.

36. This term 'requisite procession points' is inspired by Callon's concept of 'obligatory passage point' (OPP) in technological and scientific contexts (Callon 1986) and exapted to the specific requirements of legal practice.
37. There is in fact a deep link between these legal 'operatives' and the very notion of the performative that is the cornerstone of speech act theory. When Austin introduces this notion for the first time for a particular kind of linguistic utterance in which the uttering of a certain sentence is the performance of an action, he states that the existing term that is most closely related in naming this kind of utterance is the technical term 'operative' 'as it is used strictly by lawyers in referring to that part, i.e. those clauses, of an instrument which serves to effect the transaction' (Austin 1976: 7). It is interesting to note that these performatives take the kind of legal operatives that we are analysing here as the very paradigm upon which they are modelled. Ducrot has stated that the illocutionary, the kind of linguistic activity or 'force' that gives birth to performatives – is itself defined as an intrinsically juridical act. 'The illocutionary appears now as a particular case of a juridical act: a juridical act accomplished by speech' (Ducrot 1991: 78).
38. An example would be socio-biology (or evolutionary psychology) in trying to reduce behavioural dispositions of humans to our evolved genetic make-up or to strategies aimed at survival. Such explanations have also been attempted for law. The aim here is to find the 'biological roots of legal institutions' (Yarn 2000: 65).
39. According to Heidegger, the word 'cause' has a more primordial belonging in the legal context.

> In its authentic and original sense, this word [*causa*] in no way signifies 'cause'; *causa* means the case and hence also that which is

the case [*Fall*], in the sense that something proceeds and becomes claimable [*fällig*]. Only because *causa*, almost synonymous with *res*, means the case, can the word *causa* later come to mean cause, in the sense of the causality of an effect. (Heidegger 2004: 167–8)

40. Austin thoroughly realised the importance of the practice of law for his model of speech acts. In the many paradigmatic performatives he describes the words uttered within these procedures often come to do things so effectively by having their conventions backed by the force of law.
41. We could oppose a *filling out* (through) the legal forms as part of the twofold of ap-plication that extends the corpus of the dispute through conditional authorisations, with a *filling in* the blanks of a pre-fixed template.
42. As the Argentinean poet Juarróz so beautifully reminds us: 'El fondo de las cosas no es la muerte o la vida. El fondo es otra cosa. Que alguna vez sale a la orilla' ('The ground of things is not death or life. The ground is something else which sometimes comes ashore) (Juarróz 2001). The latter phrase can also be translated as: 'which sometimes rises to the surface', referring to a river drying up and temporarily exposing the riverbed . . .
43. In this context there is a link to the Deleuzian principle of contingent reason in which the rising of the ground is always related to the singularity of a contingent and problematic encounter that transforms it (and reversing the principle of necessary reason) (Deleuze 2004: 344–5; Deleuze and Guattari 1987: 93).
44. My translation. The original German text is: 'Bei allem Begründen und Ergründen laufen wir schon auf dem Weg zu einem Grund.'
45. Heidegger here specifically refers to the philosophical connections between judgment and ground as first established by Leibniz and later systematised by Kant, most specifically in his *Kritik der Urteilskraft* (Heidegger 1997: 104–7, 173–5). With Heidegger the ground is transformed from principle, ratio or causing instance to a supportive instance which is always linked to a 'while', 'during' or 'as long as', and not to a 'because' or 'since'.
46. There is a certain similarity here with Whitehead's writings on the relations between points, positions, fixing time-systems and events (Whitehead 2004). In this context he also speaks of 'event-particles', or what we could call 'dispute-particles' in our case.
47. Where Latour describes the reference produced in *scientific* practices as a series of transformations that produce information about

something, we can describe the assignation produced in *legal* practice as a series of performations that produce convictions and qualifications that gradually carry a cause into its effects.
48. This is the sense of the word in which it is used by Deleuze, not the way in which the term is often equated with 'legal theory' providing the first principles or general elements of legal systems. Deleuze has stated that 'jurisprudence is the philosophy of law, and deals with singularities, it advances by prolonging singularities' (Deleuze 1995: 153). Here legal philosophy is related to the singular event of the dispute before it.
49. In this sense it can provide new insights for a new so-called 'object-oriented philosophy'. See Harman's description at <https://speculative-heresy.wordpress.com/2009/01/06/object-oriented-philosophy/>.
50. Figures, concepts and points of view can become extracted from this middle ground of legal practice in which law becomes approached through the dispute by which practitioners are prudently engaged and which draws them into its dynamics. They can then be raised as conceptual entities in the discourse of legal theory, so that certain existing constellations and conceptual amalgams might start to shift. We could here, for instance, think of the displacement of: the role of the thing in the post-Hohfeldian Legal Realism to the extent that we can speak about 'bundles without things'; the role of facts in constructing a Hartian practice theory of legal practice from the point of view of the neutral observer; or the role of the Herculean purification of disputes in the hydra of legal practice. For a full account see Van Dijk (2013).
51. In Llewellyn's words:

> What is the relation of [...] 'the facts' to the brute raw events which happened long before? What is left in men's minds as to those raw events has been canvassed, more or less skillfully, by two lawyers. But canvassed through the screen of what they consider *legally* relevant, and of what each considered legally relevant to win the case. It has been screened again in the trial court through the rules of about what evidence can be admitted. [...] Finally, with the decision made, the judge has sifted through these 'facts' again, and picked a few which he puts forward as essential – and whose legal bearing he then proceeds to pronounce. It should be obvious that we may now be miles away from life. (Llewellyn 2008: 34)

52. As a hypothesis we could state that, when in the so-called 'normal case' the judge aligns with the translations proposed by the advocates

(and the distinction between 'normal' and 'hard cases' holds), this would further imply that normally the body of law mostly unfolds through the work of advocates! This gives a new interpretation to Cardozo's old statement that 'nine-tenths, perhaps more, of the cases that come before a court are predetermined – predetermined in the sense that they are predestined – their fate established by inevitable laws that follow them from birth to death' (Cardozo 1924: 60).

53. Not mentioned in this chapter but necessary to add to this inventory are: *jurisprudential characters* that constitute the singular figures that mediate between the legal plane of grounding and the legal concepts and which become mobilised by the singular work of establishing resonances between different disputes; and *monadic visibilities* that are installed by a double court architecture of public hearing and private deliberation.

54. A glance at the reasoning sections of the verdicts of such courts for instance, reveals very little reference to legal sources and authorisations, let alone the construction and mobilisation of legally coherent totalities.

55. Van Dijk (2011: 61).

56. Reference plays a role as an element in the transformation of the matter of dispute into a matter of fact. This is first of all the case in the practical work of affixing pieces of evidence to the case, which will allow the matter of dispute to shift into different times and situations where it can become articulated in its encounters with different actors and things. It must be realised, however, that this is above all a kind of conditioned reference according to the procedural regime of evidence, which is more properly legal than anything else. Secondly, legal practice is perfectly capable of producing its own theories and concepts of reference, which becomes especially apparent in disputes of trademark law in which the question 'To what do signs refer?' is one of the primary issues (Van Dijk 2013).

57. Shapiro (2003). This notion of the fact later migrated to other practices like experimental sciences and empiricist philosophy where it eventually attained an elevated epistemological status. The concept of the modern fact became constructed as that which grants scientists the power to become the judge of nature and to produce authoritative knowledge about this nature that was disinterested, separate from political, religious, financial or any other interests in that regard (Poovey 1998: 112–13). In order to stabilise this notion of the fact recourse was made to the rule-bound practices of law, especially the figure of first-hand witness accounts of particular

events (the *res facta* in the legal sense) and its procedures for in- and exclusion and for testing credibility.
58. This designation strategy also seems to be at work in case of the mode of existence called 'metamorphosis', which is linked to therapy and ethno-psychiatry.
59. The term 'assignation' is quite suitable for a few reasons. First its linguistic core still refers to the act of marking something out, allotting something by sign. This denomination puts it in continuity with the predecessor of the term 'mode of existence', namely 'regime of enunciation'. This semiotic background can still be seen as a vital driving force for the whole metaphysical project of devising a table of fundamental categories through the ontological equivalence thesis between enunciation and existence (Latour 1999a). Second, assignation also has the etymological meaning of 'appointing legally', which puts it in line with the thesis of legal pointillism defended in this chapter (other candidates for possible names are 'attribution', 'affixation', 'imputation' and 'qualification', although these can more properly be seen as typical partial acts on the trajectory of assignation). This denomination renders a rather Dickensian acronym in the table of modes of existence. In the words of Mr. Bumble: 'law is an [ASS]' and, following Latour's (2010) use of La Fontaine's fable, an [ASS] disburdened of the heavy relics of morality, politics, religion and even of all organization and attachment.
60. An important caveat needs to be made with regard to this naming strategy. It relates to the fact that the notion of assignation is essentially (quasi-)subject-oriented, as becomes clear in the chapter title for the legal mode of existence, 'The Passage of Law and Quasi Subjects' in Latour (2013). This denomination would however change when we shift our ontological focus from the quasi subject to the dispute as the unit of analysis. The event of the dispute (resolution) equiprimordially occasions both the processes of subjectivation and objectivation that come to mutually articulate one another in its proceedings. Here the notion of *performance* as developed in this chapter looms large, rather than that of assignation.

Bibliography

Austin, J. L. (1976) *How to Do Things with Words*. Oxford: Oxford University Press.
Callon, M. (1986) 'Elements of a sociology of translation: domestication of the scallops and the fishermen of St Brieuc Bay', in J. Law (ed.),

Power, Action and Belief: A New Sociology of Knowledge? London: Routledge, pp. 196–233.
Cardozo, B. N. (1924) *The Growth of the Law*. New Haven, CT: Yale University Press.
Cayla, O. (1993) 'La Qualification ou la vérité du droit', *Droits*, 18: 3–18.
De Vries, E. and Van Dijk, N. (2013) 'A bump in the road. Ruling out law from technology', in M. Hildebrandt and J. Gakeer (eds), *Law as Code Meets Law as Literature*. Dordrecht: Springer.
Deleuze, G. (1993) *The Fold. Leibniz and the Baroque*. London: Athlone.
Deleuze, G. (1995) *Negotiations 1972–1990*. New York: Columbia University Press.
Deleuze, G. (2004) *Difference and Repetition*. London: Continuum.
Deleuze, G. and Guattari, F. (1987) *A Thousand Plateaus*. Minneapolis: University of Minnesota Press.
Derrida, J. (1992) 'Force of law. The "mystical foundation of authority"', in D. Cornell, M. Rosenfeld and D. G. Carlson (eds), *Deconstruction and the Possibility of Justice*. New York: Routledge, pp. 3–67.
Dölemeyer, B. (2005) 'Thing site, tie, ting place. Venues for the administration of law', in B. Latour and P. Weibel (eds), *Making Things Public*. Cambridge, MA: MIT Press.
Ducrot, O. (1991) *Dire et ne pas dire*. Paris: Hermann.
Foucault, M. (1982) 'The subject and power', in H. L. Dreyfus and P. Rabinow (eds), *Michel Foucault: Beyond Structuralism and Hermeneutics*. New York: Harvester Wheatsheaf, pp. 208–26.
Greimas, A. J. (1976) 'Analyse sémiotique d'un discours juridique', in A. J. Greimas (ed.), *Sémiotique et Sciences Sociales*. Paris: Le Seuil.
Gutwirth, S. (2015) 'Providing the missing link: Law after Latour's passage', this volume.
Hache, E. and Latour, B. (2010) 'Morality or moralism? An exercise in sensitization', *Common Knowledge*, 16: 311–30.
Heidegger, M. (1997) *Der Satz vom Grund*. Frankfurt am Main: Vittorio Klostermann.
Heidegger, M. (2004) 'Das Ding', in *Vorträge Und Aufsätze*. Stuttgart: Klett-Cotta.
Jasanoff, S. (1997) *Science at the Bar*. Cambridge, MA: Harvard University Press.
Juarróz, R. (2001) *Poesía Vertical (Antología)*. Común Presencia.
Kuhn, T. S. (1996) *The Structure of Scientific Revolutions*. Chicago: University of Chicago Press.

Latour, B. (1999a) 'Petite philosophie de l'énonciation. Pour Paolo – à la mémoire de notre amie commune Françoise Bastide', in P. Basso and L. Corrain (eds), *Eloqui de Senso. Dialoghi Semiotici per Paolo Fabbri*. Milan: Costa & Nolan, pp. 71–94.

Latour, B. (1999b) *Pandora's Hope. Essays on the Reality of the Science Studies*. Cambridge, MA: Harvard University Press.

Latour, B. (2004) 'Note brève sur l'écologie du droit saisie comme énociation', in F. Audren and L. De Sutter (eds), *Pratiques Cosmopolitiques Du Droit*. Paris: Cosmopolitiques.

Latour, B. (2010) *The Making of Law. An Ethnography of the Conseil d'État*. Cambridge: Polity.

Latour, B. (2013) *An Inquiry into Modes of Existence. An Anthropology of the Moderns*. Cambridge, MA: Harvard University Press.

Leibniz, G. W. (1714) *The Principles of Philosophy known as Monadology*. Philpapers.

Llewellyn, K. N. (2008) *The Bramble Bush*. New York: Oxford University Press.

Murphy, P. (2003) *Evidence, Proof, and Facts*. Oxford: Oxford University Press.

Poovey, M. (1998) *A History of the Modern Fact. Problems of Knowledge in the Sciences of Wealth and Society*. Chicago: University of Chicago Press.

Schatzki, T. R., Knorr Cetina, K. and von Savigny, E. (2001) *The Practice Turn in Contemporary Theory*. London: Routledge.

Shapiro, B. J. (2003) *A Culture of Fact: England, 1550–1720*. Ithaca, NY and London: Cornell University Press.

Stengers, I. (2005) 'Introductory notes on an ecology of practices', *Cultural Studies Review*, 11: 183–96.

Thomas, Y. (1978) 'Le droit entre les mots et les choses', *Archives de Philosophie du Droit*, 23: 93–114.

Thomas, Y. (1980) 'Res, chose et patrimoine', *Archives de Philosophie du Droit*, 25: 413–26.

Van Dijk, N. (2011) 'Approaching law through conflicts', *Law and Method*, 1: 44–63.

Van Dijk, N. (2013) *Grounds of the Immaterial. A Transversal Approach of Legal Philosophy in Intellectual Rights*. PhD thesis, VUB, Brussels.

Whitehead, A. N. (2004) *The Concept of Nature*. Mineola, NY: Dover.

Yarn, D. H. (2000) 'Law, love, and reconciliation: searching for natural conflict resolution in Homo sapiens', in F. Aureli and F. De Waal (eds), *Natural Conflict Resolution*. Berkeley: University of California Press, pp. 54–70.

7

Plasma! Notes on Bruno Latour's Metaphysics of Law

Laurent de Sutter

§ 1 The possibility of inclusion

On 5 February 2008, in the Graham Wallas Room of the London School of Economics' Old Building, a small group of researchers gathered to listen to Graham Harman discuss the book he had devoted to the work of Bruno Latour – the latter himself being present.[1] It was a meeting destined to occur: since 1999, when he published his first article on the French thinker, Harman had never ceased to attempt to articulate the seemingly antagonistic thoughts of his two favourite thinkers: Latour and Heidegger.[2] When he wrote *Prince of Networks*, the monograph in which he explained his understanding of the work of Latour, the form taken by this articulation was finally complete, although it remained controversial – a form in which Latour was only able to half-recognise himself. Or so he told Harman, who heard it. The book that was eventually published from the manuscript discussed at the London School of Economics differed in many respects from its original version – yet, Harman persisted in maintaining the main thesis defended in it.[3] According to this thesis, the thought of Latour was caught in a process of infinite regress, since its primary *object* was the network of relationships in which things have access to something like an essence or a being. For Harman, this was a paradox that he refused, nevertheless, to regard as a flaw or a weakness – a paradox that could be formulated as a question: what is a network, if not a thing whose being, if one was to follow Latour's argumentation, should be considered in terms of relations? Even if it was a thought centred on ontological tolerance, Latour's metaphysics stumbled against the fact that there were beings excluded from this tolerance – or rather beings that this tolerance included in a form other than the form of being.[4] To this objection, Latour's response was easy: if networks did not belong to the realm of beings, it was because being could be said in multiple ways, and because that multiplicity included an ontological 'class', a 'mode of existence', which was precisely that of the network.[5] For Latour, being was not univocal, a general category modalised according to the style of appearance into existence of the various existents, but a class always already divided into a plurality of incompossible, yet jointly articulable, modes. During the conversation that opposed them in London, Latour and Harman held firm their respective positions of principle: for Latour, being was multiple from its very origin; for Harman, this multiplicity was necessarily subsumed under a more general category, foreclosed by the thought of his interlocutor.[6] However, this difference between those that Latour eventually distinguished by opposing to Harman's 'prince' a 'wolf' of its own creation was not really a difference: the main concern of both thinkers remained the one of the invention of a principle of *inclusion* which might oppose the principle of *exclusion* that characterised the history of Western thought. We had wanted to expropriate people and things of their existential status: it was time to relearn civility towards them and to give them back what was theirs – to give it back without reservation.

§ 2 What is a remainder?

Is it possible to imagine ontology or metaphysics without reserve? Is it possible to think of being in a form that does not deprive anyone or anything of that of which it is the name? In other words: is it possible to think of being *unilaterally*? To think it without double, without reverse, without negative, without border, without dumping ground, without non-being – without a category that would constitute it on the basis of an exclusion, as tenuous, as minimal, as it may be? Latour and Harman, each in his own way, tried to provide an affirmative answer to this question, although the resources that they mobilised in order to support it differed in many ways – metaphysics of relations on one side; ontology of things on the other. Harman was not alone in engaging in such an ontology, however: he could count on the loose and often contradictory group of those baptised, in an anthology, with the term 'speculative realists', a group including Quentin Meillassoux, Ray Brassier or Iain Hamilton Grant.[7] To this group, it was necessary to add the proponents of 'flat ontology' or 'object-oriented ontology', such as Ian Bogost and Levi R. Bryant, as well as various free shooters trying to develop a theory of being that could be 'all-inclusive' – for example, Tristan Garcia.[8] Similarly, it was possible to argue that the metaphysics of relations developed by Latour, as it unfolded into modes of existence that were impossible to subsume under the general heading of being, shared many features with the doctrine of truths advanced by Alain Badiou. Like Latour, Badiou refused to conceive truth otherwise than as the product of a specific procedure (Badiou distinguished four of them) that no higher philosopheme could synthesise – but that only the perspective of philosophy could describe.[9] In reality, the encounter between Latour and Harman took the unmistakable form of a crossroads: that of two routes for conceiving the possibility of metaphysics without reserve that contemporary thought was developing. Yet, as Meillassoux recalled to Garcia, one day, during a seminar held at the École Normale Supérieure dedicated to the discussion of *Form and Object*, Garcia's first great treatise, it was impossible to take for granted that this possibility could be actualised. The almost absolute ontological tolerance of Garcia, who claimed that he could give back its ontological dignity to 'whatever', was based, too, on a reserve – a reserve that Garcia admitted willingly: unfortunately his tolerance was only asymptotic; it was still haunted by some sort of remainder.[10] Unlike Garcia, however, neither Harman nor Latour claimed to succeed in thinking 'whatever': it was necessary, for Harman, to become capable of speaking of 'objects', while it was necessary, for Latour, that one could speak of 'modes of existence'.[11] Any 'object' was not 'whatever', just as what was to be considered as one of the various 'modes of existence' distinguished by Latour required, in order to exist, to, at least, not inexist – to, at least, belong to what could be called the *world* of existence. That is to say, the world in which something like the fact of existence has a meaning leading to the obligation to distinguish what exists from what does not.[12]

§ 3 Building the world

There was, however, a theory of the world in Latour – a theory whose most singular claim was the one stating that the world did not pre-exist the existents inhabiting it, but composed itself, or assembled itself, as these existents were forming themselves too.

The world, for Latour, looked a bit like the 'plane of consistency' described by Deleuze: a transversality produced by beings engaged in establishing, between them, relations governing the very distribution of being.[13] World and essence were therefore not given; they were not some kind of already-there that it would be sufficient to discover or describe; they were the last moment of a process of constitution in which they were present only as a form of latency, or as a form of virtuality. But the fact that they belonged to the virtual, as Deleuze had established it, did not mean they were not real: before the composition of a world and the constitution of an essence, there was neither chaos nor non-being – but another world and other essences.[14] Latour's theory refused to yield to the vertigo of origins, or to the archivism of genealogy, and was satisfied with attempting to read the traces through which the constitution of an essence and the composition of a world occurred. Rather than a cosmology, it offered a cosmography: an *engram* of and in the world, a listing of the provisional state of its metamorphoses, a mapping of the networks through which each trace succeeds in referring to other traces, and so on. That was why Latour had for so long pretended to be interested in sociology and anthropology: he wanted to mobilise, in the service of his metaphysics, the tools allowing the collection of the traces of the constitution of essences, and to deduce from them the map of their network.[15] This cosmography, however, involved different perspectives, each offering a unique view on the world and a unique path within the network that composed it – the perspective of sciences, politics, religion, law, art, etc. Such perspectives Latour called 'regimes of veridiction', regimes roughly corresponding to the different modes of existence defining the essences whose articulation resulted in the composition of a certain state of the world at a given time.[16] But if each of these regimes offered a sectional view of the state of the world, these views were far from being structured in the same way – just as the essences to which they corresponded differed both in nature and size. The beings of politics, for example, were defined as the permanent repetition of the discourse by which the whole of a given 'society' was represented – that is to say reformulated, repeated – again and again, so that the continuity between its elements can be maintained.[17] The beings of technology, for their part, were defined as those that allowed for a delegation such that the various resistances raised by a given state of the world might be overcome – so that this overcoming led not to their eradication, but to their redistribution.[18] And the same is true for each of the other modes of existence.

§ 4 On legal beings

The world, for Latour, was a gigantic Meccano set, whose structures and articulations could take a variety of forms, all essential to its assemblage, an assemblage whose key quality was its 'robustness'.[19] The different modes of existence contributing to the composition of the world were different operations by which its strength (the robustness of its state at a given time) was furnished: Latour's cosmography was a cosmography of the strong world. One mode of existence in particular played a key role in surviving the test of robustness that every world has to pass: the mode of existence of law – to which Latour, in his *Inquiry into Modes of Existence*, attributed the label [LAW].[20] If the role of the beings of politics was to establish a form of continuity between every component of the state of the world, the role of the beings of law was to establish a form of continuity between the actors of this world and the actions carried out by them – to attach in a robust way, and in each particular case, *this* action to *that* actor. The law ensured that actors and actions would not float in a vacuum, and that despite the ontological heterogeneity between them, they were compossibles – a robust, concrete, solid compossibility.[21] Without law, there would be no plane of composition between actions and actors, whatever they are or might be – since law recognises as actors beings as diverse as humans, animals, plants, fiction, gods, etc. Unlike politics, law has never expressed ontological reserve: it has always acknowledged that the beings whose actions it had to reconstruct might be of any species – that is to say: that they might *really* be 'whatever'. But Latour went no further. In particular, he failed to draw, from this definition, the corollary that if law was the only ontologically neutral mode of existence, it was also the only one capable of grasping within one and the same motion all the beings contributing to the composition of the world. By assigning to each being, whatever its nature or history or properties, the actions that belonged to it, or to which it belonged, whatever such actions are or may be or become, so that they also might be compossible with those of other beings, law not only, as Latour wrote in *The Making of Law*, seized the 'whole', *but law was also, crucially, the only mode to do so.*[22] The beings of politics, for example, were beings of representation: their participation in the composition of the world was participation under the guise of anxiety, inspection or verification – political beings were guards never ceasing to walk around the walls of the whole of the world of existents. However, it was law and law only that constantly fixed the relationships between beings and actions and, therefore, between beings themselves – thus defining the robustness of the relations by which, together, a world was composed. Law, as Latour also wrote in *The Making of Law*, is the factory of the fabric of the world: the factory of the network of relationships in which each being is to be caught and, because it is caught there, is related to other beings.[23] Law is the map of which the world is the territory – except that there is no territory outside of the map.

§ 5 Introducing plasma

By drawing the map of the world through the game of operations by which it connects actors and actions (operations among which the most important, for Latour, is the process of imputation), law *constructs* the world as a kind of net or mesh.[24] The world was not, according to Latour, a compact whole, a more or less structured, more or less striated, more or less broken block, but, instead, a fragile structure, made of myriad weak links articulated together by the cases giving birth to them.[25] This world, so to speak, resembled the little transparent plastic modules manufactured relentlessly by the small underground creatures from *Fraggle Rock*, the animated series for children produced by Jim Henson in the early 1980s. The tiniest of forces could smash this edifice – that is to say could destroy the ties so patiently woven by law through the operations that were strictly its, and, by destroying these links, could destroy a part of the configuration of the world itself. As Latour has often reminded us, this meant that the world, as a congeries of perspectives or points of view grounded in different modes of existence, was a world in which the overwhelmingly dominant power is that of vacuum: a net is mostly empty, so there are, as Latour wrote, innumerable beings that slip invisibly between the voids of the networks.[26] These beings, these practices, these things Latour has gathered under a generic name, revealing their rather indistinct character in his eyes: 'plasma' – a name appearing only twice in his work, namely in *Paris, Invisible City* and *Reassembling the Social*.[27] Suggestively, he admitted there that 'plasma' designated undoubtedly the great majority of what is; what the world kept in its nets constituted only a very short list – the list of all those movements of which the different modes of existence managed to keep traces.[28] *The majority of what is does not have a world*; the majority of what is only exists in the world as non-existing – as not participating in the construction of the world's consistency, structure and durability. Or rather: as *not yet* participating in that enterprise; as not yet existing, because, to borrow a phrase from Latour, such (non)-beings were 'not yet engaged in metrological chains'.[29] 'Plasma', in other words, is the generic name for all the 'missing masses' of the world, of all that exists only as non-existing, of all that is present only as absent, of all that has form only as unformed.[30] Latour did not say much more, except that it was possible to *feel*, to detect the vague intuition that these missing masses, since they do not fall within the logic of traces proper to the other modes of existence, did not really interest him. 'Plasma' designated the dumping ground of his work, the embarrassing tank of everything that either eluded capture by the constructive processes of the world, of which law formed the keystone, or had not yet acquiesced to such capture, but could perhaps one day be redeemed. Despite not providing a great deal of detail on plasma, of course, Latour never forgot to specify that this remainder was perhaps what mattered the most.[31]

§ 6 Mass and impotence

'Plasma' was the blind spot of Latour's thought, the categorical name for the decision to reject the membership of many beings to the form of the world whose multiple protocols of creation he had described and the theoretical name for what amounts to an excuse for that decision – contrarily to what he had claimed to defend through his philosophical programme. In a way, Harman was not wrong to question Latour on how he conceived the ontological nature of relations and to raise the possibility that he envisaged them as beings in themselves. As he suggested during one specific development in *Prince of Networks*, does not the category of 'plasma' also need a process of constitution?[32] Doesn't it designate, too, something that can rely on consistency, structure and robustness? Why confine plasma to the register of the formless, why *subtract* it from the system of attachments and articulations within which the other modes of existence were involved – and, by being involved in it, eventually came to produce beings in the strongest sense? Perhaps Latour's embarrassment arose there precisely because there was something compact in what might appear to be formless: the formless doesn't need bonds, because it is wholly *mass*, an adherent and plastic mass, which it was always possible to divide but never deconstruct. It was not possible to deploy viewpoints or perspectives upon plasma; it was hardly possible to turn around it or to attempt to enter it – at the risk of drowning at the inevitable moment when it would reform and envelop itself around the one who would dare to take this risk. In a sense, plasma was the apparition of Plasticine into the world of Meccano: the emergence of a system of relations so strong that it became indistinguishable from what it put in relations – whereas Latour's very thought was precisely a wager to establish the possibility of such a distinction. *Plasma was the obscure*; yet Latour's thought aimed unmistakably at the clear and distinct. Perhaps it would be possible to make of plasma a parent category to what Deleuze called the 'dark precursor', the depositary of an indiscernible virtuality, but a virtuality whose deployment would mark the destruction of any attempt to see the world as clear and distinct.[33] From this point of view, it would be possible to consider plasma as the necessary embarrassment, recognised by Latour himself, accompanying any attempt to form a representation of the world that also meets, despite his own intentions, the conditions of the programme established by Descartes. The moment of plasma, for Latour, was the moment of scruple – but a scruple that it was possible to forget once its relative importance was dutifully recognised and thus neutralised, a scruple that would not ultimately prevent the continuation of the conquering march towards truth. Because one should not be mistaken: the thought of Latour was always as much a doctrine of truth as it was a doctrine of the world or of being; it even counted, like Badiou's, among the most ambitious, most developed and most innovative theories of truth known to the late twentieth century.

§ 7 A short theory of truth

Like the world or like being, truth is not given: it is the product of a construction; it is the result of a process of manufacture, an artificial processing, a *machining* based on that which is not yet, and of which it is an impoverished form. However, contrary to the conventional view, this impoverishment preceding and leading to the production of a truth *does* imply an effect of authenticity – or rather: truth is authentic only insofar as it has been constructed (it is the fantasy of truth as given that is inauthentic). Perhaps one should speak of truth, in Latour, only as a dimension of the world or of being evidencing their fabricated, manufactured, machined, artificial or false character: the truth is that which, in being or the world, manifests itself in the traces of its manufacturing process. But if one accepts this proposition, a strange consequence would follow: this dimension of truth in the world, its *artificiality*, if deployed as a multiplicity of modes of existence, finds again its last word in law. It is law that embodies the truth of the world, as it articulates the beings whose relations and actions will eventually compose its fabric; it is law that forms its most perfect version, in the sense of perfection that belongs to facticity. It is clear that, in itself, this kind of involuntary primacy of law in Latour's grand metaphysical fresco would not matter – if this embarrassing remainder, this unexpected *return of the given* called plasma did not stubbornly exist. How to imagine the possibility of the coexistence between the fabulous cathedral of the constructed, of which law, for Latour, embodies the keystone, and the critical mass of the given around which, like a containment field, continues to dance the flexible architecture of relations constituting the world? To this question, Latour offered no more of a response than the effort that he devoted to think plasma itself, as if it was obvious that the problems differed (and that this difference warranted an even greater indifference). Latour half-confessed it: he had nothing to say about plasma – other than the mere recognition of its existence and its importance. But the recognition entailed that his metaphysics was entirely based on a gigantic exclusion, which was also a gigantic caprice. *In fact, Latour does not give a damn about plasma*: such was the unexpected finding to which were led all those who tried to interest themselves in it, or to interest themselves in how Latour, against all odds (and with an honesty that should compel admiration), consecrated it as the place of the dead. However, this indifference of Latour, redoubling the indifference that the system of relations maintained with respect to plasma, according to him, began to present a disturbing face, once one realised which categories of beings he consigned to it. Indeed, to plasma belonged everything that one could call 'beings of sensitivity': the ensemble of the beings that, without leaving any significant trace, *affect* other beings in a more or less profound, more or less durable, more or less effective way.

§ 8 Praise for the absent traces

Latour is incapable of thinking the non-existing, in the sense that the non-existing would designate everything that leaves no material, durable, visible trace; he is incapable of thinking the immaterial, ineffable, invisible trace – and even more: he refuses this with the greatest energy. The pragmatism that he has always defended was a pragmatism designed to certify the existence of the most exotic beings (gods, for example) only as long as the consequences of their existence could be *embodied* in a document.[34] Just as there is no God without a Bible, without a Church, without theology, without mass, without the sandals of the pilgrims and so on, there is no love without gifts, letters, postcards, texts, changes in dressing habits or hairstyles and so on. The truth of the beings of love and their place in the world is that of the archive boxes that disappear when love itself disappears, or the lovers who have lived it – it is nowhere else to be found, except in the indistinct plasma of feelings outside the networks. *Yet 'nowhere' is still somewhere*, just as the non-existent still exists, and a wrinkle or gray hair, an image on television or an erotic dream, as labile, as elusive, as little material as they are, are still traces. The lack of trace is a trace: this thesis may irritate Latour most, as it reflects that which his whole metaphysical system has attempted to stave off, as if it was the greatest sin which philosophy (or literature – which, for him, is almost the same thing) has been guilty of. Similarly, the absence of being is still being – as, paradoxically, the law knows very well, the law which has developed very complex, very rich and very *constraining* theories of this absence and of its more or less presumed or more or less fictitious presence.[35] For the ontological generosity of law is much broader than Latour acknowledges; it is an absolute generosity, concerning both the beings concerning which Latour accepted the possibility of traceability, and all the others that are much more complicated, if not impossible, to trace. Or else, whose traces should suggest that there is nothing that could not, in one way or another, be traceable – such as, for example, this strange being that is 'intent', the being against which Oliver Wendell Holmes railed so much and whose recognition disposes of so many cases?[36] One must choose: either everything is plasma or everything is trace. Ideas, emotions, images belong as much to being and the world as gods, loves, scientific discoveries or algorithms of high-frequency trading, even if the regime of the trace that is theirs may seem tenuous to the amateur of records and bills. *'Whatever' is entitled to the dignity of being, and 'whatever' can be a trace of this very dignity*; no theoretical necessity should be allowed to determine what is eligible for participation in the world and what, on the contrary, should be excluded from its documentation. The recognition of the ontological generosity of law should have put Latour on this track: the track of the involuntary consistency of the world, its surprising robustness, its arbitrary strength – a far less heroic track than the one that he has continued to explore, and explore, despite these shortcomings, with genius.

Notes

1. Peter Erdélyi (2011) 'Foreword', in Bruno Latour, Graham Harman and Peter Erdélyi, *The Prince and the Wolf. Latour and Harman at LSE*. London: Zero Books, p. 14.
2. Graham Harman (2010) 'Bruno Latour, King of Networks', *Towards Speculative Realism. Essays and Lectures*. London: Zero Books, p. 67 *et seq*.
3. Graham Harman (2009) *Prince of Networks. Bruno Latour and Metaphysics*. Melbourne: Re.press.
4. Ibid., p. 119 *et seq*.
5. Bruno Latour (2012) *Enquête sur les modes d'existence. Une anthropologie des Modernes* Paris: La Découverte, p. 43 *et seq*.
6. Latour et al., op. cit., p. 110 *et seq*.
7. Levi Bryant, Nick Srnicek and Graham Harman (eds) (2011) *The Speculative Turn. Continental Materialism and Realism*. Melbourne: Re.press. See also Steven Shaviro (2014) *The Universe of Things. On Speculative Realism*. Minneapolis: University of Minnesota Press, and Peter Gratton (2014) *Speculative Realism. Problems and Prospects*. London: Bloomsbury.
8. Ian Bogost (2012) *Alien Phenomenology, or What It's Like to Be a Thing*. Minneapolis: University of Minnesota Press; Levi R. Bryant (2011) *The Democracy of Objects*. Ann Arbor: Open Humanities Press; Tristan Garcia (2011) *Forme et objet. Un traité des choses*. Paris: PUF.

9. Alain Badiou (1988) *L'Être et l'Événement*. Paris: Le Seuil. On Badiou's doctrine of truth, see Peter Hallward (2003) *Badiou. A Subject to Truth*. Minneapolis: University of Minnesota Press.
10. Garcia, op. cit., p. 11.
11. Graham Harman (2010) *L'objet quadruple. Une métaphysique des choses après Heidegger*, trans. O. Dubouclez. Paris: PUF, *passim*; Latour, op. cit., p. 31 *et seq*.
12. Garcia, op. cit., p. 85 *et seq*.
13. Gilles Deleuze and Félix Guattari (1991) *Qu'est-ce que la philosophie?* Paris: Minuit, p. 38 *et seq*.
14. Gilles Deleuze (1968) *Différence et répétition*. Paris: PUF, p. 269 *et seq*.
15. Latour, op. cit., p. 37 *et seq*.
16. Ibid., p. 65 *et seq*.
17. Ibid., p. 140 *et seq*.
18. Ibid., p. 211 *et seq*.
19. Ibid., p. 166 *et seq*.
20. Ibid., p. 357 *et seq*.
21. Ibid., p. 367.
22. Bruno Latour (2002) *La fabrique du droit. Une ethnographie du Conseil d'État*. Paris: La Découverte, p. 280 *et seq*.
23. Ibid., pp. 283–4.
24. Ibid., pp. 297–8.
25. Ibid., p. 299.
26. Bruno Latour and Emilie Hermant (1998) *Paris, ville invisible*. Paris: Les Empêcheurs de penser en rond – La Découverte, pp. 154–5.
27. Ibid., p. 157; Bruno Latour (2006) *Changer de société – Refaire de la sociologie*, trans. N. Guilhot. Paris: La Découverte, p. 348 *et seq*.
28. Ibid., p. 349.
29. Ibid., p. 351.
30. Ibid., p. 354.
31. Latour and Hermant, op. cit., p. 153.
32. Harman, *Prince of Networks*, op. cit., p. 134.
33. Deleuze, op. cit., p. 156 *et seq*.
34. Bruno Latour, *Enquête*, op. cit., p. 59 *et seq*.
35. Yan Thomas (2011) '*Fictio legis*. L'empire de la fiction romaine et ses limites médiévales', M.-A. Hermitte and P. Napoli (eds), *Les opérations du droit*. Paris: EHESS – Gallimard – Le Seuil, p. 133 *et seq*.
36. Oliver Wendell Holmes (2014) *La voie du droit*, trans. L. de Sutter. Paris: Dalloz.

8

The Conditions of a Good Judgment: From Law to Internal Affairs Police Investigations

Cédric Moreau de Bellaing (trans. Solène Semichon)

One of the criticisms that has been regularly levelled in France at Bruno Latour's book *La Fabrique du Droit*[1] is that he chose to conduct an empirical investigation of law in a very particular and very powerful institution, the Conseil d'État, which supposedly only deals with a specific sort of law – administrative law. Elsewhere, we have already shown that such a criticism arises from a misunderstanding of Latour's analytical ambition, which is certainly not the development of a sociology of law nor a sociology of the Conseil d'État, but rather the empirical exploration of a mode of existence that is specific to the moderns.[2] I would like to show here that Latour's approach retains all its interest even when it is not applied to the field of the continuous production of the law but to the analysis of a very specific judicial (and administrative) investigative process which is carried out within a unit of internal control of the police institution, that is the daily work of police officers who investigate other police officers.

Such an operation is undoubtedly quite delicate. It could reduce the interest of Latour's approach to a question of method. That would be embarrassing since it is not specific to law. Latour claims[3] he has done nothing more than apply the ethnographic methods he developed elsewhere, in particular in scientific laboratories, to law.[4] There is a risk in importing a methodological process into the field of the disciplinary measures of the French national police: that of losing what it has succeeded in revealing in the case of the ethnography of the Conseil d'État, i.e. the ability of law to render disengagement productive. Admittedly, the empirical case that will be examined in the following pages will not enable us to test the notion of law as a mode of existence. However, applying to it the method of a rigorous monitoring of the files, including of their phenomenal nature, keeping in mind the idea that everything counts in the way those files are dealt with when one tries to define what a good judgment may be, and remembering that investigations revolve around what is most fragile in them, will permit us to refer to something else, to a recurrent and everlasting idea in political philosophy and the sociology of the state, i.e. legitimate violence.

This chapter applies a type of sociology which uses conflicts, arguments and mistakes as empirical starting points to apprehend the social world as a performance that is always in the process of being realised.[5] Within this framework, the police misconduct that is brought to the attention of the Inspection Générale des Services (IGS) (the internal affairs police department for Paris),[6] in particular when the grounds for complaint are illegitimate violence, may be the starting point of a sociological analysis of legitimate violence and, more specifically, of the conditions in which it is confirmed or, on the contrary, disproven.

Weber's famous definition of the state has given prominence to the concept of legitimate violence in sociology. Paradoxically enough, the effect of such a consecration has been to complicate the sociologisation of legitimate violence as it now seems to be an unexamined and unexaminable dogma no longer deserving further discussion.[7] However, adopting an approach similar to that which Bruno Latour applied to the law to deal with investigations into allegations of illegitimate violence conducted by the internal affairs officers allows us to try to 're-sociologise' legitimate violence thanks to the detailed analysis of the processes that are developed within those investigations. The approach here presented is founded on the following assumption: examining the methods of investigation used in the disciplinary cases of police violence will permit identification of the main features of the use of force according to the police. From then on, and in the same way that Bruno Latour proposed in *La fabrique du droit*, the reflection here will be guided by questions concerning the modes of elaboration of a *good judgment* that the description and the analysis of investigation files processed by the IGS will reveal. More precisely, first, the entities that must be gathered together for a 'good judgment' on the procedure under study to be formed will be identified, then the relations that must be forged during the investigation for the latter to be considered to conform with the model of a good judgment will be determined.

Before the processes involved in the disciplinary investigations are described, the exact nature of the IGS's activities must be clarified. Until recently, the IGS, which was for a long time known as the 'police of the police', had authority over Paris and the three adjacent departments. It mainly dealt with police misconduct. At the time this investigation was carried out, the IGS was made up of 70 members, distributed among three disciplinary divisions, an audit division and the administrative management division. I was assigned to one of the disciplinary divisions for several months, during which I had access to the registers, the archives of the division, the hearings of the claimants and police officers, and the routine activities of the investigators. The implementation of those disciplinary assignments results in a specific, if not an incongruous, feature as far as French administrative law is concerned: the internal affairs police department has been given judicial and administrative jurisdiction at the same time. There are three paths by which the complaints may be referred to internal affairs: (1) the administrative path: the head of a particular department, the Préfecture de police (the Police Department) or even the Direction Générale de la Police Nationale (the National Police Department) refers the case to internal affairs; (2) the judicial path: the Parquet (the Public Prosecutor's Office) of Paris or of one of the three adjacent departments refers the case to internal affairs; or (3) the public path: citizens, for whom an Office of Citizen Complaints has been created, refer the case.

When an investigation is launched, the daily work of internal affairs is to carry out hearings, to gather evidentiary elements, to establish the order of the events and either (1) suggest that the case be closed; (2) suggest that a low-level sanction (a warning, a reprimand) be imposed; or (3) conclude that the case is important enough for a disciplinary hearing to be held. In the latter case, internal affairs do not officially participate in the disciplinary hearing, even though the investigator who has worked on the case and the superintendent, who is their superior, give their opinion on the case, if only in the final report they write at the end of the investigation.

In order to classify and codify the facts that are at the origin of the claimant's complaint to the internal affairs department, the internal affairs control unit uses five categories (see Table 8.1): (1) *property damage* is divided into three sub-categories: *theft, fraud* and *property damage*; (2) *damage to persons* includes *injuries and violence* and *breaches of moral standards*; (3) *misconduct* covers *behaviour towards the administration, personal behaviour,*

Table 8.1 Distribution of the launched investigations by types of alleged facts

	Property damage	Damage to persons	Misconduct	Private misconduct	Diverse
1996–2001	640 (12.1%)	1,940 (36.5%)	1,855 (34.9%)	389 (7.3%)	488 (9.2%)

Sources: IGS annual reports 1996, 1997, 1998, 1999, 2000 and 2001.

Table 8.2 Distribution of the sanctions by types of alleged facts

	Property damage	Damage to persons	Misconduct	Private misconduct	Diverse
1996–2001	178 (16.7%)	217 (20.4%)	439 (41.2%)	138 (13%)	93 (8.7%)

Sources: IGS annual reports 1996, 1997, 1998, 1999, 2000 and 2001.

behaviour towards the public and *theft and loss* (of administrative property); (4) *private misconduct* refers to different private behaviours that are questionable from the point of view of the institution: debts, neighbour disputes or disputes with a motorist, etc.; and the last category, (5) *diverse*, comprises *administrative investigations, offences related to particular regulations* and *road traffic offences*.

The *damage to persons* and *misconduct* categories stand apart from the other motives for complaint since they represent more than 70 per cent of the remit of cases to internal affairs, the former being slightly more numerous than the latter. Such a distribution is not surprising in itself. The supremacy of *damage to persons* and *misconduct* is easy to understand in relation to the activities of the police which are the most likely to prompt criticisms, i.e. the authorisation to use force,[8] the fact that the police action is a public action and that the behaviour of the police officers is daily put to the test by the hierarchy, the colleagues and the public.

The distribution among the five main categories of misconduct is not the same, however, in the case of sanctions imposed after an investigation by internal affairs. On the contrary, there is something of a puzzle here (see Table 8.2).

It seems that *damage to property* and *misconduct* are proportionally more frequently sanctioned than reported. The reverse is true in the case of *damage to persons*, which, though it represents 36.5 per cent of the investigations, results in only 20.4 per cent of the overall sanctions.[9] Thus the recurrence of sanctions varies depending on the type of offence: *private misconduct* results in one sanction for 2.8 files; *damage to property* in one for 3.6 files; *misconduct* in one for 4.2 files; *diverse* in one for 5.2 files; and *damage to persons* in only one for 8.9 files. There exists an undeniable discrepancy between the number of complaints for *damage to persons* and the number of sanctions imposed in the corresponding cases. The difference is even more important when one considers the exact composition of the *damage to persons* category (see Table 8.3). It is divided, as we have seen, into two subcategories, *breaches of moral standards* and *injuries and violence*. *Breaches of moral standards* cover various offences: rape, sexual assault, indecent behaviour, sexual harassment, encouraging debauchery and, more surprisingly, keeping bad company (most of the time, this refers to relationships with prostitutes) and drug offences. Once such a division has been made, however, and transferred to

Table 8.3 Breakdown of the damage to persons category, 1996–2001

	Launched investigations	Heavy sanctions imposed
Injuries and violence	1,778 (91.6%)	31 (44.9%)
Breaches of moral standards	162 (8.4%)	38 (55.1%)
Total	1,940	69

Sources: IGS annual reports 1996, 1997, 1998, 1999, 2000 and 2001.

the distribution of sanctions, the difference between the number of investigations for alleged violent acts and the number of resulting sanctions increases.

When only the sanctions that result in a final termination of the relations with the administration are taken into consideration, the figures are incontrovertible. While from 1996 to 2001, 1,778 investigations into *violence* and 162 investigations into *breaches of moral standards* were launched, 31 final terminations of relations with the administration were pronounced for *violence* as opposed to 38 for *breaches of moral standards*, that is 1 in 57 in the case of *violence* and 1 in 4 in that of *breaches of moral standards*. That difference can easily be explained, at least partly so: *breaches of moral standards* include very serious cases (rapes, sexual abuses), the illegitimacy and indefensibility of which are immediately recognisable. It is impossible to impose intermediary sanctions in those cases, unlike those of *violence*, whose legitimacy may often be a matter for debate before they are established as illegitimate. Similarly, the cases that are reported to the police disciplinary authorities for drug-related offences often include in flagrante delicto evidence, which will almost surely lead to severe sanctions. In any case, the increased difference revealed by that quick dissection of the *damage to persons* category is a concrete basis for a diagnosis of the way the police institution handles the complaints of illegitimate violence. Comparing the ratio of the investigations launched into reports of violence to all the investigations conducted by the IGS and the ratio of the heavy sanctions imposed for the same facts to all the heavy sanctions imposed at the end of an investigation by the IGS in a single table, we find Table 8.4.

The unavoidable diagnosis is the following: the reports of the use of excessive force will lead less frequently to a sanction than those concerning any other type of offence. It is therefore possible

The Conditions of a Good Judgment 215

Table 8.4 Recap of the data on cases of 'violence'

	Investigations launched into violence / all investigations	Sanctions imposed for violence / all heavy sanctions
1996–2001	33.5%	16.9%

Sources: IGS annual reports 1996, 1997, 1998, 1999, 2000 and 2001.

to see, in the way the police disciplinary authorities deal with complaints for illegitimate violence, that the use of force by the police is really a problematic object, since it regularly and massively triggers complaints which, however, are less likely than the other reported offences to result in an internal sanction. Thus an enigma is taking shape: when a certain number of people file a complaint reporting illegitimate police violence to internal affairs, the latter's investigations and the decisions of the disciplinary hearing apparently interpret them as either *legitimate* violence or as cases in which the illegitimacy of violence is too difficult to establish. How can such a difference be accounted for? Is it a sign that the claimants tend to make up stories more when what is at stake is the use of force by the police? Is it a sign that the tolerance toward the physical constraint exercised by the police forces is fading away and is part of a more global process of mitigation of violence in modern societies?[10] Or is it a sign, on the contrary, of the indulgence of internal affairs towards members of the police institution, to which they too, after all, belong? Must one conclude, to quote recurrent arguments, that the police institution 'protects' its officers?

Latour's approach to law is quite useful to solve this enigma, for it allows us to step aside. Indeed, the little aggregated data that has been presented in the tables above points to a sociological problem but does not offer any solution. And for good reason: those figures have been compiled from annual activity reports of the internal affairs department and are, from that point of view, the result of an approach that consists of converting contextualised cases of reports of violence into simple bars in the columns of an assessment report. From that point of view, the annual reports, as computation centres,[11] testify to the operations of classification and categorisation performed by internal affairs. They do not, however, give any information about the qualitative process of investigation that has taken place beforehand. One must therefore look at another kind of empirical material – the disciplinary files – and open them as one would open 'black boxes',[12] to follow the way they are built up and describe the mechanisms they reveal at the same time. Indeed, those classifications only appear at the end of investigations: therefore, they are *results* that make poor starting points. To understand them, the processes they derive from, that is the practical progress of the investigations that have been launched into illegitimate violence, must be analysed. To do that, in this chapter, the sociological focus will have to be shifted toward the way the internal affairs police officers investigate, toward the constraints that weigh on the investigations and toward the effects that the latter produce.

The situations in which the actors themselves conduct investigations are ideal for the sociologist, since these investigations engage in an intensive labour of clarification. In that perspective, it is possible, with a small conversion from philosophy to sociology,[13] to quote John Dewey's definition of an inquiry as 'the controlled or directed transformation of an indeterminate situation into one that is so determinate in its constituent distinctions and relations as to convert the elements of the original situation into a unified whole'.[14] The phases through which this transformation occurs furnish the explanation of how, precisely, the investigators do their work and what people do when dealing with the controlling authority. As to internal affairs, the identification of those phases offers the possibility of understanding how an investigator establishes that a police officer deserves a disciplinary hearing or, on the contrary, that the file must be closed, because it allows us to register all the uncertainties and hesitations characteristic of the tortuous progression that the investigations carried out by a disciplinary service must survive.

This chapter is based on the thorough analysis of 70 disciplinary files, which correspond to three entire months of work of the investigation unit to which I was assigned. I was given full liberty to read the files and take notes, the only requirement being that I would change the names of the persons and places. Moreover, while I was working on certain files, the investigators who had worked on them and who were still at the IGS discussed them with me quite willingly. In that way, I was able to reconstruct the files' modes of circulation within the internal affairs department by meticulously identifying each of their transformations[15] and by enumerating the phases of the investigation during which the investigator's judgment took form, just as Bruno Latour did when he studied the files examined by the Conseil d'État.[16] That approach allowed me to identify the phases during which the circulation of a disciplinary file transforms the latter. The presentation of those essential phases – Latour also calls them objects of value[17] – helps to show how each of them implies the collection of various entities of diverse natures that the investigation links together with specific relations, and whose final networking must support a finding of 'good judgment' with respect to the entire investigation as well as a recommendation on the follow-ups that result from it, in particular as regards instances of illegitimate violence. The first part will examine how the launching of an investigation is organised: the aim of this part is to isolate the minimal conditions for an investigation to be launched and to show how those initial conditions will give direction to the investigator's work of interpretation. The second part will focus on what the investigators are regularly confronted with, and what the investigators themselves call a 'grey zone', which designates the situation in which there is a suspicion of police violence that is, however, impossible to confirm. I will identify three means of reducing the uncertainties characteristic of those situations, though they are quite few, that are available to the internal affairs investigators. The investigation must then go on, in particular with the confrontation of the versions of the claimant and the police officers under suspicion. That will be the topic of the third part of this chapter. The analysis of those confrontations reveals patterns of accusation, and symmetrically, the incriminated police officers' patterns of defence, justification or strategies of reorienting the perspective. Following the investigations will thus make it possible to clarify the internal affairs investigators' modes of launching an investigation.

Meticulously following the way the investigations proceed will also allow the analysis to go a step further. When following the way internal affairs investigators investigate the cases of alleged illegitimate violence, it is possible to understand what investigators do, concretely speaking, when they investigate. Either the investigator works on a case in which it has not been possible to reduce the uncertainties of the 'grey zone' enough and, as a consequence, the investigator chooses to close the case, or the investigator has been able to reach a decision. In that sort of case, however, his work is not only to assess the intensity of the alleged violence to measure its legitimacy, as in a ledger, in quantitative form (to identify the supernumary blow resulting in the passage from the legitimate use of force to illegitimate violence), but to fully reconstruct *legitimate violence* or *illegitimate violence*, which fundamentally depend on the situations in which they are embedded, since a version of the events capable of being considered objectively true must be stabilised.

1 Filing a complaint

For a case to be opened, the investigator must perceive that, in the complaint, what happened was indeterminate enough and the accusation's arguments are reasonable enough to justify launching an investigation. A case is opened only if the situation is considered to be problematic enough. The test of the legitimacy of the complaint begins from the very first minutes of the claimant's hearing, who is expected to respect a certain number of requirements regarding interaction. Complaints of claimants who are perceived as aggressive have very little chance of being received. The investigators may refuse to investigate any further if the claimants are too hostile. If the internal affairs investigators think that the denunciation does not show enough credibility, the story itself may also lead them to refuse to open the case. If the facts the claimants relate are considered fanciful, the investigators' psychological assessments may also be used to justify such a refusal.

Once the complaint and the claimant have passed those first tests of legitimacy, the investigator promptly collects information concerning the conditions of the interaction leading to the contested events. The investigator asks the claimant questions about the reasons for which they have been arrested, the extent to which the claimant has resisted and at what precise moment they received the blows that are the subject of the complaint. As soon as the claimant has gone, that information is supplemented with some research on their biographical details and in particular on their criminal records. The investigators think that that way, they can ensure the credibility of the claimant's testimony before checking the judicial and administrative status of the incriminated police officers. Once those records, if any, have been examined, they are added to the disciplinary file as an element that informs the whole procedure, for they are not stapled to the rest of the reports that the investigation is comprised of but are placed on loose sheets at

The Conditions of a Good Judgment 219

the beginning of the file so that the investigator may have them at their disposal at any time. From that point of view, those biographical and judicial details play a crucial role in the progress of the investigation as the complaint must meet a certain number of requirements, one of which is 'the *necessary correspondence of the testimony and of the biographical details of the victim*. As the court says, being a client of the police ruins the credibility of the testimony.'[18] Thus the very first lines of the final report that concludes the investigation – or on the contrary the last lines, which will give it a decisive value – systematically take account of whether the claimant is known by the police.

The investigator must then explain what is *problematic* in the complaint. This means that they must provide a framework for the investigation and make the alleged facts fit in one of the predefined categories used by internal affairs. The investigator who is in charge of the case writes a report on the referral, which mentions the occupation of the claimant and briefly explains the reason for the decision to open the case. A second report follows and sets out the facts: it is either the framework within which internal affairs are about to take action, if the case has been referred to them by the judicial authority, or the first hearing of the claimant. The *codification* of the legal element which is in the margins of the report and which defines the rest of the investigation is achieved by the internal affairs investigator in those first reports. This operation consists of bringing the complaint closer to pre-existing categories used by internal affairs. Such a classification is, however, neither unilateral nor given in advance. It should rather be understood as a negotiated order. There are negotiations between internal affairs and the claimant, since the investigator can characterise the situation in different ways, which sometimes leads to further discussions. There are also negotiations between the individual specificity of each case and the relative rigidity of the categories of transgressions available to internal affairs: the singularities of a given case may hinder its integration into a pre-established category. Finally, there are negotiations among the different investigators who discuss the cases, who advise one another, contradict one another and reach agreements depending on the elements that are gradually collected. The apparition of the codification in the margin of the sheets of the disciplinary files is the first ordering of the collected data and it gives a direction to the data that will be re-collected later as it creates a first series of links between the singularity of the case, the routine working categories of internal affairs and the legal necessity of respecting a legal framework.

2 Reducing the grey zone

As soon as a case of illegitimate violence has been opened, the investigator asks the claimant to go to the UMJ (the forensic department) of the Hôtel-Dieu hospital to have their injuries recorded. The UMJ certificates are the only ones able to be taken into account by internal affairs so as to avoid any false or forged certificates. The certificates give a medical description of the wounds and/or traumas which are noted very precisely and are completed by a diagram on which the parts of the body that have been harmed are indicated. The doctors who establish them then assess the number of days of inability to work that the injuries entail. The higher the number of days, the stronger the suspicion concerning the alleged blows.

The UMJ certificates serve to measure the sincerity and the consistency of the competing versions of the disputed facts. First the claimant's: if they report a rain of blows but the UMJ certificate indicates that nothing corresponds to such an intensity, the credibility of the denunciation is weakened and there is little chance that the complaint will succeed. Intensity is therefore a disputed element which is frequently an issue in an investigation. The case of a man who, in his complaint, related a real beating up by four police officers in a police van is a good illustration of this point concerning the qualification of intensity. One of the officers supposedly punched him twice in the left eye. Another put his truncheon behind his manacles and lifted him several times in a row, then put his foot on his neck to keep his head on the floor and hit him in the left eye with his truncheon. The claimant was then hit several times in the ribs with a truncheon. The UMJ certificate, however, only mentioned a blow to the left eye and did not establish any other injury. In such conditions, the internal affairs investigator mostly concentrates on the certified injury and concludes, with the reading of the initial procedure, that the injury was suffered when the claimant was arrested and fell while physically fighting with the police officers. The case was then closed.

The UMJ certificates also test the version proffered by the police officers. They allow investigators to check whether the violence that has actually been used may be due to a legitimate application

The Conditions of a Good Judgment 221

of force or whether, on the contrary, it is unsupported by accepted policing techniques. There is, after all, a series of more or less severe traumas that may be expected to result from classical, established techniques of arrest. Twisting an arm may result in injuries if the arrestee resists. If the only traces of injury that are described in the certificate are of that sort, the investigator will then focus on the conditions of the arrest, which reduces the chance for the complaint against illegitimate violence to succeed. If, on the contrary, the wound seems to be due to no application of the professional gestures of arrest, if the areas of the body that have been harmed are not those involved in general during arrests, even difficult ones, the investigation will continue. That was the case of a police officer who delivered a heavy blow to the head of an arrestee and then stated in the report that the latter had knocked his forehead in the police vehicle. The UMJ certificate, however, suggested a more violent impact, the trace and type of which did not support the conclusion that it was a simple and innocent injury due to the arrestee's inattention. From that point forward, the investigator can rely upon the materialisation of the injury to subject the police officer to a hearing and try to convince or compel the officer to acknowledge the illegitimate use of violence.

The demonstration established by the certificate rapidly shows its limits, however. The number of days of temporary inability to work are not enough to establish the police's disproportionate or, on the contrary, moderate action. They only testify to a state (traces of blows) and, possibly, support a series of assumptions (which are made based on the nature and appearance of some injuries) about the sorts of blows that were delivered. They do not account for the dynamics of the disputed situation. Serious injuries may result from a fall due to technical gestures that are authorised by the police institution and, on the contrary, injuries that may be the result of normal conditions of intervention may have been made by impermissible blows at other moments and then will potentially become illegitimate. From then on, the internal affairs' assessment of the conditions in which violence has been used by the police bears less on intensity (except in cases of traumas in which the disproportion is such that their presence alone is enough to justify the accusation of illegitimate violence) than on the adequation between the means used and the requirements of the situation. This is clearly shown in the example of a Colombian student who went to internal affairs to file a complaint against violence with a ten-day temporary inability to work. As he was drunk, he was reluctant to submit himself to the control of the police. He said he had been brutalised in the police van and hit while lying on the floor. During the hearing of the incriminated police officers, the investigator learnt that, once in the van, the student had escaped and fled to a municipal garden after clumsily jumping over the gate. He resisted when he was arrested and several police officers had to intervene to hold him on the ground. He was roughly made to go over the gate again and was brought to the police station. The days of temporary inability to work could be explained by the second arrest, which occurred after he fled and resisted the police officers and were thus due, for the investigator, to the legitimate use of force to neutralise a man that was drunk and fleeing the police.

The initial procedure (an internal police report) that was filed just after the disputed police intervention is another means for the internal affairs investigators to clarify the grey zone clouding the police's use of force. The examination of that procedure can also result in the immediate exculpation of the police officers, if its content testifies without a doubt to the truthfulness of the police's description. The case is then immediately closed. Conversely, however, the initial procedure can also serve to detect police techniques of dissimulation. The internal affairs department is, of course, part of the police institution; the investigators, thanks to their 'insider experience' (they have all been members of the daily police departments before being transferred to internal affairs), are able to detect many irregularities, the chronological impossibilities, the violations of the accepted procedure. Such a use of specifically trained professional police expertise can be found, for example, in the file on a 26-year-old man who, while going to his girlfriend's place, was detained by the anti-crime brigade at 3 o'clock in the morning in a quiet street in the close suburbs of Paris. In the initial report, the police officers claimed they intervened because he had not fastened his seat belt. They claimed they manacled him at the beginning of their intervention. The initial procedure, however, is not quite clear as to the moment he was manacled. One of the police officers said he was immediately manacled, but the offence he mentioned in his explanation was not serious enough to warrant such a response. Another stated that he was not manacled at the very beginning of the intervention, which made constraining him illegal, since he was searched and his identity was checked. Studying the initial procedure reveals the inconsistencies in the narration which will guide the developments of the investigation.

During the investigation, the investigators can also detect the purposeful orchestration of a common version by the incriminated police officers, which may point to an attempt to conceal criminal facts. During an investigation on violence resulting in a teenager's eardrum being ruptured, the internal affairs investigators discovered that the five incriminated police officers had met with their superior before they were simultaneously heard by the internal affairs disciplinary unit. Indeed, during the hearing, the police officer who was accused of delivering the blow stated that he had just leaned a little too roughly on the shoulder of the claimant to make him sit in the police station (and implied that the perforation of the eardrum occurred as a result of the conditions of the arrest), when the latter had stood up at an untimely moment to protest against what another police officer was telling him (who also assured the investigators that no violence had been committed). The other three officers claimed that one of them had been smoking outside the building, that the second was having a cup of coffee in another room, and that the third had gone to the toilets. However, except in those rare cases, the initial procedures do not contain sufficient elements to allow the investigator to satisfactorily reduce the indeterminate points of the investigation. The internal affairs investigators will then launch a third operation aiming to identify potential witnesses at the disputed scene.

Those witnesses may be different sorts of persons. There may be a witness who saw what happened as a passer-by, someone exterior to the police interaction, but there may also be irrefutable traces, such as the report of the intervention of an emergency medical unit. Looking for a form of externality to the disputed situation is a constant, a necessary point in disciplinary cases. As an element of mediation, the outsider interests the internal affairs investigator, for such a witness might be established as a referee who, without necessarily being impartial (they must take sides, otherwise they are useless, but they must not do it for any interest they share with one of the two parties), gives an unhoped for hold on the intervention in question.

Within the framework of an internal affairs investigation, the outsider plays three roles. First, looking for them gives a direction to the investigation. The investigators try to determine whether there were, in fact, any passers-by and whether they have come forward to offer to testify. In this regard neither the other police officers, nor the friends or family of the claimant, are a priori considered to be third-party referees, except in particular cases. The investigator tries to find a third party that would not be related in any way to the parties to the incident. Once found, the third party plays the part of a convincing element. A passer-by or the intervention of firemen give the internal affairs investigators testimony that they deem objective, for they are foreign enough to the claimant and incriminated officers. The testimony is thus strong not only in that it tells a story but also in that a body becomes an exhibit. Thus, in the case of a complaint against violence in which the claimant claimed he had lost consciousness after receiving a blow delivered by a police officer, the report from the intervention of the paramedics – confirming that the claimant was not unconscious – prevailed in a case in which nothing else made it possible to decide between the different versions. Finally, the testimony has strength due to the conditions of its reception. Thus, if the information given by the third party is considered to be reliable enough by the internal affairs investigator, it will be used later on in hearings as a means to test the accusation and the incriminated officers.

However, as the sociology of the police has underlined, the violent interactions between police officers and citizens are all the more likely to occur in situations of confrontation in limited physical and social spaces. Indeed, in only a few of the cases dealt with by internal affairs did the investigation result in a final version of the disputed events. Combined with the shortcomings of the initial procedure and of the UMJ certificates, the repeated absence of third-party testimony helps explain the difference between the number of alleged acts of violence and the number of sanctions that are imposed in response to those acts. The conditions in which police violence occurs (in situations of confrontation, in the margins of the social spaces) determine the path taken by the internal affairs investigations because of the small quantity of contradictory information made available for the investigation. Thus the elements that allow the investigator to move on from an initial situation affected by a general indeterminacy to a consistent and stabilised version of 'what happened' are extremely incomplete. In the absence of irrefutable evidence, the police's use of force remains legitimate. That process is, moreover, supported by two other mechanisms that are identifiable in the analysis of the files: the presumption of innocence which, in French law, results in each citizen being considered innocent as long as their guilt has not been proven, and the presumption of credibility that the police officers enjoy in the eyes of the other police officers, which concretely results in the police's words having more weight than the words of the claimants, other things being equal.

3 Comparing the different versions

In these conditions, the investigation must proceed with hearings. The reports on hearings are, in that respect, what the disciplinary cases investigated by the internal affairs are mostly made up of. It is thanks to their succession and the subtle intertwining of the versions of events that they display and which the investigators try to understand that the investigation can move forward. A report on a hearing will generally take the following form: after they have given a certain amount of basic information, the person that is being heard is invited to give their own version of the facts that are being investigated. What they say takes up an important part of the report. A few questions of clarification, which are presented as such, are asked during the account. They show the direction that the investigation is taking by progressively invoking elements that the investigator selects as relevant. When it is the police officer who is being heard, the internal affairs investigator gives the officer the version that the alleged victim has provided and asks them to react to it. They are then led to contest it, to put things into perspective, to deny everything and to reaffirm their own version not as a version in itself, but adapted to take account of someone else's story.

As the hearings proceed, the transformations of the versions of the different parties and the questions of the investigator pile up and can be read in the reports. It is through the increasingly precise formulations of the same related facts, the sharpening of the questions that are being asked to the persons who are being heard, that the work of *stabilisation* that results can be observed. Those hearings are then a double source of information for the investigator: they multiply the versions which are at the basis of their work. They produce justifications that inscribe the questions that the internal affairs investigator himself asks – as they appear in the statement of the claimant, in the precise questions that are asked, the points on which the description must be refined, etc.

– at the heart of the refinements provided by the person that is being heard. It is thanks to the coexistence of those two movements that the work of the investigation, which then proceeds through progressive refutations and confirmations of the segments of the versions that are questioned, can progress. As the reports on the hearings multiply the versions and increasingly point out the disagreements, the inaccuracies, the inconsistencies or confirmations, the authentifications and the clarifications, the disciplinary process progresses and draws to its end, for the 'objects' of the investigation are identified with increasing precision and tend to stabilise. Most of the time, however, the confrontation of the different versions favours the incriminated officers.

The moment of confrontation nonetheless makes possible the comparison of concurrent versions of the disputed situation and in particular of the nature of the force that has been used. If the investigative approach implies submitting the versions of each of the parties to the disputed events to a space of variations, then the investigation consists in collecting the contradictory *stories* that relate the situation in which the police have allegedly used violence. Those stories, which are all descriptions of the use of force by the police, will then be submitted to a work of objectification by the investigator. The analysis of the files reveals patterns of accusation of illegitimate violence and, symmetrically, of justification of the use of force and/or of different perspectives on the force used in the situation. Three categories of accusation, matched by three sets of justification, have thus been identified but cannot be detailed too much here.[19] To mention them briefly, there is: lack of discernment, which consists in the denunciation of a disproportion between the action of the police and the situation of the claimant; relentlessness, which is also based on a disproportion, but points out an intentional disproportion in the actions of the police; and omnipotence, which, contrary to the other two, is not related to a disproportion, but appears in situations in which, for a moment, even a very short one, the claimant found herself in a state of almost complete subjection in relation to the police.

For each type of accusation, the defence of the police officers is the same: in the case of lack of discernment, the police officers try to reverse the interpretation of the points on which the judgment of disproportion is based to show, on the contrary, how the elements of the situation made their control or intervention legitimate. As to complaints about relentlessness, the defence of the police officers consists in recontextualising or putting into perspective the behaviours targeted by the complaint by transferring the accusation of disproportion onto the claimant. Unlike what happens in the case of lack of discernment, the balance is not restored thanks to a re-adaptation to the facts alleged by the claimant and reinforced by the investigation, but by the presentation of new facts which are meant to raise doubts as to the behaviour of the claimant. Finally, in the case of omnipotence, the police officers try to show that, *in reality*, the claimant still had degrees of freedom at their disposal and, starting from that analysis, they reduce omnipotence to a simple asymmetry, which can then be justified by the powers with which the police are legitimately vested or to an unintentional mistake that results from the organisation of the department.

One point in particular is essential here. In the three categories of accusation, as in the three sets of defence arguments, the illegitimate violence alleged by the claimant and the legitimate violence claimed by the police officers are always assessed from the logical framework of the situation in which the disputed intervention took place. Indeed, and to take only the example of lack of discernment (but the argument applies to the other sets of arguments), the allegation of illegitimate violence is founded on the claimant's attempt to demonstrate that the police officers committed an error of appreciation, which triggered the use of force based on a mistaken evaluation of the nature of what was happening. The illegitimacy of violence is not due to its mere use, but to its adjustment to the given situation. In the same way, the police officers' attempts to demonstrate that they are innocent is based on the account, during the hearing, of all the elements which, in the situation, made them reasonably think that they must control and/or arrest the person in question, whose resistance entailed the use of force. From that point of view, the accusation of *lack of discernment* is autonomous with respect to the regulated measure of the intensity of violence as it was experienced. Indeed, the denunciation of illegitimate violence is not only based on the description of some physical force used against the person who files the complaint, but above all on the incapacity of the police officers to correctly assess the framework of the situation. From then on, the denounced violence can only be questioned by the internal affairs investigator in relation to the conditions of its use and, in particular, to its legitimacy regarding the requirements of the situation.

This means that when they investigate complaints filed at the internal affairs unit against facts of illegitimate violence, the investigator never, or very rarely, undertakes an independent assessment of the quantity of force used by the police officers before measuring its legitimacy in relation to the circumstances. Instead, the reverse happens: force and legitimacy are never separated by the claimant, nor by the incriminated police officers, and even less by the internal affairs investigator. The latter is not satisfied with measuring the level of violence. They do not try to decide whether three blows would have been enough in an intervention in which the police officers delivered five. They want to know when they were delivered, who delivered them and in what circumstances, as a response to what sort of behaviour, etc.

In this regard, each of the three categories of accusation contains cases in favour of the claimant and others which exculpate the police officers. The essential is elsewhere, and is revealed thanks to Bruno Latour's method of analysing files. The identification of those processes of accusation shows that violence and legitimacy are inseparable, and permits an explanation of the tangible and material composition of what is being accounted for, *in fine* as being 'legitimate violence'. From that perspective, the descriptions the files give access to cannot be reduced to simple exhibitions of cases of use of force. They are the stories of the use, be it legitimate or illegitimate, of force by the police, but they offer the possibility to understand that the way investigations are carried out by internal affairs rarely aim to determine the quantity of violence that has been used. On the contrary, they rather aim to establish the ecology of the use of force by the police officers based on the logic of situations. This does not mean that the determiners of the use of police force are only those related to the situation, as they might incorrectly be assumed to be, but that from the moment the investigator tries to qualify the legitimacy of the violence, they can only do so by measuring, in the strong sense of the word, the disputed situation. The measurement, and the identification of such a differentiator, results from the comparative analysis of the versions that have been presented during the investigation. The constant search for elements that will make the division possible – on the one hand, the investigation establishes that the violence that was used was illegitimate, on the other it concludes that it was legitimate – prevails in practice because violence and legitimacy are inseparable.

The Conditions of a Good Judgment   229

5 Closing the investigation

Once the other possibilities that could clarify the grey zone have been explored and the confrontations of the versions have been completed by the investigator, the latter must close the file. This is done following three phases: leaving the file to rest, proceeding to the final condensation and reaching a decision.

The *pauses* are an integral part of the progress of the investigation. They belong to two categories. The first kind overlaps with the phase of stabilisation and that of the closure. The file is left to rest to mature, as in the case of the Conseil d'État presented by Latour. The investigators say that it is necessary to leave a file aside for some time to be able to look at it in a different way later on. An internal affairs investigator works on several cases at the same time rather than solving them one by one and systematically concentrating on a specific case. They do not wish to deal with many files at the same time either, for fear of feeling indifferent to the cases or even of being tempted to neglect them when they leave the files aside for a while. A second type of pause is more directly related to the closing phase since it is the moment when the file is transferred, if need be, to the judicial authority. The transfer entails a duplication of the file. The first copy leaves the internal affairs building to go to that of the judicial authorities. The second only leaves the office of the investigator to be put on a shelf in the office of another officer where it is classified, based on the year, next to other files that are awaiting a judicial decision. It will stay there for a time, for it then becomes dependent on the judicial temporality. The file must wait before undergoing other transformations, if necessary.

All the files always end with the same document: the investigator's report to the superintendent who is at the head of the disciplinary unit to which the investigator belongs. That document is a *shortened* version made from the versions that have been identified during the investigation, the stable segments put end to end to form an ordered version, namely that of internal affairs. The report enumerates the essential facts of the case. The facts that have not been proven are there, as well as those that have been established, and come in two forms. Either there has been no further investigation because they were not deemed to be worth the trouble, and they are barely mentioned in the report (minimal facts that have not been established or are too bizarre are sometimes completely omitted), or they are mentioned to be better contested by the demonstration of the report. What remains in the file, therefore, is what has been linked together by the investigation, the connections that are materially accessible by the long succession of reports in the file. The report contains all the elements that are prominent: the conditions of the opening of the case, a relatively detailed synthesis of the hearing of the claimant, a comparison with the other versions that have been collected, a mention of the contradictory points and of the means to decide (or not) upon what really happened. That account is at least a page long, and might take up three or four pages.

Such an exercise of condensation is essential because it will be the basis for the superintendent's proposal of a sanction or of a classification to the relevant authorities. The investigator is obliged to carefully choose what to relate if they wish their recommendations to be accepted as the valid result of a disciplinary process and likely to be followed by the different authorities they are going to be sent to. The report is therefore the final link in the file between the daily work of the internal affairs investigators, the motive for the complaint, the codification that was chosen, the different versions collected during the investigation and the proposition which was at the origin of the disciplinary decision. Thus it puts an end to the file in all the meanings of the word.

Once the investigation report and the proposal of the superintendent have been written, the document which contains and provides a synthesis of them both is sent in the administrative system. When that precious document has received the different necessary signatures, it goes back to the internal affairs department and replaces the photocopy that was put in its place to fill the void left by its departure. If the conclusion of the internal affairs investigation is that the case must be closed, the file is put in the archives where it is classified according to its identification number, not to move from there unless another case would benefit from a quick look at it, or if a researcher were to go through those well-organised shelves. If, on the contrary, the final internal affairs report recommends a first-level sanction (a warning, a reprimand) or a simple written observation/caution, the proposal is sent to the DGPN (the National Police Department) and the file is, once again, classified (after the final decision has been added to it). Finally, if internal affairs ask that the case be submitted to a disciplinary hearing, the latter must meet before the file is classified. A letter is afterwards systematically sent to internal affairs to announce the decision of the disciplinary hearing. When that letter arrives, it is immediately put at the end of the disciplinary file while the decision is written on the front page. Most of the time, though, internal affairs also receive a new report, which is hardly comparable to those whose intertwining make up the architecture of the disciplinary file, and which recaps the whole session of the CD, the words of each representative, the questions asked to the police officer(s), the debates and, eventually, the decision. It is also put in the file, which can then go and rest on the densely occupied shelves of the archives. The investigation is *closed*.

Conclusion

Following the internal affairs investigations and looking at the instruction of the disciplinary files with a sociological eye allows us to make a list of the necessary conditions for objective certainties to be established during the investigation – certainties likely to warrant a discharge or a sentence, and other certainties, too, based on which it will not be possible to know precisely how the disputed events happened. Thus the examination of the files reveals the difficulties of the internal affairs investigator trying to resolve the uncertainties that are at the heart of the 'grey zone' of the situations during which the police officers have used force. As the violent interactions between the police officers and their clients are much more likely to occur when they meet face to face, without external witnesses, the indeterminacy of the problematic situations that are submitted to the judgment of the investigators remains in many cases.

The internal affairs officers are, in short, confronted by three investigative situations. The first leads to the establishment of legitimate violence. The investigations establish either that violence was used within a legally authorised framework, or that the claimant has made up the story by denouncing infringements that are without common measure to what is established by the forensic certificates, or that the allegation of blows conceals the claimant's ulterior motive, etc. In these conditions, the complaint is established as illegitimate. The second situation is related, on the contrary, to the instances in which the internal affairs investigation establishes that violence was illegitimate. They might be revealed by the UMJ certificates, the testimony of a third party, suspicious contradictions in the initial procedure or during the hearings. The violence identified by the investigator is disproportionate, it was exercised while the arrestee was already manacled or in custody, or does not correspond to any of the professional gestures and permissible techniques of intervention. The complaint is eventually considered to be legitimate. In those first two cases, the assumption of the illegitimacy of the exercise of violence, which is progressively submitted to a series of tests, has not been offended, in the sense that it has been established with certainty or, on the contrary, positively invalidated in the case at hand. Finally there is the third situation, in which the investigator does not manage – for good or bad reasons – to establish the validity or invalidity of the alleged facts. There remains a doubt: it is quite possible that some illegitimate force has been used, but the investigation does not permit its establishment. Thus, the level of evidence necessary to establish a violation in a disciplinary procedure is as high as in a criminal procedure, which also explains why sanctions are so rare.[19] The persistence of those uncertainties then makes it impossible for the investigation to succeed, if this means passing from an indeterminate situation to a situation that is so determinate that is gives some consistency to the scattered elements that first characterised it, as Dewey suggests.

From that point of view, it is important that the analysis of the processes that are developed during the internal affairs investigations also shows that the investigators do not assess quantities of violence to establish whether it is proportionate or not, but rather try to identify, describe and reconstruct *legitimate violence* or *illegitimate violence*, from a prior reconstruction of the situational proceedings, by asking questions about what really happened (what, in the alleged facts, is certified?) and about the surrounding circumstances in which what happened really happened (which draws on, *inter alia*, the investigator's expertise with police techniques of covering up their colleagues' misdeeds). The identification and differentiation of legitimate violence and illegitimate violence is then achieved without requiring the confrontation of the two terms of each of those syntagmas. As a consequence, what makes the investigator lean toward finding some illegitimate use of force or, on the contrary, to the establishment of adequate use of force by the incriminated police officers is always the recomposition of the relations existing when force was used. It follows that the legitimacy of violence is not established in relation to a quantified measure. Either it is inscribed from the moment the violent gesture was made, because it was made in circumstances that assured it was, as a gesture, the exercise of legitimate violence, then and always, or it is excluded from the moment the violent gesture was made, for nothing in the situation could allow the use of force, even minimally, by the police officers. In that, the police's use of force always carries a certain normativity at the very moment it happens, precisely because it is inextricably linked to the situation in which it is exercised.

This does not mean that internal affairs have a monopoly on the qualification of violent legitimate acts and violent illegitimate acts. However, their investigations can be understood as explanatory tests of what is at stake in that social process that the police's use of force is, insofar as the investigators manage to decide, and insofar as they must, somehow, decide, produce a work in the form of a file capable of stabilising competing, unstable versions of truth, through a meticulous and comparative description of the disputed scene. Such investigations show that the issue of the measure of violence – which we immediately seize upon in hearing of any case of police brutality or excessive force – is in fact secondary in the internal affairs investigation, that such a measure is taken only *after* the legitimacy or the illegitimacy of the force has been determined, and that it is an *effect* or a consequence of the investigation, rather than a guide for it. What is explained here, then, in the purest Latourian tradition, is what the actors care for – which is something rather different than we had, perhaps, imagined at the outset.

Notes

1. B. Latour (2009) *The Making of Law. An Ethnography of the Conseil d'État*. Cambridge: Polity Press.
2. F. Audren and C. Moreau de Bellaing (2013) 'Bruno Latour's legal theory', in R. Benakar and M. Travers (eds), *An Introduction to Law and Social Theory*. Oxford: Hart, pp. 181–94.
3. B. Latour (2012) 'Biographie d'une enquête – à propos d'un livre sur les modes d'existence', *Archives de philosophie*, 75: 549–66.
4. B. Latour and S. Woolgar (1979) *Laboratory Life. The Construction of Scientific Facts*. Beverly Hills: Sage.
5. Y. Barthe et al. (2013) 'Sociologie pragmatique : mode d'emploi', *Politix*, 103: 175–204.

6. Since September 2013, the IGS has merged with its national counterpart, the Inspection Générale de la Police Nationale (General Inspection of the National Police Forces).
7. An assessment that is similar, though it supports quite a different demonstration, has been made in F. Jobard (2002) *Bavures policières? Sociologie de la force publique et de ses usages*. Paris: La Découverte.
8. E. Bittner (2001) 'Florence Nightingale à la poursuite de Willie Sutton. Regard théorique sur la police', *Déviance et Société*, 25 (3): 285–305.
9. The important number of sanctions that are imposed for *private misconduct* (7.3 per cent of the launched investigations, 13 per cent of the cases resulting in a sanction) can be explained by the fact that the deviancies included in that category are brought to the attention of the IGS by the administrative services and will create fewer problems of clarification by an investigation since the alleged facts are often supported by a factual report, an in flagrante delicto or an internal investigation.
10. N. Elias (1975) *La dynamique de l'Occident*. Paris: Calmann Levy.
11. B. Latour (1999) *Pandora's Hope. Essays on the Reality of Science Studies*. Cambridge, MA: Harvard University Press.
12. B. Latour (1988) *Science in Action*. Cambridge, MA: Harvard University Press.
13. C. Lemieux (2012) 'Philosophie et sociologie: le prix du passage', *Sociologie*, 3 (2): 199–209.
14. J. Dewey [1938] (2007) *Logic: The Theory of Inquiry*. New York: Saerchinger Press.
15. B. Latour (1995) 'The "Topofil" of Boa Vista – a photo-philosophical montage', *Common Knowledge*, 4 (1): 145–87.
16. Latour, *The Making of Law*, op. cit.
17. Ibid.
18. Jobard, *Bavures policières?*, op. cit., p. 154.
19. On that point, see D. Linhardt and C. Moreau de Bellaing (2005) 'Légitime violence? Enquêtes sur la réalité de l'État démocratique', *Revue Française de Science Politique*, 55 (2): 269–98.
20. L. W. Sherman (1978) *Scandal and Reform: Controlling Police Corruption*. Berkeley: University of California Press.

9

In the Name of the Law: Ventriloquism and Juridical Matters

François Cooren

From John Langshaw Austin (1962) to Jacques Derrida (1992) through Harold Garfinkel (1967), scholars studying language and social interaction have often been intrigued by the judicial scene, a scene where testimonies, exhibits, evidence, texts of law and precedents regularly define the fate of specific cases and individuals (Heritage 1984; Bruner 2003). If Austin insisted on the performative dimension of judicial utterances, Garfinkel analysed the interpretive methods jurors use to justify their decisions for another next first time, while Derrida explored the gap that seems to always separate law from justice.

Beyond their differences, however, all these contributions point to the performative or eventful character of law, i.e. the fact that law should be considered an achievement or accomplishment in its *haecceity*, as Garfinkel (2002) would say. However, they also point – and this is the paradox – to its iterative, uneventful and institutional character, that is, that this performativity should *also* be considered the product of a specific context, structure or frame that authorises or legitimises certain moves and dictates or prescribes how imputations should be established. Something called 'Law' is thus supposed to iteratively and repeatedly find its *passage* through these performances, since any judicial decision has to be the application, incarnation or embodiment of specific rules that permit, justify or substantiate it.

In this chapter, I will explore this tension by showing how the judicial scene can be considered a *dislocated locus* where various entities can be *made to speak* and *present themselves*, defining the contours and substance of a given case. According to this approach, we do not need to choose between eventfulness and iteration or even between action and structure/system. What we need to show, however, is how different elements of the so-called 'context' of a given scene are, in fact, *made to say things* in a situation of interlocution, thus becoming active participants in what is happening. Using the metaphor of ventriloquism (Cooren 2010, 2012; Goldblatt 2006), I will show – both theoretically and empirically – how participants in legal processes constantly make facts, principles, precedents and texts of law, i.e. *say and do things*, which come to define what Bruno Latour (2010) would call the making and passage of law.

The fragile force of law

In many respects, this exploration will consist of analysing what Kyle McGee rightfully calls 'the fragile force of law' (2012: 1), a law that has to, both iteratively *and* eventfully, find its way through multiple deliberations. As he points out:

> Without the litigants and their legal counselors, the judge would have nothing to oversee, consider, pontificate about, or finally judge. Litigation or criminal prosecution proceeds in a manner not altogether dissimilar from the parliamentary model of interlocution. Documents are prepared and submitted to the court, lawyers come to the courthouse for oral argument or hold conference calls with judges and their clerks, witnesses are interviewed and deposed and put on the stand, evidence is collected and produced, perhaps jurors are impaneled and made to suffer through the tedium of a trial concerning which the lawyers are, in contrast to the jurors, strangely excited. (McGee 2012: 5)

A contrast cannot fail to be noticed between the heat of these interactions/interlocutions and what is often depicted as the coldness of a coherent and autonomous system/structure of laws (Luhmann 1992, 1995), a system/structure that somehow manages to express itself through this intense traffic.

This tension between the context in which litigation takes place and litigation itself indeed haunts legal studies, as it seems to inhabit any social science confronted with the debate between realism and constructivism (Hacking 2000; Latour 2013). While various forms of realism tend to highlight the contextual elements that iteratively determine the judicial scene, constructivism tends to focus on the eventful character of this scene and the capacity participants have to define the outcome of a given case. In their oft-cited article titled 'Governed by Law?', Nikolas Rose and Mariana Valverde propose, for instance, what appears to be a constructivist stance when they suggest replacing 'The Law' with the term 'legal complex', a terminology that allows them to refer to 'an assemblage of legal practices, legal institutions, statutes, legal codes, authorities, discourses, texts, norms and forms of judgment' (1998: 542).

Law is therefore denounced as a fiction, even as

> the mother of all legal fictions, the always receding specter that forever haunts lawyers and judges. As a specter it has, of course, a certain effectivity (Derrida 1994) – people do many things in the name of law. However, *what people do when invoking the law or facing legal difficulties is never law as such.* (Valverde 2003: 10, my italics)

According to this constructivist position, the term 'law' would not be really useful to explain what is happening in legal processes. Since law has, according to Valverde (2003), no agency per se (we will see later how this chapter departs from this position), we, as analysts, would be better served to investigate legal complexes empirically, that is, as she says, 'how it's all done' (p. 11).

Studying how legal processes are done would thus amount, according to Valverde (2003), to developing what she calls, echoing Valéry (1932), Deleuze (1990) or even Foucault (1977), a *dermatological* approach, that is an approach that would not reproduce binary oppositions between what would pertain to the surface and the depth of a given situation or phenomenon. According to her, a dermatological approach allows us to focus on the skin, i.e. the legal process that we can actually observe, without resorting to invisible entities or structures that would determine it. As she points out:

> Deconstructing the surface/depth binary that has plagued both philosophy and commonsense, metaphysics as well as astrology, for many centuries now, Nietzsche's main advice on method – which I think Foucault followed – was to caution us against ascribing the deeds and events studied by the human sciences to transcendental entities such as the free will or to invisible forces such as structural causation. What people do should be studied neither as acts of the individual's Kantian will nor as the product of relentless natural necessity but simply as a set of effects. (Valverde 2003: 13)

Instead of looking for invisible causes behind visible effects, Valverde (2003) thus proposes to analyse the body of law by *opening it out flat*, so to speak. In other words, her approach does not amount to questioning the existence of causality, but to observing and following empirically *what a legal process is concretely made of*. Opening something out flat is the equivalent of *mettre à plat* in French, which roughly means unfolding something in order to make its components visible. Echoing Deleuze (1988), whose work on *the fold* she explicitly mentions, Valverde thus encourages us to *unfold* the legal process, that is to remain on its surface while examining all its meanders, sinuosity and curves.

As we know, this approach is also the one implicitly proposed by Bruno Latour (2010b) when he invites us to 'remain on the surface of things' (p. 143) in order to grasp what he calls 'the making of law'. Staying on the surface of things indeed means that we follow

> the hesitant course of judgment, in which judges quite clearly admit their prejudices while asserting at the same time that they alone cannot determine the solution, or in which they attach themselves quite passionately to legal forms while constantly rejecting the dangers of what they call 'legalism' or 'formalism'. Neither by recognizing social violence nor by focusing on the presence of rules can one predict the movement of the law. At this point, there might be no need to go in search of some invisible layer of reality other than this *winding* of reasoning itself in order to explain how it forces its way through all these obstacles. (Latour 2010b: 143, italics in the original)

Remaining on the surface of the judicial scene thus allows us to observe the *eventful* character of law while noting that this surface is also the *dislocated locus* where many elements seem iteratively conveyed, staged, re-presented and made visible, although through a form of hesitation that seems to characterise the judicial process.

It is indeed this *hesitation* that seems to fascinate Latour, a hesitation that, according to him, prevents law from being either completely autonomous (a self-governing system à la Luhmann, so to speak) or completely heteronomous (a form of social violence, à la Bourdieu, if you will). In one of the most beautiful passages of his book *The Making of Law*, Latour comments on this hesitation:

> Justice only writes law through winding paths. In other words, if she has refused to make mistakes, if she had applied a rule, if she had summed pieces of information, we could not identify her as having being either just or indeed legal. For her to speak justly, she must have hesitated. (Latour 2010b: 151–2)

Justice – if there is such a thing (*s'il y en a*), as Derrida (1992) would have said – thus requires what Latour (2013) identifies as the overcoming of a specific *hiatus*, *leap*, *gap* or *step* that characterises and defines its hesitant passage.

Latour (2013) identifies this hiatus as the *dispersal of cases and actions*, that is the gap that always separates the documentation of the constitutive elements of a given situation and the (judicial) action that could be undertaken from such identification. In order to fill this gap, participants (plaintiffs, juries, judges, lawyers, prosecutors, etc.) thus have to find the *means* that will establish the link between the case they want to establish and the actions they want to see undertaken. Commenting on these means, Latour writes:

> Either there is a legal means and it works – the means is sometimes said to be 'fruitful' – or else there are no legal means and 'there the matter rests.' You wanted to stop a factory from polluting? Yes, but here's the problem: you lack the 'quality to act,' you have no standing: you can make as much fuss as you like, but nothing will happen on the legal level. You wanted to have your French nationality recognized? Yes, but you don't have your parents' naturalization certificates; you can go ahead and alert the media, but nothing will happen on the legal level. You can make what you will of the stalled affair: fiction, religion, science, scandal, but not law. The linkages of law thus have this distinctive feature: through the intermediary of a particular hiatus they allow means to follow a highly original trajectory in a series of leaps from facts to principles. (2013: 365)

Echoing Valverde (2003), Latour thus invites us to study law *as it happens*, that is to determine the specific leap, gap or hiatus that characterises its mode of existence. This leap – the legal means – is the specific way by which a certain continuity can be established between cases and (judicial) actions.

Acting and passing

So we know that we should remain on the surface of things when studying law, since this is where it is supposed to literally be made or performed. However, we also know that there is something called 'law' that is apparently *passing* through this performance. The term 'passing' is indeed crucial for Bruno Latour (2013), since it is, according to him, the way by which law, as an institution, expresses its own mode of existence. As he notes:

> Law is not made 'of' law; but in the final analysis, when everything is in place and working well, a particular 'fluid' that can be called legal circulates there, something that can be traced thanks to the term 'means' but also 'procedure.' There is, in fact, a pass particular to law; something that leaps from one step to the next in the work of procedure or in the extraction of means. (Latour 2013: 39)

The hesitant passage of law would thus both express forms of activity and passivity: a form of activity because it is happening before our eyes (it is *made* visible); a form of passivity because something is also always already *passing* or *transiting* through these occurrences (*it* is made visible).

As Latour (1996, 2013) notes, the key is to think in terms of causing to do or 'faire faire', as the French would say. Since there is no absolute origin to action, any action or activity can indeed be envisaged according to *what makes it possible or impossible*. Action is therefore always *doubled*, which means that its source is always partial and can be shared between various authors, participants or contributors (Latour 2013: 157–8). For instance, acting *out of* anger means that a specific feeling – here, anger – leads me to act the way I do. Similarly, positioning myself as speaking *in the name of* equity means that a specific value or principle is supposed to express itself through my position. Finally, talking or acting as the spokesperson *for* an institution means that this institution is supposed to be saying something through my talk.

In these three examples, a feeling, a principle and an institution should be considered as literally and figuratively expressing themselves *through* what I am saying or doing, hence the idea of *passing*, literally because it is *really* and *actually* what is happening and figuratively because this reality/actuality can express itself through specific *figures* (of speech), e.g. 'anger struck again' (feeling), 'equity dictates that we proceed this specific way' (principle), 'the government of the United States thinks that . . .' (institution). In other words, speaking figuratively is a way to recognise other authors/contributors/actors who or that are literally participating in what is happening when a given actor is talking or doing something. It is what makes any acting a form of passing, that is *what makes an actor a passer for another actor who/that is acting through him/her/it.*

A similar idea can be indirectly found in Garfinkel (1967, 2002) when he highlights the *accountable* character of *any* action, that is that any action can be reconstructed according to what makes it intelligible, explainable or understandable. For instance, if you are recycling plastic bottles, cans, containers, cardboards and newspapers at home, you might account for this activity by saying that you do this *out of respect* for the *environment*. It is your *attachment* to the environment that can be identified as what, among other things, explains your conduct, i.e. makes you do what you are doing. Accounting for any action thus consists of reconstructing/identifying/delimiting *what led this action to take place*, that is what passed or circulated through what happened. Similarly, when someone defends a specific position in the name of justice, it means that it is her attachment to this principle that, among other things, makes her position intelligible, explainable or understandable (Cooren 2010, 2012). Justice is supposed to pass through what this person is saying.

Interestingly, Latour also notes that recognising this doubling of action also leads us to acknowledge that *the direction of action is always uncertain* (2013: 158). For instance, speaking in the name of an institution means that we make this institution speak through what we are presently saying. However, we could as much notice that this institution also leads us to say specific things to the extent that we are precisely constrained, attached or bound in terms of what we can say and cannot say in these kinds of circumstances (i.e. we are, for instance, supposed to defend *its* interests). The same reasoning applies for the environment illustration: recycling is certainly a way for you to express your attachment to the environment, but this attachment is also, as we saw, what leads you to recycle. In other words, it is also the environment's interests that are supposed to express themselves through this routine you perform or habit you have.

To illustrate this oscillation/vacillation, Latour gives the example of the puppeteers who, as he says, can always be surprised by the puppets they manipulate. As he points out:

> We find the clearest instance of this oscillation pushed to an extreme with marionettes and their operators, since there can be no doubt about the manipulator's control over what he manipulates: yes, but it so happens that his hand has such autonomy that one is never quite sure about what the puppet 'makes' his puppeteer do, and the puppeteer isn't so sure either. The courts are cluttered with criminals and lawyers, the confessionals with sinners whose 'right hand does not know what the left hand is doing.' (2013: 158)

Since action is always something that is *shared* (Latour 1996), the source of what is happening is always distributed, which also means that who or what is the producer/author and who or what is the product/outcome is a matter of perspective or focus.

But if action is always shared/doubled, as well as uncertain/indeterminate, it can also be considered *good* or *bad*, which is, for Latour 'the third and most decisive ingredient of the composite notion of construction' (2013: 159). It is indeed not enough to acknowledge that the puppeteer is carried away by her puppet, but this carrying away has to be *well executed*, that is the audience has to be not only marvelled by the way the puppeteer interacts with her puppet, but also impressed by the fluidity of the marionette's behaviour, that is by its (relative and apparent) *autonomy*. In other words, if there is co-construction in both directions, it remains that what happens needs to be well constructed in terms of *what matters* or *counts* to a given audience.

For instance, it is not enough to show that scientists participate, of course, in the co-construction of the facts they claim to discover (Latour 1987), it remains to be shown that these facts are *well*-built or *well*-constructed, that is that the experiment they designed allows these said facts to express themselves as *autonomously* as possible (Latour 2013: 158; Pickering 1995). In other words, and echoing Austin's (1962) Speech Act Theory, any type of action has its own *felicity conditions*, making it successful or unsuccessful (felicitous or infelicitous) according to specific criteria (Cooren 2000). For a scientific audience, the experiment indeed matters a lot, but what matters the most is the capacity for this experiment to faithfully express the factuality of the world.

Similarly, any novelist knows that she can be carried away by her characters, but what matters for her readers (and, we could imagine, for her too) is whether this co-execution appears fluid enough to carry away the readers, too (Latour 2013). In French again, there exists a nice expression that conveys this idea: *ça passe* or *ça ne passe pas*, which literally means 'it passes' or 'it does not pass', as does the English idiom, 'it goes down well' or 'it does not go down well'. In any activity of co-construction, *specific things or beings matter* and it is these things or beings that need to pass well, since they are the ones that ultimately *count* for a given audience. When it does not go down well (when it does not pass through well), it means that something that was supposed to count does not materialise itself very well in what is taking place.

For instance, it is not enough to make an institution speak, i.e. to act as its spokesperson, *this institution has to be made to speak well*, which means that its interests, style and preoccupations have to be well represented, embodied, materialised and made visible in a given performance. In other words, the audience or interlocutors need to *recognise* this institution through what someone is saying. The idea of passing thus means that a specific being – here, an institution – is able to *pass* through a given action/performance, whatever this action/performance might be, whatever form this institution might end up taking in order to pass and be made present.

Similarly, it is not enough to speak in the name of equity or justice, we have to *speak well* about it, that is we have to demonstrate that it is indeed this principle that not only expresses itself through our intervention, but also counts or matters when evaluating the present circumstances. In other words, speaking or acting *in the name of*, *for* or even *under the influence* of something or someone (which is what we always do in *all* circumstances) always has its own share of risk even if this risk also is the condition of the intelligibility/explainability/understandability/accountability of what we say and do.

Acknowledging the doubling of action, the uncertainty of its direction as well as the condition of its felicity thus leads us to explore questions of materiality or even substantiality, that is questions related to what is supposed to *stand under* what is accomplished or performed. The Latin word *materia* means 'the substance from which something is made' or the 'grounds, reason or cause for something', while the term 'substance' etymologically refers to 'what stands under something else', that is what explains its mode of existence or being (see Cooren et al. 2012).

What counts or matters in a given situation thus *defines* what this situation is supposed to be about. It is what is supposed to characterise or qualify it. For instance, if we start speaking in the name of equity or justice, it means, by definition, that the question of equity is supposed to preoccupy, concern or worry us. If it preoccupies, concerns or worries us, it means that it is something that appears to count or matter to us in the present circumstances; we are attached to it. Equity (or lack thereof) is therefore what *substantiates* our position, i.e. what stands under what we end up saying or doing. It is, in other words, what is supposed to (literally and figuratively) *materialise itself* through our interventions.

Acknowledging the question of *passing* thus means that specific beings haunt or inhabit others and their performances. For instance, acting as a physician means being preoccupied or even sometimes obsessed with a patient's health or well-being. It is what is supposed to (ideally) count or matter in these circumstances (both for the physician and the patient) and this is especially what is supposed to *substantiate* and *dictate* a medical intervention. To act well as a physician thus means that we know how to preserve or improve what we are supposed to care for, in this case the patient's health. It means that a specific expertise or know how is also supposed to express itself through what we say and do.

A specific expertise or know-how can therefore be defined as knowing how to express or translate what the elements of a given situation dictate, require or demand, according to what counts for us in this situation. This is where, of course, disagreement might take place, since what counts or matters in a given situation always depends on our respective attachments, preoccupations or interests. For instance, what counts or matters for a physician might not be what counts or matters for a lawyer, a priest or a politician. Each expertise, specialty or interest has its own matters of concern, which means that they might have different ways of expressing/translating/conveying what a given situation dictates.

In contrast with the *dermatological* approach advocated by Valverde (2003) and Latour (2010b), we thus see that it is possible, as analysts, to remain on the surface of things while still acknowledging what is supposed to *stand under* this surface. Although Latour (2013) explicitly rejects the term 'substance', which he considers to be too static and to which he prefers the term 'subsistence', it is noteworthy that everything that constitutes or stands under a given action, situation or position can, in fact, be unfolded not only by the analysts, but also by the participants themselves. In other words, and following Kenneth Burke, we could point out that 'in banishing the term [substance], far from banishing its functions one merely conceals them' (1945/1969: 21).

For instance, a physician can perfectly explain to her patient what brings her to prescribe such or such a medication, that is everything that is supposed to *stand under* (substantiate) her diagnosis and recommendations. Unfolding/explaining what stands under a given medical act thus consists of presenting – i.e. making present – the sources of authority that end up telling what should be done with the patient in the present circumstances. In other words, what stands under an action is the *author* that participates in its accomplishment. All these authors, which participate in the authority of the act, are *co-authors* of what is happening, lending their own respective weight to what authorises a particular move.

Unfolding, whether it is done by the analyst or by the participants themselves, thus consists of staging all the beings that participate in the *authoring/authority* of a given action (Cooren 2010; Taylor and Van Every 2011). Justifying, explaining or accounting for what is accomplished or proposed thus amounts to articulating what or who *dictates* it. As Latour (2013) rightfully notices, 'if we speak in an articulated manner, it is because the world, too, is made up of articulations in which we are beginning to identify the junctures proper to each mode of existence' (p. 152). In other words, *the world is not mute*, it tells us things, as Charles Sanders Peirce (1955), the founder of both pragmatism and semiotics, noticed more than a century ago (Misak 2013).

Ventriloquism

I proposed elsewhere to call *ventriloquism* this way of passing, through which the world articulates itself in what we say and do (Cooren 2010, 2012). Ventriloquism is indeed an interesting way to talk about passing, since this lower form of popular art constitutes, as Goldblatt pointed out, 'illusion without deception' (2006: 37). The audience who attends this type of performance knows that the ventriloquist is a type of illusionist, which means that they are not really deceived by the ventriloquist. They, of course, know that the ventriloquist makes her puppet say things, but they also marvel at the way she fosters this illusion by throwing her voice.

Goldblatt (2006) also notices that ventriloquism is marked by an oscillation/vacillation which is, as we already saw with Latour (1996), constitutive of the shared character of *any* action. If the ventriloquist artfully makes her puppet say and do things, she is also and paradoxically ventriloquised by the puppet she is supposed to manipulate. Why is this so? Because what the puppet says is always, to some extent, what the ventriloquist also says, meaning that the puppet also makes the ventriloquist say things. Although ventriloquism is based on a form of *self-effacement* on the part of the person who manipulates the puppet, this self-effacement is always limited and partial, not only because the ventriloquist is usually holding the puppet on her lap and often *responds* to what her puppet is saying (she is usually engaged in a heated dialogue with her puppet, which is usually what arouses laughter in an audience), but also because what the puppet says is also coming, as we know, from the ventriloquist's mouth.

Scholars interested in phenomena of polyphony also used this idea of ventriloquism: not only Jacques Derrida (1977, 2007), of course, but also Mikhail Bakhtin (1994), even if the latter never used this notion explicitly (but see Carroll 1983; Holquist 1981; Wall 2005). Ventriloquism is an interesting way to talk about communication in general to the extent that it problematises the question of the origin of what is communicated (Cooren 2010). If the performance is well executed, the puppet can appear completely *autonomous*, that is an effect is fostered such that the puppet really looks like it does and says things *on its own*. As I will try to show, the same effect can be identified whenever people communicate with each other.

In order to identify this phenomenon, we have to precisely *unfold* the numerous voices that can be heard or reconstructed whenever we hear people talking to each other, whether we are dealing with persons conversing about the weather, politicians debating on television or lawyers representing their clients in front of a jury. In all these situations, as varied as they are, we deal with what Garfinkel (1967) calls the accountable character of what is happening, that is it will always be possible for both analysts and participants to account for what led the participants to say or do what they said or did.

How does this unfolding take place? First, we have to notice that often times, participants themselves stage what leads them to say what they say or do what they do in their conversation. In other words, our work as analysts is often facilitated by the fact that *people often talk about what ventriloquises them*, i.e. what makes or leads them to say what they say or do what they do. They implicitly or explicitly specify *in the name of what* they talk or act. In order to illustrate this point, let us look at an example that is very familiar to conversation analysts, i.e. the way people usually justify a decision when they have to decline an offer that was just made to them:

A: We're going to the movie tonight. Would you like to join us? (0.5)
B: Hmm, I'm sorry, I have too much work. I wish I could come. It's really too bad.
A: I understand, no problem.

As we see in this example, justifying your decision not to join your friends at the movies usually amounts to implicitly staging what leads you to decline their offer. In terms of ventriloquism, this means that you are implicitly explaining/unfolding *in the name of what* you are declining this invitation. In this case, it is the amount of work you are supposed to have. Although B does not explicitly phrase it that way, everything happens as though she were saying that the amount of work that she presently has *dictates*, *requires* or even *demands* that she decline her friends' offer. This kind of translation should be heard both literally and figuratively: literally because the amount of work is actually and really presented by B as what explains her inability to join them, and figuratively because we see that she is implicitly staging a figure – her work (or the amount of work she has) – that is presented as what, for all practical purposes, prevents her from going to the movies.

The term 'figure', which was surreptitiously introduced earlier in this chapter, is not innocently mobilised here because ventriloquists themselves sometimes call the puppets they manipulate figures. This term, which comes from the Latin *fingere*, means to form or build and can also be used, as we know, to refer to someone's physical appearance, to faces, to a specific jump executed in skating or gymnastics (a double somersault, for instance), but also 'to an illustration, a (written) character, a number, a diagram, a musical motif, a status, a role, or the special usage of a word or phrase (as in figure of speech)' (see Cooren and Matte 2010).

If these figures are made (up), this aspect does not prevent them from having a specific mode of existence or autonomy. Of course, we all know that this kind of justification could be completely *made up* by B, that is that this figure could have just been used as a polite way to decline A's invitation. For instance, we could imagine that B does not want, for various reasons, to join A and his friends or that she feels too tired to go to the movies. Whatever the reasons, what matters is that her refusal to join A and his friends is potentially accountable (even if some accounts are more acceptable than others), which means that other figures could have been staged or mobilised to justify or explain this decision.

'Hmm, I'm sorry, I'm really too tired' would consist, for instance, of implicitly staging her fatigue, tiredness or sleepiness as the figure that justifies/explains her declining the invitation. Interestingly, this fatigue could not only be staged in what B says, but also in how she looks (the fact that she indeed looks tired or exhausted), which would then add to its potential existence. Similarly, responding 'Hmm, I'm sorry, I have too much work,' as she did, could also be accompanied by a gesture showing her desk and all the books and articles she has to read in preparation for an exam. Showing the indices of a very busy person is also a way to *add* to the existence of this figure she is invoking in her response.

What I mean here – and this is a crucial point in my argument – is that some work can always be done by B to show that the invocation of this figure – whether it is her fatigue or the work she has – is not *just* made up on the spot, so to speak, but that other aspects of the situation points to its existence, to its (always) relative *autonomy*. This does not mean that 'making up' the figure is not something that is taking place, since we already saw that *a figure is, by definition, made up*, but it is important to resist the idea that what is made up is non-existent (an argument that is similar to what Latour (2013) points out when he asks us to resist the temptation to equate what is fabricated with what is non-existent, for instance in the case of facts).

As Étienne Souriau (1939, 2009) points out, and as, of course, Latour (2013) implicitly reminds us, figures – and for that matter *anything* – should be conceived as having *more or less existence* (see also Bencherki and Cooren 2011). A figure that is called upon, invoked or evoked, that is *made to say or do something*, in an interaction is always, by definition, made up (this eventfulness is irreducible and incontrovertible), but this 'making up' does not mean that its existence should be reduced to this invocation (here, we could refer to Latour's (1988) principle of irreduction). Since the world speaks, other elements can ventriloquise, translate or convey a figure's existence, adding to its (always relative) autonomy and independence.

I hope that at this point, a link with the first part of the chapter is becoming clear. While constructivism has historically insisted on the eventful character of (inter-)action, we saw that various forms of realism have always retorted that the world as we know it is never completely made up, on the spot, so to speak, and insisted on its iterative, uneventful and institutional character. For them, any form of performativity should *also* be considered the product of a specific context, structure or frame. What we see with the metaphor of ventriloquism is that we do not need to choose between iterativity and eventfulness, i.e. between realism and contructivism. There is always a form of eventfulness, but this eventfulness is the product not only of what humans do and say, but also of what the world does and says *through* them.

If we go back to the interaction example I used, saying 'Hmm, I'm sorry, I have too much work' is certainly a way to ventriloquise the figure of work, but the autonomy or existence of this figure is also reinforced by what B just says afterward ('I wish I could come. It's really too bad'). Saying this is supposed to show or convey that B really wants to join them at the movies and is disappointed. By unfolding two figures that are supposed to animate or inhabit her – her desire to come and her disappointment in not being able to come – she is supposed to *increase the existence* of what prevents her from fulfilling the first (her desire to come) and what causes the second (her disappointment in not being able to come, a disappointment that she can also express/unfold by looking disappointed). Furthermore, we already saw that other things could testify to the amount of work she invokes as the reason not to come. For instance, she could be pointing to the books and articles she has on her desk.

Acknowledging all these forms of ventriloquism is a way to show that we can indeed remain at the surface of things, as Latour (2010) and Valverde (2003) recommend that we do, a surface made of meanders, sinuosity and curves, as long as we also understand that what stands under this surface can also be made visible. Unfolding all the figures that animate or populate a given discourse or interaction is therefore a way (for the analysts and the participants) to *show that they are literally part of the situation*, that they are not only intelligible, but also 'experienceable', that is visible, hearable, touchable, even sometimes tastable and smellable.

Any interaction can thus be considered a *dislocated locus* where various entities or figures can be *made to speak* and *present themselves*, defining the contours and substance of a given situation. However, and in keeping with Latour (2013), what also matters is that these activities of unfolding and ventriloquising need to be *well performed*. For instance, declining an invitation, as a speech act, requires that we have *good reasons* to do so, which also means that these reasons need to *look* real to interlocutors and observers: you are not only invoking the work that you have to do, but you are also showing what is on your desk and you seem indeed disappointed. Admittedly, it could still be completely 'made up' on the spot, but at least three elements – what you are saying, what you look like, what is on your desk – appear to point to the existence of this figure – work – that justifies your declining the invitation.

Ventriloquism is therefore something that you perform when you do, say, write or show something, but it is also – and this is also a crucial point in my argument – something that you do *whenever you interpret, translate or make sense of a situation*, as an observer, interlocutor or participant. Interpreting, translating or making sense of a painting, a text or any interaction is indeed a way to make it *say* or *do* something. If B is ventriloquising her work as the cause of her declining the invitation, A is also in a position to ventriloquise this situation and make it say something, something that might differ from what B wants to convey. In other words, A also notices that B looks indeed disappointed and acknowledges what is on her desk. These indices tell him that A might be sincere. In other words, 'it goes down well' or *ça passe*.

Although accounts are always made up or fabricated, they have, as both Latour (2013) and Speech Act Theory (Austin 1962; Cooren 2000; Searle 1979) remind us, to be well fabricated. That is, what they point to or ventriloquise has to *pass well* because this is *what matters* in these circumstances (Cooren 2010).

How to make law speak well

So what does it mean to speak about law as an act of ventriloquism? Latour characterises this being called law as having a specific mode of existence, which he identifies through a specific leap, gap or hiatus that he calls the 'dispersal of cases and action' (2013: 487), as well as a specific trajectory, which consists of 'linking ... cases and actions via means' (2013: 487). Regarding its felicity and infelicity conditions, he respectively identifies them as *reconnecting* levels of enunciation and *breaking* levels of enunciation. This thing called law is thus able to *pass down well* when the means mobilised seem to be acknowledged as securely linking or connecting cases and actions. It does not pass down well when these means are deemed ultimately absent or questionable.

Law, that which needs to pass down well in the cases that interest us here, would therefore be made up of all these means that are ventriloquised in order to link a specific situation to what is called a judicial action. Bruno Latour (2010) empirically showed how law functions and passes down by studying the Conseil d'État in France, which is the equivalent of a supreme court of administrative law. In what follows, I will analyse a case taken from a different court of justice, the Superior Court of Quebec, Civil Division. This division has jurisdiction over civil and commercial cases, as well as administrative and family matters.

Over the course of two days, I was lucky enough to follow the unfolding of a specific case which involved two groups of rehabilitation centres suing one of Quebec's health and social services agencies as well as the hospital they were working for. These rehab centres offer specialised health and social services to these agencies and were recognised, from 1 April 2001, as accommodation resources (also called 'intermediate resources') when a big reform of the health system took place in this Canadian province. As accommodation resources, they are supposed to 'act as an intermediary between a public facility [such as a hospital] to which they are bound by contract and the users entrusted to them by the facility' (RAMQ). According to this contract, these centres offer these users 'a residential environment as close as possible to a home environment and in which they receive the support and assistance they require' (RAMQ).

After the official recognition of these centres as intermediate resources in 2001, their remuneration was, according to the reform, supposed to be raised. The litigation that interests us concerns a transitory period during which the centres – the plaintiffs – considered that their remuneration was illegally paid in three-year instalments from 1 April 2001 to 31 March 2004. The defendants, that is the social services agencies as well as the hospital that is contractually bound to these rehab centres, considered, on the contrary, that these instalment payments were legal in accordance with legislation concerning centres recognised as intermediate resources before 1 April 2001. According to the co-defendants, the plaintiffs belonged to this category of centres, while the plaintiffs claim that they were officially recognised as intermediate resources only after 1 April 2001.

With these legal actions, which started in 2007 and 2008, the two groups of plaintiffs pleaded that the co-defendants owed them close to 2 million dollars. Although more than six years separated the introduction of the new system of remuneration from this legal action, the accusers alleged that their delay to act was due to the fact that the defendants misinformed them about their new status and how the law would be applied. As for the defendants, they pleaded that this legal action had not been taken within the statutory time and that the plaintiffs had, in fact, been correctly informed. In other words, they alleged that they had informed the plaintiffs within the scheduled timeframe and that they had made them aware of how the reform would be applied and how it would impact the centres.

Although I was able to attend some of the pleas made by the lawyers for this specific case, I will concentrate my analysis on the judge's final decision. Even if this methodological choice does not allow me to talk about the various phases of hesitation that this judge might have experienced throughout the case, it will constitute a way for me to retrospectively evaluate what ended up *mattering* in her reasoning in this situation, i.e. what *substantiated* her verdict. Her judgment can indeed be envisaged as a specific way to depict and reason about the case, a case, as we will see, in which some specific elements were granted the right to *tell us things* about what should be done. In other words, I will try to show that what constitutes a judgment mainly consists of showing what some elements/figures of the situation require, demand or call for, which is what I metaphorically propose to call an activity of ventriloquism.

So how does this happen and to what extent can the judge's written judgment be analysed as a sort of phonation device, that is a device by which various entities are made to say or require things? In order to answer this, I propose that we follow the way this written judgment is structured. Since this verdict was written in French, I translated all the passages quoted. A version of the judgment can be found through the following link: <http://jurisprudence.canada.globe24h.com/0/0/quebec/cour-supe rieure/2009/01/28/nadon-c-hopital-sacre-coeur-de-montreal-20 09-qccs-583.shtml>.

After having presented the file numbers corresponding with this case, the document specifies the judge's name, followed by the names of the different parties involved – the two groups of plaintiffs and the two groups of defendants. The section devoted to the judgment per se then begins with an introduction where the judge presents what is supposed to be factual aspects of the case, an introduction that roughly corresponds with my own summary. This introduction, which is not supposed to be controversial, is meant to condense what the litigation is all about, that is :(1) the compensation the plaintiffs are asking for as well as why they are asking for it; and (2) what the defendants allege in defence in order to reject this judicial action.

At this point, only a few elements appear to be mobilised by the judge to support what she says in this introduction. In two separate footnotes, she indicates which file documents – all submitted to the judge – specify the amounts of money the two groups of plaintiffs are asking for, while in a third footnote, she indicates in what paragraph of another document – called the *motion to institute a proceeding* – the reasons the plaintiffs put forward to justify their delay in litigating can be found, i.e. that the defendants misinformed them about their new status and how the law would be applied.

Through these three footnotes, the judge explicitly ventriloquises three file documents that support/substantiate/stand under what she is saying. But note the phenomenon of oscillation, which is typical of ventriloquism: she is making these documents say something – to the extent that they are presented as indicating the amount of compensation requested (close to 2 million dollars) and the reasons for the delay in litigating – but these documents are also what allow/authorise/enable her to say what she is saying. In other words, they also constitute what leads her to say what she is saying, i.e. they ventriloquise her too. They are literally and figuratively co-*authoring* some aspects of what she is saying.

In a first part called 'Context', the judge then presents the two parties, starting with the plaintiffs. They are presented as accredited intermediary resources, implying that they provide health and social services to persons facing mental illness or a loss of autonomy. This is substantiated by another footnote where the judge mobilises a section of the *Compilation of Quebec Laws and Regulations*. It is a law called the Act Respecting Health Services and Social Services, which appears in this compilation, that stipulates what these intermediary resources are required to do. At least two authors can thus be identified again in this presentation to the extent that it is both the judge and this legal Act that specify what intermediary resources are mandated to do.

Then follows a paragraph where the judge discusses the energy the people in charge of these intermediary resources put into helping their patients. As she points out, 'They are passionate about their mission and they do not count their hours. By their own admission, they bear little attention to, or even neglect the financial management of their establishment' (p. 3). This situation, unveiled by the judge, thus presents these persons as (literally and figuratively) absorbed by their work. But what is especially interesting is how the judge ventriloquises them as admitting that they neglect the financial aspect of their mission. In other words, it is not only the judge who says that they neglect this aspect, but also the plaintiffs themselves, according to their own testimonies. As we will see later, this aspect of the situation will assume significant proportions in her final judgment.

The judge then mentions the successive contracts these establishments signed with the Montreal health and social services agency prior to 2001, as well as the contract that they signed as intermediary resources with the hospital in the winter of 2003. This contract, whose file number is indicated in a footnote, is presented as 'includ[ing] in its section 3 as well as in its appendix 7 dispositions relatives to the installment of their remuneration' (p. 4). In other words, this contract is presented as stipulating that the signatories would be paid through instalments. And this contract is, of course, supposed to bind its signatories.

At this point, let us pause briefly to note how the beginning of this judgment allows the judge to ventriloquise a series of figures that are presented as supporting important aspects of what she is saying. These figures are, as we saw, the various file documents (the motion to institute a proceeding, the contract, etc.) as well as the *Compilation of Quebec Laws and Regulations* that are referred to in the footnotes. These figures also include the plaintiffs themselves who, in their testimonies during the hearings, admitted a lack of concern for the financial aspect of their mission.

Through these elements, it is another figure, the *situation* depicted by the judge, which is supposed to tell the readers two important things: (1) that the plaintiffs did sign a contract in the winter of 2003 and (2) that they, to their own admission, tended to be absorbed by their work, which led them to neglect the financial aspect of their business. Although she draws no conclusion at this point, for those who can read between the lines, the conjunction of these two aspects of the situation tends to implicitly portray the plaintiffs as people who might not have paid too much attention to the contract they signed. This portrayal already appears to diverge from what the plaintiffs allege, which is that the defendants misinformed them about their rights and remunerations.

In keeping with Latour (2013), we thus see a judge *connecting levels of enunciation*, that is, in my own vocabulary, making figures say things at specific points in her judgment. It is not only she who depicts a specific situation, but also the various figures she ventriloquises, mobilises or invokes. If she is the author of her judgment, she also makes co-authors say things, to the extent that file documents, laws and testimonies are presented as authoring key aspects of the situation she depicts, lending their own weight to what she puts forward.

But let us go back to the judgment. The introduction of the plaintiffs continues as she presents each of them (a total of ten, eight presented as individuals, one as a couple and one as an establishment). In each presentation, the judge spends the first paragraph describing when these persons started to be in charge of their respective centres and what these centres consist of. She then addresses the question of how they were each informed about the transition period, what they thought they agreed on when they signed the contract and what they generally remember about what happened during this period.

Although I do not have enough space to analyse these ten descriptions, I will reproduce one of them which summarises, I think, their spirit. Speaking about one of the ten plaintiffs, the judge writes:

> Mr. Filteau remembers the information meetings during which the Contract, as well as the modification and three-year installments were addressed. He reads the Contract and the hospital explains it to him before he signs it. On 1 April 2001, he realises that his resource does not receive 100 per cent of the expected remuneration, regardless of a mention to the contrary by the hospital. Nevertheless, he does not undertake any action to correct this situation. (p. 4)

Through these descriptions, the judge thus portrays the plaintiffs who remember, for most of them, having been informed about their new status and their payment instalments.

While the judge specifies that some of them understood that a three-year instalment would take place, she also points out that others did not realise this aspect and were surprised or even shocked when they found out. However, she also mentions that no one, at that time, undertook any legal action to redress what some perceived as a form of misleading on the defendants' part. The case in itself could be understood as a nice illustration of ventriloquism to the extent that signing the contract amounts, for most of the ten centres, to committing themselves to something they had not foreseen. In other words, these contracts *make them agree* on a three-year instalment that they were unaware they had agreed to or thought did not concern them.

After having briefly presented the two defendants – the agency and the hospital – the judge then addresses three other dimensions of the context, which are substantiated by several file documents mentioned in numerous footnotes: (1) how the reform of Quebec's health system took place; (2) how the new remuneration was paid in three instalments; and (3) how a previous judgment concerning another intermediary resource – the Claire Daniel House – was explained by a lawyer to the plaintiffs in the summer of 2007. I will focus on how the judge presents this last element of the context (the three footnotes 39, 40 and 41 appear in the judgment itself and refer the reader to the file documents mentioned in the text):

> [50] On 10 January 2007, the court of appeal passes a judgment on the *Claire Daniel House* case.[39]
>
> [51] A few months later, in the summer of 2007, the Assembly of Adult Residential Resources of Quebec ('AARRQ') organises an information meeting for their members with the prosecutor

> for the Claire Daniel House, Mr. Carignan. The latter explains his comprehension of the court of appeal's conclusion in this judgment, i.e. that the transitory regime effective from 1991 to 1 April 2001 prevents the recognition of a resource as an intermediary resource before 1 April 2001. He adds that, in a similar way as for the Claire Daniel House, it renders the installation of their remuneration inapplicable, and informs them that they have the right to a judicial remedy in order to obtain compensation for loss of earnings generated by this installment. Only the following plaintiffs participate in this meeting: Michael Sauvé, Jean Barlotti, Michelle Caseneuve and Genevieve Bertrand.
>
> [52] The plaintiffs file their motion to institute a proceeding respectively on 19 December 2007[40] and 8 May 2008.[41] (p. 10)

As we see, this last element of the context allows the judge to introduce another figure in the landscape, the Claire Daniel House case. This judgment, which was mobilised by the plaintiffs' lawyers during the trial, is not presented in its details by the judge – she only refers the readers to this past case through a footnote. What matters for her at this point is how this judgment was understood by the lawyer, that is how he *made it say* that the three-year instalment was illegal. This ventriloquism is made possible, according to this lawyer, by another element – the transitory regime effective from 1991 to 1 April 2001 – which was mobilised by this judgment to determine this inapplicability.

In other words, we see here a small cascade of acts of ventriloquism implicitly staged by the judge: the lawyer – Mr Carignan – ventriloquised the Claire Daniel House judgment, a judgment that itself ventriloquised a transitory regime. All these authors – the lawyer, the judgment and the transitory regime – are themselves ventriloquised by the judge as saying something about a mistake that might have been made about the plaintiffs' remuneration. Note, however, that the judge does not mark her endorsement of this way of ventriloquising this ruling. As she points out, this interpretation is the lawyer's comprehension, i.e. the way *he* makes this verdict say specific things.

Having presented the context, the judge then presents, in section 2, the matters of litigation:

> [53] The litigation raises two questions:
> - Has the plaintiffs' right to recourse expired?

- Were the plaintiffs erroneously remunerated as intermediary resources from 1 April 2001 to 4 December 2003? Did they qualify as intermediary resources before 1 April 2001? (p. 11)

As we see, the judge operates a sort of *self-effacement* as she is summarising the case. She does not present herself as raising these two questions. It is *the litigation itself* that is presented as doing this.

This self-effacement is comprehensible to the extent that it is one of the conditions of her authority regarding the matters at stake. Although these three questions are, of course, *also* raised by the judge, selecting this form of ventriloquism allows her to *lend weight* to this reduction. By effacing herself in her own judgment, she thus stages the litigation – and all the matters that were staged through it so far – as *calling for* these three questions and only these three questions, three questions that will allow her to simplify the decision-making process. To the extent that it is the litigation itself that raises these questions, this reduction/simplification is presented as authorised and legitimate.

We thus observe here an *act of selection* that is also typical of ventriloquism. As we know, any act of ventriloquism consists of making figures say things. However, this activity also presupposes that these figures *count* or *matter* to the ventriloquist. If they deserve to be ventriloquised, it is because *they speak to* the problems at hand, i.e. they are deemed relevant or pertinent. They have a say about these matters. Some elements do not count while others do, which means that the ones that do count will materialise themselves in the judgment. They will stand under or substantiate it.

In a third section called 'Position of the Parties', the judge then presents the two parties' respective stances, which could be considered the most obvious cases of ventriloquism in this ruling. She starts with the plaintiffs who, as we will see, are themselves presented as ventriloquising a series of figures. As she writes:

[54] In invoking their recognition as intermediary resources since 1 April 2001, the plaintiffs claim that the second paragraph of the transitional provisions of the statute law was illegally applied to them. This second paragraph, which is at the heart of the current litigation, provides for a three-year instalment of the remuneration increase. (p. 11)

In the Name of the Law   259

Then follows a reproduction of the two paragraphs of the transitional provisions (which corresponds with Article 200) of the statute law. Having quoted this article, the judge then adds:

> [55] They claim that they were entitled to an immediate payment of this raise in accordance with the first paragraph of the aforementioned Article 200. Yet, in paragraph 18 of their motion to institute a proceeding, they put forward that they were deceived by the defendants' erroneous interpretation and consequently were made aware of the violation of their rights only in summer 2007 on the occasion of the information meeting with the Claire Daniel House prosecutors. (p. 11)

This is followed by a quote from paragraph 18. She then writes:

> [56] The plaintiffs add in paragraph 20(b) and 20(c) of their motion that the defendants' fault put them in a situation of legal impossibility to act before 2007, the year a lawyer informed them of their rights. (p. 12)

What follows is a reproduction of paragraphs 20(b) and 20(c). Having reproduced these two paragraphs, she then concludes:

> [57] Finally, in insisting on the inequality of the parties in presence and on their unfavourable position, the plaintiffs invite the tribunal to discard the Contract that links them to the hospital. (p. 12)

As we see, the plaintiffs are implicitly staged as ventriloquising figures that are supposed to authorise them to make their case. In Latour's (2013) vocabulary, these figures are the *means* by which the accusers claim they can establish a link between their case and their legal action. These means are, among others: (1) their official recognition as intermediary resources on 1 April 2001; (2) the first paragraph of Article 200 of the statute law; (3) their situation of legal impossibility to act before 2007; and (4) their unfavourable position in terms of balance of power with the hospital.

All these elements are implicitly presented by the plaintiffs as demonstrating or showing that they are entitled to the compensation they are asking for, which corresponds with the second question that the judge identified when summarising the litigation.

Their official recognition as intermediary resources (means no. 1) was supposed to entitle them, according to the first paragraph of Article 200 of the statute law (means no. 2), to get immediate compensation. Regarding the first question: 'Has the plaintiffs' right to recourse expired?', the plaintiffs are staged by the judge as invoking their status of legal impossibility to act before 2007 (means no. 3). It is this status of legal impossibility that dictates that they were still entitled to institute this legal action even if their right to recourse had apparently expired.

Finally, since the contract they signed in 2003 made them officially agree on the three-year instalment, they invoke another status – their unfavourable position in terms of balance of power with the hospital (means no. 4) – in an attempt to discount this document from what should be considered in this case. In other words, it is a specific situation that, according to the plaintiffs, figuratively and literally authorises them to take action. This situation is made up of four key figures – the four *means* we just identified – that are supposed to count or matter because they all dictate that the plaintiffs get compensation for their loss of income.

As already noted by narratologists such as Jerome Bruner (2003) or Algirdas Julien Greimas (1987), this part of the judgment functions like a little story with heroes (the plaintiffs and their lawyers) trying to mobilise helpers (the first paragraph of Article 200 of the statute law, their status of legal impossibility, their unfavourable position in terms of balance of power) while thwarting opponents (the prescription period, the contract, the hospital, the provincial agency) in order to fulfil their mission (getting the compensation they deserve). What the ventriloquist analysis adds, however, is that this way of telling their story is made possible because the helpers they mobilise are literally and figuratively presented as *doing things* in this narrative. More precisely, they are supposed to be saying things that the plaintiffs are also saying.

As for the opponents – the prescription period and the contract – they are supposed to be *rendered mute* by two of the helpers, i.e. the plaintiffs' status of legal impossibility and their unfavourable position in terms of balance of power. It is indeed this status and position that hinder, according to the plaintiffs, the opponents' argument that the plaintiffs are not entitled to get their compensation. In other words, the judge should not consider these opponents, since they *do not have a say* in these matters. What Latour (2013) calls *means* are therefore figures that are made to say things that allow the plaintiffs to progress in their trajectory, a trajectory that is supposed to lead them to the object of their mission, i.e. their compensation, which is the goal of their legal action.

If we now turn to the way the judge presents the defendants, here is what we find in her verdict:

[58] The defendants plead the limitation of remedies, a means of inadmissibility that was already raised unsuccessfully through a motion to dismiss the case, since the court did not have at its disposal, at this preliminary stage, sufficient evidence to discard the plaintiffs' argument founded on their legal impossibility to act.[43] In this regard, they put forward the lateness of the legal recourse taken in 2007 and 2008, since the last allegedly illegal payment dates from December 2003. They add that the plaintiffs do not allege any new investitive fact between 2003 and 2007, except the Court of Appeal's judgment in the *Claire Daniel House*'s affair. They also point out that if the Claire Daniel House – a housing resource placed in the same situation as the plaintiffs, according to their own thesis – was able to institute its recourse within the prescribed time, nothing justifies nor excuses the delay in acting

[59] Regarding the fact of the matter, the hospital pleads the absence of fault in the execution of the Contract with the plaintiffs, as well as its good faith and transparency in the transmission of information in accordance with the Ministry's and Health Authority's decisions. As for the Agency, they argue that they did not commit any fault. They contend that they paid the plaintiffs, within the timeframe, all the credits put at their disposal by the Ministry to apply the new scales of remuneration. (p. 12)

As expected, according to the judge, the defendants are telling a different story regarding the two questions raised by the litigation. The figures rendered mute by the plaintiffs – the prescription period, the contract – are, of course, now fully capable of speaking out. Conversely, the figures ventriloquised by the accusers are now muted: the legal impossibility to act cannot be invoked, since no fault was committed: the plaintiffs were properly informed and remunerated and the contract properly executed.

But what is also noteworthy in this story is the alleged absence of *investitive facts*, a technical term jurists use to refer to facts 'by means of which a right comes into existence' (law dictionary).

Indeed, pleading this absence of facts allows the defendants to portray a situation where nothing changed between 2003 and 2007 in terms of new rights that could emerge from new facts. Had these investitive facts emerged, they could have *told* or *showed* us a different story about what the plaintiffs are entitled to, but this is not the case, according to the defendants.

We now arrive at the fourth section entitled 'Analysis' at the end of this judgment. In this section, the judge decrees her judgment and the axe falls, so to speak.

> [61] For the following motives, the tribunal concludes that the right to recourse expired.
> [62] The plaintiffs had a delay of three years to allege their personal right,[44] here the one claimed for the one-off payment of the adjustment of their remuneration.
> [63] Even assuming that the basis of their thesis holds water, which the tribunal will not decide upon given its conclusion on the limitation of the remedies, the plaintiffs must have instituted their legal action in the prescribed delay, except in the case of suspension or interruption. (p. 13)

As we see, the judge decides on the matter by addressing only one of the two questions that this litigation raised. This is, indeed, the expiration of their right to recourse that ends up mattering, notwithstanding the plaintiffs' thesis regarding the unfair character of the three-year instalment of their remuneration. In other words, this *means* – the prescription of the recourse – is what allows her to make her decision. It is also the means that leads to her decision.

As expected, this means does not come from thin air and takes the form of a footnote (44), which refers the readers to Article 2925 of the Civil Code of Quebec. Although this article is not reproduced in the judgment, it reads: 'An action to enforce a personal right or movable real right is prescribed by three years, if the prescriptive period is not otherwise established.' It is this article that, according to the judge, *speaks to* this specific case. It is the principal means by which she will establish a link between the established case and her decision. According to the tribunal, which the judge ventriloquises at this point, this article literally and figuratively tells us that the right to recourse is, in this case, expired.

But even if the verdict has already come down, the judge now elaborates on the case itself. She needs to show that more than three years indeed separates the official information about the instalment from the action to enforce the plaintiffs' personal rights. Interestingly, we will see that this elaboration seems to reproduce some of the *hesitations* she might have had during the hearings:

> [64] So, the dispute concerns the starting point for the running of the prescription period. Must we retain the information meetings organised by the hospital in 2001, during which, according to the preponderance of evidence, the plaintiffs learn about the instalment of their remuneration adjustment? Would it rather be 4 February 2002, the date of the first instalment? 2 December 2002, the date of the second instalment? The signature of the contract in 2003, a contract that calls for instalments in its appendix 7? 4 December 2003, the date of the last instalment and of the reception of the letter from the hospital confirming the final payment of the adjustment? The plaintiffs invite the Tribunal to consider at best the date of 4 December 2003 as the starting point of the prescription. So, in the best-case scenario, the actions filed respectively on 19 December 2007 and 8 May 2008 would be prescribed since 4 December 2006. (p. 13)

Having selected the article that appears to count or matter regarding the case at hand, the judge now selects the fact that this article is supposed to speak to, i.e. when the prescription period started.

Interestingly, we see her enumerating the five dates that could possibly count as the ones on which the three years could commence, an inventory that allows her to demonstrate the exhaustive character of her investigation. But what is even more interesting is the way she attributes the selection of the last date to the plaintiffs themselves. It is, according to the judge, they who invite the tribunal to select this date – 4 December 2003 – as the right one from which to count the three-year prescription. It is their words, not hers, which, of course, lend weight to this selection. In other words, it is as if it were the plaintiffs themselves who were saying that it is unfortunately too late for them if we retain what Article 2925 stipulates.

But what if the prescriptive period could not be otherwise established, as specified, as we saw, at the end of this article? In other words, what if other dates could be selected as the starting point, which is what, as we saw, the plaintiffs allege? This is what the judge now addresses. It is indeed not enough to put forward the means of your own conclusion. As a judge, you also have to call into question alternative means that might lead to other conclusions:

> [65] Each of the plaintiffs testified that they were not made aware of any new investitive fact since 4 December 2003, except for the judgment of the Court of Appeal in 2007. So, to retain their position that the prescription started to run in 2007, one needs to conclude that there was impossibility to act.[46] Yet the burden shouldered by the one who alleges impossibility to act proves to be heavy.[47] (p. 13)

In order to mute Article 2925, the plaintiffs – through their lawyers – indeed mobilised another article of the Quebec Civil Code, namely Article 2904, which the judge refers to in footnote 46. This article reads as follows: 'Prescription does not run against persons if it is impossible in fact for them to act by themselves or to be represented by others.' The entire affair thus seems to now stand on this specific question: was it indeed impossible for the plaintiffs, as they allege, to act by themselves or to be represented by others regarding this case? Although the judge does not start to answer this question explicitly, she already points out that this is hard to prove.

Ventriloquising Article 2904 is indeed a possibility, but one needs to be well armed or prepared, a claim that the judge backs up with another footnote (47), which this time refers to a jurisprudential decision (*Mobarakizadeh against Koritar*, AZ-50084032 (CS), para. 34). In other words, she is saying that it is not only her, the judge of this present case, who says that it is hard to prove that one was unable to act, it is also the judge who made a decision regarding a previous case, a decision that creates a legal precedent. This precedent, as any precedent, can therefore be ventriloquised to substantiate this position.

Let's see now how she finally examines whether or not the plaintiffs are able to shoulder this burden:

> [66] The plaintiffs allege that they were deceived by misleading information from the defendants regarding the application of the transitory period. However, they do not document any concealment or deceptive manoeuvre.[48] They simply plead that they

relied on the defendants' indications, either because they represented the authority, or because they were too engaged with their resource's daily business to take a close look at financial questions, or because their limited knowledge did not enable them to understand that their rights were violated. (p. 14)

Again the footnote (48) is noteworthy because it allows the judge to stage another jurisprudential decision that could have had a say on her judgment. Had the plaintiffs been able to document forms of concealment or deceptive manoeuvres on the defendants' part, they could have, according to this past judgment, found their means for a legal action. However, we see the judge ventriloquising the plaintiffs as exposing other reasons for not paying attention to what the defendants were telling them during these information meetings. This legal means, again, does not hold water. Consequently, the plaintiffs' case does not pass down well.

But could other ways be found to prove that the plaintiffs were unable to act? The judge ends her judgment with what now appears like the last nail in the coffin of the plaintiffs' means.

[67] Yet, quickly during the elaboration of the reform, that is, from 1997, the Ministry informs the partners of the network, including the resource associations, of their plan to spread the future adjustments of remuneration during a three-year transitory period.[49] Then the decision of the Authority on this instalment is taken publicly,[50] and this question is openly discussed in the network.[51]

[68] Some plaintiffs who were until then satisfied with their remuneration find matters of reproach only after the information session of summer 2007 when they learn that another housing resource placed in a similar situation as theirs won its case, the Claire House, and that, consequently, they too have a right to an effective appeal.

[69] However, the prescription applies to all, and ignorance of the law or existence of a right[52] does not constitute an impossibility to act. Knowledge of recourse should not be confused with knowledge of the facts that could lead to its opening.[53]

[70] Furthermore, in the absence of any evidence, a fact remains unexplained: the Claire Daniel House instituted its recourse as soon as 2003. The evidence does not reveal a privileged situation compared with the plaintiffs or the reception of

information that differs from the ones conveyed to them. In addition, what distinguishes the Claire Daniel House's situation from the plaintiffs'? How can we understand that, faced with a similar situation, it did not find itself in an impossibility to act and instituted a legal action within the prescribed delay? One cannot help but conclude that the plaintiffs did not pay the same attention, nor did they demonstrate the same diligence and vigilance as the Claire Daniel House in following up of their business. The case of suspension of prescription for impossibility to act remains an exception to the rule according to which the prescription runs for all.[54] The plaintiffs do not find themselves in such exceptional situation.

[71] Finally, the plaintiffs, who are members of a resource association that represents them, do not establish any fact that would allow us to conclude that there is a contractual illegality that would excuse the delay to institute the recourse. (pp. 14–15)

We are now familiar with the footnotes that both lead and allow the judge to add other voices in support of what she is putting forward. In footnotes 49, 50 and 51, we see her mobilising three file documents submitted by the defendants, three documents that, according to her, demonstrate that a lot was actually done to publicise the three-year instalment. These documents are therefore supposed to counter any allegation that information might have been concealed or that deceptive manoeuvres were undertaken. This means also disappears. The plaintiffs' charge cannot pass.

In paragraph 68, the judge then recalls the period – summer 2007 – when the plaintiffs realised that the defendants might have misled them. However, she then ventriloquises, in paragraph 69, two principles that, according to her, show that there was no impossibility to act: (1) ignorance of the law or existence of a right does not constitute an impossibility to act; and (2) knowledge of recourse should not be confused with knowledge of the facts that could lead to its opening. These two principles are themselves backed up by two jurisprudences indicated in footnotes 52 and 53. Again, it is not only the judge who is telling us and the plaintiffs that it is too late. These two judicial precedents, which put forward these two principles, also demonstrate that there is, indeed, prescription.

In paragraph 70, we then see the judge asking a question to which she proposes what appears like a devastating answer. How come the Claire Daniel House was able to institute legal action from 2003 while the plaintiffs did not? As she points out, another figure called the evidence – that is, all the facts considered material to the case – was not able to reveal that the plaintiffs' case was different from this rehabilitation centre's. The plaintiffs almost appear to pass from the status of accuser to one of culprit: if there are persons to be blamed, it should be them, not the defendants. They are the ones who should have taken care of their business, which is what the Claire Daniel House did. They are in the wrong. They should have been vigilant. The tables have turned.

The judge then ends her judgment with this conclusion, followed by her signature:

FOR THESE MOTIVES, THE TRIBUNAL
[72] **REJECTS** the action in the file 500-17-042915-085
[73] **REJECTS** the action in the file 500-17-041439-087
[74] **WITH COSTS.** (p. 15, capital letters and bold in the original)

The case is now sealed. One after the other, the judicial means proposed by the plaintiffs were discarded, while some of the means put forward by the defendants were retained.

Although it is, of course, the judge who is making these two decisions, we also saw the many voices that were invoked to lead her to this verdict. All these voices – the ones of precedents, principles, facts, articles of the civil code, other judges, the plaintiffs themselves – point, according to this judgment, to the existence of means by which she can reject the two legal actions. Conversely, we also saw how these voices pointed to the absence of means put forward by the plaintiffs. In order to *go down well*, their legal case should indeed have been carried by multiple figures, figures that were, one by one, dismissed. They were supposed to count. They did not.

Conclusion

Did I mobilise a dermatological approach to analyse this case? To be sure, I remained on the surface of things, as Latour (2010) recommends that we do. I limited myself to examining this verdict, although I also attended some of the hearings, which helped me understand other aspects of this judgment. In any case, attending these hearings gave me access to additional aspects of this case, to other ranges of its surface, so to speak. As any trope, the skin metaphor, however, has its limits as we saw that what *stands under* a specific position or judgment appears to be constantly *brought to the surface*, something that, of course, does not always take place with an epidermis.

What is supposedly behind the surface will not count or matter as long as someone (e.g. a lawyer) or something (e.g. an article of law) does not excavate or dig it up. A jurist's skill consists of knowing or determining what could make a difference or matter in a given case. If an element that could have counted remains uncovered, it will not count, which means that it will not be able to substantiate a decision. It will formally not be part of the case, per se. And what is true for a lawyer, a judge and an article of law is, of course, true for the analyst herself. What stands under one or several judicial decisions can also be revealed by bringing to the surface motives or facts that might have remained hidden but that might have actually counted in the decision. In all these cases, what we deal with is an activity of surfacing or digging, whether it is done by the participants themselves or by the analyst.

In contrast with the skin metaphor, I proposed the image of the ventriloquist and her figures. As we saw, acts of ventriloquism consist of giving a voice to what or who could have otherwise remained mute. In other words, what a case is made of, what its substance consists of, needs to be staged by the lawyers so that these elements or figures can tell the judge what conclusions should be reached. Law is thus able to *pass down well* if a form of self-effacement takes place, that is if we feel or sense that it is the case itself that *calls for* this specific judgment.

Echoing the debate between realism and constructivism, we realise that we do not need to choose between iterativity and eventfulness, between legal formalism and law-as-it-happens. On the contrary, studying law-as-it-happens (or *law in action*, as Latour could call it) allows us to examine how the judicial context is constantly ventriloquised in the hearings and judgments we observe. Instead of sterilely opposing the realm of court interactions from the reign of forensic structures, we now understand that the judicial scene is a dislocated locus where articles of law, precedents, documents, facts and principles are *made to tell us* what should be done with a specific case. The so-called context constantly invites itself in the text of the debates.

But what characterises this scene is that only specific beings are, of course, allowed to speak out. On one side, there is what constitutes the evidence or proof, that is whatever is considered as a body of facts admissible to the court, an admissibility that is a matter of debate. These facts, which, as we saw, travel to the court through the form of documents and testimonies, basically tell us what should matter or count in what happened. On the other side, we have the judicial texts, made of articles of law and precedents, which are supposed to indicate what should be done with what this body of evidence tells us.

As shown in the previous analysis, the *authority* of what is put forward, whether by the lawyers or the judge, is literally and figuratively made up of the various *authors* or figures that will join their respective voices to what has to be demonstrated. These authors or figures are, of course, not only *selected* but also *interpreted* by the lawyers and, subsequently, by the judge. However, selecting and interpreting are precisely the acts by which a specific author is *made to say something* about a specific case (interpreting always is making something or someone say something). If there is a form of self-effacement on the jurists' part, ventriloquism is always at stake to the extent that lawyers and judges *have to make these authors or figures speak well*.

Making these elements speak well means that their relative *autonomy* must be acknowledged, which is, of course, a matter of debate. A good ventriloquist is, as we know, someone who is capable of entertaining the illusion that her dummy is really saying something *by itself*. Although there is no deception, this illusion is important, since the audience needs to be able to 'suspend its disbelief', so to speak. Law is therefore capable of passing down well if its (always relative) autonomy is recognised, that is if we feel or sense that law is indeed literally and figuratively speaking through the jurist, that it is indeed the law that speaks at this very moment (even if it is also always someone or something that makes it speak).

But please, do not make me say something I did not mean to say! I am not claiming that the law always speaks clearly, plainly or in a straightforward manner, or that it is easy to ventriloquise it. If ventriloquism works in one direction, we also saw that it always works the other way as well. In other words, jurists are themselves preoccupied, inhabited or even haunted by the voices they ventriloquise. This is the *hesitation* that Latour (2010) very nicely analysed with the Conseil d'État and that we can only skim through with this case. Making a good decision consists of constantly and painfully *testing* which voices should count and which ones should not. A ventriloquist is *also* a figure that is led or made to say specific things and not others.

Although the ventriloquist metaphor could be accused of reducing judicial matters to a simple game or show, we see that it also allows us to acknowledge what is supposed to be the painful character of any decision, whether judicial or other. This is probably what Derrida (1992) had in mind when he pointed out that we, paradoxically, need to experience the *undecidable* character of a decision in order to truly decide. Experiencing undecidability or hesitation for a judge means that she is *preoccupied or concerned by this law that has to pass down well through her voice.* Hesitating thus consists of weighing which voices should come from her, that is which ventriloquists deserve to speak through the figure that she embodies.

My deepest thanks to Richard Janda for providing great feedback about this chapter.

À Guylène Beaugé
Avec toute mon admiration.

Bibliography

Aid Programmes (n.d.) *Régie d'assurance maladie du Québec (RAMQ)*. Retrieved 17 April 2014 from <http://www.ramq.gouv.qc.ca/en/citizens/aid-programs/Pages/accomodation-in-intermediate-resource.aspx>.

Article 2925 (n.d.) *Civil Code of Québec*. Retrieved 16 April 2014 from <http://ccq.lexum.com/ccq/en#!fragment/sec2925>.

Austin, J. L. (1962) *How to Do Things with Words*. Cambridge, MA: Harvard University Press.

Bakhtin, M. (1994) *The Bakhtin Reader: Selected Writings of Bakhtin, Medvedev, and Voloshinov*. London: Edward Arnold.

Bencherki, N. and Cooren, F. (2011) 'Having to be: the possessive constitution of organization', *Human Relations*, 64 (12): 1579–607.

Bruner, J. (2003). *Making Stories: Law, Literature, Life*. Cambridge, MA: Harvard University Press.

Burke, K. (1945/1962) *A Grammar of Motives*. Berkeley: University of California Press.

Carroll, D. (1983) 'The alterity of discourse: form, history, and the question of the political', in M. M. Bakhtin, *Diacritics*, 13 (2): 65–83.
Cooren, F. (2000) *The Organizing Property of Communication*. Amsterdam/Philadelphia: John Benjamins.
Cooren, F. (2010) *Action and Agency in Dialogue: Passion, Incarnation, and Ventriloquism*. Amsterdam/Philadelphia: John Benjamins.
Cooren, F. (2012) 'Communication theory at the center: ventriloquism and the communicative constitution of reality', *Journal of Communication*, 62: 1–20.
Cooren, F. and Matte, F. (2010) 'For a constitutive pragmatics: Obama, Médecins Sans Frontières and the measuring stick', *Pragmatcs and Society*, 1 (1): 9–31.
Cooren, F., Fairhurst, G. T. and Huët, R. (2012) 'Why matter always matters in (organizational) communication', in P. M. Leonardi, B. A. Nardi and J. Kallinikos (eds), *Materiality and Organizing: Social Interaction in a Technological World*. Oxford: Oxford University Press, pp. 296–3.
Deleuze, G. (1988) *The Fold: Leibnitz and the Baroque*. Minneapolis: University of Minnesota Press.
Deleuze, G. (1990) *The Logic of Sense*. New York: Columbia University Press.
Derrida, J. (1977) 'Fors', *Georgia Review*, 31 (1): 64–116.
Derrida, J. (1992) 'Force of law', in D. Cornell, M. Rosenfeld and D. C. Carlson (eds), *Deconstruction and the Possibility of Justice*. New York and London: Routledge.
Derrida, J. (2007) *Psyche: Inventions of the Other*. Stanford: Stanford University Press.
Foucault, M. (1977) *The Archaeology of Knowledge*. London: Tavistock.
Garfinkel, H. (1967) *Studies in Ethnomethodology*. Englewood Cliffs, NJ: Prentice Hall.
Garfinkel, H. (2002) *Ethnomethodology's Program: Working out Durkheim's Aphorism*. Lanham, MD: Rowman & Littlefield.
Goldblatt, D. (2006) *Art and Ventriloquism: Critical Voices in Art, Theory and Culture*. London and New York: Routledge.
Greimas, A. J. (1987) *On Meaning. Selected Writings in Semiotic Theory*, trans. P. J. P. F. H. Collins. London: Frances Pinter.
Hacking, I. (2000) *The Social Construction of What?* Cambridge, MA: Harvard University Press.
Heritage, J. (1984) *Garfinkel and Ethnomethodology*. Cambridge: Polity Press.
Holquist, M. (1981) 'The politics of representation', in S. J. Greenblatt

(ed.), *Allegory and Representation: Selected Papers from the English Institute, 1979–80*. Baltimore: Johns Hopkins University Press.

Investitive Fact (n.d.) *The Law Dictionary*. Retrieved 17 April 2014 from <http://thelawdictionary.org/investitive-fact/>.

Latour, B. (1987) *Science in Action: How to Follow Scientists and Engineers Through Society*. Cambridge, MA: Harvard University Press.

Latour, B. (1988) *The Pasteurization of France*. Cambridge, MA: Harvard University Press.

Latour, B. (1996) 'On interobjectivity', *Mind, Culture, and Activity*, 3 (4): 228–45.

Latour, B. (2010) *The Making of Law: An Ethnography of the Conseil d'État*. Cambridge: Polity.

Latour, B. (2013) *An Inquiry into Modes of Existence: An Anthropology of the Moderns*. Cambridge, MA: Harvard University Press.

Luhmann, N. (1992) 'Operational closure and structural coupling: the differentiation of the legal system', *Cardozo Law Review*, 13: 1419–40.

Luhmann, N. (1995) 'Legal argumentation: an analysis of its form', *Modern Law Review*, 58: 285–98.

McGee, K. (2012) 'The fragile force of law: mediation, stratification, and law's material life', *Law, Culture and the Humanities*, 1–24.

Misak, C. (2013) *The American Pragmatists*. Oxford: Oxford University Press.

Peirce, C. S. (1955) *Philosophical Writings of Peirce*. New York: Dover.

Pickering, A. (1995) *The Mangle of Practice*. Chicago: University of Chicago Press.

Rose, N. and Valverde, M. (1998) 'Governed by law?', *Social and Legal Studies: An International Journal*, 7 (4): 541–51.

Searle, J. R. (1979) *Expression and Meaning. Studies in the Theory of Speech Acts*. Cambridge: Cambridge University Press.

Souriau, É. (1939) *L'instauration philosophique*. Paris: Félix Alcan.

Souriau, É. (2009) *Les différents modes d'existence, suivi de Du mode d'existence de l'oeuvre à faire*. Paris: Presses universitaires de France.

Taylor, J. R. and Van Every, E. J. (2011) *The Situated Organization*. New York: Routledge.

Valderde, M. (2003) *Law's Dream of a Common Knowledge*. Princeton: Princeton University Press.

Valéry, P. (1932) *L'Idée fixe*. Paris: Gallimard.

Wall, A. (2005) *Ce corps qui parle. Pour une lecture dialogique de Denis Diderot*. Montreal: XYZ éditeur.

10

Laboratory Life and the Economics of Science in Law
David S. Caudill

Introduction

> [T]he application of the term 'sociology' to a study of scientific activity will be regarded by many scientists as dealing primarily with . . . a variety of behavioral phenomena which . . . unavoidably impinge upon scientific practice by virtue of the fact that scientists are social beings; but they are essentially peripheral to the practice itself. In this view, social phenomena occasionally make their presence felt in instances of extreme secrecy, fraud, or on other relatively infrequent occasions. It is only then that the kernel of scientific logic and procedure is severely threatened and scientists find their work disrupted by the intrusion of external factors. (Latour and Woolgar 1986: 20–1)

The significance of Bruno Latour and Steve Woolgar's *Laboratory Life* (1979, 1986) for science studies can hardly be exaggerated – it provided a theoretical framework and a working model for so many 'second-wave' (rejecting the Mertonian 'first wave') sociologists of science, some even critical of Latour and Woolgar, who were dealing with diverse questions of science/society interactions in numerous settings. It also anticipated the science wars and provided a (frequently unrecognised) pragmatic alternative to the stereotypical images of social constructivism. Moreover, Chapter 5 of *Laboratory Life* (exploring the 'cycle of credibility' among scientists) anticipated the current interest in the economics of science in science studies. As to law and legal contexts, *Laboratory Life* anticipated both the *Daubert* revolution in evidence law, where philosophical questions about the nature and reliability of science would be the subject of US Supreme Court speculation, as well as contemporary concerns over the effects of financial bias on scientific research and expertise.

The term 'economics of science' has multiple connotations, referring in the first instance either to the application of economic models to the scientific enterprise, or to the behaviour of scientists as they compete in the 'market' for scientific knowledge, perhaps trading in reputation or credibility (e.g. Bourdieu's 'symbolic capital') instead of money. Secondarily, the term can refer narrowly to the effect of financial support on research outcomes, or more broadly to the effect of the economy on the scientific enterprise, whether (in either case) positive or negative. It is my view that *Laboratory Life* is important for understanding all of these aspects of the economics of science (although a targeted focus on Chapter 5 of *Laboratory Life* would suggest that the authors were primarily concerned with the market metaphor and how scientists trade in credibility – however, not only does the cycle of credibility involve funding, but Michel Callon's recent economic model of the interaction between private firms and public laboratories (Callon 2002) is an extension of actor-network theory – grounded in and inspired by *Laboratory Life*).

The purpose of this chapter is to explore the debate that continues over the impact of the social aspects of science, especially its economic aspects, even after everyone concedes that science is a social and economic activity. In the quest for a realistic image of science and scientists, I turn in the next section to the science wars, as they have been mediated by Goodstein and Woodward on the one hand, and by Latour and Woolgar on the other. I then consider the legal context – the post-*Daubert* evidence wars – where concerns about adverse 'social' influences on expertise, including economic pressures, are evident. Next, I introduce the discourse of the economics of science, popularised by Mirowski, and I question the fairness of Mirowski's critique of Latour. Finally, I consider Mirowski's intervention into legal contexts; I argue that he veers away from the insights of science studies (with which he begins) by, for example, postulating that one of the clearest examples of economic harm to science is exacerbated by Latourian symmetry (Mirowski 2011: 304). I conclude that a seemingly anachronistic (in terms of Latour's *oeuvre*) return to *Laboratory Life* gives a firmer ground to Mirowski's attempt to identify the systemic, and not merely individualistic, effects of the economy on science, including the expertise that is acquired in legal processes and institutions.

Laboratory Life and the Economics of Science in Law

Stories about science: the science wars

Modern science . . . resembles much more a stock market speculation than a search for truth about nature . . . The picture of the scientist as a man with an open mind, someone who weighs the evidence for and against, is a lot of baloney. (Shapin 2001: 99–100)

Science is basically a collaborative enterprise aimed at discovering important truths about the world, carried out by individuals who are generally more strongly motivated by their own interest than by the collective good. The Reward System and the Authority Structure serve to regulate and channel this collaboration-cum-competition to produce useful results . . . And, oh yes, Science costs a lot of money. That may have something to do with it, too. (Goodstein and Woodward 1999: 90)

At first glance, such contrasting aphorisms seem to capture the essence of the 'science wars', an academic debate that flourished alongside (but seemingly had nothing to do with) the *Daubert* revolution in evidence law. That is, when the US Supreme Court in *Daubert* (in 1993) established new standards for judicial admissibility of expertise in federal (and, it turned out, many state) courts, its effort was followed both by several years of voluminous commentary (alternatively explaining, praising and criticising the opinion) and two more Supreme Court opinions (*Joiner* in 1997 and *Kumho Tire* in 1999) clarifying and resolving persistent questions concerning the new regime (Caudill and LaRue 2006: 4–11). Meanwhile, the growing field of science studies, including the history, philosophy, sociology and cultural studies of science and technology, witnessed an attack (on science studies) by Paul Gross and Norman Levitt's *Higher Superstition: The Academic Left and Its Quarrels with Science* (1994), followed in the spring of 1996 by the 'Sokal hoax', wherein physicist Alan Sokal first

> wrote an article [for 'The Science Wars', a special issue of *Social Text*] . . . [that] seemed to argue [in the jargon of postmodernism] that language, politics, and interests, rather than objective reality, determine the nature of scientific knowledge . . . After publication Sokal immediately issued a disclaimer in the journal *Lingua Franca* . . . revealing that the first article was a parody . . . to determine whether the cultural studies community . . . could tell the difference between serious

scholarship and deliberate nonsense. (Labinger and Collins 2001: 1; Sokal 1996a, 1996b)

And just as the legal debates concerning the standards for admissibility of courtroom expertise have continued in the twenty-first century (Caudill and LaRue 2006: 49–83), particularly with respect to discredited forensic 'science' identification technologies (National Research Council 2009), the ongoing science wars appear to reflect an 'irresolvable' conflict resembling some of the 'oldest and most contentious theological controversies' (Dear 2001: 199–200).

Returning to my epigraphs, the problem of the science wars is that the debate relies upon, for its maintenance, somewhat exaggerated or caricatured positions – those who believe that scientific knowledge is socially constructed (and who impliedly deny any causal role to the natural world (Dear 2001: 198)) versus those who believe in accessible nature, truth and reality (and who impliedly deny that scientific knowledge is in any sense culturally determined, rhetorical or negotiated). Indeed, the first epigraph above, written by historian of science Steven Shapin, who is associated with science studies and therefore would be expected to make such statements (i.e. science resembles stock-market speculation; open-mindedness among scientists is baloney), is itself a hoax. After making the statements quoted above (and adding many more aphorisms, such as 'there is no such thing as The Scientific Method', 'new knowledge is not science until it is made social', 'scientists [put] order in nature' and 'scientific explanations have both social determinations and social functions'), Shapin reveals that none

> of these claims about the nature of science that I have just quoted, or minimally paraphrased, does in fact come from a sociologist, or a cultural studies academic, or a feminist or Marxist theoretician. Each is taken from the metascientific pronouncements of distinguished twentieth-century scientists... (Shapin 2001: 99–100)

Shapin's response to the science wars is twofold: (1) the claims 'that have occasioned such violent reaction on the part of some recent Defenders of Science have been ... repeatedly expressed by scientists' and therefore (2) highlighting the social aspects of science, for example worrying about the links between publicly funded science and the commercial world', is not anti-scientific (Shapin 2001: 101, 114).

My second epigraph, written by physicist David Goodstein and philosopher James Woodward, is also a response to the science wars, albeit a somewhat arrogant response as indicated at the outset of their article: (1) referring to the 'fashion' of social scientists 'who visit the strange continent of Science and send back reports on the natives' behavior and rituals'; (2) suggesting that the science wars 'are becoming amusing'; and (3) claiming that it might be 'useful' for somebody to describe the social organisation of science 'from the inside' (Goodstein and Woodward 1999: 83). While it is true that ethnographers who visit laboratories to investigate the cultural aspects of science do not 'go native' and therefore remain 'outsiders' in some sense, it is hard to see how the philosopher Woodward is an 'insider' except insofar as he, alongside Goodstein, promotes an idealised self-image for scientists – for example, 'science is a true meritocracy', wherein success depends on 'who has the best ideas and who works the hardest' (Goodstein and Woodward 1999: 88). In any event, the reader of Goodstein and Woodward's article, who might be expecting (after such a sneering introduction) a critique of those sociologists of science who seek to *reveal* the *hidden* system of institutional gatekeeping in science, is treated to a brazen revelation of science's system of institutional gatekeeping! The science wars were supposed to be between (1) insiders/scientists who either denied the inevitability of social features in science or who saw them as merely constituting a context of supports; and (2) those who argued that the scientific enterprise is essentially (though, in Latour's so-called 'naturalist turn', not exclusively) social, rhetorical and institutional, merging methodology and facticity with elements of credibility, persuasion, negotiation and funding (Labinger and Collins 2001: 5). Moreover, those social aspects of science were seemingly hidden:

> The result of the construction of a fact is that it appears unconstructed by anyone; the result of rhetorical persuasion in the [agonistic] field is that the participants are convinced that they had not been convinced; the result of *materialization* [e.g. detection and measurement technologies] is that people can swear that material considerations are only minor components of the 'thought process'; the result of investments of credibility, is that participants can claim that economics and beliefs

are in no way related to the solidity of science; as to the circumstances, they simply vanish from accounts ... (Latour and Woolgar 1986: 240)

In Goodstein and Woodward's insider account, however, it is no secret that the scientific enterprise, since the seventeenth century, is all about gaining admiration, esteem and glory (the Reward System) in order to attain the power and influence that comes with becoming gatekeepers (the Authority Structure); it's a race for prestige, reputation, financial support and invitations to speak (Goodstein and Woodward 1999: 84–7). Aspiring scientists are encouraged to attend conferences, get doctorates and post-doctorates from and become professors at prestigious universities, bring in research support, get published, get tenure, get more funding, get appointed to boards, get noticed and get prizes (Goodstein and Woodward 1999: 86).

Several observations are in order concerning Goodstein and Woodward's exposé. First, it was introduced as a 'useful ... description of the social organization of science as seen from the *inside*', in contrast to the reports of 'outsider' social scientists (Goodstein and Woodward 1999: 83). And yet, Bruno Latour and Steve Woolgar's (mid-1970s) sociological fieldwork at a Salk Institute laboratory resulted in a strikingly similar description; indeed, Chapter 5 of *Laboratory Life* details the same quest for credibility and career strategies in science, including the importance of 'accumulat[ing] a stock of credentials', getting invited to meetings, getting noticed, gaining prestige, getting published and getting positions (Latour and Woolgar 1986: 195–6, 199–200, 202, 210–11). There is, of course, a difference in the two accounts, as Latour is concerned throughout *Laboratory Life* with the construction or production of scientific facts (under certain circumstances, using certain inscription devices, in a particular culture), while Goodstein and Woodward are explaining how important truths are discovered and how science advances: 'science cannot exist – certainly cannot flourish – without the Reward System and the Authority Structure' (Goodstein and Woodward 1999: 90). They do acknowledge that the Reward System might appear to some as

> merely a capricious lottery, with the Matthew effect [i.e. 'For unto every one that hath shall be given, and he shall have in abundance; but from him that hath not shall be taken away even that which he hath'],

Laboratory Life and the Economics of Science in Law 279

the old boy network, and other similar inequities helping to distribute credit unfairly. (Goodstein and Woodward 1999: 88–9)

That was the lesson taught to the protagonist Justin Childs, in Rebecca Goldstein's popular novel about quantum physicists, by his mentor:

> The last thing in the world I ever expected was to be ignored ... I thought that it was only the objective merits of the work itself that mattered, especially in science ... I didn't know how things really work ... how it gets decided what should be paid attention to ... The big shots decide and the little shots just march lock-stepped into line. (Goldstein 2001: 38)

But for Goodstein and Woodward, that is 'scientific folklore' – 'the Reward System is a mechanism evolved for the purpose of identifying, promoting, and rewarding the star performers who will propel science forward' (Goodstein and Woodward 1999: 89).

Second, it should be acknowledged that Goodstein and Woodward, notwithstanding their modesty ('We can hardly hope to bring the science wars to an end ...' (Goodstein and Woodward 1999: 83)), do make some serious progress in tamping down the controversy over the social aspects of science. Instead of describing the social aspects in pejorative terms, to explain only failures in science, Goodstein and Woodward seem to adopt the symmetrical approach that characterises the sociology of science, wherein 'achievements held to be correct should be just as amenable to sociological analysis as those thought to be wrong' (Latour and Woolgar 1986: 23–4). Of course science is a social enterprise, thus the 'main reaction' of the scientists who were the subject of Latour and Woolgar's study in *Laboratory Life* 'was that it was all rather unsurprising, if not trivial' (Latour and Woolgar 1986: 274). Goodstein and Woodward, by contrast, revel in the contingencies of the social: a Reward System that 'beggar[s] the etiquette of a medieval royal court', the need to be 'in the right place at the right time' and the 'infinitely subtle layers of influence and prestige' wherein 'no one is quite sure who is keeping score but everyone knows roughly what the score is' (Goodstein and Woodward 1999: 84–5, 88). Although there are plenty of things left to fight about, such as whether the notion of credibility 'blurs [conventional] divisions between economic, epistemological, and psychological factors' (Latour and Woolgar 1986: 239) – Latour, yes; Goodstein and Woodward, not really – all seem to have agreed on a realistic and less idealised account of science, which was genuine progress in a dialogue that (Goodstein and Woodward joke) 'has not always been entirely amicable' (Goodstein and Woodward 1999: 83).

Third, and finally, Bruno Latour occupied an uncomfortable position in the science wars – he became the signifier of and whipping boy for science studies in the eyes of its realist critics, notwithstanding the riven state of science studies and its cottage industry of criticising Latour.[1] Latour's association with science studies is clearly justified, but in the science wars, the enemies of science studies were attacking social constructivism as a critique or reduction of science's accomplishments, and while very few science studies scholars would fit that particular caricature, Latour is famous for his rejection of social constructivism due to its maintenance of the social/natural distinction – for merely replacing natural explanations of scientific progress with social explanations (Latour 1987: 132–4). Having taken (or engendered) both the linguistic and the naturalist turn in science studies, Latour does not privilege the 'social' – scientific facts are too discursive, and too natural, to be reduced to the 'social' (Latour 1993: 6). Latour recognises his lack of credibility, for scientistic critics, who accuse him of trying to debunk 'science itself'; even after writing a dozen books 'showing every time in great detail the complete implausibility of' socially accounting for the objects of science and technology, 'the only noise readers hear is the snapping of the wolf's teeth':

> You can dust your hands with flour as much as you wish, [but] the black fur of the critical wolf will always betray you; your deconstructive teeth have been sharpened on too many of our innocent labs – I mean lambs! – for us to believe you. (Latour 2004: 232)

To be fair, even if such critics rose above oversimplification and stereotyping through a more sophisticated engagement with Latour, they probably would not like him. Steve Fuller, therefore, in his critique of Latour, exaggerates Latour's (alleged) complicity with and (supposed) popularity within the scientific establishment (Fuller 1999, 2005). Fuller also exemplifies the fact that, despite his influence in science studies, Latour can be just as maddening to his fellow sociologists of science for his rejection of critique, of denouncement, as the task of social scientists:

> Many see the ... task of the intellectuals ... as a critique of the foundation. They need to develop a metalanguage that will unveil and denounce the false appearances ... [A]ll debunking makes people believe in the thing being debunked. The attitude of unveiling and denouncing the falseness of the scientific method always reinforces the argument of the scientist [because it] makes you believe it is important to find the true method. (Latour, in Crawford 1993: 250, 255)[2]

One way to understand Latour's concern, and also the criticism of Latour (which is curiously reminiscent of the alleged failure of critical legal studies to provide answers, to propose solutions, to rise above 'debunking'), is to see Latour breaking down conventional categories and distinctions, especially those offered by the subjects of study:

> When I say there is no inside/outside distinction, I mean that we should not believe in the existence of inside and outside. We should sit exactly at the place where the inside and the outside of the network are defined ... [W]e have to see inside-and-outside as an active category, created by the actors themselves, and it has to be studied as such. (Latour, in Crawford 1993: 247, 257)

If there is a critique (and there is), it should not be on the same terms (or grant the same categories and distinctions) as the target of the critique. Thus the flaw in social constructivism was to preserve the nature/society dualism and end up privileging the social; the flaw in modernism was to divide natural science from social science, non-human from human; the flaw in postmodernism was to believe in the modern as the object of denunciation.

> So then the question is can we play another game? Can we redefine the task of the intellectual so that it is no longer denouncing from one of two poles? (Latour, in Crawford 1993: 258)

To the extent that the science wars represented the realism/ constructivism debate, Latour promises that 'you do not need to believe in either of these two poles':

> Things become active, and the collective becomes made of things – circulating things – [and] these hybrids (quasi-objects) start resembling what our world is made of. It is not that there are a few hybrids; it is that there are only hybrids. And the ... purely social relation [and] the purely natural construction ... don't exist. (Latour, in Crawford 1993: 261)

Careful divisions 'between what is natural and what is social' do not interest Latour (Latour, in Crawford 1993: 262).

Another distinction in science studies worth mentioning in this context is that between 'upstream' and 'downstream' contexts in the production of scientific knowledge. The term 'ELSI', ethical, legal and social implications, became popular in science studies to designate a role for the social scientist in the production of scientific knowledge. Instead of waiting 'downstream' for the results of science, and then considering the implications for society, the suggestion was made to move 'upstream', into the laboratory, with a team of ethicists and lawyers and sociologists (Rabinow 2009). However, that conception risks eclipsing the already-present ethical, legal and social aspects of laboratory life and unwittingly grants social independence to the scientific enterprise (Caudill 2009).

Placing Latour in law's evidentiary wars

After his mediating response (with Woodward) to the science wars, Goodstein played a very similar role in the *Daubert* revolution in evidence law; following the trilogy (*Daubert, Joiner, Kumho Tire*), which established a judicial role in evaluating expertise, and contemporaneously with the 2000 Amendment to Federal Rule of Evidence 702, which was anchored in and elucidated the trilogy, Goodstein published (in the Federal Judicial Center's *Reference Manual on Scientific Evidence* (2000)) an article entitled 'How Science Works' (Goodstein 2000). In a 'mildly irreverent spirit', and in order to 'demystify the business of science just a bit', Goodstein conceded that notwithstanding the central roles in *Daubert* of (1) the scientific method and (2) Karl Popper's notion of falsification, 'we don't really know what the scientific method is', and 'the behavior of the scientific community is not consistent with Popper's notion ...' (Goodstein 2000: 69–71). And although science is (contra paradigm theory) 'truly progressive', science is also (contra idealised conceptions of science as non-rhetorical) 'an adversary process' among scientists who are not 'skeptical and tentative' with respect to their hypotheses (Goodstein 2000: 74). Goodstein repeats (and makes reference to) his earlier account (with Woodward) of the Reward System and the Authority System, adding that peer review frequently does not work 'as a means of choosing between competing valid ideas' and then he dismantles the myths that 'reason [always triumphs] over authority', that scientists 'must have open minds' and that 'real science is easily distinguished from pseudoscience' (Goodstein 2000: 75–8). Notably, Goodstein also challenges the myth that science is 'just ... theories ... eventually proved wrong', and distinguishes between 'the frontiers of knowledge ... where theories are indeed vulnerable' and 'textbook science that is known with great confidence' (Goodstein 2000: 79).

Missing, however, from Goodstein's lesson (for lawyers and judges about how science works), which did mention that science is *funded* by foundations, government and industry (Goodstein 2000: 75), was any mention about the *impact* of money on science. Indeed, Goodstein and Woodward ended their 'insider' intervention into the science wars with an undeveloped afterthought: 'And, oh yes. Science costs a lot of money. That may have something to do with it, too' (Goodstein and Woodward 1999: 90). They had already mentioned that obtaining external research support was essential to success as a scientist – Robert Boyle's personal wealth (external, in a sense) and Galileo's ability to land government and private (e.g. the Medici's) sponsorship were necessary to early scientific progress (Goodstein and Woodward 1999: 86, 90) – but does money have anything to do with science beyond externally sustaining an otherwise internal dynamic?

One of the defining features of the science wars was the issue of whether the social aspects of science matter in some non-trivial sense, or 'influence the results of research in any critically distinctive way' (Harding 1998: 3). That is, some would assume that

> the success of modern science is insured by its internal features[, its methods and standards, such that] all social values and interest that might initially get into the results of scientific research [can] be firmly weeded out ... through subsequent critical vigilance. (Harding 1998: 2, 3)

In this perspective, social factors can clearly be mobilised to explain false beliefs, errors, fraud and other disruptions of

> the proper operation of scientific norms[, while] the facts themselves determine truth ... The consequence of this is that with true belief there [is] nothing to explain, save for how the conditions for proper scientific inquiry came about and how those conditions are undermined. (Potter 1996: 19)

Thus in idealised accounts of the characteristics of science, we read that 'the evolution of scientific knowledge is the result of research not external pressures', and that 'basic science has no external value system', but also that there are bad scientists 'whose peers will not hesitate to expose their flaws' (Mahner and Bunge 1996: 103–4).[3] From the opposite vantage in the science wars, sociologists of science either (1) 'focus on the role of human factors in science and how scientific knowledge is contingent on and constructed by the operation of these factors' (Labinger and Collins 2001: 5), or (2), following Latour in treating the conventional science war categories as one more object of inquiry, blur the division between 'intellectual' (or epistemological) and 'social' (including cultural, institutional, rhetorical, psychological and economic) factors (Latour and Woolgar 1986: 22–3, 239):

> [T]he distinction between 'social' and 'technical' factors is a resource drawn upon routinely by working scientists. Our intention is to understand how this distinction features in the activities of scientists, rather than to demonstrate that emphasis on one or the other side of the duality is more appropriate for our understanding of science ... [O]ur explanation of scientific activity should not depend in any significant way on the uncritical use of the very concepts and terminology which feature as part of that activity. (Latour and Woolgar 1986: 27)

Economic factors (or, more properly, aspects), however, have generally received less attention in science studies than, for example, the roles of institutional gatekeeping and credibility, language and rhetoric, or even gender. As Mirowski and Sent explain:

> Deep down, all scientists understand that at some fundamental level, there is some sort of economic process or processes channeling and fortifying their science; it is indisputable that someone, for some

reason, has been picking up the tab. Yet, the tendency until recently has been to deny that process has any substantive bearing on the real activity of scientific research. (Mirowski and Sent 2002: 1)

Not only is there a sense that economists 'of various persuasions ... are rediscovering the phenomena analysed by sociology of scientific knowledge' (Rip 2003: 428), but also a sense that because

> something rather drastic and profound has been happening to the social organization of science in America and Europe at the end of this [twentieth] century ... a serious reconsideration of the 'economics of science' is long overdue. (Mirowski and Sent 2002: 3)

Steven Shapin highlights the 'ethical and intellectual erosion' that attends the 'commercialization of science', even in the view of some scientists (Shapin 2001: 112–14).

As to the worry is that commercial interests tend to set limits on scientific research, Ian Hacking finds it

> patently obvious that when questions get asked, taken seriously, investigated, funded, reported, analyzed, and so forth is the result of social processes, human interaction, and current interest. Very few detailed questions are asked about the most widespread tropical diseases because there is no money in it for drug companies ... (Hacking 2000: S69)

Ethical erosion is documented by Daniel Greenberg in *Science, Money, and Politics* (2001) as a 'systemic, persuasive invasion of the money ethic on the conduct and presentation of research' (Greenberg 2001: 348–64). Worries about the effects of money on science are also evident in legal contexts. Professors McGarity and Wagner have argued for a realistic view of how public health science can be 'bent', not only by special interests upon arrival into public policy deliberations, but (by the same interests) in the 'normal processes of science' (McGarity and Wagner 2008: 2–6).

Regarding the role of economics and the economy in the scientific enterprise, Latour and Woolgar's *Laboratory Life* highlighted the issue in their Chapter 5, entitled 'Cycles of Credit'. As D. Wade Hands points out, 'Cycles of Credit' was not an exercise in 'the economics of science' in many of the senses of that term. First, the chapter was neither an attempt to 'apply' economics to science, nor to model science as a 'competitive market process'. (Wade suspects that Latour and Woolgar would 'consider neoclassical economics to be naively reductionist, narrowly individualistic, and in general a quite uninteresting approach to studying (any) social process' (Hands 2002: 526–7).) The 'economics of science' more likely refers to works 'in the language and discursive format of contemporary economics', such as Diamond's theory of the rational scientist maximising a utility function under constraints, or Wible's explanation of fraud in science by specifying first-order conditions and optimisation uncertainty (Hands 2002: 535–6; Diamond 1988; Wible 1991, 1992). Second, Latour and Woolgar describe a quasi-economic 'market for credibility that determines what scientists work on', and use economic analogies to describe science in capitalist terms (e.g. supply, demand, and value of information)' (Hands 2002: 525). Finally, Latour and Woolgar do not address the issue of the effects of the economy on science, except to say (in passing) that (1) the 'link between the scientific production of facts and modern capitalist economics is probably much deeper than a mere relation', and that (2) scientists' 'final realization of capital, through their movement into clinical studies, industry, and culture, is not examined' in *Laboratory Life* (Latour and Woolgar 1986: 231 n. 9, 233 n. 22).[4]

That examination has been carried out by Philip Mirowski, an economist, science studies fellow-traveller and critic of Latour (and of actor-network theory, especially its socio-economist, Michel Callon). Mirowski's critique of neo-liberalism and privatised science regimes goes a long way toward revealing and shifting attention toward the systemic effects of the economy on science, and he offers examples of the economic effects on science in law. In the end, however, he relies upon and reifies categories and distinctions that render his critique of commercialisation in science ineffective.

Science and the economy

[O]ne of the most repeated complaints about Latourian actor-network analysis is that it leaves everything pretty much just the way it found it. (Mirowski and Sent 2002: 58)

[I]nstead of arguing [for] and reinforcing the strict opposition between open science ... and a market with clearly defined boundaries ...

[network theory] aims to show the possibility of scientific research that is both autonomous and strongly connected with firms. (Callon 2002: 281)

The growing privatisation of science raises questions about whether science is degraded or enhanced by relationships with (or financial support from) commercial industry. Does the increase of collaboration between scientists and industry decrease the collaborative behaviour of scientists (i.e. freely sharing knowledge) toward one another? Everyone knows science costs money – always has – but then the debate begins, with three identifiable positions on financial interests or entanglements: (1) they are relatively benign, because the internal workings of scientific methodology are unaffected by external support (except in the case of fraud, the occasional bad apple); (2) they are seriously influential and generally good for science by fostering efficiency and innovation; (3) they are seriously influential with pernicious effects that degrade the quality of science. The first position is represented by physicist David Goodstein, discussed above, who has written extensively on scientific fraud (Goodstein 2010). The second position is found in Paula Stephan's *How Economics Shapes Science* (2012), which raises no cause for alarm – there's always room for improvement, of course, but '[s]cience costs money and incentives play a key role in science . . .' The third position has been taken up by Philip Mirowski, who fiercely claims to be neither naive nor Pollyanna-ish about any purported golden age of disinterested science, and also insists that the commercialisation of science is not in itself a marker of decline – 'accusations of corruption must be judged on a case-by-case basis' (Mirowski and Van Horn 2005: 508). Taken as a whole, however, Mirowski suspects that commercialisation has changed the structure of science for the worse, even as he concedes the difficulty of measuring that decline (Mirowski 2011: 266).

To be clear, Mirowski is *trying* not to talk about individual responsibility, scientific fraud or the intentional manipulation of data by a scientist with an obvious conflict of interest due to funding. In the tradition of science studies, Mirowski views science and the economy as 'mutually constituted' – for example, in the re-engineering of 'university science around more commercial pursuits', we notice that 'some forms of funding and organization of credit [i.e. from authorship to ownership of intellectual property] promote certain kinds of creative or innovative activity, while other forms actively discourage them' (Mirowski 2004: 117, 132). This is clearly a challenge to the idealistic notion that social interests are not

> systematic or structural, [but] merely serve to focus our attention ... [They do not affect] how we do research or what it is we find there ... [In the view of science studies, however,] different social alignments can produce different scientific outcomes. (Mirowski 2004: 21, 24)

While everyone acknowledges that decades of industry funding

> may have had some minor influence on changing the means by which research is prosecuted, [few imagine that] it transformed the ends of science [–] whatever it is that we get at the end of the process ... (Mirowski and Van Horn 2005: 531–2)

Examples of other systemic analyses of science and the economy as co-productions include David Tyfield's study of the 'economic impacts on the directions of scientific thought, argument, and controversy', which conceptualises science and the economy as a 'process of ongoing (re)construction [wherein] each conditions the development of the other' (Tyfield 2012: 25–6). Like Mirowski, who attempts to trace the harms of commercialisation upon 'good' science (Mirowski 2011: 160), Tyfield argues that social influences 'on science are not ... only relevant when science goes wrong or is corrupted, in some way' (Tyfield 2012: 18). Another example of systemic analysis is Daniel Lee Kleinman's study of the commercialisation of academic science, which acknowledged the popular criticism that 'commercially motivated collaborations between university biologists and science-based companies can skew research agendas, prompt inappropriate restrictions on the flow of information, and create conflicts of interest' (Kleinman 2003: x). Kleinman, however, is more interested in the 'subtle landscape' of academic capitalism – not the direct results of corporate influence, but how 'corporate domination of a field of scientific investigation early in its development', even absent subsequent industry funding, 'can indirectly affect the questions that are asked and the answers that are acceptable at a later time' (Kleinman 2003: xi). The laboratory studied by Kleinman was neither restricted by industry sponsors, nor showed any signs of 'egregious violation of academic norms' (e.g. secrecy, conflicts

Laboratory Life and the Economics of Science in Law 289

of interest), but 'indirect, systemic effects' of commercial culture (e.g. the chemical industry's effects on agricultural pest-control research) were identifiable, including

> the way scholarly writing in the field is framed, the way experiments are organized, the measures of success that are used, and the tools that are available ... [N]o direct intervention ... by industry needed to occur for the influence to be felt. (Kleinman 2003: 4, 6, 17, 88–9)

Mirowski, notably, does not limit his analysis to the commercialisation of university science, but identifies the parallel 'creation of new social structures of research ... new forms of intellectual property, new communication technologies, new research protocols, new career paths, and new institutions' such as 'contract research organizations' (Mirowski and Van Horn 2005: 504). As examples of the decline in science brought on by commercialisation, Mirowski (in *Science-Mart*) first identifies 'just-in-time' science ('the forced inducement of quick and dirty techniques to produce attenuated results on schedule, under budget, and within the parameters of contractual relations') (Mirowski 2011: 290). Second, Mirowski identifies the 'sound science' (or anti-junk-science) movement wherein hidden organisations (e.g. 'neo-liberal think-tanks') promote industry friendly, or in terms of litigation defence friendly, science by casting doubt on good science as 'uncertain', demanding more research to confirm the validity of good science and harassing good scientists (Mirowski 2011: 297–9). Finally, Mirowski identifies the degradation of patent quality, a phenomenon which finds support in intellectual property law literature (Mirowski 2011: 305–6; Henderson et al. 1998; Miller 2013).

My question is whether Mirowski has identified systemic economic pressures; his examples do not appear to be 'good science', but rather to fall into his category of individual responsibility (the first and third examples) or fraud (the second example), thereby undermining his claim that he is not talking about the obvious deleterious effects of commercialisation on science. I want to link that blind spot in Mirowski's work (1) to his criticism of Latourian actor-network theory and, in the economics of science literature (2) to Callon's application of actor-network theory as a response to Mirowski's distinction (crucial to Mirowski's analysis) between open and privatised science.

Mirowski v. Latour

> [S]ince ... we wish to attack scientist's hegemony on the definition of nature, we have never wished to accept the essential source of their power: ... the very distribution between what is natural and what is social and the fixed allocation of ontological status that goes with it. We have never been interested in giving a social explanation of anything, but we want to explain society ... (Callon and Latour 1992: 348)

Rejecting the 'social explanation genre', Latour and Callon seek to 'obtain' nature and society through 'network building, or collective things, or quasi-objects ...' (Callon and Latour 1992: 348). Tired of being labelled conservative or reactionary for their supposed realism, they claim to be *genuine* co-productionists (and they scold their science studies critics for being 'exactly as reactionary' as their scores of natural-realist critics):

> The perfect symmetry in the misreading of our work by 'natural realists' and 'social realists' alike is a nice confirmation that we are in a different, although for them unthinkable position. (Callon and Latour 1992: 349–50)

It's not *either* social relations (intentional human subjects) *or* things (brute material objects), but 'the circulation of network-tracing tokens, statements, and skills' to be observed and documented (Callon and Latour 1992: 351). And it seems to be the agency of non-humans that attracts the accusation of realism; for 'realist' readers of Callon's study of St Brieue Bay fishermen, the scallops must either be 'out there [forcing] themselves on naïve realists, or ... in there made of social relations of humans talking about them'; but Callon and Latour do not attribute 'out-thereness' to the various forms 'under which 'scallops exist' (Callon and Latour 1992: 347; Callon 1986). The key to the accusation, in any event, is the criticism that accounts of science by Callon or Latour do not differ from those of conventional historians of science – explaining a scientific discovery by 'granting agency to things in themselves' (Callon and Latour 1992: 354). Callon and Latour concede the difficulty of finding an 'unbiased vocabulary', but 'negotiation' is not 'discovery' and 'actant' is not 'actor' – 'We should be credited with having tried to [establish a symmetrical vocabulary], and when no other selection was available, to have chosen a repertoire which bears no insult to nonhumans' (Callon and Latour 1992: 354).

This (minimalistic) background is important because Mirowski has joined the harshest science studies critics of Latour and Callon. Steve Fuller, for example, blames the Parisians and their actor-network theory for the decline of science studies – its 'aversion to normative judgment and ... open antagonism to the adoption of "critical" perspectives' (Fuller 1999: 6). By their invocation of 'natural factors', Latour and Callon have apparently caused science studies to jump the shark:

> Not surprisingly, scientists ... have welcomed the Parisian turn, since it clearly reopens the door to traditional ... explanations of science that incorporate both natural and social factors 'interacting' to produce ... an experimental outcome. It would seem we have reached one of those ... Molièrean moments ... when a move that appears radical within the terms of a paradigm is equivalent to the prose that everyone else outside the paradigm has been always speaking (albeit now with a French accent). (Fuller 1999: 8)

Fuller is wildly suspicious, because a 'seemingly radical innovation that quickly acquires widespread currency probably serves some well-established interests that remain hidden' in its reception (Fuller 1999: 18). After all, didn't fascist ideology combine 'an animistic view of nature, a hyperbolic vision of the power of technology, and [a] diminished sense of individual human agency', just like actor-network theory (Fuller 1999: 23)?[5]

Mirowski frames *Science-Mart* (2011), his study of the negative effects of privatisation on American science, as a story about the fictional, 'intrepid academic researcher Viridiana Jones' (Mirowski 2011: 1). Early in the book, she meets a few fellow faculty members in the field of science studies, which sounded interesting enough for her to go to a conference at her university to hear some 'of their more famous representatives like Bruno Latour, Steve Woolgar ...' (Mirowski 2011: 3). But she

> was distressed to find that when they weren't indulging in opaque jargon about 'actants' ... they tended to confuse 'excellence' (whatever that was) with the crudest sorts of proxy measures for scientific output. (Mirowski 2011: 3–4)

Mirowski drops an endnote here to Latour's *Reassembling the Social* (2005) and Latour and Woolgar's *Laboratory Life* (1979), among others (Mirowski 2011: 4, 351 n. 5). Fast forward fifty pages, in a discussion about how most 'intellectuals simply took both the priority and primacy of science over technology as gospel before 1980' and most 'disavowed it afterward', we read that some, like 'Bruno Latour, went so far as to claim there had existed only one ontological entity called 'technoscience' all along ...' (Mirowski 2011: 54).[6] Mirowski sees this 'loss of faith' in science as having 'everything to do with the economy' – the bending of science and technology to economic ends' (Mirowski 2011: 54; Godin 2005: 287). Latour, in this narrative, adopts the 'trademark neo-liberal doctrine' that science has always been commercial, 'an utter travesty of the actual history' (Mirowski 2011: 327).[7] If Latour is not a card-carrying neo-liberal, but rather an accidental one, it is because he turned his

> attention to microscale studies of laboratory life, ignoring how the laboratory's macroscale relationship to society was being reengineered all around, not to mention the changing identities of the paymasters for all those DNA sequencers and inscription devices. (Mirowski 2011: 90)[8]

Fuller echoes this concern, remarking that when laboratories become 'objects of fascination', science studies scholars might fail 'to see how science reflects larger societal forces' (Fuller 1999: 27).[9]

In discerning whether this set of criticisms is fair – indeed, whether Latour is an appropriate target of a critique of neo-liberal privatisation of science – the accusation that laboratory studies ignore social and economic forces is far from compelling. Of course an ethnographic study is neither grand theory nor a broad quantitative analysis. Nevertheless, the chapter on cycles of credit in *Laboratory Life* (1979) traces several (actual, not metaphorical) economic forces on the scientific community (grants, money, equipment) (Latour and Woolgar 1986: 197–233); more importantly, the laboratory provides 'a model on which you can actually do empirical studies about the technologies of society and knowledge production' (Latour, in Crawford 1993: 282). The remaining criticisms reveal Mirowski's position in the debates over the economics of science, which Callon has described as a plea for the restoration of the autonomy of an open, academic science, in opposition to a 'market with clearly defined boundaries' (Callon 2002: 279–81). Callon does not dispute the need for non-profit research (for diversification) and scientific autonomy (from the economic market), but wants to show, using network theory, 'the possibility of scientific research that is both autonomous and strongly connected with firms' (Callon 2002: 281).

In fairness to Mirowski and Fuller, it is difficult to extract a normative argument from Callon, paralleling and opposing Mirowski's concerns over the degradation of science, that firm/laboratory interactions produce better science, but Callon does argue that his description (not the scientific knowledge)[10] is more accurate: overflowings (from conventional frames, like the strict division between the 'open' academy and commerce) happen; they are likely to be 'irresistible and irrevocable'; and laboratory autonomy is not necessarily threatened by 'connections between fundamental research and the economic market' (Callon 2002: 312–13). For my purposes, I simply want to highlight how Callon proceeds by challenging the assumptions and categories that provide the foundation for Mirowski's concerns.

Structural effects of the economy on science in law

> Economists stage a play with double-bound actors: [firms and laboratories] must interact without crossing boundaries! The only relationships that these straitjacketed actors are allowed are those that emerge from the circulation of information. The conditions for their production are simply ignored. This is simple exchange economics, whereas one of the key points of science studies is that the circulation and production of knowledge are inseparable: they are one and the same process. (Callon 2002: 287)

The scientific enterprise can be conceived of as virtually independent from the economy – except in cases of fraud driven by monetary greed, external financial support of science does not affect the internal workings of science. It is perhaps a minor advancement in the economics of science for some to argue that financial support is an unqualified good, as it fosters efficiency and innovation – they point to 'hard-won' advances in medical and surgical care' due to industry collaborations (Stossell 2012). But others, while conceding the inevitability of funding as well as the 'social pressures and political agendas result[ing] in significant scientific progress', warn that the pressure of commercialisation could reduce collaboration among scientists, undermine 'scientific progress, and contribute to premature application of technologies' (Caulfield 2012). The 'statistically significant association between industry sponsorship and pro-industry conclusions' has raised questions about whether we can trust biomedical research findings (Bekelman et al. 2003: 454). This is a major advancement, to recognise both positive and negative effects of the economy on science. Mirowski's work constitutes yet another advance, by distinguishing between an individualistic and a systemic or structural perspective on the potential problems of interaction between the economy and science. If the problems are conflicts of interest, low methodological quality or 'accepting remuneration geared to the outcome of a research project', all on the part of individual scientists, then we encourage transparency and disclosure, better methodology[11] and ethical guidelines (Rowe et al. 2009: 1288). But those solutions do not begin to address the sort of recent structural changes brought about by economic forces on science.

Recall Latour's version of the sociology of scientific knowledge, where the phenomena under analysis

> have the characteristics of being narrative, collective, and outside [of us]. They are quasi-objects; they are not of our own making. That is it: real, narrated, social. (Latour, in Crawford 1993: 264)

In the discourse concerning financial bias in science, many of the solutions offered to counteract the pernicious effects of the economy on science seem aimed at ensuring that scientific knowledge is not rhetorical or social. Get rid of the bad apples who fabricate data for financial gain and look past or behind the false promises of the bad pharmaceutical company to discern the promotion of the 'quick and dirty result over the calm and measured finding . . . to get those new discoveries out the door and into the world as soon as possible' (Mirowski 2011: 289). Even Mirowski's critique of so-called 'litigation science' (research performed after a case has been brought), allegedly a structural analysis (aimed at 'good science', not 'scientific fraud') of the commercialisation of science (Mirowski 2011: 288), is also an avowed critique of science studies.

In *Daubert* on remand to the Ninth Circuit Court of Appeals,

Judge Kozinski expressed a preference for science that pre-exists litigation, because research

> conducted independent of the litigation provides important, objective proof that the research comports with the dictates of good science[, and experts relying on] existing research are less likely to be biased toward a particular conclusion by the promise of remuneration. (*Daubert* 1995: 1317)

That conclusion is questionable, given (1) that existing pharmaceutical research is sometimes tainted (Krimsky 2006: 63–81), and (2) that there is no structural reason that litigation science is necessarily of a low quality. (Judge Kozinski went on to say that law enforcement forensic science, which is clearly litigation science, does not raise the same concern (*Daubert* 1995: 1317 n. 5). That conclusion is also questionable in light of the recent National Academy of Sciences study of forensic science, which raised concerns about the independence of laboratories administered by law enforcement agencies and recommended public forensic laboratories (National Research Council 2009: 183–4).) Yet Mirowski joins in the condemnation of litigation science, (1) viewing it as a corporate enterprise (even though in cases against pharmaceutical companies it is the plaintiffs that need litigation science); (2) labelling it just-in-time science and retaining the boundary 'between purpose-built science for litigation ... and academic science in standard peer-reviewed journals'; and (3) blaming science studies for taking a symmetrical approach toward assessing critically both litigation science and peer-reviewed science:

> This is not the first time we observe science studies beginning to make a pact with neoliberal conceptions of knowledge, but it is certainly one of the most dispiriting. (Mirowski 2011: 304–5)

Notwithstanding his starting point, that commercialisation alone is not a marker of the decline of science (Mirowski and Van Horn 2005: 508), Mirowski seems to revert to an earlier (Mertonian) sociology of errors with respect to science – only bad science is characterised by co-production. Given that Mirowski's examples of the structural effects of the economy on science *in law* are quite individualistic (corporate production of defence-friendly science, and applying for low-quality patents, although the latter is arguably a result of *systemic* commercial pressures), we might say that it is difficult for Mirowski to sustain a systemic or structural analysis of science and the economy while maintaining such normative distinctions between academic science and commercial pursuits, open and privatised science, and basic and applied science. As an example of an analysis of the interaction between science and the economy that does not assume such distinctions, we have Callon's network model (Callon 2002), which blurs conventional boundaries to include hybrids (1) of basic and applied science (in consolidated networks), (2) of academic and commercial pursuits (in boundary configurations and hybrid firm/laboratories), and (3) of public and private domains (e.g. science is not intrinsically a public good but becomes a public good in the network as 'a source of diversity and flexibility' (Callon 1994: 416)[12]).

Conclusion

> [When sociologists of science] try to reconnect scientific objects with their ... web of associations ... we always appear to weaken them, not to strengthen their claim to reality ... [W]e want to add reality to scientific objects, but, inevitably, through a sort of tragic bias, we seem always to be subtracting some bit from it. (Latour 2004: 232)

I'm beginning to appreciate Latour's goal of description in advance of critique, of groundwork, of trying to understand how given or conventional categories and distinctions might eclipse certain features of the interactions between law, science and the economy. It is not simply that we need to acknowledge the complexity of that interaction by creating new categories (such as hybrids) or by adding more pieces to the analysis, but that we need to acknowledge a particular kind of complexity that is not visible when conventional boundaries are honoured – we may need to get rid of some assumed pieces (such as inside/outside distinctions) and do away with short-cuts (whether that short-cut is assuming commercialisation always degrades science or always fosters efficiency and innovation). Distinctions can remain – science is neither the law nor the economy – but the boundaries are blurred when a scientific expert appears in court or a scientific report is delivered to a governmental agency, because the acquired science is a co-production or hybrid of legal recognition, scientific practices and economic structures. Expertise is mutually constituted and conditioned by all three enterprises, and because each enterprise is equally rhetorical, social, institutional, political and historical, there is no priority or privileging based on one enterprise escaping from culture. Establishing that analytical framework is a descriptive project and is easily criticised for leaving everything as it is – 'Fine, it is a co-production, but the scientific enterprise, the economy and the law open for business tomorrow and do not change or improve on the basis of a more accurate description.'

On the other hand, to say that all of the science that is appropriated by law (on terms established in law but informed by science) is structured and constituted, not merely influenced or supported, by economic forces, is a critique. It is a critique of Judge Kozinski's categorisation of litigation science as suspect (and the categorisation of law enforcement laboratory forensic science as reliable) in *Daubert* on remand; it is a critique of David Goodstein's 'insider' description (for federal judges) of how science works (with social, economic and rhetorical supports that have little effect on the results of research); it is a critique of Paula Stephan's mundane acknowledgment of the economy 'shaping science' with no cause for alarm; and it is a critique of Professors Thomas McGarity and Wendy Wagner, who in *Bending Science: How Special Interests Corrupt Public Health Research* (2008) sound the alarm, but focus on direct influences on science by bad actors. These critiques, however, are only constructive if judges and regulators can understand that revealing science as a co-production of social, rhetorical and natural 'forces' is not a critique of the scientific enterprise, but an arguable description of our state of affairs.

Notes

1. Science warriors Gross and Levitt (1994) 'choose me wrongly. Of course it's ridiculous to say it's all politics, all signs, or all gender. It is ironic, because the French postmodernists hate the stuff I do – I believe in objectivity, options, democracy. They see me as reactionary. They think I've gone back to naïve realism' (Latour, in Berreby 1994).
2. For example, Latour finds that Feyerabend's 'denouncing presupposes the existence and importance of what is at stake' (Latour, in Crawford 1993: 255).
3. The authors concede that external pressures 'can only accelerate or slow down a research process that has an internal dynamics', and

that science has a complex internal value system with '*logical* values such as exactness ... and logical consistency; *semantical* values such as meaning definitiveness ...; *methodological* values such as testability ...; and *attitudinal* and *moral* values such as critical thinking ...' (Mahner and Bunge 1996: 103–4). Their description of the scientific enterprise (which I would characterise as somewhat idealised in its claims that 'scientific knowledge is the result of reason[,an internal dynamic,] not of external pressures' and 'science has no external value system') includes as essential elements the community of scientists and the 'hosting' societies (Mahner and Bunge 1996: 103).

4. Michel Callon chooses to 'get rid of notions like markets of ideas, scientific capital, credibility cycles, etc., which erase the differences between activities that are obviously different' (Callon 2002: 281 n. 5).
5. As to the diminished sense of human agency in actor-network theory, Fuller paradoxically also sees an eerie similarity between 'totalitarian and actor-network theorists' in their 'glorification of the heroic practitioner' (Fuller 1999: 23)!
6. The claim attributed to Latour echoes his argument that we have never been modern ('We have never been cut off from our past; we have never been different'), and that the supposed scientific revolution never happened (Latour, in Crawford 1993: 259).
7. That is, historically, the academy was 'relatively sheltered from commercial considerations' (Mirowski 2011: 97). However, perennial concerns over 'corporate influences on ... university research agendas, corporate restrictions on the free flow of information, and ... control over intellectual property' often reflect a contrast of our current situation with an assumption that 'the academy was once an isolated ivory tower' (Kleinman 2003: 33, 35). Kleinman rejects this contrast, both because

> periods of relatively high levels of faculty autonomy regarding their capacity to define research agendas and set priorities are relatively few in the history of the American university[,and because] the attention on the impact of direct relations between academic scientists and science-based firms ... overlooks the indirect but pervasive influences of the world of commerce ... (Kleinman 2003: 35)

8. Mirowski notes that while Latour and Woolgar 'gleefully resort[ed] to economic metaphors' in *Laboratory Life* (1979), they essentially

ignored 'any substantive economic structures' (Mirowski 2011: 360 n. 6).

9. The 'critiques' of Fuller and Mirowski seem forced and smug – focused on an allegedly fake radicalism, arcane language and undeserved popularity – not unlike Bourdieu's 'critique' of Latour in *Science of Science and Reflexivity* (2004) which, according to Evan Kindley, never

> amounts to an actual critique of Latour, or science studies, or really anything (except maybe interdisciplinarity as an academic phenomenon) . . . Bourdieu is mostly content to summarise and describe Latour's work and then sit back with an air of satisfaction, as if the enterprise were so patently absurd he doesn't even need to poke holes in it. If there is a charge, it's of semiotic bias, or 'textism,' based on the fact that (again, in early work like *Laboratory Life* and *The Pasteurization of France*) Latour reduces all scientific practice and phenomena to inscriptions and texts: 'Science is . . . just a discourse or a fiction among others, but one capable of exerting a "truth effect" produced, like all other literary effects, through textual characteristics . . .' (Bourdieu 2004: 28). This is not a particularly sophisticated accusation: it sounds, indeed, like nothing so much as the angry voices of reactionary anti-deconstructionists circa the early 1970s . . . [Bourdieu's text] amounts to a decent preliminary introduction to the (early) work of science studies for those oriented toward critical sociology, but little more – certainly not a serious critique . . . Bourdieu barely touches the substance of Latour's arguments: he takes them either to be depressingly familiar (just more postmodern 'textism'/deconstruction) or patently absurd ([human and automatic, non-human] door closers! come on!). (Kindley 2010)

As to the *fact* of reductionist 'textism', refer to note 1 above ('Of course it's ridiculous to say it's all . . . signs . . .').

10. 'To call a claim "absurd" or knowledge "accurate" has no more meaning than to call a smuggler trail "illogical" and a freeway "logical"' (Latour 1987: 205).
11. On the issue of methodological quality, a perceived problem, most investigations into commercial funding of scientific research have 'found no association between sponsorship and overall methodological quality' (Sismondo 2008: 1910–11).
12. '[P]ublic and private science are complementary despite being distinct: each draws on the other . . . A firm that funds diversity by

supporting new collectives is producing a public good[,] and the government agency that contributes to a yet stronger linkage between the research it funds and the perfecting of Tomahawk missiles [is] supporting a science that can doubtless be called private' (Callon 1994: 416).

References

Bekelman, J. E. et al. (2003) 'Scope and impact of financial conflicts of interest in biomedical research: a systematic review', *Journal of the American Medical Association*, 289: 454–65.

Berreby, D. (1994) '... that damned elusive Bruno Latour', *Lingua Franca*, September/October, 22–32, 78.

Bourdieu, P. (2004) *Science of Science and Reflexivity*, trans. R. Nice. Chicago: University of Chicago Press.

Callon, M. (1986) 'Some elements of a sociology of translation: domestication of the scallops and the fishermen of St Brieue Bay', in J. Law (ed.), *Power, Action, and Belief: A New Sociology of Knowledge?* London: Routledge & Kegan Paul.

Callon, M. (1994) '"Is science a public good?" Fifth Mullins Lecture, Virginia Polytechnic Institute, 23 March 1993', *Science, Technology, and Human Values*, 19: 395–424.

Callon, M. (2002) 'From science as an economic activity to socioeconomics of scientific research', in P. Mirowski and E.-M. Sent (eds), *Science Bought and Sold: Essays in the Economics of Science*. Chicago: University of Chicago Press.

Callon, M. and Latour, B. (1992) 'Don't throw the baby out with the bath school! A reply to Collins and Yearley', in A. Pickering (ed.), *Science as Practice and Culture*. Chicago: University of Chicago Press.

Caudill, D. (2009) 'Synthetic science: a response to Rabinow', *Law and Literature*, 21: 431–44.

Caudill, D. and LaRue, L. H. (2006) *No Magic Wand: The Idealization of Science in Law*. Lanham, MD: Rowman & Littlefield.

Caulfield, T. (2012) 'Pressured to commercialize: is the push for science to save the still flailing economy a threat to scientific research?', *The Scientist*, 28 May 2012. Available at <http://the-scientist.com/?articles.view/articleNo/32158/title/Opinion-Pressured-to-Commercialize/>.

Crawford, T. H. (1993) 'An interview with Bruno Latour', *Configurations*, 1 (2): 247–68.

Dear, P. (2001) 'Overdetermination and contingency', in J. A. Labinger and H. Collins (eds), *The One Culture? A Conversation About Science*. Chicago: University of Chicago Press.

Diamond, A. D. (1988) 'Science as a rational enterprise', *Theory and Decision*, 24: 147–67.

Fuller, S. (1999) 'Why science studies has never been critical of science: some recent lessons on how to be a helpful nuisance and a harmless radical', *Philosophy of the Social Sciences*, 30: 5–32.

Fuller, S. (2005) 'Is STS truly revolutionary or merely revolting?', *Science Studies*, 18 (1): 75–83.

Godin, B. (2005) *Measurement and Statistics in Science and Technology: 1920 to the Present*. New York: Routledge.

Goldstein, R. (2001) *Properties of Light*. Boston: Houghton Mifflin.

Goodstein, D. (2000) 'How science works', in F. M. Smith (ed.), *Reference Manual on Scientific Evidence*, 2nd edn. Washington, DC: Federal Judicial Center.

Goodstein, D. (2010) *On Fact and Fraud: Cautionary Tales from the Front Lines of Science*. Princeton: Princeton University Press.

Goodstein, D. and Woodward, J. (1999) 'Inside science', *American Scholar*, 68: 83–90.

Greenberg, D. (2001) *Science, Money, and Politics: Political Triumph and Ethical Erosion*. Chicago: University of Chicago Press.

Gross, P. and Levitt, N. (1994) *Higher Superstition: The Academic Left and its Quarrels with Science*. Baltimore: Johns Hopkins University Press.

Hacking, I. (2000) 'How inevitable are the results of successful science?', *Philosophy of Science*, 67: S58–S71.

Hands, D. W. (2002) 'The sociology of scientific knowledge: some thoughts on the possibilities', in P. Mirowski and E.-M. Sent (eds), *Science Bought and Sold: Essays in the Economics of Science*. Chicago: University of Chicago Press.

Harding, S. (1998) *Is Science Multicultural? Postcolonialisms, Feminisms, and Epistemologies*. Bloomington: Indiana University Press.

Henderson, R. et al. (1998) 'Universities as a source of commercial technology: a detailed analysis of university patenting, 1965–1998', *Review of Economics and Statistics*, 80 (1): 119–27.

Kindley, E. (2010) 'Beneath contempt, beyond critique: Bourdieu on Latour'. Blog post available at <http://wehaveneverbeenblogging.blogspot.com/2010/01/beneath-contempt-beyond-critique.html>.

Kleinman, D. L. (2003) *Impure Cultures: University Biology and the World of Commerce*. Madison: University of Wisconsin Press.

Krimsky, S. (2006) 'The ethical and legal foundations of scientific "conflict of interest"', in T. Lemmens and D. R. Waring (eds), *Law and Ethics in Biomedical Regulation*. Toronto: University of Toronto Press.

Labinger, J. A. and Collins, H. (2001) 'Introduction', in J. A. Labinger and H. Collins (eds), *The One Culture? A Conversation About Science*. Chicago: University of Chicago Press.

Latour, B. (1987) *Science in Action: How to Follow Scientists and Engineers Through Society*. Cambridge, MA: Harvard University Press.

Latour, B. (1993) *We Have Never Been Modern*, trans. C. Porter. Cambridge, MA: Harvard University Press.

Latour, B. (2004) 'Why has critique run out of steam? From matters of fact to matters of concern', *Critical Inquiry*, 30: 225–48.

Latour, B. and Woolgar, S. (1986) *Laboratory Life: The Construction of Scientific Facts*, revised edn. Princeton: Princeton University Press.

McGarity, T. O. and Wagner, W. E. (2008) *Bending Science: How Special Interests Corrupt Public Health Research*. Cambridge, MA: Harvard University Press.

Mahner, M. and Bunge, M. (1996) 'Is religious education compatible with science education?', *Science and Education*, 5 (2): 101–23.

Miller, S. P. (2013) 'Where's the innovation? An analysis of the quality and qualities of anticipated and obvious patents', *Virginia Journal of Law and Technology*, 18: 1–58.

Mirowski, P. (2004) *The Effortless Economy of Science?* Durham, NC: Duke University Press.

Mirowski, P. (2011) *Science-Mart: Privatizing American Science*. Cambridge, MA: Harvard University Press.

Mirowski, P. and Sent, E.-M. (2002) 'Introduction', in P. Mirowski and E.-M. Sent (eds), *Science Bought and Sold: Essays in the Economics of Science*. Chicago: University of Chicago Press.

Mirowski, P. and Van Horn, R. (2005) 'The contract research organization and the commercialization of scientific research', *Social Studies of Science*, 35: 503–48.

National Research Council (2009) *Strengthening Forensic Science in the United States: A Path Forward*. Washington, DC: National Academies Press.

Potter, J. (1996) *Representing Reality: Discourse, Rhetoric, and Social Construction*. London: Sage.

Rabinow, P. (2009) 'Prosperity, amelioration, flourishing: from a logic of practical judgment to reconstruction', *Law and Literature*, 21: 301–20.

Rip, A. (2003) 'Constructing expertise: in a third wave of science studies?', *Social Studies of Science*, 33: 419–34.
Rowe, S. et al. (2009) 'Funding food science and nutrition research: financial conflicts and scientific integrity', *American Journal of Clinical Nutrition*, 89: 1285–91.
Shapin, S. (2001) 'How to be antiscientific', in J. A. Labinger and H. Collins (eds), *The One Culture? A Conversation About Science*. Chicago: University of Chicago Press.
Sismondo, S. (2008) 'How pharmaceutical industry funding affects trial outcomes: causal structures and responses', *Social Science and Medicine*, 66: 1909–14.
Sokal, A. (1996a) 'Transgressing the boundaries: toward a transformative hermeneutics of quantum gravity', *Social Text*, 46/47: 217–52.
Sokal, A. (1996b) 'A physicist experiments with cultural studies', *Lingua Franca*, May/June, pp. 62–4.
Stephan, P. (2012) *How Economics Shapes Science*. Cambridge, MA: Harvard University Press.
Stossell, T. P. (2012) 'What's wrong with COI [conflicts of interest]?', *The Scientist*, 12 June. Available at <http://the-scientist.com/?articles.view/articleNo/32190/title/Opinion-What's-Wrong-with-COI-/>.
Tyfield, D. (2012) *The Economics of Science: A Critical Realist Overview*, Vol. 1. New York: Routledge.
Wible, J. R. (1991) 'Maximization, replication, and the economic rationality of positive economic science', *Review of Political Economy*, 3: 164–86.
Wible, J. R. (1992) 'Fraud in science: an economic approach', *Philosophy of the Social Sciences*, 22: 5–27.

Cases

Daubert v. Merrell Dow Pharmaceuticals, Inc. (1993) 509 US 579–601.
General Electric Co. v. Joiner (1997) 522 US 136–55.
Kumho Tire Co., Ltd. v. Carmichael (1999) 526 US 137–59.

11

Bartleby, Barbarians and the Legality of Literature
Faith Barter

In *An Inquiry into Modes of Existence*, Bruno Latour offers a sweeping account of his 'Anthropology of the Moderns'. The title is, to deploy one of the book's key terms, a 'preposition' that orients the reader in several directions. By framing the project as an 'inquiry', it claims that modes of existence are susceptible to organised, textual and anthropological examination. Second, it establishes that existence occurs within and among various 'modes', making clear that existence is diverse, varied and multifaceted. By describing types of existence as 'modes', the title invokes the concepts of habit and behaviour; according to Latour, a defining feature of a mode is that each one 'possesses its own particular type of veridiction'.[1] Thus we recognise a mode by looking to its own habits of '*explicitly* and *consciously* . . . decid[ing] what is true and what is false' (*Inquiry* 53).[2]

Throughout the book *Modes of Existence*, Latour proceeds from his extensive work in actor-network theory (ANT) to identify and develop more than a dozen modes of existence, such as law, politics and, perhaps surprisingly, fiction. He examines each as part of what he calls a 'regional ontology' (*Inquiry* xxv); by using the term 'regional' as a modifier of 'ontology', Latour suggests a spatial component to these modes of existence. The word 'regional' also implicates Latour's claim of 'local' ontologies that are specific to various modes of existence. This regional delineation does not isolate the modes from one another; rather, Latour uses the term 'crossing' to suggest a means of putting modes into conversation with one another: 'A crossing makes it possible to compare two modes, two branchings, two types of felicity conditions, by revealing, through a series of trials, the contrasts that allow us to define what is specific about them, as well as the often tortuous history of their relations' (*Inquiry* 63). The result of such crossings demonstrates, for Latour, 'the irreducible character of [the modes'] viewpoints: this is where we shall be able to see why the conclusion of a [legal] trial bears no resemblance to that of a scientific proof ...' (*Inquiry* 63). In Latour's framework, though crossings shed light on relationships among various modes' histories, the more useful application of crossings is to identify the boundaries and borders of modes that set them apart from each other.

My interest here focuses on Latour's treatment of two specific modes, law and fiction. While this chapter addresses law and fiction, I examine a particular structure of crossing – worldbuilding – that blurs the boundaries between law and fiction and makes visible their shared interest in troubling the definition of the human. The result is a mechanism through which both law and fiction muster institutional strength. I explore specific texts – American judicial opinions and statutes and several works of fiction – in order to identify what is actually legal about literature and how Latour's work on law has the potential to bring a fresh critical perspective to legal theory as well as literary criticism. Specifically, I examine Herman Melville's 1853 short story, 'Bartleby, the Scrivener', J. M. Coetzee's 1980 novella *Waiting for the Barbarians* and the 1857 US Supreme Court decision in *Dred Scott v. Sandford*.[3]

The concept of world-building arises in literary criticism – frequently with respect to science fiction – as the use of narrative to build both the beings of fiction[4] and the worlds they inhabit. In literature, a text obeys implicit laws governing what happens within its literary world. These 'rules' in fiction may be more or less explicit – they become most visible in science fiction, where the 'rules' of science and Earth cease to be limitations on the world of the text. Realist literature, however, also participates in the same process of world-building, even if its rules are more familiar – and therefore less visible – than those in science fiction. The human labour of authorship produces worlds structured by the behaviour of the fictional beings who inhabit them as well as the text's circle of self-referentiality. As Pavel writes, 'Literary texts are neither natural phenomena subject to scientific dissection, nor miracles performed by gods and thus worthy of worship, but fruits of human talent and labor' (2003: 202). In *Reassembling the Social*, Latour cites Pavel in a discussion of literature's potential for building a 'diversity of ... worlds' (2005: 55). In *Reassembling the*

Social, Latour (2005: 24) rejects as too narrow the term 'world-making' for its tendency to suggest a single coherent world. The capaciousness of 'world-building' and its suggestion of numerous 'possible worlds' lends Pavel's term the traction necessary for a Latourian examination of discursive crossings.

Perhaps counter-intuitively, the unquantifiability of possible worlds is the characteristic that makes literature particularly hospitable to Latourian analysis; literature's tentacles possess practically limitless reach, not only creating new networks but also re-imagining existing ones. Lubomir Dolezel writes in 'Possible Worlds of History and Fiction' (1998: 786), 'The universe of discourse is not restricted to the actual world, but spreads over uncountable possible, nonactualized worlds.' Therefore literature need not construct a fantastical, implausible universe in order to participate in this discursive practice. Rather, the fictional world that is a 'possible world' need only be a non-actualised version of the actual world.[5] Moments of collision between the actual world and a possible world are sufficiently arresting that the law often intervenes to regulate fictional texts by requiring familiar legal disclaimers to the effect that similarities to 'real' persons are purely coincidental. More commonly, authors avoid litigation by changing the names of 'fictional' characters based on living persons. Beneath these examples of legal and literary friction lurks an anxiety about how to separate the 'actual' from the 'fictional' – an anxiety that bespeaks the extent to which the two categories are interrelated.

This connection between the 'actual' and the 'fictional' suggests that world-building has applicability beyond fiction, and specifically to law. Like fiction, law uses sets of facts to structure the legal narrative at the heart of a judicial opinion or a statute. In both law and fiction, instauration – in which a work of art comes through, but not 'by' an artist – seems an applicable concept, though Latour discusses it primarily with respect to fiction. In both cases, creators work through textual production to generate worlds that obey the rules circumscribed by the texts themselves. The question of authorial intent is a complicated one in literary criticism, in which many critics tend to employ the conceit that a literary work has an agency of its own; the resulting tension between intent and effect illustrates the extent to which we think of authors as the vehicles for the works they produce. By comparison, legal writing embraces instauration via judicial opinions and statutes. In each type of legal text, the actual 'author' (more properly, writer) of the work becomes subject to erasure; instead, it is the institution (a court or a legislature) that is deemed to have 'written' the text. Cultural narratives about law would take instauration one step further, insisting that specific legal institutions are merely vehicles through which law becomes recorded.

In a judicial opinion, for instance, the recitation of facts circumscribes the scope of the legal reasoning to follow. Robert Cover has written that '*nomos*, as a world of law ... is a present world constituted by a system of tension between reality and vision' (1983–4: 9). Cover's formulation of *nomos* refers to 'a normative universe' in which '[n]o set of legal institutions or prescriptions exists apart from the narratives that locate it and give it meaning' 1983: 4). The normative nature of this universe does not refer to the oppressive nature of social norms. Rather, as Cover writes, 'law becomes not merely a system of rules to be observed, but a world in which we live' (1983: 5). Cover's formulation envisions a material world, but one that depends on laws and legal meaning to set its terms. Not only does law set terms for the material world, but it brings into being, through legal work, the very materiality in which we live.

The law sets its terms through legal narratives – such as those created in judicial opinions. Though the law purports to inhabit the realm of the actual, the judicial practice of establishing – essentially re-narrativising – facts operates to create alternative non-actualised versions of the so-called 'real world', bringing legal world-building and literary world-building crashing directly into one another's orbits. The availability of world-building in both law and fiction endows each mode of existence with the capacity to trouble, among other things, the definition of the human. Beyond having a shared capacity for this work, each mode of existence has an *interest* in doing so; for law, the definition of the human organises and assigns rights and privileges, while literature's manipulation of the human enables us to imagine alternatives to law's organising principles. Not only do both law and fiction practise world-building, but they both do so *intertextually*. In other words, legal texts and literary texts engage in world-building not only within specific works but through those works' relationship to other texts.

The intertextual dimensions of law and literature accrue meta-intertextuality when we place the modes of law and fiction in conversation with each other. Scholars have grappled with how best to bring law and fiction together, usually through critical legal studies or, more generally, the field known as law and literature. Critical legal studies, focused mainly on law and legal institutions, fit somewhat more neatly within Latour's work on the passage of law, given Latour's work on the sociology of law. Law and literature, on the other hand, strive to join the disciplines of law and literature. This union has tended to be an uncomfortable one that forces scholars to choose between two general critical postures: (1) law *in* literature, or (2) law *as* literature. These two category titles make visible the field's propensity for attracting literary scholars with an interest in law, as well as legal scholars with an interest in literature. Both types of scholars are susceptible to criticism; literary critics have accused legal practitioners of dabbling irresponsibly in literary analysis, while legal theorists have bristled at the suggestion that non-lawyers might have something to say about the law. These questions of appropriation manifest in the binary that inflects the field at every level, insisting always that one discipline bow to the other. Latour's work enters this conversation as an opportunity to imagine an alternative to this binary, an alternative critical posture that permits law and literature to coexist simultaneously in a given text – even a critical posture in which it becomes possible to read literature as law.

In *An Inquiry into Modes of Existence*, Latour focuses largely on the 'beings of fiction'. His positioning of the beings of fiction encompasses not only literature, but all works of art; specifically, his use of instauration networks art and literature with artists and authors in an ANT-inflected framework. By presenting art works as arriving *through* their creators without whom the artworks could likewise never exist (*Inquiry* 160), Latour preserves the status of both artists and artworks as actants within their networks. Despite his assignation of fiction to numerous artistic disciplines, his work focuses largely on the characters of fiction as the beings that possess the most 'realness'. By engaging them in this manner, Latour seems to want to restore to them the objectivity they have been 'too hastily denied' (*Inquiry* 239) despite their unchallenged cultural value.

As I have already suggested, the question of what constitutes a fictional being is not self-evident; a fictional character may be identified with an actual person, frequently the author, or an actual person or event may appear in a fictionalised work.

Depending on the author's degree of realism, the reader may or may not recognise these actual beings as fictional entities. For instance, in the preface to her 1856 novel, *Dred, A Tale of the Great Dismal Swamp*, Harriet Beecher Stowe acknowledges that she has included in her fictional text a trial transcript from a North Carolina slavery case. Stowe writes of herself, 'The writer has placed in the mouth of one of her leading characters a judicial decision of Judge Ruffin, of North Carolina . . . The author having no personal acquaintance with that gentleman, the character to whom she attributes it is to be considered as created merely on a principle of artistic fitness' (2006: 4). In this fascinating moment of legal and literary collision, Stowe acknowledges the realness of the text she quotes even while she insists on the fictionality with which she ventriloquises Judge Ruffin. Stowe's ventriloquisation of Judge Ruffin, rather than acting as pure citation of his opinion, operates instead as a critique of it. Such moments in literature suggest the relative ease with which actual persons and events are susceptible to transformation into beings of fiction.

Latour recognises the tendency of both law and literature to encroach on one another's discursive domains. Even in focusing on fiction, Latour acknowledges its relationship to law, making this affinity a central aspect of the contours that form fiction's modal boundaries. Throughout his treatment of fiction, Latour continuously places it into conversation with law – usually for the purposes of establishing the two modes' common ground and then drawing distinctions between them. For instance, Latour observes that '. . . the beings of fiction, like those of law, indeed possess full and complete reality in their genre, with their own type of veridiction, transcendence, and being' (*Inquiry* 239). In other words, fiction is like law for its generic realness, but it differs from law in its type of veridiction, among other things. With fiction, this veridiction consists for Latour mainly of coherence and believability (*Inquiry* 245). Moreover, Latour's analysis claims that fiction differs from law (and from the other modes of existence) as follows: 'Here we have a mode of existence like no other, defined by hesitation, vacillation, back-and-forth movements, the establishment of resonance between the successive layers of raw material from which are drawn, provisionally, figurations that nevertheless cannot separate themselves from this material' (*Inquiry* 244). Latour identifies fiction's vacillation as a distinction between the raw materials (a lump of clay that forms a statue, to use his example) and the artistic *value* that we attach to art objects. The fictionality of fiction depends on the raw materials that produce it – the words on the pages, the clay, the paints – even as we perceive it to exist apart from or above these items.

The back-and-forth movement to which he refers resides mainly in the relationship between artwork and audience and the manner in which fiction follows its audience beyond the limits of its own mode. Latour writes of fiction's 'continuous creation [as] distributed all along [the beings of fiction's] path of life, so much so that we can never really tell whether it is the artist or the audience that is creating the work' (*Inquiry* 242–3). Here is what Latour suggests is fiction's sharpest contrast with law; with fiction, Latour calls attention to the capacity of art to infiltrate our daily lives to such an extent that we may hesitate to draw bright lines between fictional beings and the beings we touch, address and engage throughout the day. However – and as I will discuss later with respect to specific legal texts – the mystification of 'who' creates law produces a similar result. Do we not have a similar vacillation when we perceive the badge of a police officer? In that encounter, we move back and forth between the object itself (an unremarkable bit of metal) and what it stands for, and we almost always ultimately give permission for it to engage with us on its own terms. Of course, it is this continued act of permission – stopping when an officer flashes a badge – that sustains the badge's power. Here again, we cannot be certain who is doing the badge's work – the police officer or all of us who obey him.

For Latour, another distinguishing characteristic of fiction is its ability 'to add segments without ever taking any away' (*Inquiry* 243). Here he discusses the capacity of art to make relevant – essential, even – each detail contained within it. He offers individual pixels as examples of such details, though Latour's larger focus is on the 'beings of fiction'. Latour makes a subtle elision between fiction itself and the so-called beings of fiction. Even while decrying the reduction of fiction to the realm of the 'symbolic', Latour focuses largely on the symbolic realness of the beings of fiction without devoting comparable attention to the texts themselves. It cannot be the case that literary texts exist solely as vehicles to give life to fictional beings; the texts themselves establish worlds that simultaneously intrude upon the reader and invite the reader to enter them. One imagines a poem or story, for instance, in which the literary landscape is entirely inhospitable to beings.[6] These works do not exist along a continuum in which the more 'symbolic' the piece, the less 'real' it is.

The question of 'plausibility' therefore becomes important to the veridiction required for fiction. The issue is not whether a fictional work represents a plausible version of our world, but whether the world it builds is plausible *on its own terms*. What Latour identifies as the believability of a character, literary work, etc. rests entirely on this question of plausibility.[7] One way that fiction references its own predication on plausibility is through the capacity for fictional texts to engage in dialogue with each other. In literature, this intertextuality manifests most frequently in several possible ways – one is genre and another is through citational re-imagination. In short, the worlds of literature produce 'typeness' of one form or another[8] that is only recognisable as 'typeness' when numerous texts coexist simultaneously. Regardless of when two texts were created, we recognise certain affinities, relationships and literary features that constantly reappear. By viewing texts as polytemporally networked, we thus derive a third layer of meaning in addition to the meaning residing in each of the texts separately.

I examine several specific literary texts in order to unpack these claims; my examination specifically considers literature's capacity to engage intertextually in a dialogue on the human. Whereas law does so through (usually) visibly linked citations, literature undertakes this conversation through the repetition of themes, characters and plots in multiple texts – the 'typeness' identified above. Both Herman Melville's 1853 short story 'Bartleby, the Scrivener' and J. M. Coetzee's 1980 novel *Waiting for the Barbarians* trouble the definition of the human in ways that inextricably – though not always explicitly – place the texts in relation to each other. Through the worlds created in the texts, Melville and Coetzee each introduce fictional beings who challenge traditional definitions of the human and therefore call attention to the constructedness of all definitions of the human, including legal definitions.

David Attwell formulates Coetzee's intertextuality in *Doubling the Point* where he writes that 'reflexive self-consciousness ... characterises all Coetzee's work' (1992: 3). Read this way, Coetzee's self-consciousness to the intervention of literature in broader cultural histories enables a dialogue with earlier texts that does not depend on hierarchies. Rather, Coetzee's works can speak back to other texts that are already part of a larger literary history *and future*. Coetzee self-consciously calls attention to the temporal shiftiness of his literary works by frequently making overt or obvious connections to other texts.[9] In the case of 'Bartleby' and *Barbarians*, I suggest that the two texts occupy a precedential relationship to each other, though not in the sense of original and copy or even in the sense of contingency. Instead, imagine that 'Bartleby' and *Barbarians* are two points along the continuum of a particular trajectory. These two moments then speak back and forth to each other across time to give each text new meaning.

In both 'Bartleby' and *Waiting for the Barbarians*, the narrator, a mid-level legal official, forges an intimate and puzzling relationship with a mysterious other whose personhood is tenuous. The narrator in 'Bartleby', a legal official in 1850s New York City, says of himself, 'I am a man who, from his youth upwards, has been filled with a profound conviction that the easiest way of life is the best' (Melville 3). Later, he writes, 'All who know me consider me an eminently *safe* man' (Melville 4). His position as a master of chancery is, in his words, 'not a very arduous office, but very pleasantly remunerative' (Melville 4). The narrator thus establishes himself as a prototypical lawyer – risk-averse, steady: someone who never rocks the boat. Likewise, the Magistrate in *Waiting for the Barbarians* – also an unnamed lawyer-narrator – opens his text in a similar fashion. Though he inhabits an unnamed time and place, he writes:

> I am a country magistrate, a responsible official in the service of the Empire, serving out my days on this lazy frontier, waiting to retire. I collect the tithes and taxes, administer the communal lands . . . preside over the law-court twice a week. For the rest I watch the sun rise and set, eat and sleep and am content. When I pass away I hope to merit three lines of small print in the Imperial gazette. I have not asked for more than a quiet life in quiet times. (*WB* 8–9)[10]

Here the narrator characterises his life as a gap or a trace that he hopes will 'merit three lines of small print in the Imperial gazette'. The desire to exist as a mere textual trace suggests a hollowing out of his material self and structures his humanity as a textual relic or afterthought – an artifact of, and in furtherance of, the Empire. There is a relationship here to Latour's concept of hesitation.[11] The narrator anatomises his life, teasing apart the individual components of eating, sleeping and carrying out administrative tasks, as a prerequisite to reading his own life as evidence of imperial continuity – hence the imagined memorialisation of his life in the Imperial gazette.

Both narrators, at the outset of their respective texts, establish their personal histories as men who follow rules, honour structures of power and authority, and avoid discomfort wherever possible. Neither narrator has an interest in activism or radical politicking. Rather, both men seek to live out their lives with minimal disruption. Moreover, given that both narrators occupy positions as quasi-state-actors in the law,[12] we might read each character as a kind of commentary on the law's lazy posture with respect to its own machinations. This narrative framing of the texts calls attention to the power of authorship – the narrator's point of view in each text completely controls the reader's access to the worlds being described. Much as Melville and Coetzee are the implied authors, they each create narrators (who are therefore fictional beings); we are invited to believe that these fictional beings are the ones creating the literary worlds they narrate. Ironically, this technique adds to the plausibility of the literary worlds, in which a country magistrate and a city lawyer call us to visit the nearly realistic worlds they describe.

Against this backdrop, the two men encounter mysterious others who destabilise profoundly the ordered and easy world of each narrator. The worlds of the texts bear only tenuous similarity, on their surfaces, to anything we might reasonably call 'the real world'. Though set in nineteenth-century New York, 'Bartleby' quickly becomes an almost supernatural tale about a man with no history and no home, who appears to require neither sleep nor food for much of the story. By contrast, the world of *Waiting for the Barbarians* refuses to locate itself in a particular time or place; it suggests a primitive culture (as in the opening sentence, when the narrator encounters sunglasses as new technology) even as it has the feel of a post-apocalyptic dystopian future (as when the narrator puzzles over archaeological artifacts from civilisations past). It is only because the narrators of each text have qualified themselves to us as plausible beings – a lawyer, a magistrate – that we accept their descriptions of the worlds they inhabit.

Having introduced the reader into these worlds, each text offers characters whose personhood is up for debate, even among the other characters in their worlds. Bartleby is a scrivener whose primary function is to hand-copy legal documents and transcripts.

His career in the narrator's office begins as one of industry and diligence, but it quickly devolves into stubborn refusals to do any work or even to leave the office itself (where he eventually takes up residence). As Bartleby gradually stops doing any of his work, he instead repeatedly utters the phrase 'I prefer not to', whether in response to requests for his labour or eventually to the narrator's pleas for Bartleby simply to quit the premises. Bartleby's unwillingness to elaborate confounds and preoccupies the narrator who is at a comedic loss to engage Bartleby in more satisfying explanations. Their dynamic escalates until the narrator eventually moves to a new office. Bartleby, to use the narrator's description, 'remain[s] as ever a fixture in [the] chamber' (Melville 27) and refuses to leave the building, even when the narrator offers to bring Bartleby home with him. Consequently, the new tenants have Bartleby arrested and jailed in the Tombs where his refusals to eat or speak occasion his death. Throughout this bizarre series of events, the narrator is haunted and baffled by his inability to read or understand Bartleby. Moreover, the narrator repeatedly describes Bartleby as being without a history,[13] and his efforts to learn about Bartleby's past compel him to research Bartleby's biography at some significant (though ultimately unsatisfying) length. Bartleby remains as mysterious to the narrator at the end of the story as he is at its beginning. Bartleby's inscrutability, however, transcends mere mystery; the text questions whether Bartleby is 'ordinarily human' (Melville 13), suggesting not only that Bartleby is somehow extraordinary but also that the classification of 'human' is an improper site in which to locate him at all. The narrator likens Bartleby to a 'fixture' in the office and compares Bartleby to a 'millstone' around his neck (Melville 27). These rhetorical moves that figure Bartleby as an object or a non-human creature place Bartleby's humanity at the centre of the text's greatest mystery: is Bartleby even human at all?

The narrator undertakes an obsessive biographical search for Bartleby's history, finally learning only of his former employment in the Dead Letter Office.[14] At every turn, Bartleby denies access to his interior, if he has one. Instead, Bartleby is constituted almost entirely through a preference of negation, producing an endless cycle in which the narrator only comes to know Bartleby by that which Bartleby is *not*. The narrator even writes, 'I might give alms to [Bartleby's] body, but his body did not pain him – it was his soul that suffered and his soul I could not reach' (Melville 23).[15]

These efforts to reach Bartleby's interior – both through researching Bartleby's past and through his attempts to gain insight into Bartleby's thoughts – evince the narrator's emotional interest to Bartleby as much as his efforts to assist Bartleby in prison evince his sense of obligation to his former employee. It is an obligation that makes even less sense because Bartleby had refused to do any work or even leave the office itself, thereby creating a cascade of problems for the narrator. Bartleby's opacity gives him power over the narrator and takes him from a position of subjection to authority and then back to subjection when the narrator fails to successfully rescue Bartleby from the violence of state power. This power likewise disrupts traditional narratives about the human – if Bartleby is something other than human, his ability to acquire power over the narrator arguably positions him as somehow *superhuman*, even while the narrator's characterisations – a creature, a fixture, a millstone – suggest that Bartleby is *subhuman*.

In *Waiting for the Barbarians*, the Magistrate encounters an unnamed barbarian girl, the victim of the Imperial government's brutal tactics of torture and interrogation against the native population. By the time the girl arrives at the Magistrate's doorstep, the scars of her previous torture taunt the Magistrate as an unreadable text that preoccupies him. He writes, 'It has been growing more and more clear to me that until the marks on this girl's body are deciphered and understood I cannot let go of her' (WB 36–7). An amateur archaeologist, the Magistrate approaches the girl's body much the way he approaches the ancient wood slips he excavates from the surrounding territory. He attempts to decipher the text of her body through physical examination and repeated questioning, never to his satisfaction: 'But with this woman it is as if there is no interior, only a surface across which I hunt back and forth seeking entry' (WB 49).

Like the narrator in 'Bartleby', the Magistrate searches single-mindedly for evidence that the girl has an interior at all – he questions her repeatedly about her past and the Empire's torture of her, and he lingers over the scars on her body as though using his hands to read the marks on her skin. The Magistrate finds the girl unyielding and recalcitrant in her reluctance to answer questions about her scars, writing that she 'remains as obscure to [him] as ever' (WB 73). Like Bartleby's 'I prefer not to', the barbarian girl resists providing information about her life but also resists even the provision of any further explanation for her refusals. The absence of personal history raises the question of her humanity from the Magistrate's perspective; this occurs against the backdrop of an Imperial government that likewise legally regards her as non-human on account of her racial identity as 'Barbarian'. In 'Bartleby' and *Waiting for the Barbarians*, the law occurs as the site across which these questions of the human do battle with each other; the law office of 'Bartleby' acts as the literal setting for this debate, while the law in *Waiting for the Barbarians* struggles to manage categories of beings who are legally, in the world of the novel, non-persons.

For both 'Bartleby' and *Barbarians*, then, a certain family resemblance across characterisations emerges from the relationships of the narrators to mysterious and largely silent figures who disrupt the definition of the human; not only do Bartleby and the Barbarian girl call into question their proper classification as human, but they also draw attention to the curious lack of 'humanity' in their respective narrators. Each narrator, having professed a preference for quiet and inactivity, finds a version of his extreme double in the mysterious others who interrupt their existences. These encounters destabilise profoundly the narrators' experience of themselves as human. In both texts, the question of ethics interrupts the lawyer-narrators' actions, producing different results – the Magistrate in *Barbarians* ultimately risks his life by returning the girl to her people, whereas Bartleby's employer never manages to rescue Bartleby from the Tombs. The narrators recognise as human these beings who do not match up with the accepted definitions of 'human' within their own fictional worlds; the resulting conflict dramatises the friction between individuals and the institutions that constantly manage their daily lives. If a system proscribes categories for organising its subjects, a subject that fails to fit into one of those categories is extraordinarily disruptive both to individuals and to the system as a whole, which suddenly risks being exposed as a construction of flawed origins.

This systemic disruption is more evident in *Waiting for the Barbarians*, where the Magistrate's relationship to his state evolves from one of complicity to one of resistance. He challenges his government in undeniably hostile fashion, threatening to expose Colonel Joll for the sadistic torturer he really is; the government has little choice (acting, as most governments do, out of an instinct for self-preservation) but to imprison and torture the Magistrate before he can incite others. It is important here to distinguish the multiple layers on which world-building occurs: (1) Coetzee has built the world of the novel; (2) the Magistrate has built the world of his own narration; and (3) the Magistrate's government has built the world it narrates about the existence and threat of the Barbarians. Even as the latter two worlds break down, Coetzee's world remains sufficiently intact that we are able to read the entire work of fiction as a coherent, if not disorienting, text. Nevertheless, this multi-layered structure makes visible the power of world-building to manage literary worlds as well as 'real' ones, especially in terms of how these worlds continually redefine their own limits and police their inhabitants. Totalitarianism itself is a version of world-building, in which institutions produce representations of the world, to which the world in turn shapes itself. Totalitarianism therefore illustrates the extent to which representation produces the present, rather than simply recording it.[16]

Given the similarities in character, plot and theme, both 'Bartleby' and *Waiting for the Barbarians* appear to participate in a shared literary tradition that becomes recognisable through the 'typeness' that repeats across the two texts. However, a Latourian reading of this relationship should compel us to resist the urge to draw a straight line that begins with Melville and ends with Coetzee.[17] Rather than reading Coetzee as simply the heir to Melville's original or originary canonical text, acknowledge the two texts as existing simultaneously in a polytemporal network. Taken this way, Melville is an inheritor – both an inheritor to whatever came before him and an inheritor to Coetzee's later work – as much as Coetzee is. Dispensing with a reductive linear chronology allows the texts to accumulate additional meaning as participants (or actants, to import the terminology of ANT) in a shared conversation. Not only does 'Bartleby' produce commentary on nineteenth-century American labour, but it also engages with the questions raised by *Waiting for the Barbarians*. Moreover, reading *Waiting for the Barbarians* alongside 'Bartleby' produces alternatives to Melville's text; it demonstrates an alternative course for the lawyer-narrator, and it also imagines the larger implications of institutional establishment of categories of the human.

As effective as these texts are in dramatising the problem of defining the human, this analysis has pushed us ever closer to the mode of law – explicitly through the presence of legal institutions in these works, and implicitly through the questions being raised about who has the authority to adjudicate the rights of beings who do not fit into accepted categories of 'human' or 'person'. At this point, it is necessary to make a closer examination of Latour's treatment of law and to explore how legal texts use world-building to trouble the human. For Latour, law's modality has the following 'distinctive feature: through the intermediary of a particular hiatus [it] allow[s] means to follow a highly original trajectory in a series of leaps from facts to principles' (*Inquiry* 365). Here Latour addresses how a hiatus in law – the discontinuity of something like what we commonly call a 'legal fiction', for instance – actually reinforces legal institutions by imbuing even 'a little case of no importance' (*Inquiry* 365) with the weight of legal rules and principles.[18]

It is difficult to argue with this proposition, as attested to by anyone who has unsuccessfully challenged a traffic ticket.[19] Latour crystallises the manner in which legal regulation hovers like a fog above everyday interactions, threatening always to introduce the full material and psychological force of The Law, a fairly terrifying presence that remains on call to either rescue a wronged party or punish a bad actor. It is worthwhile, however, to pause – hesitate – here to interrogate some of the 'legal' conceits that underlie Latour's analysis. Most striking about his language is the presumed clarity of the boundary between facts on the one hand and principles on the other. The dichotomy between the two sounds at first fairly obvious, and the law itself treats the two as diametrically opposed. For instance, in judicial opinions and legal briefs, it is common for the drafter to include a section titled, with rhetorical obviousness, 'Facts'. This portion of the document recites a set of events, names interested parties and lists other information that takes on the hue of 'background material'. The recitation of facts, however, is critical for the immediate litigation (in which stipulated facts and facts in evidence represent the entirety of the legal 'world' in which the matter will be adjudicated), as well as future litigation (where, for instance, the legal rule of Case A is held to apply to Case B only if the facts in both cases are substantially comparable). In this context, the inclusion or omission of certain facts has a transformative effect on the law being made: the representation of facts pre-shapes and then merges with the law which purports to indifferently await them.[20] Given this tension, the dichotomy between 'fact' and 'law' begins to disappear. This disquisition on legal facts illuminates their importance, but does not disrupt Latour's formulation; on the contrary, it makes visible one example of legal hiatus or legal fiction.

More murky is the role of facts in American jury trials, where the division of labour in the courtroom putatively depends upon them: juries answer questions of fact while judges address questions of law. The problem of separating out questions of fact from questions of law can be tricky – they are 'questions', after all. The Federal Rules of Evidence contemplate this problem in Rule 104 ('Preliminary Questions'). Rule 104(b) addresses the problem that arises when the relevance of evidence depends on the existence of a fact, providing that in such cases 'proof must be introduced sufficient to support a finding that the fact does exist'.[21] In other words, juries alone do not determine whether or not facts exist; only upon a judicial determination of a fact's 'existence' does the jury decide how much weight to give particular 'facts' and how to resolve apparent discrepancies among the facts offered. Latour's earlier work in *On the Modern Cult of the Factish Gods* unpacks the relationship between 'fact' and 'fetish' in part by mystifying the dichotomy between construction and reality. He writes: ' . . . we shall use the label *factish* for the robust certainty that allows practice to pass into action without the practitioner ever believing in the difference between construction and reality, immanence and transcendence' (2010b: 22). This conflation of fact and fetish hints at the fiction necessary for 'practice to pass into action'. In *The Making of Law*, Latour likewise suggests that, in the legal context, facts are a hinge that facilitate the passage of law. In that work, Latour (2010a: 89) cites an administrative decision in which the tribunal writes that a legal conclusion (notice) 'emerges from the documents in the file'. Having ratified the fact of actual notification, the tribunal concludes that a legal requirement – notice – has been met.

In *An Inquiry into Modes of Existence*, Latour also discusses the spectres of 'straight talk' and 'undisputable facts' as obscuring and flattening discourse, going so far as to label straight talk 'a literary genre' (*Inquiry* 138–9). This classification of straight talk as 'literary' calls attention to the relationship between legal texts and fiction; legal texts insist on straight talk and have as their project the evacuation and reconciliation of disputed facts. The legal conceit of the separation between facts and law, once exposed to be less than a bright-line boundary, complicates Latour's claim of law's ontological uniqueness. If legal institutions are constantly selecting which facts to include – whether through admissibility or recitation in an opinion – and adjudicating the existence of facts in the first place, the movement from facts to principles begins to look less like an arrow moving in one direction and more like a circle tracing back upon itself. As Latour might claim, these movements of law from fact to principle may be expressing the hiatus that reinforces law's staying power in the end – the discontinuities that facilitate the continuity of law as an institution. This dynamic does, however, raise questions about the *directionality* of law. Does law always and only move forward, or does law contain the capacity for temporal shiftiness and bidirectionality?

In *An Inquiry into Modes of Existence*, Latour hints at the possibility that there is something more happening with respect to law's directionality. In comparing law to other modes, Latour writes that 'all the modes identified up to now have this distinctive feature: they *pass*, they move forward, they launch into the search for their means of subsistence. Each one does it differently, but they have in common the feature that they never *go back* to the conditions under which they started' (*Inquiry* 368). In this theoretical move, Latour suggests that law, unlike the other modes, does, or can, return to the conditions under which it started; in this framework, law's constant proliferation of text behaves differently from the proliferation of texts in religion or literature. As Latour writes, 'Thanks to law, you can *multiply the levels of enunciation without causing them to disperse*' (*Inquiry* 369). In other words, law's proliferation ceaselessly produces new levels of enunciation, new interpretations and new rules that nevertheless remain like irons around a powerful magnetic core. Law by necessity constantly 'return[s] to the conditions under which it started' (*Inquiry* 368) through citation of itself to justify or authorise its own proliferation.

The common law tradition, through precedent, provides a visible example of law's self-referentiality to support its continued existence: the common law judicial decision remains a powerful cultural icon of the law's permanence, stability and institutional legitimacy. With few exceptions – and usually only then in an attempt to literarise a judicial text, as with my earlier example from Harriet Beecher Stowe – American public discourse rarely recognises individual judges as having authored opinions. Rather, both legal and cultural norms treat decisions as coming from 'courts' rather than individual human beings. Common law precedent pushes further what Latour implies about the directionality and temporality of law.

In 'Violence and the Word', Robert Cover captures the speculative nature of law: 'Law is the projection of an imagined future upon reality' (1985–6: 1604).[22] The future in the law is 'imagined' in part because of the judge's latitude in inscribing the narrative of his or her choice; it is through the legal ruling that this largely imagined narrative – Cover's 'imagined future' – enacts material effect.[23] As Robin West has asserted, '[L]aw is also an ever-present *possibility*, potentially bringing good or evil into our future' (1985: 146). Both Cover and West use the language of possibility and imagination, raising again the concept of world-building, and imbuing it with a polytemporal quality. The speculative nature of law is the mechanism through which Cover's 'imagined future' is a future that simultaneously reverberates through the actual past, present and future. One decision, issued in a case, becomes precedent for future cases – any single judicial decision therefore both contemplates the previous decisions that came before it and anticipates, by virtue of its enactment, its transformation into a future text on which yet more judicial decisions rest. This moment where the present incorporates the past and becomes the new, slightly different future is the transaction in which the law creates and constantly reaffirms the ritual that acts as a discursive legal tradition. In enacting the ritual, a judge inherits the legal reasoning last rendered by another author-judge, qualifies the narrative with new facts, and re-imagines the legal rule with a difference.

The difference is critical. If legal precedent were fully capable of contemplating every possible permutation or distinction in a legal issue, there would be no need for later decisions on similar questions. In order to modify, or transform, legal precedent without disturbing the weight of legal texts in general, judges face a precarious task. Though they retain the option of public policy-based rulings, it is much more common for judges to invoke factual differences in order to justify new legal rulings or modifications to existing precedent. While Latour suggests that law revisits the conditions of its own birth (a move backwards in time), Cover focuses instead on law's constant visitation of conditions that have not yet occurred. In *The Making of Law*, Latour observes that 'there is now a legal obligation for each new text of law to make a study of the impact that it can have on the other texts of law – a bit as if the law were . . . a second nature, whose transformations are difficult to foresee' (2010a: 65 n. 87). Latour's observation underscores a particular tension in law between the weight of existing law and the spectre of future law.

In this light, law possesses a remarkable propensity for bidirectionality. It both looks backward to its own origination and also looks forward to its future status as history (precedent). Moreover, through this bidirectionality, legal texts acquire new meaning that accrues only from reading them in the context of their temporal shiftiness. Imagine a line of cases, beginning a century in the past and extending into the present, each of which absorbs the earlier cases and produces a slightly modified rendition of the applicable legal rules. It is common to read two decisions from this series as participating in a legal history of sorts. In this reading, the earlier decision is a predecessor, an ancestor, an antecedent to the later case. Likewise, the later decision is considered to be more evolved than its predecessor, a refinement. Each of the two cases are separately reflections of the historical and factual conditions that produced them; together, they represent a relationship whereby the earlier case is somehow responsible not only for the adjudication of its own dispute but also for the formation of the later case. Now imagine that instead of reading these cases chronologically, we interpret them as networked in a polytemporal system that allows them to exist *simultaneously*. By altering this understanding of their relationship to one another, a new, third layer of meaning emerges in which they each anticipate and respond to the other.

At this point it is useful to introduce an example from legal history to offer some context for these claims. In the American legal system, few cases are so well-known as *Scott* v. *Sandford*.[24] In the Dred Scott Decision, the Supreme Court notoriously held that African-Americans had no claim for citizenship and the privileges that accompany citizenship. This decision, though eventually legally overturned by the 14th Amendment, has never been judicially overturned. Therefore, despite the vast implications of the decision – and though the legal principles enunciated within it have been overturned by the Constitution – the Supreme Court never formally invalidated *Scott*. By the time it reached the Supreme Court, the case had already been heard by numerous lower courts; the Supreme Court absorbed both the factual findings from the lower courts in this case, as well as the legal holdings from relevant precedent. This collision of adjudicated facts and legal precedent set the stage on which the Court would promulgate one of its most infamous, most derided opinions.

Because this case concerns mainly definitional questions – the legal definition of 'citizen' in particular – and because it demonstrates an acute awareness of its own futurity, it is a particularly apt exemplar for the issue of legal fact-finding as well as the polytemporality of law. The Court in *Scott* enunciates the facts of the case in a manner that largely proscribes its later legal findings. The Court formulates the central legal issue as follows: 'Can a negro, whose ancestors were imported in this country, and sold as slaves, become a member of the political community formed and brought into existence by the Constitution of the United States, and as such become entitled to all the rights, and privileges, and immunities, guaranteed by that instrument to the citizen? One of which rights is the privilege of suing in a court of the United States in the cases specified in the Constitution.'[25] As a threshold matter, at this point, the Court intertwines the issues of fact and law; the formulation of the legal question before the Court incorporates into itself the recitation of various facts that have been carefully and deliberately formulated. Though this language abstracts Dred Scott himself from the question posed, the Court establishes (1) that he is a Negro; (2) that he is not a member of the political community of the United States (because the Court poses the question in terms of whether or not it is possible for him to *become* such a member); and (3) that, because he is not a member of that political community, he is not currently entitled to any privileges of citizenship.

It is apparent, at this early stage, where the Court is headed in terms of its findings. Though Dred Scott had spent considerable time living in free states,[26] the Court omits this 'fact' from its formulation of the circumstances that control the legal consideration of Scott's claim to citizenship. The Court's definition of Scott – before it has even considered the definition of 'citizen' – omits the word 'free' from any of its framing of the legal issue. Moreover, it establishes him as an outsider, an alien and a stranger to the political community in which he lives. Though the Court also includes a brief recitation of Scott's various travels and owners, the framing of the legal issue strips him of any claim to citizenship before even engaging any formal legal arguments. Significantly, the only noun in that framing that applies directly to Scott is 'a Negro'.

This intermingling of fact and law underscores the operation of law's conceit that the two are entirely separate, and it makes visible law's need to engage in the calculated framing of facts at the moment of adjudication. Facts are not immutable, indisputable *items* but are carefully constructed arguments that advocate for legal principles. To be more precise about the Court's movement in *Scott*, it repackages principles as facts – and then in turn it uses these 'facts' to justify the principles from which it began.[27]

The Court displays an awareness of its own position within history and legal history through its keen consciousness of the opinion's future as history or precedent. In *Scott*, the Court goes through the regular motions of discussing earlier precedent, situating itself along a trajectory of forward-moving legal decisions. It also, however, self-consciously positions itself toward the future, taking full advantage of its own future as precedent. Despite having no legal obligation to do so, the Court opined in *dicta* about the decision's effect on the ability of slaves to exist as other legal subjects in light of the pronouncement that they were incapable of citizenship. This positioning makes logical sense since one of the privileges of citizenship is the right to sue. In deciding *Scott*, the Court considered the implications of this decision in light of the case history, which previously treated as inseparable the right to sue and the capacity to be sued.[28] The Court in *Scott* wrote: 'Besides, we are by no means prepared to say that there are not many cases,[29] civil as well as criminal, in which a Circuit Court of the United States may exercise jurisdiction although one of the African race is a party; that broad question is not before the court.'[30] Thus the Court explicitly leaves open the possibility for African-Americans to be named as civil or criminal defendants – an undeniable nod to the future life of the opinion, in which this language might be cited in support of an attempt to sue or prosecute an African-American.

These different 'shades' of personhood demonstrate the law's capacity to adjudicate the human – is a legal person a citizen, a plaintiff, a criminal defendant? Is it possible for a human to fall into some, but not all, of these categories? The resonance here with 'Bartleby' and *Waiting for the Barbarians* suggests that these different definitions of personhood are connected intimately with a text's structures of world-building. A court's, or an author's, answers to these questions about personhood control the rights and obligations of the characters, or beings of fiction, that inhabit the texts. There is also a way in which the parties to litigation are themselves beings of fiction. Given that legal texts build particular worlds with only the facts deemed relevant to the case at hand, judicial opinions necessarily flatten the characters of the parties; the 'Dred Scott' who appears in *Scott* v. *Sandford* is just one version of the 'Dred Scott' who brought the lawsuit. While Dred Scott the person lived and died, the 'Dred Scott' of the opinion exists as a snapshot frozen in time, yet this version of Scott travels well beyond his natural lifetime into future opinions and statutes.

In *Scott*, the Court reveals its own awareness of the decision's futurity. As noted, its later life has remained technically undisturbed in the chain of Supreme Court opinions that have since issued. Nevertheless, the 14th Amendment to the Constitution, in its extension of citizenship to 'all persons born or naturalized in the United States',[31] legally overrides the judicial holdings in *Scott*. That Amendment, ratified in 1868 (twelve years after the decision in *Scott*), obviously responds directly to the *Scott* holding; in that respect, we might think of *Scott* as the Amendment's precursor or predecessor. However, what happens if we allow *Scott* and the 14th Amendment to *coexist*? In this instance, it becomes clear that the two texts both anticipate and respond to one another. What appears in *Scott* as a pre-emptive argument against the later Amendment appears in that latter text as an answer that – though in a different genre of legal text – tracks the language of the *Scott* opinion. Without referring to African-Americans or former slaves in particular, the Amendment is written in such a way as to deny the possibility of an alternative outcome based on the *Scott* reasoning. In explicitly granting citizenship and its attendant rights to 'all persons . . .' the Amendment both anticipates the argument that African-Americans are not citizens and responds to it by reframing the category definition for citizens entirely. The Constitutional Amendment's structure – 'all persons' – explicitly avoids the dismantling of *Scott*'s legal holdings, subsuming them instead into this new formulation of citizenship.

It is significant that both *Scott* and the Amendment also participate in a dialogue with the remainder of the Constitution. *Scott* turned in no small measure on the reasoning that the original Constitution could not possibly have intended to include African-Americans in the category of 'citizen'. Of course, the Constitution made no such specification about African-Americans. Therefore, what the 14th Amendment was really amending was not the original constitutional language, but the *idea* as expressed in *Scott* that African-Americans were categorically incapable of citizenship. What began as the bidirectionality of law emerges as a rich polytemporality that makes visible law's larger participation in the construction of the human. Once we allow them to coexist, these debates about citizens, subjects and persons across a variety of legal texts assemble a narrative about categories of the human. The narrative consists of competing arguments for the proper conditions under which the state may intervene in the human to 'produce' various categories of persons – the persons themselves have always already existed and persisted as the field on which these battles are fought.

The legacy of *Scott* v. *Sandford* illustrates and complicates Latour's formulation of law as a mode of existence. The polytemporal behaviour of legal texts cuts against conventional understandings of law as moving in only one direction – forward. Latour hints at law's power to resist unidirectional interpretation; *Scott* and its legal relatives make visible the potential for a polytemporal legal network that nevertheless retains the law's momentum as an institution. If law behaves in this manner, does it retain Latour's claim for it as a completely singular mode of existence? This vacillation of law between past and present mystifies the separation between fact and principle, bringing it significantly closer to the mode of fiction. Fiction, for its part, seems to want to meet law halfway. Structures of crossing, such as world-building, open up these questions about the conditions necessary to trace discursive lines across various modes. What emerges is a shared tendency in law and fiction to engage and trouble the notion of the human. If law adjudicates the categorisation of the human, fiction – at the very least – critiques and reimagines the grounds for law's adjudications. However, as suggested by the application of Latour, the relationship between law and fiction is far more complex, nuanced and intimate than action and critique: not only does law require fiction's regional ontology in order to implement legal action, but fiction also imports law's regional ontology in establishing fictional worlds and engaging polytemporal dialogues among texts.

Acknowledgments

The author wishes to thank Colin Dayan and Mark Schoenfield for their guidance and feedback in producing this essay.

Notes

1. *Inquiry* at 53. Hereafter, references to *Inquiry* refer to *An Inquiry into Modes of Existence*.
2. Emphasis in original.
3. I have chosen these texts for the degree to which they each deal in the valences of the human, but also as an example of how these crossings can occur across broad spans of time and genre. At some level, the choice of text is arbitrary; I seek to provide only an exemplar of the mechanism of the law–fiction crossing.
4. Here I use 'beings of fiction' as a term of art in keeping with Latour's use of that term.
5. By definition, all fiction, as imagined text, inhabits non-actualised worlds.
6. One matter of confusion here is Latour's implication that the beings of fiction are the anthropomorphic characters in fiction. An important question, for instance, concerns whether non-human characters within fiction qualify for Latour's definition of 'beings'. The speculative answer, given Latour's earlier work on ANT, is 'yes'. Examples of non-human beings of fiction might include the town of Middlemarch in that novel (as many literary critics have argued that the town itself is a character), so-called 'it narratives', in which a story is told entirely from an object's point of view, or even works such as *The Call of the Wild*, which takes place primarily from a dog's perspective.
7. Here again the comparison to law is instructive. In rendering a judicial opinion, a court likewise must account for plausibility: do the facts presented warrant the court's legal ruling? Has the court adequately accounted for the limitations imposed by existing precedent? Within the world the court has built around the dispute at hand, does the legal ruling disrupt or displace the continuity of the narrative being offered?
8. This 'typeness' could rest on genre (for example, the 'typeness' that we recognise of a lyrical ballad or an epistolary novel) or it could rest on specific themes or characters, as in the two literary texts I address, *Waiting for the Barbarians* and 'Bartleby, the Scrivener'.
9. For example, the titular character in *The Life & Times of Michael K* recalls the character of Josef K. in Kafka's *The Trial*. In his more recent work, Coetzee himself becomes a fictional character in his novels' worlds, as in *Summertime*, a series of fictional interviews conducted following 'the author John Coetzee's death'.

10. Hereinafter, citations to WB refer to *Waiting for the Barbarians*.
11. See below n. 18.
12. A master of chancery was an appointed position as an officer of the court. Though the narrator in 'Bartleby' maintains his own private office, he is nevertheless a government employee and therefore an extension of the court itself. Likewise, the narrator in *Barbarians* is a magistrate judge who actually hears cases in the law court but also presides over more mundane administrative procedures in his territory. Though all lawyers are considered 'officers of the court', the proximity of both narrators to government institutions reinforces the intimacy of their connections to legal institutions.
13. 'Bartleby was one of those beings of whom nothing is ascertainable except from the original sources, and, in his case, those are very small' (Melville 3).
14. The Dead Letter Office was a government office devoted to processing, and destroying, undeliverable mail.
15. While Bartleby is in prison, the narrator also writes that Bartleby was 'greatly to be compassionated' (Melville 41).
16. As I discuss later in this chapter, law effects a similar condition, whereby the representation of facts actually renders facts, rather than merely recording them.
17. In the years before writing *Waiting for the Barbarians*, Coetzee taught nineteenth-century American fiction, including Melville, and he was probably familiar with 'Bartleby'. See Coetzee (1992: 103). Coetzee recalls teaching 'Bartleby' several times in the years prior to writing *Waiting for the Barbarians*, but does not recall whether he maintained a conscious connection to the Melville piece while writing his novel (Coetzee email to F. Barter, 2 March 2014). Nonetheless, this biographical [fact] is not sufficient authorisation for claims of influence or allusion, and indeed my argument does not depend on the existence of a conscious authorial reference.
18. We might contrast hiatus with Latour's conception of hesitation in *The Making of Law* as that 'which produces freedom of judgment by unlinking things before they are linked up again' (2010a: 195). Hesitation is a stage that occurs in the making of individual law, while hiatus refers to a kind of system-wide hesitation in the law.
19. And, to keep fiction on the table, Kafka's *The Trial* follows to terrifying absurdity what fate awaits an ordinary citizen who attempts to challenge the law's intrusion into his life.
20. The susceptibility of facts to representation or misrepresentation underscores the fictive nature of the law; a judge authors an opinion

by making *narrative choices* about how to characterize certain 'facts' and whether to include other 'facts' at all.
21. Federal Rules of Evidence 104(b).
22. Hereafter, citations to 'Violence' refer to 'Violence and the Word'.
23. Cover, in 'Violence' (1611), refers to this process as follows: 'The judicial word is a mandate for the deeds of others.' His use of 'mandate' explicitly speaks the legal text into the future, highlighting both the complex temporal relationships across legal texts and the future material effects brought into being through a judicial decision.
24. *Scott* v. *Sandford*, 60 US 393 (1857).
25. *Scott* at 403.
26. *Scott* at 397–8.
27. Cf. my earlier example of notice in *The Making of Law* (2010a: 89).
28. See *Scott* at 423, citing *Legrand* v. *Darnall*, in which a slave had been permitted to bring suit.
29. This formulation echoes Bartleby's habit of 'preferring not to' do tasks in the office. The Court's use of numerous negatives constitutes its legal holding through negation, much the same way Bartleby's interior can only be constituted, if at all, through negation.
30. *Scott* at 425.
31. *US Const.*, Amend. XIV.

References

Coetzee, J. M. (2010) *Waiting for the Barbarians* [1980]. New York: Penguin.

Coetzee, J. M. (1992) *Doubling the Point: Essays and Interviews*, ed. David Attwell. Cambridge, MA: Harvard University Press.

Cover, Robert (1983–4) 'The Supreme Court, 1982 Term – Foreword: Nomos and Narrative', *Harvard Law Review*, 97: 4–68.

Cover, Robert (1985–6) 'Violence and the word', *Yale Law Journal*, 95: 1601–29.

Dolezel, Lubomir (1998) 'Possible worlds of fiction and history', *New Literary History*, 29: 785–809.

Federal Rules of Evidence, Pub. L. 110–322, §1(a), 122 Stat. 3537, eff. 1 Dec., 2013.

Latour, Bruno (2005) *Reassembling the Social: An Introduction to Actor-Network Theory*. New York: Oxford University Press.

Latour, Bruno (2010a) *The Making of Law: An Ethnography of the*

Conseil d'État, trans. Marina Brilman and Alain Pottage. Cambridge: Polity.

Latour, Bruno (2010b) *On the Modern Cult of the Factish Gods*, trans. Catherine Porter and Heather MacLean. Durham, NC: Duke University Press.

Latour, Bruno (2013) *An Inquiry into Modes of Existence: An Anthropology of the Moderns*, trans. Catherine Porter. Cambridge, MA: Harvard University Press.

Melville, Herman (2003) 'Bartleby the Scrivener' [1853]. Penn State Electronic Classics Series.

Pavel, Thomas (2003) 'Literary genres as norms and good habits', *New Literary History*, 34 (2): 201–10.

Scott v. Sandford, 60 US 393 (1857).

Stowe, Harriet Beecher (2006) *Dred: A Tale of the Great Dismal Swamp* [1856]. Chapel Hill, NC: University of North Carolina Press.

US Constitution., Amend. XIV, Sec. 1.

West, Robin (1985) 'Jurisprudence as narrative', *New York University Law Review*, 60 (2): 145–211.

12

The Strange Entanglement of Jurimorphs

Bruno Latour

Since I have had the privilege of reading all the chapters of this edited volume and since I don't have nearly as much experience of legal practice as most of the authors, I think it is more appropriate that I limit my piece to comments and emendations of what they themselves have done. Actually this is in keeping with my own way of pursuing the inquiry into modes of existence (AIME) that orients several of the arguments developed in those pages. So I will use the material presented in the preceding chapters to offer *contributions* to the inquiry in the same style and format as the many snippets I have assembled over the years and which are still being collated by co-inquirers in the site www.modesofexistence.org. It is through that process of assembling multi-coloured tesserae that the mosaic begins to conjure a more or less coherent figure. By following this habit, I won't have to apologise for the disjointed nature of the following paragraphs. Let's just hope that in the end they will make some sense. (I also apologise for a wide use of the jargon of the AIME book and site to facilitate connections with the material assembled there.)

Before I really start, I want to stress how reassuring it is for me to see that it is actually the mode of existence I call [LAW] that has been so generously commented on by English speaking jurists. By the way, I fully agree with Van Dijk (p. 184) that *Assignation* should really be used to name the mode in question so as to avoid confusing it with the multi-faceted domain of Law, but I feel that the acronym [ASS] will create some unwanted diplomatic frictions![1] So far, it is the only mode where the conversation has progressed to the point of allowing a few fascinating diplomatic encounters.[2] I am really grateful to the authors of this volume and especially to its editor, Kyle McGee. Actually I began to really believe in my own project when reading Kyle's book (2013) on how I should have studied law!

I

I.1

Overall, I take this volume as a confirmation of my claim that [LAW] has resisted much better than all the other modes the crushing weight imposed by an exclusively epistemological definition of what true and false really mean. If I employed the legal institution to offer a tentative protection to the diversity of all the modes before the notion of preposition [PRE] was firmly instituted, it is because everyone seems to agree that law has its own way of defining true and false, although everyone also agrees that such a way does not resemble what is needed for extending the scope of referential statements [REF]. Even if this original way of the law is ridiculed for its formalism, belittled for its archaic dramaturgy, mocked for its wide use of imaginary solutions, it remains the case that it is always recognised that what *holds legally*, well, holds for good – in some fashion to be determined.

In that sense, Law has been respected by the Moderns in a way that has never been the case for divinities, gods or fictions, whose dignity has been so thoroughly crushed that they have been taken as 'things in the head', that is for things which have no existence at all. By contrast, when confronted with law, Double-Click [DC], my nemesis, remains toothless. Because the successes of Science have never intimidated them that much, I don't take it as a coincidence that jurists have understood the AIME project long before any other group of practitioners paid attention to their own modes. I wish others could work on the project as efficaciously as jurists, but I gather that they prefer nursing the wounds that [DC] has inflicted on them instead of rejecting the diktat of its epistemological claims – which, I remind you, crush scientists just as much as they do psychologists, theologians or economists. It is because law has a way to affirm its existence in the world without apologising that it plays a crucial role in the project of the Inquiry. The difficulty is to exactly weigh its ontological dignity.

I.2

That there is an exteriority, an objectivity, or rather an objectity, a solid outside presence of legal ties is essential to reconstitute the strange materiality of what we call 'the social world'. And this is true even when legal statements are taken to be nothing but a formal work of imagination, a *cosa mentale*. The claim of actor-network theory (ANT) is that the social world is what should be explained and not what provides any explanation. In this volume, it is striking to see how much of what, in earlier years, would have been 'put into a social context' before being 'socially explained' is much more powerfully rendered by following the complex detour of legal ties. Class actions against industrial pollution,[3] sovereignty and the 'Honour of the Crown',[4] police disciplining itself,[5] the organisation of hospitals,[6] all those matters of concern are not explained by being put into some bigger frame that would have given sense to the 'black letter law'. On the contrary, it is by paying close attention to the meandering trajectory of what could be called the 'red and bright letter of the law' that some of the aspects of what we render in shorthand as 'the social' are accounted for. In that sense, the *vinculum juris* seems to retrace the path of associations better and more powerfully than any other.

Such an attention marks a paradigm shift from Critical Legal Studies, which, as a rule, has been critical *of law*, but has swallowed the usual definitions of what the social was supposed to be made of without the least critical distance. Thus, for me, this volume is also a vindication that there exists an alternative to critical studies that is no less critical because it takes the ingredients making up the social of sociologists with just as much distance or rather as much *critical proximity* as that of legal formalism. Law has its own social theory and social practice that is much more powerful than the social explanations offering to 'embed' it 'in' society. This point seems to be understood much better by legal practitioners than by sociologists of Law. I subscribe to de Sutter's remark[7] that law possesses an intrinsic philosophy much more articulate than what philosophers have attempted to offer as its 'foundation'. I could say that AIME tries to reverse the effort by philosophers to give law any foundation and to spur jurists into respecting even more the way in which legal ties are able to see through and to perform society.

Of course, to fully grasp the span of the AIME project, this argument should be made for the other modes as well, so that all types of associations (the alternative definition of the 'social' that ANT provides) are being simultaneously granted their own social theory, social practice and specific ontology. Attempts at studying a few embranchments are made in this volume, for politics [POL], for fictions [FIC], a little bit for reference [REF] and techniques [TEC] with some passing allusions to religion, organisation and economics. I will come back to some of these examples to clarify a point of method: the difference between comparing modes (through what I call *crossings*) and comparing *domains* (a hopeless undertaking, in my view). Several chapters offer a good occasion to clarify this confusion of methods and establish on a firmer basis how the sociology of associations could benefit from an analysis of modes (in our jargon the rather undeveloped crossing we call [NET.PRE]).

II

After those two remarks about what I take as a vindication of my attempt to highlight the profound originality of law in the anthropology of the Moderns, I'd like to summarise in my own words what I see as broad agreements among the chapters before shifting to more contentious matters.

II.1

I was pleasantly surprised by the view developed in most of the contributions that there is no way to speak *of the law* without speaking *legally*. What a relief from the obsession around norms and the normativity of law.[8] To expand what I have just said about law's intrinsic philosophy and social theory, law has no reflexivity except its own, or, to put it in another way: *law is its own metalanguage*. Which is true of all the modes, one could say, since this is actually the general principle of method of the whole AIME project: there is no metalanguage, except that of prepositions [PRE] which say nothing at all about any content but just provide the key with which what comes next should be qualified.

Yet the authors in this volume have made this general claim much more specific: what they mean is that either you talk legally about some aspects of the law and you *direct your attention* to one segment of the *legal institution* – be it a case, or a professional expert, or a text, or even a building, an artifact – or you don't speak at all about the [LAW]. (Remember that the acronym [LAW] designates the mode, the enunciation trajectory, the assignation, what Serge Gutwirth would call law2,[9] and that Law, capital L, would code for the domain, that is Law1 in Gutwirth's parlance,[10] or, depending on how we clarify the matter further, the institution – the relation between the two being still in need of some clarification (see below).)

The modest expression 'direct your attention' is here crucial because it means that either you *follow the trajectory* leading to some really existing case or enter into contact with some practitioners, and then you speak legally about the law, or you talk nonsense about something that bears only a vague relation with the 'legal' – no more than some sort of homonymy. Without such a *directionality*, any argument about the normative power of law is groundless. Conversely, this means that any course of action becomes 'legal' [LAW] when it is *streamlined* to direct attention to any part or aspect, past, present or future, of the case law. (I use this expression easily understood in the Anglo-American tradition as a shorthand for the whole material set of entities gathered under the label Law.) McGee, in my view, has offered the best word to describe what those attention-orienting devices look like when they begin to be *streamlined* to pave a trajectory leading to some aspect of the case law: *jurimorph*. Most of the papers in this book deal with how to handle, pile, limit, discard, combine or dismiss jurimorphs. In effect, I am going to expand on McGee's presentation of the problem that he himself says might be a bit obscure:

> Risking a degree of obscurity, we can say that the content of law is not only irremediably bound up with its conditions of enunciation, but is *fully identical with those conditions*. And some of those conditions are packaged in legal devices that we can unwrap and explore. Provisionally, we can define legal devices as assemblages of *mostly non-legal beings* deployed for a legal purpose, namely to give consistency and objectivity, as well as direction, to a specific *legal trajectory*. The device formats, translates the diverse strata bound up in a disputed matter into legal discourse, but while this entails certain technical reductions, it entails no ontological reduction of agency. Technically, the various entities and agents at stake are semiotically refigured – *jurimorphised*. This, we will see, amplifies their agency rather than (or in addition to) diminishing it. (p. 64) (my emphasis)

Either there is a path leading to some aspects of the case law and the jurimorphs can be said to be 'true' in the [LAW] sense of the adjective, or the path is interrupted and there is no way those pointing arrows that direct our attention to the case law can be said to be legally truthful, no matter how much normative virtue they are supposed to carry. Which is just a way of saying that without the institution of law, no statement or action may be said to have legal force. They might gesture toward an absent state of law, or they might exert or resist violence, but there is nothing legal to their course of action. The difference between the two regimes of action can be captured thanks to a somewhat shaky metaphor: attention-orienting-devices-to-some-aspects-of-the-case-law are like signposts leading a cohort of tourists through the Louvre Museum to shoot selfies with the *Mona Lisa* in the background. Either the signposts lead there and they are true to form (in this case the [ORG] type of truth conditions), or they are piled in the office of the janitors and they can't possibly have any attention-orienting role. Either jurimorphs point their arrow-like ends toward the institution of law, and someone paying attention to what they do is moved from one jurimorph to another until they reach some place that we recognise as having some relation with the legal establishment, or they are a disorderly heap like signposts in the janitor's office where they just gather dust. In other words, to speak legally you need a *ground*, to use the word that is closest, according to Richard Janda, to what the French lawyers I studied call *moyen* or *moyen de droit*. And no matter how much you try to materialise and to spatialise this word 'ground', you will never fathom enough how mundane, material and technical law can be. For this reason you would have dealt only with what I have called its *superficiality* or what François Cooren prefers to call its 'dermatological' character! (That law is a question of filaments and membranes will be clear in a minute.)

As Graham Harman shows in his chapter, such a sensitivity to conditions is also true of group-making (what is taken in AIME as the political [POL] Circle) and, I will add, which is even truer of religion [REL]. I will come back to this odd property common to the third group, those who deal with *quasi-subjects*. For the moment, it's sufficient to point out that the three of them gain or lose the meaning of what they say or how they act on the basis of a tiny difference of tone or direction. What Austin had captured with the notion of the *performative*, something so sensitive to the situation that it can be either amazingly fecund, to the point of creating what it says, or totally moot, just adding more verbosities upon verbosities. Any preacher knows that what she says loses its meaning at once if she is not able to transform the millenary old words read during the service as something that renders the Word present in the situation, in this temple, to this flock. And so does any politician (not necessarily a professional of politics) when she feels that she is unable to *roundly* assemble, by the way she behaves and she talks, those to whom she is offering a representation of what they would wish to say and to act if only they were speaking by themselves – except they don't, she does the speaking. But assignation [LAW] is specific in the sense that it has no other content than the institution it directs attention to. The whole history of Churches has been made by people who claim that they are starting afresh to define what should be preached – and most often *against* the established Churches. And the same is true of politics. But someone who would claim to speak legally *beyond*, *above* and *in spite of* what the complex apparatus of the law is able to do, would simply be a fool – or else, as Oliver Wendell Holmes would say, someone who has totally mixed up law with morality, justice or political militancy. The reason law is often deemed 'slow', 'weak', 'conservative', even 'reactionary', is also the reason its truth conditions are so harsh: either you are in it or you are not. It is not about the Church but about the Law that one should say: 'Outside the Law, there is no salvation' – *legal* salvation, that is.

II.2

This is also the reason why it is so tricky to define its autonomy. Because of this truth condition, it is tempting to say that Law consists of a homogeneous *domain* that is clearly delineated by a membrane (as I just said, you are inside it or outside it). And the temptation is irresistible if you consider that law has no other metalanguage than itself. Very few have resisted this temptation, and some, like Niklas Luhmann, have made a systematic doctrine out of it! And yet, a distinction should be made between the *tautological* nature of legal action (now redescribed as the arrow shape of many jurimorphs) and the *autonomy* of a domain that could be called the Law. Several chapters of this volume explore the paradox of a mode that is simultaneously the *most tautological* of all (since it does nothing but connect jurimorphs to one another) and the *least autonomous* of all (since it is able to deal with any entity, to absorb any matters of concern while being sensitive to multiple influences). An argument on law *as a mode* becomes interesting or futile depending on whether it sustains the full tension of that paradox. As soon as you try to weasel out, you lose any chance of defining the conditions of felicity of this most peculiar mode of existence. (And of course, once the specifications have been listed, its paradoxical nature will disappear: we will be dealing with a bona fide mode).[11]

That law is always defined tautologically has been underlined so many times that I can move on quickly. Still, I can't resist commenting on a nice proof of that well known point inadvertently offered by Serge Gutwirth when he claims to provide at last a *non*-tautological definition of law. For him (this volume pp. 130–2) the directionality of jurimorphs is defined because they always point their arrows toward what a judge might possibly decide. He writes:

> The distinctiveness of law lies in the *singular mode in which it seizes cases*. In other words: everyone can practise law, everyone (who is called to do so) can become a legal practitioner, and that is, when *she is moving or moved forward* by the legal regime of enunciation with its many particular constraints and value objects (...). But eventually this way of 'moving forward' and 'making the law' always, and it can't be said enough, amounts to *anticipating* how and what a judge or court would *decide*. (p. 130) (my emphasis)

This is a clear restatement of Holmes's famous dictum that law has no other content than the expectation of judges' 'oracles' (1897: 457–8)[12] and a nice way of summarising law's specificity as what paves trajectories toward some segments of the case law.

But what interests me is the *endnote* appended to this passage. It reads: 'I think it is worth noting that this is a description of law *that avoids the tautology* (cf. Latour 2012: 359)'. I was greatly amused that defining law as anticipation of what *a judge* would decide be considered by such an astute legist as being *less tautological* than the many definitions I refer to in the cited passage where the adjective 'legal' is repeated over and over again to explain to the outsider what the hell law is (six times, for instance, in McGee's quote above!)! Defining what a judge does is just as difficult, as Gutwirth acknowledges, as what 'legal' means in the legal enunciation regime. If anything, defining law by the path potentially able to pass through a *judge's* decision is an even more tautological way than defining law by what is *legally* binding. The connection with the material, corporeal and corporate nature of the legal institution is rendered even stronger. Which is an excellent way, once again, to *ground* any recourse to law. As Serge says: 'it can't be said enough'.

II.3

Clearly tautology is part of the specifications. What about autonomy? Why is it that this sharp membrane between inside and outside remains unable to stop the infinite permeability of legal paths to any sort of influence? In every legal case you take, *extra-judicial* elements immediately begin to multiply. (We will soon see why this is a calamitous adjective.) If law is like a protective roof, it leaks aplenty; if it is a border, it is so badly defended that it is crossed by thousands of migrants! Here is the heart of the matter and a difficult point to make because, as Harman says, it is a problem of *topology*; we seem to lack the conceptual tools for mapping trajectories and differences between modes. Graham's metaphor is apt: 'Luhmann tends to locate each of his "social systems" in a *distinct* professional *place*, Latour conceives of his modes as separate radio *frequencies* all occupying *the same air space*' (p. 50) (my emphasis).

Somewhat uncharitably, I will use one passage of the present volume to clarify this point. In his chapter, David Saunders offers a critique of my book *The Making of Law* by claiming that I stick too much to law as such, to the point of making impossible any reconnection with the social and historical context. This critique is especially puzzling since all the cases I have followed show the constant influence on the decisions of many extra-judicial elements. Indeed, the peculiar body of 'judges' I studied (the French Conseil d'État) is composed of characters who pride themselves for *not* being full-time judges but politicians, managers, militants or administrators who constantly move back and forth from the executive, legislative and judiciary branches (and also the private sector), making a mockery of Montesquieu's division.[13] And yet they engineer statements that are legally binding not *in spite* of but *because* of this complete permeability – at least in their eyes. As I said earlier, this is the paradox that should be kept in full force if we hope to have a chance of detecting law's peculiar mode of existence.

Saunders, however, does not see it that way: on the contrary – he insists on peeling away the superficial and tautological dimension of [LAW] I uncovered and to sandwich it between layers that are said to be deeper or higher – the social forces, the normative dimension – and which cannot be 'aligned' with the law for the same reason that bacon and Gruyère cannot be 'aligned' with the bread above and below. Here is his critique:

> Latour's response is to elevate 'irreduction' to a 'principle'. But with this move, is he himself *closing-off the possibility* that we can be 'anti-reductionist' and yet remain capable of *recognising that in certain social and historical conjunctures* law and legal institutions have been *fully aligned* with religious, political or *other social* institutions and functions? This more historically open form of 'irreduction' is *absolutely precluded* when Latour's 'principle' *forecloses* on the possibility – or the fact – of law *sometimes* being '*reduced*' to or *aligned* with what's taken to be a '*deeper*' or '*higher*' level of reality, be this an *underlying social structure or a set of overlying norms*. (p. 25) (my emphasis)

'Closing off', 'absolutely precluding' and 'foreclosing'! This is harsh, especially when addressed to an actor-network theorist who prides himself on freeing connections in all sorts of ways! In effect, we witness here why the topology that distributes the world by domains cannot possibly account for a mode. Once you have this idea of the social as a certain type of stuff and a certain type of material, when you wish to pour it inside another equally homogeneous domain, they never mix, but at best *sediment* on top of one another. Saunders' topological principle is that of a cassata with, inevitably, the 'social structure' below and the 'norms' 'overlaid' upon them, the domain of Law being squashed in the middle.

The principle of irreduction mocked by Saunders, on the other hand, draws upon a totally different topology. If there are no extra-judicial factors in accounting for legal decisions, it is because everything in law is extraneous! This is exactly why McGee's term jurimorph is so apt for capturing what is going on: *everything in law is extra-legal and streamlined to pave the trajectory* of moving toward the law or being moved by the law. If we return to the janitor of the Louvre Museum, we easily understand that his signposts are made of cardboard, paper or zinc and that this extraneous materiality doesn't 'absolutely preclude' or 'foreclose the possibility' of being streamlined to act as signposts for tourists looking for the *Mona Lisa*. It is the opposite that would be surprising: how would a signpost work without the standing it gets from the substance of paper, cardboard or zinc? Similarly, what else could law be made out of *if not out of extra-legal elements*? Law is what happens to extra-legal features when they are jurimorphed! To give shape to something, that is to 'morph' it, you need this thing there first.

This is why it is more than an understatement to 'recognise *that in certain social and historical conjunctures* law and legal institutions have been *fully aligned* with religious, political or *other social* institutions and functions'. Here is a clear topological mistake. It is *constantly* the case and at all points that law is bound to history and society, but it is never a question of 'alignment'. Just like signposts are *continuously* made of cardboard, paper or zinc and not at some point or in a certain layer. What Saunders does not get is that the difficulty of 'aligning' law with 'social structure' and 'overlying norms' is precisely due to what the irreductionist social theory of actor-network has been fighting all along. Once you accept the sociology of the social handed down by (Durkheimian) sociologists, all phenomena disappear from view and you are left with mysterious puzzles to distribute the material into distinct pots much like Luhmann had to do. It is such a topology that creates the amalgams that 'absolutely foreclose' any anthropology of the Moderns. Saunders and I are not using the same definition of what it is to connect, to align and to trace. The failure of Critical Legal Studies – and critical thought more generally – to make more than a dent in the practice of Law has no other explanation: the topology they use is so far removed from that of practitioners that it passes over them like rain on a duck's plumage.

By the way, this a nice confirmation that the two projects – ANT and AIME – that some people have difficulty reconciling pertains, from day one, to the same enterprise [NET.PRE]: without redescribing sociology as the science of associations – and not of the 'social' – it's impossible to see why it is so crucial to define precisely the different ways to *connect* associations – precisely what modes of existence do well.[14] Jurimorphs are simply one of those ways of building associations entangled within many others.

II.4

I have to concede that this alternative topology, that is so obvious for practitioners and so bizarre for commentators influenced by sociologists of the social, is more difficult to receive in Law than elsewhere. The three modes that I have listed under the label of 'third group' share this same property of being made entirely of 'extraneous' material. It is actually why I call them *quasi-subjects*: they morph or they streamline elements, entities, matters of concern that come from elsewhere[15] generating some of the constituents of what we used to call 'subjectivity'.[16] It is also why, when you begin to analyse them, you feel some form of disappointment at how little substance they carry. And yet, it is obvious in politics as well as in religion that those two domains are a hotchpotch of totally disjointed features vaguely assembled so that it is very hard to take them for homogeneous sets. Just witness the endless fights political scientists and students of religion have to wage simply to define what is common to their respective fields. If Law gives the appearance of a real domain (and that might excuse Luhmann's as well as Saunders's cassata metaphysics) it is precisely for the reason well-articulated in this book by the dispute between Gutwirth and McGee about the right extent of the Law. Here too we come upon another discussion about the limit between outside and inside, or rather between past and present.

It is risky for an amateur to offer a settlement to such a technical controversy, but it seems to me that once you accept the notion of jurimorphs, both parties agree with one another more than they think. The more law develops, the more it populates the world with jurimorphs, to the point where you end up inhabiting an ecosystem where every aspect is made of arrow-pointing entities, some still closely connected to a judge's decision (Gutwirth's position), others removed by so many steps that the judge's presence is made totally invisible (McGee's and Susan Silbey's position). The two arguments are rendered comparable once you begin considering the *number* of jurimorphs that have to be aligned for any juridical trajectory to circulate. And the only difference between the two positions is how many steps you are prepared to take. If I click without thinking on the 'Agree' button at the bottom of a new version of some software, or if I slow down because of a speed bump, I might feel far away from any bench; except that, at some point in the past, lawyers had been much closer to some adversarial encounters where it is very plausible that lawyers, attorneys, judges and prosecutors could have been seated. If not, I would *not be asked to* click on the button or I would *not be forced* to slow down to save my car's shock absorbers instead of obeying the 'slow' sign. If they are there, some decision has been made.

A metaphor might help here: everyone knows that a magnetised needle indicates *directly* where the North pole roughly lies; but, in addition, geologists know, through very elaborate and *indirect* steps, how to extract from any rock that's part of the ocean floor the direction of the magnetic pole at the time when it solidified out of the magma.[17] (In the long history of the Earth, the magnetic poles keep reversing dramatically – much like jurisprudence!) In the same way, every element touched by the morphing activity of law freezes in a shape that most of the time – but not always – keeps the arrow-like quality typical of law even long after the 'passage' of the legal fluid. But in that case, it requires more work to detect the morphing than when you are filing for a divorce or being summoned to a criminal court. So in the end, Law1 and law2, to use Gutwirth's classification, are the same, just as Science-made is the same as Science-in-action, but simply taken at different moments in their process of crystallisation.[18]

What gives a certain domain-like tonality to the practice of law (to the point that observers are always tempted to speak of the Law with a capital L) is that no matter how remote the jurimorphs are from one another they establish connections *only* with other jurimorphs – just like Lego blocks. So, from the same viewpoint, you can either detect only legal ties – the connections – or only extralegal elements – the blocks. And since there is no other *content* to the legal mode than establishing this sort of continuity, it is just as true to say that it 'covers' everything – through connections – or that it is almost invisible – when you look at the blocks. This is why speaking about legal matters is always a matter of dealing with membranes and filaments. If ever the metaphor of a net had a meaning it is with law since its span is just as striking as its emptiness. It is just as true to say that it is the best totalising instrument since, from any point, you may call all the other arguments to help you out, and yet what is coming to your rescue is only the tiny thread of *vinculum juris* – nothing else, nothing more.

This is also why there is never any way to agree about the 'fragile force of law' since it is either amazingly strong (jurimorphs snap nicely into one another and allow claims to travel along vast distances to the astonishment of observers) or amazingly weak (it says nothing substantial about any state of affairs and fails miserably to 'defend civilisation against evil' to the great lamentation of the same observers). How odd to consider that, of all the modes, it is the one most easily confused with a domain whereas its ability to reign, cover, swallow, absorb, replace what it is supposed to 'dominate' is so limited. If it is true that the Romans were the first to have extracted this mode as such, it is easy to understand their enthusiasm for a mode so powerful and yet so devoid of content. No! A mode so powerful because it is so astutely devoid of any other content than its connectedness through every possible entity.

The reason why it is so important to articulate a topology made of membranes and filaments is that it provides a way to overcome the *disappointment* that strikes so many critiques at this slow and meandering account of legal practices. 'Where is justice?' one could ask. How would you fight exploitation and domination with such a weakened, slow, limited, down-to-earth definition of law? Where is law 'speaking truth to power'? Where is morality? And yet, what could pass for a deflationary move is not a return to 'black letter law', to positivism and to formalism. Attention to the 'red and bright letter of the law' leads very precisely to the *crossings* with the other modes. Not expecting too much from Law is the first move necessary to differentiate the many components making up this apparent domain. However, the whole project of the Inquiry is to prepare the second move: searching for an alternative *institution* that would respect its peculiar ontology. It is at this point that diplomacy could begin. Since we are not there yet, let me conclude on a few more remarks on how to pursue the task of disamalgamation.

III

III.1

One of the advantages of AIME, in my view, is that it allows for an extension of the comparative method until we begin to be articulate enough to grant each mode its exact ontological weight without always resorting to the two conventional templates: objects-out-there-in-the-world and ideas-humans-have-in-their-head. The distinction I just made between an analysis in terms of modes and an analysis in terms of domains could be clarified even further by commenting on the nice final chapter of this volume on what could have been the crossing coded [FIC.LAW] in our jargon. Naturally, we would go nowhere were we to start with a

The Strange Entanglement of Jurimorphs   345

'collision between the actual world and the possible world'. This would be trying to shoehorn all entities into the two usual templates of object and subject. 'Actual world' has no more meaning than 'underlying social structure' or 'overlying norms'. Those expressions are tantamount to saying 'complex amalgams of so many things that we abandon the idea of disentangling them'. The ANT and AIME joint project is to replace those meaningless terms by actionable and negotiable expressions. This is what I mean by shifting from modernism to anthropology of the Moderns.

Contrary to Law, fiction [FIC] is not a domain at all but what infuses all the subsequent modes because of its very simple phenomenon that semioticians have called *shifting* or *shifting out*.[19] Among the enterprises that make full use of this ability, the Western tradition has developed a specialised art form that we can call literature. Once this art form is established, it is fairly possible to bring any other text to resemble or bear upon literature. However, when this is done, it is what could be called a *fictionalisation* of whatever has been brought in.[20] The key to interpreting the course of action [PRE] has been shifted from [LAW] to [FIC]. Take, for instance, a passage of Cooren's case. Read as fiction [FIC], you immediately detect how much it depends on a *previous work of figuration*.

> [53] The litigation *raises* two questions:
> - Has the plaintiffs' right to appeal *expired*?
> - Were the plaintiffs erroneously remunerated as intermediary resources from 1 April 2001 to 4 December 2003? Did they *qualify* as intermediary resources before 1 April 2001? (pp. 257–8)

The decision could not even begin to be understood without recruiting and streamlining a large number of actors – the litigation, plaintiff's right, intermediary resources – and actions – raising, expiring, remunerating, qualifying – shifted out and delegated to different spatial, temporal and 'actantial' roles – 'plaintiffs' transformed into 'intermediary resources' on '4 December 2003'. It is actually the multiplicity of those shiftings out that Cooren underlines with his concept of 'ventriloquism'. I have myself done this extensively with scientific literature, taking it out of the [REF] key to reveal how much it depends on [FIC] to succeed in its referential work.[21]

Such fictionalisation, however, cannot maintain the other key in focus; it's like taking a close-up photograph with the result that the background will be blurred. This is clearly the case with Barter's example. The comparison established by her chapter works nicely but only among texts seized *qua texts*. To the corpus selected out of novels in which characters have been given the figure of judges or 'master of chancery',[22] has been added one other item written by a collective author known as 'the Supreme Court'. The fact that some items come from novelists and another one from judges is immaterial here since they have been made part of the same corpus by coming upon the terrain of literature. But through such a move, the 1857 US Supreme Court decision in *Dred Scott* v. *Sandford* has been lifted out of the legal trajectory and, if we build upon what has been said above, has quickly lost its quality as a jurimorph (except for the para-textual elements – italics and coded reference – so important for eventually redirecting the argument back toward the source). From then on, the analysis *does not compare literature and law* but characters in literature whose writers employ vastly different styles, effects and narrative strategies. It is of course of great interest to compare those little world-building activities, but the difference between, let's say Melville and McEwan or Coetzee, are just as great as those between McEwan and the Supreme Court. All along, we remain inside literature, at no point moving on to law. Here again fiction does not trace a border with law in the way Germany does with Belgium. Fiction is inside every single element of law just as much as the cardboard, paper or zinc remains 'inside' the signposts I mentioned above. To use Graham's metaphor, you have moved the radio tuner and captured another frequency 'in the same air space'.

To detect the crossing [FIC.LAW] we would need to get some interference between the two modes, a category mistake or at least some hesitation as to which key to use, which radio frequency to select. Cases of plagiarism brought to court would offer a symmetric case from the one studied by Barter, the key being shifted, this time, from [FIC] to [LAW] by clerks poring over a corpus of novels to detect whether or not the intertextual exchanges qualify as a fraud – while the lawyer for the defence would plead the rights of 'artist imagination'. And it would be the case, again, with the very notion of 'author'.[23] It would also be the case, but in reverse, if an artist not only fictionalises but this time *aestheticises* a text of law, making the viewer sensitive to the style, to the typography, to the materiality of the inscription, and in doing so points out the oscillation or the vibration between form and matter which is one of the odd features of beings of fiction. This is the case, for instance, of Armin Linke's book on the Law Courts.[24] Such an aestheticisation is often used to underline the 'melodrama' of the theatre of law, a common enough cliché of critical discourse, transforming the jurimorphs into so many props and characters of some pageantry on stage. Examples could be multiplied, but what should be clear is that the presence of fiction throughout the legal trajectory does not allow us to confuse the two because law *streamlines* and jurimorphs all characters it gets from fiction to get at its own goal – keeping the shifted frames connected even though it is drastically impossible to do so.[25] As soon as this goal is interrupted, law stops being law. The same phenomenon happens with reference [REF], whose use of fiction is just as extensive as that of law, but which streamlines all the characters to achieve a different goal, this time access to the far away – a task just as impossible but which the referential chain succeeds in doing nonetheless. In that sense, it is just as accurate to say that fiction and law never connect – since the shifting out is reversed – as to say that assignation [LAW] totally depends on fiction, just as much as does reference [REF].

III.2

Another deamalgamation that would be of great interest is the one alluded to in the fascinating chapter by Mariana Valverde and Adriel Weaver on the 'honour of the Crown'. Here we witness judges juggling with politics, morality, religion and law in the most clever and devious way.[26] I often wonder why the modes in AIME have assembled themselves by groups of three, as if it was imposed by some mysterious 'system' or by some numerological trick. It is hard, however, not to recognise the filiation, in the history of the Moderns, that the three modes making up the third group of quasi-subjects have with one another. A fascinating feature of most of the chapters in this volume is that they seem to accept the idea that normativity is not at all a feature of assignation [LAW] but a multimodal term if any is. I concur. What is called normative power is the list of all the conditions of felicity of all the modes added to one another, beginning with those of reproduction [REP] all the way to those of morality [MOR]. Thus any understanding of the 'state of law', this most ambiguous term, should be preceded by tearing apart the various threads making up what 'enforces' it. Any law enforcement relies on a relay race where so many different entities are passing the baton to so many teams made of so many different characters that something is immediately missed when an analysis is made in terms of layers or domains.[27] Here again we need to be able to define the nature of the connections [PRE] without losing sight that they have the shape of networks [NET].

Such an enterprise is especially important to reopen the question of *sovereignty*. If there is one amalgam that precludes the analysis in philosophy, in sociology as well as in economics and political science, it is the State, this makeshift pile of arcane emblems. Politics, law and religion have so greatly exchanged their properties that it is very difficult to disentangle them and the last thing you want to have is a 'theory of the State'. 'State', like 'society', is not what provides an explanation but what should be explained, especially when the question of enforcing the law is being raised. The modernist obsession with the sovereignty of the State has been a way to settle the religious wars of the sixteenth century by way of some sort of armistice rather than providing the time necessary to arrive at a peace treaty. To stop atrocities, another monster has taken the stage but without allowing any settlement of what should be expected from religion [REL], what should be expected from politics [POL] and what should be expected from law [LAW].[28] The productions of the three modes have been compressed into the Leviathan rendered even more monstrous by the added fight between State and Market. The State has become the most obscure amalgam of all.

This is why there is something reassuring in the calamitous irruption of ecological mutations. At least the bundle of features stuffed into the inflated Body of the State can no longer stay there. Because ecology brings back the question of *where* the State resides, it also breaks down the abstract, utopic and simply confused *absence of place* over which sovereignty is supposed to reside.[29] The Leviathan is still around but it resembles an exploded Body Politic. If it is so important, as this volume shows, not to ask too much from assignation [LAW], it is because a mode succeeds much better at doing only one thing well. In the general reconfiguration of the older questions of sovereignty impacted by the intrusion of Gaia, what we should expect law to do is to stick to jurimorphs and to reopen the key question of what it is for a claim to have a *ground*. Disappointment in what politics, law and religion may achieve is essential to regain some modicum of hope.

Acknowledgments

English kindly corrected by Michael Flower. This research has been carried out thanks to a grant of the European Research Council, politiques ERC 269567.

Notes

1. In an older version of the project law was defined in French as LIAISON, religion as PRESENCE, politics as RASSEMBLEMENT, fiction as ENVOI, attachment as EMPRISE and organisation as REPARTITION, which would have probably been better. I now regret having created a confusion between domains and modes for the sake of not introducing jargon.
2. Richard Janda from the McGill Law School in March 2014 had kindly hosted the AIME team, together with anthropologists Eduardo Kohn and Peter Skafish, in what has been one of a few diplomatic encounters where the *Middle Ground* has really been drawn in the way anticipated in the Inquiry. We are still debriefing this amazing experience. See modesofexistence.org/mcgill-workshop-on-diplomacy-atelier-a-mcgill-sur-la-diplomatie/. Several of the authors chaired by McGee participated in an AIME meeting in Paris in April 2014.
3. McGee: 'One unique *quality* of law is that it is well-suited to *forging connections* between actions and harms despite insurmountable disagreement between those summoned by a common divisive issue' (this volume, p. 71).
4. Valverde and Weaver: 'Thus the honour of the Crown functions to impose duties on government even in the absence of – or prior to the establishment of – the kind of specific aboriginal interest that would be sufficient to give rise to a fiduciary obligation' (this volume, p. 103).
5. De Bellaing: 'However, their investigations can be understood as explanatory tests of what is at stake in that social process that the police's use of force is, insofar as the investigators manage to decide, and insofar as they must, somehow, decide, produce a work in the form of a file capable of stabilising competing, unstable versions of truth, through a meticulous and comparative description of the disputed scene' (this volume, p. 233).

6. Cooren (this volume).
7. Laurent de Sutter (2009) *Deleuze: La pratique du droit*. Paris: Michalon.
8. Normativity, in AIME, is a multimodal term since each mode is defined by its own felicity and infelicity conditions. Even morality [MOR] cannot claim hegemony over the notion of norms – nor does law.
9. Gutwirth: 'Now, they will invariably consist of an enumeration of legal professionals: judges, advocates, attorneys, public prosecutors, paralegals, the jurists in the legal services of enterprises and administrations, bailiffs, registrars and so forth, not the political representatives that populate the representative assemblies nor the members of bodies with legislative powers, but all those who are involved in the production not of rules but of decisions, among which the judges and the members of courts are the most emblematic examples' (this volume, p. 129).
10. Gutwirth: 'Law1 is thus intimately interwoven with government and governance, economy, power balances, geopolitics, ethics, religion, history – it carries, expresses and imposes the content and values of the material sources – but nonetheless, it remains persistently characterised as "law"' (this volume, p. 128).
11. Such is the test for every mode: that it is defined enough on its own terms that it does not have to bow to others, or apologise for not being like the others, but that, on the contrary, it is now able to shed its own light on all the modes. Exactly what was impossible when every entity was made visible at the wavelength of [DC].
12. Holmes: 'These are what properly have been called the oracles of the law. Far the most important and pretty nearly the whole meaning of every new effort of legal thought is to make these prophecies more precise, and to generalize them into a thoroughly connected system' (O. W. Holmes (1897) 'The path of the law', *Harvard Law Review*, 10: 457).
13. To the point that the European Court decided that *commissaires du gouvernement* are not really part of the judiciary.
14. People who have been interested in ANT sometimes feel 'betrayed' by the AIME project as if it was a return to the social theory they have learned to abandon without realising that the two projects have been set concurrently.
15. The AIME project is so far organised in four groups: those who totally ignore the subject/object relation; those who are said to be object-oriented; the third group which is subject-oriented (and to

which [LAW] belongs); and the fourth which gathers the modes which establishes complex relations between objects and subjects.

16. In AIME, subjectivity is not the starting point of the analysis, but what is generated by each mode, each mode providing a different layer or tone or flavour or constituent of what it is to be subject.

17. By the way, contrary to de Sutter's bizarre critique in his chapter, geologists know perfectly how to reverse what is magma and what is solidified rock, which is apparently impossible for philosophers who want to have 'plasma' on the one hand and 'trace' on the other without realising they are exactly the same but at two stages in time. To try to distinguish the two would be like asking if a fishing net is made of threads or of voids!

18. Gutwirth: 'The interplay between values and their institution, transposed upon the relations between law2 and Law1, shines a light on different aspects of law. First, it explains the complex conjunction between the age old and rather stable regime of enunciation of law2 (or [LAW]) that subsisted and persisted since the Romans, and the always changing (sometimes even volatile) normativity and rules of Law1 which are dependent on a lot heterogeneous factors and their common history' (this volume, p. 140).

19. modesofexistence.org/ime/en/voc/334

20. The pivot table is a good site to follow how the key of one mode may be used to read (that is, to specifically *mis*read) all the others. In the same way that it is possible to read all the modes as examples of law – juridicisation – including reproduction [REP.LAW], it is possible to read all modes as cases of fiction [FIC]. It is the task of preposition [PRE] to counteract those attempts at hegemony by showing how they are made and what they reveal or hide of the interpreted mode. This is what I mean by extending the comparative method inside the anthropology of the Moderns.

21. More tellingly in the (in)famous paper on Einstein's little book on relativity (Bruno Latour (1988) 'A relativist account of Einstein's relativity', *Social Studies of Science*, 18: 3–44), written, by the way, the same year as *Science in Action* proving, once again, how ANT and AIME have worked together all along; and also Deleuze on delegated characters cited in AIME at pp. 250–1.

22. A nice recent example could be Ian McEwan's (2014) *The Children Act*, London: Doubleday, where the main character is Fiona, a London judge.

23. Mario Biagioli, and Peter Galison (2002) *Scientific Authorship: Credit and Intellectual Property in Science*. London: Routledge.

24. Aestheticisation brings the topic at hand inside the domain of art forms, a limited and recent subset of what could be fictionalised. An interesting example of such a hybrid study has been made by Gustav Kalm and Robert Hamacher on the aesthetic dimension of law firm offices and lawyers' demeanours (modesofexistence.org/ime/en/cont/13915/).
25. McGee puts it best:

> Examples of the problem are easy to imagine: placed before me is a document containing my name signed in ink, dated May 23, 2008 in Philadelphia, Pennsylvania. In the non-legal modes – say, that of the persistence of my body [REP] – this document's contents do not coincide with the actually existing individual sitting at his desk writing these words. The document reflects a series of shiftings-out. The 'author' of the document, or one of its signatories, *has my name but is not me*: presently, this 'author' looks in fact like a 'character' in another drama. The time and place are also entirely different: it is not May 2008, I am not in Philadelphia. There are, in other words, a series of *disjunctions* between the figures populating this document and the author of the present text. It is only in the enunciative regime of law that these disjunctions are *bridged*. By a series of legal mediations, the document's figures—which are or seem to be beings of fiction [FIC] – are connected to the enunciative level that I occupy at any subsequent time, with the consequence that, thanks not only to this document but also, and more importantly, *to the legal means of connection*, I am legally married to another that has signed her name, wisely or unwisely, to the very same document. By way of law, this specific sequence of enunciative planes is identified and selected from a staggering multiplicity of others. They are *telescoped* and made to *coincide*. (Kyle McGee (2014) *Bruno Latour: The Normativity of Networks*, New York: Routledge, p. 214, my emphases)

26. A beautiful example of the [POL.LAW] crossing mentioned by Harman can be found in the way judges take it upon themselves to use law for the benefit of the political Circle in Valverde and Weaver: 'And addressing the question of why the government of the day – today's "Crown" – should be obligated to do things not contained in any treaty and not arising from the law of fiduciary duty, the answer given is that the Crown of today, judges feel, has to make an effort to repair *"the ongoing rift in the national fabric"* (Manitoba Métis

para. 140) that the history of aboriginal-white relations has created' (this volume, p. 111) (my emphasis).
27. This is why de Bellaing's chapter is so interesting on the detailed manner by which the law enforcement quality control of law enforcement itself may be achieved. If you 'put it into context' (Society, the State) the efforts of policemen to police themselves become incomprehensible.
28. Eric Voegelin [1952] (1987) *The New Science of Politics* (new foreword by Dante Germino). Chicago: University of Chicago Press.
29. Kenneth Olwig (2011) 'The Earth is not a globe: landscape versus the "globalist" agenda', *Landscape Research*, 36 (4): 401–15.

List of Contributors

Faith Barter is a PhD candidate in the Department of English at Vanderbilt University. Her dissertation examines the relationship between literary and legal personhood in the antebellum United States. In particular, her work focuses on how black discursive practices structured contemporary legal narratives, even while those legal narratives sought to dismantle or erase black subjectivity. Prior to beginning her PhD programme, she practised law at a global law firm.

David S. Caudill is Professor and Arthur M. Goldberg Family Chair in Law at Villanova University, where he teaches expert evidence, sports law and property. After law school, he clerked for the Hon. John Brown of the US Court of Appeals for the Fifth Circuit, and then practised law in the US for several years. After receiving his PhD in philosophy from the Vrije Universiteit, Amsterdam in 1989, he joined the Washington & Lee University law faculty from 1989 until 2005 and has also taught as visiting faculty at the University of Texas, Southern Illinois University, Cardozo School of Law and the University of Florida. He is currently a Senior Fellow at the University of Melbourne Law Faculty in Australia and is the author of *Lacan and the Subject of Law* (1997), *No Magic Wand: The Idealization of Science in Law* (2006) and *Stories about Science in Law: Literary and Historical Images of Acquired Expertise* (2011). His research interests focus on law and science studies, and law and literature.

François Cooren is Chair and Professor of the Département de communication at the Université de Montréal. He has authored several books on communication theory and conversation analysis, including *Action and Agency in Dialogue: Passion, Incarnation,* *and Ventriloquism* (2010) and *The Organizing Property of Communication* (2000).

Laurent de Sutter is currently a Senior Fellow at the Käte Hamburger Center for Advanced Study in the Humanities, Bonn, Germany. Author of several books, including most recently *Après la loi* (2014), *Métaphysique de la putain* (2014) and *Théorie du trou* (2013), his work spans a broad array of themes, including legal and political theory, cinema, pornography, law and literature, and law and science studies.

Serge Gutwirth is Professor and Director of the Law, Science, Technology, and Society (LSTS) programme at the Vrije Universiteit, Brussels. He has authored many legal-theoretical articles as well as numerous empirical studies in technology and privacy law, and has edited or co-edited several collections of legal research into European privacy law.

Graham Harman is Distinguished University Professor at the American University in Cairo. He is the author of twelve books, most recently *Bells and Whistles: More Speculative Realism* (2013) and *Bruno Latour: Reassembling the Political* (2014). He is also Editor of the Speculative Realism book series at Edinburgh University Press and Co-Editor (with Bruno Latour) of the New Metaphysics series at the Open Humanities Press.

Bruno Latour is Professor at the Institut d'études politiques. He is the author of studies falling into a number of genres, including science studies (*Laboratory Life*, *The Pasteurization of France*, *Science in Action*, *Pandora's Hope*), technology studies (*Aramis*), philosophical anthropology (*We Have Never Been Modern*, *An Inquiry into Modes of Existence*), religion (*Rejoicing*) and, of course, law (*The Making of Law*), among others.

Kyle McGee is a legal practitioner struggling to find a few hours per year in which to do philosophy. He is the author of *Bruno Latour: The Normativity of Networks* (2014) and several articles, as well as co-editor of *Deleuze and Law* (2012).

Cédric Moreau de Bellaing is Assistant Professor, Department of Social Sciences at the École Normale Supérieure. He is the author of articles appearing in *Politix*, *Déviance et société*, *La Revue française de science politique* and *Genèses*. He is currently co-holder, with Dominique Linhardt, of a collective research programme entitled *No War, No Peace? The 'Knots' of Violence and Law in the Formation and Transformation of Political Orders*.

David Saunders is Professor Emeritus at Griffith University. A specialist in early modern European political and legal thought, he is the author of a number of books weaving together law, religion, history and politics, including *Anti-Lawyers: Religion and the Critics of Law and State* (1997) and *On Pornography: Literature, Sexuality, and Obscenity Law* (1993).

Mariana Valverde is Professor of Criminology at the University of Toronto. She is the author of a variety of critical socio-legal studies, including *Diseases of the Will* (1998), *Law's Dream of a Common Knowledge* (2003), *Everyday Law on the Street* (2012), and most recently, *Chronotopes of Law* (2015).

Niels van Dijk is a Lecturer in the Law Department at the Université Saint-Louis, Brussels, and Visiting Fellow in the Law Department at the London School of Economics. He has authored several articles on themes encompassing law, privacy and technology. His first monograph, a philosophical ethnography of law in practice, is forthcoming.

Adriel Weaver is a graduate student in the Centre for Criminology and Sociolegal Studies at the University of Toronto. Weaver also practises law at a firm specialising in aboriginal law.

Index

Arnot, D., 98, 107
Attwell, D., 311
Austin, J. L., 178, 235, 242, 250, 336

Badiou, A., 199, 204
Bagehot, W., 118–19
Bakhtin, M., 246
Barshack, L., 100
Benjamin, W., 102, 111
Berlusconi, S., 32
Binnie, J., 99, 107–8, 115–16
Bodin, J., 28, 117
Bogost, I., 199
Borrows, J., 118
Bourdieu, P., 2, 238, 274
Boyle, R., 283
Brassier, R., 198
Bruner, J., 260
Bryant, L., 199
Burke, K., 245

Callon, M., 13, 274, 286–7, 289ff.
Campos, P., 30–1
Cartwright, C. J., 105
Cayla, O., 127, 131–2, 133
chains of obligation, 48, 51, 57, 75, 78
Cicero, 135
Coetzee, J. M., 14, 305, 311ff., 346
Coke, E., 98, 105

conditions of felicity *see* felicity conditions
Cover, R., 307, 321
critical legal studies, 2, 165, 281, 308, 333, 341

Daubert v. Merrell Dow Pharmaceuticals, Inc., 273ff., 294–5, 297
Deleuze, G., 9, 10, 11, 122, 200, 204, 237–8
Derrida, J., 111, 235, 237, 239, 246, 270
Descartes, R., 204
descendentalism, 5–6
Dewey, J., 43, 70, 216, 232
Dicey, A. V., 28, 95, 114
Dingpolitik, 34
diplomacy, 34
Dolezel, L., 306
double-click, 40, 42, 52, 55, 63
Duguit, L., 28
Dyzenhaus, D., 27

Engster, D., 117
Ewick, P., 122

factish, 319
felicity conditions, 44, 162, 174, 177, 184, 242–3, 251, 304, 338, 347
Foucault, M., 43, 53, 148, 237
Fuller, S., 280–1, 291–2, 293

Gaia, 6, 7, 22, 34–6, 348
Galilei, G., 283
Garcia, T., 199
Garfinkel, H., 12, 235, 241, 246
Goldblatt, D., 236, 245–6
Goldstein, R., 279
Goodstein, D., 274ff., 287, 297
Grant, I. H., 198
Greenberg, D., 285
Greimas, A. J., 78, 260
Gross, P., 275
Grotius, H., 28

Habermas, J., 53
Hacking, I., 236, 285
Hands, D. W., 285–6
Harding, S., 84, 283
Hart, H. L. A., 2
Hayek, F., 52
Hegel, G. W. F., 28
Heidegger, M., 35–6, 178–9, 197
Hobbes, T., 28, 52, 53, 57, 117
Holmes, O. W., 78, 130, 206, 337, 338

instauration, 8, 78, 131, 306ff.
international relations, 57

James, W., 78, 131
Janda, R., 336
jurimorph, 7, 14, 64–84, 131, 150, 335ff.
jusnaturalism *see* legal naturalism

Kant, I., 28
Kantorowicz, E., 94–5, 114
Kleinman, D. L., 288–9
Kozinski, J., 295, 297
Kuhn, T., 174

La Fontaine, 165
Lamer, C. J., 99
legal formalism, 2, 15, 238, 268, 332–3, 344
legal naturalism, 56, 57
legal pointillism, 10, 168, 177, 181

legal positivism, 2, 56, 57, 138, 344
Leibniz, G. W., 10, 169
Levitt, N., 275
libido judicandi, 3, 78
Linke, A., 347
Lippmann, W., 43, 53
Llewellyn, K., 180
Loughlin, M., 28–9
Luhmann, N., 25, 50, 63, 236, 238, 337, 339, 341, 342

Macdonald, J., 109–10
McEwan, I., 346
McGarity, T., 285, 297
Machiavelli, N., 43
McLachlan, C. J., 99
Maitland, F. W., 95
Marx, K., 52, 53
Meillassoux, Q., 198–9
Melville, H., 14, 305, 311ff., 346
Mirowski, P., 13, 274, 284, 286ff.
Montesquieu, B., 339

neoliberalism, 13, 286, 289, 292
Nietzsche, F., 54, 237
nomos, 307

Pavel, T., 305–6
Pickering, A., 242
Pierce, C. S., 245
plasma, 11
Pocock, J. G. A., 29–30
political circle, 39–43, 52, 54, 56, 57
Pope Benedict XVI, 54
Popper, K., 282
positivism *see* legal positivism
Potter, J., 284
Pratter, J., 75, 77–80, 81
publics, 41, 43, 53, 65–6, 68, 70
Pufendorf, S., 28

Rabinow, P., 282
Rip, A., 285
Rose, N., 237

Rousseau, J.-J., 52, 81
Rubin, E., 28

Schiavone, A., 132, 138
Schlag, P., 30–1, 36
Schmitt, C., 43, 53, 54, 57
Scirica, J., 79–80
Scott v. Sandford, 14, 305, 322ff., 346
Searle, J., 250
Shapin, S., 275, 276–7, 285
Silbey, S., 122, 342
Smith, S., 30
Socrates, 52
Sokal, A., 275–6
Souriau, E., 248
Stengers, I., 9, 130, 131, 150
Stephan, P., 287, 297
Stowe, H. B., 309, 320
Strauss, L., 53

tautology, 66, 164, 183–4, 337–9
Teubner, G., 25–6
totalitarianism, 317
Tyfield, D., 288

Uexküll, J. von, 54

Valéry, P., 237
Vries, G. de, 42

Wagner, W., 285, 297
Watson, A., 26–7
Weber, M., 210
West, R., 321
Whitehead, A. N., 10
Woodward, J., 274ff.
Woolgar, S., 273ff.

Xunzi, 184

EU representative:
Easy Access System Europe
Mustamäe tee 50, 10621 Tallinn, Estonia
Gpsr.requests@easproject.com

www.ingramcontent.com/pod-product-compliance
Lightning Source LLC
Chambersburg PA
CBHW061705300426
44115CB00014B/2568